BLAKE

Peter Ackroyd is a prize-winning writer. His biographies include *T.S. Eliot* (1984), winner of the Whitbread Biography of the Year Award and joint winner of the Royal Society of Literature's William Heinemann Award; *Dickens* (1990), short-listed for the NCR Book Award; *Blake* (1995), the acclaimed *The Life of Thomas More*, which also won the James Tait Black Memorial Prize and the bestselling *London* (2000). His most recent novels are *Dan Leno and the Limehouse Golem* (1994), *Milton in America* (1996) and *The Plato Papers* (1999). He lives in London.

ALSO BY PETER ACKROYD

Fiction

The Great Fire of London
The Last Testament of Oscar Wilde
Hawksmoor
Chatterton
First Light
English Music
The House of Doctor Dee
Dan Leno and the Limehouse Golem
Milton in America
The Plato Papers

Biography

T.S. Eliot
Dickens
The Life of Thomas More
London

Poetry

The Diversions of Purley

Criticism

Notes for a New Culture

Peter Ackroyd

BLAKE

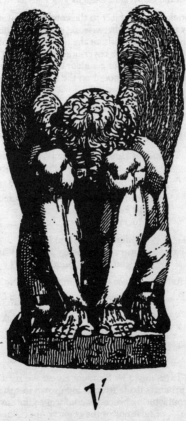

V

VINTAGE

Published by Vintage 1999

15 17 19 20 18 16 14

Copyright © Peter Ackroyd 1995

The right of Peter Ackroyd to be identified as the
author of this work has been asserted by him in accordance
with the Copyright, Designs and Patents Act, 1988

First published in Great Britain by Sinclair-Stevenson in 1995
Published by Minerva in 1996

Vintage
Random House, 20 Vauxhall Bridge Road, London SW1V 2SA

Random House Australia (Pty) Limited
20 Alfred Street, Milsons Point, Sydney,
New South Wales 2061, Australia

Random House New Zealand Limited
18 Poland Road, Glenfield,
Auckland 10, New Zealand

Random House (Pty) Limited
Isle of Houghton, Corner of Boundary Road & Carse O'Gowrie,
Houghton 2198, South Africa

The Random House Group Limited Reg. No. 954009

www.randomhouse.co.uk/vintage

A CIP catalogue record for this book
is available from the British Library

ISBN 978 0 7493 9176 8
ISBN 0 7493 9176 6

Papers used by Random House are natural,
recyclable products made from wood grown in sustainable forests.
The manufacturing processes conform to the environmental
regulations of the country of origin.

Printed and bound in Great Britain by
Cox & Wyman Ltd, Reading, Berkshire

In memory of Brian Kuhn

O how couldst thou deform
those beautiful proportions
Of life & person for as the Person
so is his life proportiond

WILLIAM BLAKE

Qui n'a pas l'esprit de son âge
De son âge a tout le malheur

VOLTAIRE

CONTENTS

LIST OF ILLUSTRATIONS

Black and white plates

Self-portrait by Samuel Palmer. Ashmolean Museum, Oxford
Self-portrait by John Linnell
Painting on ivory of Blake by John Linnell.
 Fitzwilliam Museum, Cambridge
Life-mask of Blake by Deville. National Portrait Gallery, London
Blake on the heath at Hampstead by John Linnell.
 Fitzwilliam Museum, Cambridge
Sketch from Blake's Notebook: the 'traveller'. British Museum
The last page of *Jerusalem*. British Museum

Colour plates

The Book of Thel (title-page). British Museum
Songs of Innocence: 'The Ecchoing Green'. British Museum
Songs of Innocence: 'The Shepherd'. Fitzwilliam Museum, Cambridge
Songs of Experience: 'The Chimney Sweeper'. British Museum
Songs of Experience: 'London'. British Museum
The Marriage of Heaven and Hell (title-page).
 Fitzwilliam Museum, Cambridge
Visions of the Daughters of Albion (title-page).
 Pierpont Morgan Library, New York
Plate from *The Book of Urizen*. British Museum
Plate from *The Book of Urizen*. British Museum
Plate 6 from *Europe*. British Museum
Plate 11 from *Europe*. University of Glasgow
Plate from *The Song of Los*. British Museum
Plate from *The Song of Los*. British Museum
Newton. Tate Gallery, London
Nebuchadnezzar. Tate Gallery, London
The Agony in the Garden. Tate Gallery, London
The Body of Christ Borne to the Tomb. Tate Gallery, London
David Delivered out of Many Waters: 'He Rode upon the Cherubim'.
 Tate Gallery, London
The Raising of Lazarus. Aberdeen Art Gallery
Illustrations to the Book of Job: 'When the Morning Stars Sang together'.
 Pierpont Morgan Library, New York
*Sir Jeffery Chaucer and the Nine and Twenty Pilgrims on
 their Journey to Canterbury* (detail).
 Glasgow Museums, Stirling Maxwell Collection, Pollock House
Jacob's Dream. British Museum
Six Illustrations to Milton's 'On the Morning of Christ's Nativity':
 'The Descent of Peace'. Huntington Library, San Marino, California
Twelve Illustrations to Milton's 'L'Allegro' and 'Il Penseroso':

ACKNOWLEDGEMENTS

I would like to thank the curators and staff of the following institutions for allowing me to study their collections of Blake material: Department of Prints and Drawings, British Museum; Manuscript Room, British Museum; North Library, British Museum; The Tate Gallery; The Victoria & Albert Museum; The Preston Blake Library, Westminster City Libraries; The Museum of Fine Arts, Boston; The Fogg Art Museum, Harvard; The Houghton Library, Harvard; The Fitzwilliam Museum, Cambridge; The Stirling Maxwell Collection, Pollock House, Glasgow; The Whitworth Art Gallery, Manchester; The Beinecke Rare Book and Manuscript Library, Yale; The Yale Center for British Art, New Haven; The Frick Collection, New York; The Metropolitan Museum of Art, New York; The Pierpont Morgan Library, New York; The Berg Collection, New York Public Library; The Ashmolean Museum, Oxford; The Philadelphia Museum of Art; The Rosenbach Foundation, Philadelphia; The National Gallery of Art, Washington; The Library of Congress, Washington.

I should also like to thank David Scrase, G. E. Bentley jnr, Robin Hamlyn, George Goyder, Tim Heath, Heather Howell, George Lawson, William Rees-Mogg, R. John Linnell, Claire Tomalin and Ron Parkinson.

BLAKE

ONE

O why was I born with a different face?

In the visionary imagination of William Blake there is no birth and no death, no beginning and no end, only the perpetual pilgrimage within time towards eternity. But we cannot follow him into that bright world, not yet, and his story must begin above a hosier's shop in Soho where, at 7.45 on a November evening in 1757, he came crying into the rushlight and candlelight of a London winter. We may be able to see, if we look hard enough, the doctor's lantern and the fire of sea-coal that greet the piping infant; but the outlines of those who attended the birth remain shrouded in the deepest obscurity. Blake was later to invoke the 'Angel at my birth'[1] and 'The Angel that presided oer my birth',[2] but he remained strangely silent about his own more immediate family. The little that is known about them can be related here, as the infant is bound tightly in swaddling clothes before being returned to his mother.

The father, James Blake, was a hosier. The available records suggest that he had been a draper's apprentice from Rotherhithe, but there is also a possibility that he was one of two infants with that name born in the parish of St Anne's, Soho. This at least would have the advantage of neatness since, in one of those peculiar examples of territorial clustering, there were nine families with the name of Blake living in the adjacent parish of St James's, Westminster, where William Blake himself was born on that twenty-eighth day of November.[3] He was not, at any rate, of Irish extraction – this was the theory of William Butler Yeats, who believed that the father of a visionary must spring from somewhere west of Dublin. Visionaries can be born and nurtured within the very depths of London.

James Blake married Catherine Hermitage in the autumn of 1752.

They were both Dissenters, according to Blake himself, and thought so little of the state ceremony that they were content to be united at St George's, Hanover Square, a church which specialised in expeditious and inexpensive marriages, at a guinea a time, without the encumbrance of banns or licences. They married on Sunday 15 October (one of the fifteen services performed that day), and so avoided closing the shop on a workday and the prospect of losing customers. Catherine Hermitage had previously been married to a hosier in Broad Street, who had subsequently died, and in the hasty formalities in St George's two businesses were joined together.

William Blake was the third child in a family that grew steadily to include four more (an older brother had died at infancy); he adored one, as we shall see, but hated another as 'the evil one'. There was a sister, Catherine, who on various occasions in the future helped Blake in domestic crises, and was considered a useful if somewhat irritating familial assistant. He appears to have been largely indifferent to the rest of his siblings, if it were not for certain stray phrases buried within the sublimities of his epic poetry; as he exclaimed 'to the Jews' in *Jerusalem*,

> A mans worst enemies are those
> Of his own house & family.[4]

Since Blake's parents were of 'a dissenting sect',[5] they were eventually placed in the soil of the Nonconformists' burial ground in Bunhill Fields, but the identity of that sect has never been determined. James Blake may have been a Baptist from the little church in Grafton Street, or a Moravian from the chapel in Fetter Lane, and his wife might equally well have been a Muggletonian since there was another Hermitage in the parish of St James's who composed Muggletonian hymns.[6] They might have been Sandemanians or Hutchinsonians, Thraskites or Salmonists, or, alternatively, they might have been part of a sectarian congregation with no settled name. It is of no consequence at this late date, except in one respect – all the evidence of Blake's art and writing suggests that he was imbued with a religion of piety, enthusiasm and vision. His older brother, who settled into trade as a hosier, claimed to have seen Moses and Abraham. He was also reputed to 'talk Swedenborg', which, in the language of the period, meant that he espoused some visionary faith bearing traces of the radical mysticism of the seventeenth century or earlier. This was Blake's inheritance, and it can truly be said that he is the last great religious poet in England.

Emmanuel Swedenborg, the prophet and visionary, had already marked the year of Blake's birth as one of peculiar significance. England was at war with France, and in the July of 1757 Chesterfield had written, 'We are no longer a nation. I never yet saw so dreadful a prospect',[7] but Swedenborg had witnessed more beneficent spiritual agencies at work: 'The Last Judgment was accomplished in the Spiritual World in the year 1757 . . . the former heaven and the former earth are passed away, and all things are become New.'[8] Blake read this prophecy at an age when he was able to understand it, and he replied in the cadence and vocabulary of his London faith:

> Now Art has lost its mental Charms
> France shall subdue the World in Arms
> So spoke an Angel at my birth
> Then said Descend thou upon Earth
> Renew the Arts on Britains Shore
> And France shall fall down & adore . . .[9]

He was baptised in Christopher Wren's church of St James Piccadilly, one of twenty-three William Blakes in London to receive 'the Water of Life' during this period.[10] The font was designed by Grinling Gibbons; it is supported by the tree of life, and the serpent is seen offering the fruit to our first parents, while the sides bear the images of Jesus, the Baptist, St Philip and the ark of Noah. Seven other babies were baptised in the same font that day, 11 December, and we may see them as Blake later depicted them: 'many Infants appear in the Glory representing the Eternal Creation flowing from the Divine Humanity in Jesus'.[11] After the service was over, the family party went out into the cold London air, crossed Piccadilly and walked up Air Street towards Golden Square.

Their house was on the corner of Broad Street and Marshall Street, not numbered for many years but unmistakable because of its position; like all proper houses it reflected the condition of its inhabitants – solid if not exactly prosperous. It had a stock brick front, in the fashion of London building after the Great Fire, with some discreet pilasters and cornicing that dated it to the early eighteenth century; it was four storeys in height, with a basement, and was three sash windows wide along Broad Street. In such a house as this the interior was of the plainest sort, lined with simple panelling and finished off with deal floors and stairs, which soon acquired that whitish patina so peculiar to London homes in the period. The ceilings were low, and the main room on each storey was some twenty feet square: it was in one of these rooms, close by a window, that William Blake first saw God. James Blake's shop was on the ground floor facing Broad Street, while above it was the sitting room; the bedrooms and other chambers were on the two remaining floors, while a little wooden staircase led from the top storey onto the roof. It was protected by a parapet of some three feet, but from here the young Blake could have seen the sun rising above the dome of St Paul's or declining westwards into Kensington Gardens.

> Then the Divine Vision like a silent Sun appeard above
> Albions dark rocks: setting behind the Gardens of Kensington
> On Tyburns River, in clouds of blood . . .[12]

At night the stars would have seemed brighter over London than they can ever do in our own time, and from this roof he could have seen all the swords and spears held by the figures in the sky, as well as such exotically named constellations as The Printing Office and The Sculptor's Studio. Blake knew them well, and traced their movements within the very texture of his poetry.

Broad Street itself was not completed until the 1730s but, even by the time of Blake's birth, some of the more prosperous inhabitants had moved further west in step with the great march of the city; many of the houses were now owned by shopkeepers or had been converted into apartments for lodgers. By the end of Blake's life it had become a squalid area of tenements, and worse, but in this period it was the abode of citizens of the 'middling' sort such as engravers, carpenters and harpsichord-makers. The Blakes came from the same stock, and James Blake, the hosier, was typical of the many thousands of small tradesmen who made up the commercial life of the city. It was in every respect a family business (Catherine Hermitage's father, as well as her first husband, had also been a hosier), and those scholars who have located the enduring concern of Blake's verse with looms, with garments and with the details of weaving might care to remember that as a child he was brought up among nightcaps, gloves, socks and stockings.

The Blakes were of a recognisable London type, in other words, and it is no surprise to learn that, as Dissenters and small tradesmen, they also espoused radical politics: Blake's father later voted for Charles James Fox in the Westminster parliamentary elections, and we may be sure the boy was brought up in a household which remained deeply opposed to the Court and to Old Corruption. The presumption must be that James Blake was a shrewd, plain tradesman of the old-fashioned sort, whose unorthodox politics and Dissenting faith materially influenced his son's more extravagant speculations. We catch a glimpse of him sometimes in the face and demeanour of William Blake himself, the journeyman engraver – patient, disciplined, workmanlike – and it should not be forgotten that the poet of the sublime and terrible came from this solid stock of Dissenting Londoners.

James Blake had a more obvious influence on his eldest son, also named James, who continued the family business well into the nineteenth century. Blake wrote later that 'the Eldest brother is the fathers image',[13] and one of his first biographers describes this more conventional sibling as 'an honest, unpretending shop-keeper in the old world style . . . as primitive as his brother he was, though very unlike: his head not in the clouds amid radiant visions, but bent downwards and studying the pence of this world'.[14] The young Blake was not so competent with pence, or with figures, and in later life manifested an extreme horror for financial concerns of any sort. When he denounced 'the merchants thin / Sinewy deception' he might even be supposed to be mounting an attack upon the trade or manner of his father,[15] and in fact there have been critics who have diagnosed all of his work as an extended exercise in Freudian subversion.

It is true that his epic poems disclose a great familial saga in which the various members struggle with each other for pre-eminence and mastery, but did these metaphysical wars start within the small house in Broad Street? It has been remarked that 'Blake's associates in later years remember to have heard him speak but rarely of either father and mother',[16] and he only ever recorded real affection for his younger brother. He remained profoundly uncomfortable with the rest of his family, as if he felt betrayed or compromised by any natural tie, and indeed he was marked by such wonderful and wilful gifts that he might almost have been self-created. He never agreed with Locke that the infant came into the world as a *tabula rasa* without aptitudes of any kind, and he had a sense of fate close to that of Shakespeare's Coriolanus, who stood 'As if a man were Author of himself, And knew no other kin'.[17] At a later date Keats was to remark, 'That which is creative must create itself',[18] but the process was not an easy one for Blake. He might have been some star-child, or changeling, who withdrew into himself and into his own myth because he could not deal directly or painlessly even with the human beings closest to him. Certainly part of the momentum of his great epic poetry derives from his need single-handedly to create a new inheritance and a new genealogy for himself. Yet there may be anxiety and guilt attendant upon such a pursuit, and the sense of separation may lead to the threat of punishment. In old age he tried to read the parable of the Prodigal Son, but broke down and wept when he came to the passage, 'When he was yet a great way off, his father saw him.'[19] It was as if he were then confronting the nature of his own life for the first time.

In his poetry there are various signs and symbols; fathers are slain, mothers are weak or faithless, and 'soft Family-Love' is denounced.[20] There is a continual threat of paternal tyranny, and the father becomes easily translated into a serpent or a priest; in the great saga of Los and Orc, the father betrays himself and then chains down his son in guilty fearfulness. There are also less familiar images among his drawings – women with huge erect phalli, old and young men in erotic poses together. Yet the most powerful impression is not one of Freudian subversion or discontent, but a more general sense of loss and attenuation – of faculties dimmed, of possibilities denied and energies foreclosed. It is one of Blake's great themes, and cannot be reduced to the conflicts and quarrels above a hosier's shop.

And what, in any case, were these familial dissensions? To the end of his life Blake remembered how his parents had favoured a younger brother, John: 'William often remonstrated,' according to his earliest biographer, '& was as often told to be quiet.'[21] It was John he called 'the evil one',[22] although he seems to have been no more than dissolute: he was a failure as a gingerbread baker, absconded from his house without paying the rates, and became a soldier in the wars against the French only to live 'a few reckless days'.[23] But the fact that he had risen higher than Blake in his parents' esteem was enough to earn him undying enmity, which suggests how sensitive the poet remained to any presumed slight or neglect. He never found it easy to compete with the rest of the world, and as a result regarded it with scorn, dismay, or what he called 'Nervous Fear'.[24]

There was another cause of disquiet in the Blake household when, at one time, his mother beat him for declaring that he had seen visions. On another occasion his father threatened to do the same for precisely the same reason, but his mother then intervened. The exact circumstances will be discussed when we enter Blake's visionary world; the salient point here is that he was beaten only once. Yet for Blake it became a source of perpetual discontent; the threat remained with him in various ways, and out of it he wove fantasies of horror and evil that have nothing to do with his parents themselves. The distinction is between memory and vision. Memory was for Blake an aspect of time and thus part of the fallen world; for him the true 'regions of Reminiscence' were visionary spaces, where he could 'behold our ancient days before this Earth appear'd in its vegetated mortality to my mortal vegetated Eyes'.[25] So he created pictures of his childhood which have the formal clarity and ultimate significance of all timeless things; he believed himself to have acquired as a child, for example, the same visionary intensity that he possessed in middle age. He once said that death was simply the movement from one room to another, and in his recollections he moves into a bright room where he can shake hands with his idealised younger self.

That is why, in the light of his visionary remembrance, his parents remain obscure. The reports, such as they are, are bland and muted. Frederick Tatham was the poet's first biographer, and had the advantage of knowing both Blake and his wife towards the end of their lives. It must have been from their report, therefore, that he described James Blake as a man 'of moderate desires, moderate Enjoyments, & of substantial Worth [by which he means moral, not financial, stature], his disposition was gentle, & by all accounts his Temper amiable, & was by his Sons description, a lenient & affectionate Father, always more ready to encourage than to chide'.[26] The father also excused his young son from the duties of family business, kept him from school, and even purchased engravings and plaster casts for his private study. There is nothing here, then, to explain Blake's reluctance to be associated with him. Of the mother, Tatham goes on to say that she was 'represented as being possessed of all those Endearing Sympathies, so peculiar to maternal tenderness'.[27] We also learn from another early biographer who had the opportunity of talking to Blake's companions and contemporaries that Blake's artistic proclivities were 'privately encouraged by his mother' and that he used to hang his early verses and drawings on the walls of her chamber.[28] There is nothing here, then, to explain Blake's later belief that Christ 'took much after his Mother. And in so far he was one of the worst of men.'[29] This is not the place to discuss Blake's apparent misogyny, as well as his hatred of what were then considered to be the 'female' virtues, but it is worth remarking that the natural landscape has often been associated with the maternal embrace and the female body – Blake despised landscapes, and utterly refused to draw from nature.

All the evidence suggests, however, that his parents were more than usually affectionate and considerate. Theirs was a liberal household in every sense, and confirms that a Dissenting tradition could be maintained without the brooding pieties so extravagantly depicted by nineteenth-century novelists. There is no obvious reason for Blake's later attempts to disown or to dismiss his parents as of no consequence in his own life. Yet he did always remember that they had once 'threatened' to beat him, and that they seemed to prefer another child over him; as we move from Broad Street into the greater world we will come to see how he remained deeply nervous and resentful of any authority, even when it took the most benign form. Perhaps that is why the children within his own poetry tend to be spirited, enraged or simply afraid. He was a born antinomian whose 'Nervous Fear' could express itself either in violent anger or mechanical obedience; the family itself, that first home for authority and the lessons of submission, was therefore something to be banished from his life and from his memory. It might be called egotism, solipsism, paranoia but, however it is defined, it remained the true soil of his genius.

So he could never be taught. It is Tatham who explains that 'he despised restraints & rules, so much that his Father dare not send him to School. Like the Arabian Horse, he is said to have so hated a Blow that his Father thought it most prudent to withhold from him the liability of receiving punishment. He picked up his Education as well as he could.'[30] As Blake himself put it, more succinctly,

> Thank God I never was sent to school
> To be Flogd into following the Style of a Fool.

He did not attend any of the Dissenting academies, at Hoxton or Homerton or Hackney, and he was never even despatched to a local dame school or 'horn book' school; he was not to taste the delights of Latin until a much later date, and was never given the opportunity to master another of the set subjects, Navigation. Blake once explained to a persistent enquirer, 'There is no use in education, I hold it wrong. It is the great Sin. It is eating of the tree of Knowledge of Good and Evil.'[31] But he may just have been reverting to the Dissenting tradition of his own family – that *radical* milieu may indeed be the *root*

– since, in many antinomian sects, Reason and Education were also considered the great sin. As one songbook puts it, in a cadence close to Blake's own occasional verse,

> By edducation most have been mislead
> So they believe because they were so bred.[32]

If for a moment we return to the birth of William Blake in Broad Street, that moment of twilight and darkness, which in his poetry is often identified with the emergence of new life, we may recall his belief that 'Man Brings All that he has or Can have Into the World with him. Man is Born Like a Garden ready Planted & Sown This World is too poor to produce one Seed.'[33] Yet no garden can remain unworked, and Blake once declared he was someone who 'has not lost any of his life since he was five years old without incessant labour & study'.[34] This may be an example of the Protestant ethic that is inspired by the virtues of self-help and obedience, but it may equally be the first indication of his passionate desire to create a cloistered and separate identity. He was at first encouraged and assisted by his mother, but much of his education certainly came from solitary and incessant reading. In the illustration to one of his lyric poems, 'The School-Boy', a child sits in an arbour made of two trees and contentedly studies an open book. There may have been disadvantages in such an autodidactic course – his spelling and grammar are never orthodox, and he was maladroit with figures of any kind – but this solitary education must have encouraged that single-mindedness, obstinacy and even pugnaciousness for which he was later remarkable. Yet he also received a wide and varied education, and from his reading he eventually was able to fashion a mythic system that has no equal in his own, or any other, century.

His education was necessarily as informal as it was varied. He would, for example, have acquired a knowledge of words and cadences even before he began to read: nursery rhymes would have been the first poetry he heard, and in later years his wife formally wrote out 'Mr Blake's Nursery Rhyme', which begins

> The sow came in with the saddle,
> The little pig rocked the cradle,
> The dish jumped o' top of the table
> To see the brass pot swallow the ladle.
> The old pot behind the door
> Called the kettle a blackamoor.

'Odd bobbs' said the gridiron, 'can't you agree?
I'm the head constable, bring them to me.'[35]

Mrs Blake may have believed that it was her husband's invention, but
actually it is a rhyme of ancient date. There were other words in the
air around him, and in his own work he often quotes from popular
ballads, rhyming proverbs and halfpenny street ballads; here, then, is
one source of juvenile inspiration. But on his actual reading, he
remains generally silent. Most writers are happy to divulge an early
taste for fables, romances, or fairy tales, but he says nothing at all
about them. The staple reading for all children in the period of Blake's
infancy was the chapbook – stories from British history, the true
confessions of criminals about to be executed at Tyburn during
'Paddington Fair', myths and legends of uncertain provenance such as
The History of the Two Children in the Wood – printed on cheap thick
paper and accompanied by clumsy if vivid woodcuts. These 'cuts'
show children dancing 'in the round', chasing butterflies, and
spinning hoops; but there are also images of forests 'dark and drear', of
crippled beggars and wayfarers offering an appropriate subject for
infant contemplation, of deathbed scenes to remind the little
children of mortality. Blake may also have read such illustrated books
as Pine's Horace and Croxall's Aesop, and his later interests suggest
that he had at least glanced at The History of Jane Shore as well as at
The History of Joseph and His Brethren; but it is important only to note
that, from the beginning, he saw words and images together in the
morbid mid-eighteenth-century equivalent of comic books. Yet Blake
rarely admitted any debt to predominantly secular literature. If he
mentions it at all, it is only to dismiss its influence – as he declares in
one of the furious annotations he made within the books he later
purchased, 'I read Burkes Treatise when very Young at the same time I
read Locke on Human Understanding & Bacons Advancement of
Learning . . . I felt the Same Contempt & Abhorrence then; that I do
now.'[36] If he did indeed read these solemn volumes when he was 'very
young', he was right to reject them. All his life he looked back at a
visionary childhood in which the signs of an emerging spiritual life are
of paramount importance. Perhaps that is why he appears to have
been so solitary a child. There is never any mention of shared sports
such as football or skating, no games such as prisoner's base or
pitch-in-the-hole (although in Songs of Innocence he does depict
snap-the-whip), no pastimes such as kite-making or fishing. It is as if

nothing ordinary could touch him, and in his recollection of childhood he sees himself already pursuing his own lonely course.

His early biographers do agree upon a single aspect of his childhood, however, since it is one that affected his entire life – his closest and most significant attachment was to the Bible. It would have been the staple reading of his family, the object of continual meditation and interpretation. It is hard to re-imagine a culture in which that book was the central and pre-eminent text, through which the world itself was to be understood, but the sectaries of mid-eighteenth-century England still retained the old radical traditions of commentary and exegesis. It has been said that there is nothing in Blake's work which is not first to be found in the Bible; it is an overstatement, but it does emphasise an important truth. His poetry and painting are imbued with biblical motifs and images; the very curve and cadence of his sentences are derived from the Old Testament, while his passages of ritualistic description and denunciation come from the words of the great prophets that were heard in the house in Broad Street.

TWO

The Whole Bible is fill'd with Imagination & Visions

There are two images that help to illustrate the study of the Bible in a household of Dissenters. On the title page of Blake's *Songs of Innocence* a woman sits with an open book upon her lap, from which two children are reading. There are variants of this scene in other contexts, where Blake has the child reading aloud to the parent or pointing upwards in fervour.

Thou art the anointed cherub that covereth, and I have set thee so: thou wast upon the holy mountain of God; thou hast walked up and down in the midst of the stones of fire . . . and I will destroy thee, O covering cherub, from the midst of the stones of fire.[1]

The second image appears in a series of engravings from the Book of Job that Blake completed late in life. It shows the patriarch, with his children crouched beside him, pointing toward painted images of his biblical sufferings. It was customary in Dissenting houses to display wall-hangings of biblical scenes as a testament to their faith; there were also painted cloths and 'godly tables' displaying various homilies or messages from the sacred texts.

Thus saith the Lord God; An evil, an only evil, behold, is come. An end is come, the end is come: it watcheth for thee; behold, it is come.[2]

In Blake's mature poetry the biblical imagery of fire and furnace, of the wine press and the threshing floor, of stars and spears, of engraved tablets and opened tombs, of bones and temples, is a continual reminder of his early reading. In his poetry, too, reappear the Ancient of Days and the Last Vintage within a landscape of mournful desolation.

For our God is a consuming fire.[3]

The images which Blake saw in the household Bible were quite different from those of the chapbooks or the printed street ballads. Here were altars of squared stone, tents and dwellings set up in desert places, arks and pillars erected to alien gods, visions appearing as light among the clouds.

After this I looked, and, behold, a door was opened in heaven: and the first voice which I heard was as it were of a trumpet talking with me; which said, Come up hither, and I will shew thee things which must be hereafter. And immediately I was in the spirit . . .[4]

In the illustrated pages of the Bible there were also visions of cities in flame, of broken walls and terraces, of bearded prophets making gestures of threat or admonition – visions that Blake saw for the rest of his life.

Therefore is your land a desolation, and an astonishment, and a curse . . .[5]

In the sixth night of *Vala*, or *The Four Zoas*, Blake repeats a similar trinity of curses with 'The throb the dolor the convulsion'.[6] The words of Job are not forgotten, either.

But where shall wisdom be found? and where is the place of understanding? Man knoweth not the price thereof . . .[7]

But they are wonderfully altered by Blake into a deep lament:

What is the price of Experience do men buy it for a song
Or wisdom for a dance in the street?[8]

Nor, in his lyrics, did he ever forget the prophecies of Isaiah,

The wolf also shall dwell with the lamb, and the leopard shall lie down with the kid; and the calf and the young lion and the fatling together; and a little child shall lead them.[9]

He assimilated the very shape and structure of the biblical narrative, which, in strangely changed form, is to be glimpsed in his own epic poetry. As one eighteenth-century theologian expressed it, the sacred book comprised 'things to come, many, various; near, intermediate, remote; the greatest, the least; terrible, comfortable; old, new; long, short; and these interwoven together, opposite, composite; relative to each other at a small, at a great distance; and therefore sometimes as it were disappearing, broken off, suspended, and afterwards unexpectedly and most seasonably appearing again'.[10] It is close to a definition of Blake's own art, but the household Bible also forcibly impressed upon him its particular themes. In Ezekiel he read that

The sword is without, and the pestilence and the famine within: he that is in the field shall die with the sword; and he that is in the city, famine and pestilence shall devour him.[11]

Over a period of thirty years he continually worked upon watercolours with the subjects of 'Pestilence', 'Fire', 'Famine', 'War' and 'A Breach in a City'. One of the most famous of his images illustrates the lyric poem 'London'; an aged and bearded man, upon crutches, is guided by a child.

Thus saith the LORD of hosts; There shall yet old men and old women dwell in the streets of Jerusalem, and every man with his staff in his hand for very age. And the streets of the city shall be full of boys and girls playing in the streets thereof.[12]

In this household of dissent he would have learned that the righteous must eventually triumph over those set in high places, that there is no abiding city upon this earth, that prophets and visionaries have an especial calling, that the old order will be utterly consumed at the moment of revelation. He might have glimpsed, too, something of his own visionary childhood.

Before I formed thee in the belly I knew thee; and before thou camest forth out of the womb I sanctified thee, and I ordained thee a prophet unto the nations. Then said I, Ah, Lord GOD! behold, I cannot speak: for I am a child. But the LORD said unto me, Say not, I am a child . . .[13]

THREE

All that we See is Vision

It is characteristic of so lonely and separate a boy that Blake's principal childhood memory is of solitary walking. He walked to Peckham Rye, and he walked among the haymakers on the outskirts of London, although his great nineteenth-century biographer, Alexander Gilchrist, has also pictured him 'sauntering about the quiet neighbouring streets'.[1] 'Found the Word Golden,' he wrote in his notebook on 23 May 1810, but he had always known the word.[2] Golden Square was just south of Broad Street; it had been finished in the 1670s and the square itself, with its grass plots and gravel walks and wooden railings (with a statue of King James in the centre), was a token of early eighteenth-century urban gentility. Like Broad Street, it was losing its former status; the houses of the nobility and the great merchants were now occupied by painters and cabinet-makers. Even wholesalers began to arrive in the 1770s, heralding the louche desolation that Charles Dickens would describe in the opening pages of *Nicholas Nickleby*. So, growing up in the 1760s, in the immediate area around his family home, Blake was exposed to some of the variety of London life.

The house itself was erected upon an old burial ground once known as Pesthouse Close; it was completely filled by 1733, but the residents of Broad Street still complained of the stench that sometimes erupted from its ancient soil. The parish workhouse had been built upon a neighbouring burial ground behind Blake's house, known less noisomely as Pawlett's Gardens, and the inmates of that institution also complained that 'the Grave Digger neglects to cover the Coffins of the Dead with Earth when buried, which occasions a very offensive smell to the Neighbourhood and Persons in the workhouse'.[3] The workhouse was supposed to harbour some three hundred of the poor, but it was severely overcrowded; a contemporary report speaks of 'the stench hardly supportable, poor creatures, almost naked, and the living go to bed to the dead'.[4] These were the conditions with which the poet of 'London' was closely acquainted. A school of industry was later set up in 1782 to train the indigent children of the parish and there was also an infirmary in the same area, thus completing a trinity of institutions that echo within Blake's poetry of loss and denunciation – from the charity school children raising their voices in St Paul's to the women who labour at the workhouse looms in Lambeth This is not a simple matter of topographical coincidence, either, since there was at least one strong connection between the parish overseers and his own family: James Blake supplied haberdashery to the workhouse and the infirmary, and perhaps it is not too fanciful to consider the young poet delivering some of the stock to the guardians of the poor. Around the corner from Broad Street, in Carnaby Market, there was an abattoir which was famous for its female butchers. One of the plates of *Jerusalem* depicts three women removing the entrails of a fallen man, and it has been suggested that this scene of disembowelment is borrowed from Poussin or from an Italian engraving after Fiorentino. But Blake might also have turned for inspiration to the foul shambles of Carnaby Market.

It would be wrong to depict the parish of St James's in an entirely disagreeable manner, however, and there are aspects of it more akin to Rowlandson than to Hogarth; the Pantheon, an elaborate edifice for assembly rooms and galleries, was being built at the corner of Oxford Street during Blake's childhood and he was within easy reach of small theatres and places of musical entertainment –one of the most celebrated of them, Carlisle House in Soho, was conducted by J. C. Bach. The Crown pub was on the corner of Broad Street, while Piccadilly itself was well known for its china shops and fruit shops. There were sculptors' yards along Piccadilly, too, and certain eminent men of culture or fashion frequented the area.

And of course beyond the streets of his early childhood lay 'Infinite London', which is 'the spiritual Four-fold London eternal',[5] and which is also, as one contemporary put it, 'the confused *Babel* which now appears to us, with the *Hotch-Potch* of half-moon and serpentine narrow Streets, close, dismal, long Lanes, stinking Allies, dark, gloomy Courts and suffocating Yards'.[6] In Blake's childhood it was still an old London before the acclaimed 'improvements' of morals, manners and social amenities that occurred in the last years of the century. The heads of the condemned were still rotting on Temple Bar, the stocks were still a great public spectacle, and soldiers were lashed on the streets. It was a time when mobs and rioters often controlled large areas of the city; there were riots by sailors, silk-weavers, coal-heavers, hatters, glass-grinders; there were violent and bloody demonstrations over the price of bread, and the supporters of 'Wilkes and Liberty' could muster such large numbers in London that the disturbances reached 'almost to the point of revolution'.[7] Oxford Street was a 'deep hollow road, and full of sloughs', while many of the smaller lanes and alleys were no more than repositories of ordure and offal, the haunt of scavengers and nightmen.[8] These are the streets through which Blake wandered as a child.

> I see London blind & age-bent begging thro the Streets
> Of Babylon, led by a child. his tears run down his beard . . .
> The Corner of Broad Street weeps; Poland Street languishes
> To Great Queen Street & Lincolns Inn, all is distress & woe.[9]

He walked south, towards Dulwich and Camberwell and Croydon; he saw the mulberry trees of Peckham Rye, and crossed the brook that ran through the Vale of Lambeth. He had a very strong sense of place, and all his life he was profoundly and variously affected by specific areas of London; when he was young he rarely travelled to Hampstead or Highgate, Hornsey or Muswell Hill, because they provoked a 'torment of the Stomach', which sometimes affected him for two or three days.[10] But let us accompany him on one of his long walks, those expeditions that exhibited 'the Vigor I was in my Childhood famous for'.[11] He was a short child (his mature height was five feet five inches), but thickset and powerfully built with wide shoulders; his head was rather large, and in youth boasted a crop of reddish-yellow hair that tended to stand on end; he had a flat and pugnacious face, with large brown eyes and a snub nose. He was a tough little boy, known for his 'Vigour & activity',[12] while tending to be 'daring' as well as 'impetuous'.[13] He would have worn a cloth coat, sheepskin breeches and stockings with knee buckles; he was a typical child of his century, in this respect if in no other. These are the haunts of his childhood that he commemorated in verse:

> The fields from Islington to Marybone,
> To Primrose Hill and Saint Johns Wood:
>   Were builded over with pillars of gold,
>   And there Jerusalems pillars stood . . .
>
> The Jews-harp-house & the Green Man;
> The Ponds where Boys to bathe delight:
>   The fields of Cows by Willans farm:
>   Shine in Jerusalems pleasant sight.[14]

He left Broad Street and walked north across Oxford Street towards Tottenham Court Road. This was a populous area of the city but still badly paved with round stones, taken from the quarries, which rolled about under the impress of carriage wheels and pedestrians; there were puddles and causeways of dirt scattered the length of the main thoroughfares, while the carriages moved endlessly in opposite directions along two files, 'which never cross or disturb each other'.[15] He turned left at St Giles High Street, past some old almshouses and brick houses from the reign of Queen Anne (famous for the grotesque masks carved on the keystones), and crossed the boundary stone where the charity boys of St Giles parish were whipped; he turned north up the Tottenham Court Road, passing a brewhouse to his right and Hanway Street to his left. The Blue Posts Inn was here, one of the many along this expanding thoroughfare. As he continued northwards past some straggling houses he came to Percy Street and Windmill Street before passing a timber yard on his right; the yard itself abutted onto the fields of Capper's Farm, which was then occupied by two elderly maidens of that name. As a contemporary remembered them, 'They wore riding-habits and men's hats; one rode an old grey mare, and it was her spiteful delight to ride with a large pair of shears after boys who were flying their kites, purposely to cut their strings . . .'[16] (One of Blake's small emblems shows an old man with shears, cutting the wing from an angel child.) There were now open fields on both sides of the Tottenham Court Road, just after Blake passed Whitfield's tabernacle and almshouses, which had only recently been erected. On the opposite side of the road was a group of dwellings with two rows of trees to shelter them; the trees were covered with a greenish moss or down, because of the humid and foggy air, which could be rubbed off with the hand. He passed through the fields here, known as Crabtree or The Crab and Walnut Tree Fields, before coming to the turnpike that marked the crossing of the

New Road from Paddington to St Pancras. On this site stood the Adam-and-Eve public house, depicted in Hogarth's 'The March to Finchley'; it possessed a skittle ground and Dutch-pin alley, but it was most famous for its rather sad menagerie, which included a monkey, a heron and a goldfish pond. Here there were also remnants of an ancient house known as King John's Palace, and it is one of the features of London in this period that ruins were to be found among the modern buildings as a perpetual reminder of the city's past. In this area were the familiar fields, ponds and hawthorn hedges of the countryside around London, but it was hardly a scene of sylvan bliss; there were also fetid ditches and piles of stinking refuse, smoking brick kilns and hog pens, ugly pipes belonging to the New River Company that were propped up at a height of some six or seven feet and beneath which grew abundant watercress. Here, Blake would have turned left to see the Green Man shining in the light of Jerusalem; in his childhood it was better known as the Farthing-Pie-House, and it has the distinction of being mentioned not by Blake alone but also by Defoe, Pope and Dickens. It was at this place that Tottenham Court Fair was held, with its cudgelling contests and operatic puppet shows, as well as an annual 'Smock Race' organised for women of a more than usually developed physique. Then he could have turned northward and rambled up Green Lane through the fields until he came to the Jews-harp-house tavern, which overlooked some small tenements and the hills of Highgate and of Harrow. The inn had boxes in an enclosure outside, where the customers drank their tea or their ale, while in the vicinity there were signs that proclaimed 'Steel-traps and spring guns all over these grounds' or 'N.B. dogs trespassing, will be shot'.[17] From there it was a short ramble further north to Willan's farm.

And when he returned to the great city after his excursions north, he would come back to the footpaths thronged with people, the songs and the street cries, the hackney chair men and the porters, the thoroughfares crowded with carriages and dustcarts and postchaises, the dogs and the mud carts, the boys with trays of meat upon their shoulders and the begging soldiers, the smoke from the constant exhalation of sea-coal fires, the whole panoply of urban existence. Londoners are variously described in this period as being grave and serious in conversation, as being clean in dress and neat in appearance, as being violent and sadistic, as being good-humoured and tolerant; they were in fact like Londoners of all times and all periods. 'Never mind it' was a catchphrase of the era, and travellers remember the same set phrase about directions through the city: 'Go down the street, as far as ever you can go, and ask anybody.' A gentleman was addressed as 'sir' and a labouring man as 'master'. There was much swearing and bawdiness, of course, in a city famous for its violence; a contemporary recalled one of the many obscene songs bawled out in the streets, the Chair Clubs and the Cock and Hen Clubs: '. . . I am sure she'll go to Hell / For she makes me fuck her in church time.'[18] It was also an era of war and rumours of war (the fact that England was engaged in violent conflict for most of Blake's life may in part account for his continual invocation of battles and warfare), but the prevailing complaint among contemporary moralists and divines was that London itself was in thrall to effeminacy and luxury. The genteel, in particular, were given over to '*Dress, Gaming, Entertainments* and *Equipage*'.[19] England may have 'founded a mighty empire' in this period, as Macaulay testifies,[20] but all the evidence suggests that it was a time of unease and irresponsibility, laxness and uncertainty, which was to lead to the prophetic dissent and apocalyptic moralism of the 1770s. Blake himself rarely alludes to such things, and so the biographer must mention them for him – even if, in the process, he becomes one of those whom Blake denounces for their blindness to the true and spiritual state of the world. 'And many said We see no Visions in the darksom air'.[21]

For the young child saw visions, even as he walked among the ditches and the brick kilns of the countryside around London. His mid-Victorian biographer tells the story best, or, at least, most plausibly: 'On Peckham Rye (by Dulwich Hill) it is, as he will in after years relate, that while quite a child, of eight or ten perhaps, he has his "first vision". Sauntering along, the boy looks up and sees a tree filled with angels, bright angelic wings bespangling every bough like stars. Returned home he relates the incident, and only through his mother's intercession escapes a thrashing from his honest father, for telling a lie. Another time, one summer morn, he sees the haymakers at work, and amid them angelic figures walking.'[22] The vision of Peckham Rye may not, however, have been his 'first'; his wife once reminded him of an earlier apparition. 'You know, dear, the first time you saw God was when You were four years old. And he put his head to the window and set you ascreaming.'[23] And then again, 'even when a Child his mother beat him for running in & saying that he saw the Prophet Ezekiel under a Tree in the Fields'.[24] The story of his father's threat to beat the child, for seeing a tree filled with angels, may be the source of a note made by a close friend after Blake's death: 'belief in his inspiration reprov'd by his Father for asserting it'.[25] These visions were indeed his inspiration and, as Blake declared in one of his 'Proverbs of Hell', 'A fool sees not the same tree that a wise man sees.'[26] What Blake saw was not the crepuscular and dirty city of the historian's imagination, but a city filled with angels and prophets. He saw a biblical city.

He was a child of uncommon imagination. 'Do you call *that* splendid?' he once enquired of a traveller, bringing news of a foreign city. 'I should call a city splendid in which the houses were of gold, the pavements of silver, the gates ornamented with precious stones.'[27] The biblical echoes are noticeable here again, but equally important is the evidence of a strongly visual sensibility. It seems that he demonstrated an 'early talent of design' at the age of three,[28] and that he was 'always sketching'.[29] Such a powerful visual sense, when aligned with vigorous creative abilities, can in certain people provoke or create exceptionally clear images, which have a hallucinatory reality. One early biographer has explained how 'the Scripture overawed his imagination' – to such an extent that he saw it materialising around him.[30] It is not an uncommon gift and one friend, George Richmond, commented in the margin of Gilchrist's *Life*, 'He said to me that all children saw "Visions" and the substance of what he added is that all men might see them but for worldliness or unbelief, which blinds the spiritual eye.' Jonson and Coleridge saw their own visions, too, which Coleridge described as 'vivid spectra' or 'flash images',[31] and it is related of Shelley that he 'could throw a veil over his eyes and find himself in a camera obscura, where all the features of a scene were reproduced in a form more pure and perfect than they had been originally presented to his external senses'.[32] But visions do not only vouchsafe themselves to men of genius. The imperatives of industry and technology had not yet closed the 'spiritual eye' of the eighteenth century, and there were many such cases as that of 'Henry Prescott, commonly called Joseph', who began having visions of angels at the age of eight.[33]

The phrase commonly employed by psychologists for such phenomena is 'eidetic imagery', and textbooks supply numerous instances of hallucinatory images that 'are always *seen* in the literal sense'; they are not memories, or afterimages, or daydreams, but real sensory perceptions.[34] In the late nineteenth century, Francis Galton noted that this faculty 'is very high in some young children, who seem to spend years of difficulty in distinguishing between a subjective and objective world'. He went on to suggest that 'like all natural gifts, it has a tendency to be inherited',[35] and this might explain why Blake's older brother insisted that he had seen Moses and Abraham. In any event, Blake's early visions are not unusual. What is remarkable, however, is the extent to which an ordinarily childhood capacity was maintained by him until the end of his life. Perhaps there is a sense in which, with all his contrariness and extreme sensitivity, he remained a child; perhaps the experience of his infancy was so strong that he was always the small child whose 'inspiration' was questioned by his father. Certainly, at times of more than usual stress and difficulty, his visions became a way both of lending himself a coherent identity and of confirming a special fate; they afforded him authenticity and prophetic status in a world that ignored him, they acted as a comfort and a consolation in circumstances when he felt unloved or unwanted. Yet they were real, and the child who returned from communion with angels or with Ezekiel knew that he had been blessed with a second sight. Such a gift, however, can lead to isolation or humiliation.

> O why was I born with a different face?
> Why was I not born like the rest of my race?[36]

FOUR

I devoted myself to Engraving in my Earliest Youth

He could never have been a tradesman. He was 'totally destitute of the dexterity of a London shopman' and was 'sent away from the counter as a booby';[1] the tone of this early report suggests the actions of disappointed or unsympathetic parents, but in fact they encouraged and actively supported their son's genius. We know that Blake hung his verses and drawings in his mother's chamber; he once showed friends the drawing of a grasshopper among his juvenilia, and in the same period he completed a lyric which begins

> How sweet I roam'd from field to field.
> And tasted all the summer's pride.[2]

So there was evidence of skill, even precocity, and in his tenth year his parents sent him to the major school for promising young artists in London. Henry Pars Drawing School was at No. 101 the Strand, on the right-hand side as you travel towards the City; it was among the grand shops that were to be found between here and Holborn, with their great glass doors and ornate architectural decorations. For a Londoner with so strong a sense of place, it is also appropriate to note that William Blake was to die, singing. in a lodging house only a few feet away. The Pars establishment was considered to be the preparatory school for the Academy of Painting and Sculpture in St Martin's Lane (the Academy had been established by Hogarth and, until the advent of the Royal Academy Schools in 1769, was by far the best in London), and the instruction which Blake received over the next five years was along traditional and clearly defined lines. He had first to be trained in draughtsmanship, while at the same time being given the rudiments of an artistic education, and so the emphasis was upon the faithful copying of engraved prints and plaster casts from the antique. Another pupil at the school has described the habit of 'copying drawings of Ears, Eyes, Mouths and Noses'.[3] It was the finest possible tuition he could have received. Michelangelo himself had once remarked that it was necessary to learn how to draw correctly in early youth in order to adopt the best 'manner of study'.[4] Ingres said that it took thirty years to learn how to draw, three years to learn how to paint. Blake always was a wonderful draughtsman; indeed dexterity and inventiveness in drawing became, for him, the key ro all the mysteries of form and composition. But he was also being trained to appreciate what was called the language of art and, in particular, the work of the 'Ancients'. Henry Pars' brother, William, had recently returned from a drawing expedition through Greece and Asia Minor; he had been commissioned by the Society of Dilettanti to sketch the statues and public buildings of the classical past, and he returned to London with a portfolio of work. The first volume of his *Ionian Antiquities* was published during Blake's second year at the school and although in certain respects it is a 'pattern book' for aspiring architects it also provided Blake the opportunity of imaginative entry into the remote past. For many of his contemporaries it was simply a method of learning by rote, but Blake's work is haunted by images of ruinous stone, of temples and heroic statuary; part of the landscape of his imagination was to be found in the little school along the Strand. In his second year, too, he was allowed to draw from the casts of classical sculpture in the Duke of Richmond's Gallery in Whitehall; here he studied the Apollo Belvedere and the Medici Venus, for example, in the company of teachers such as Giovanni Cipriani and Joseph Wilton. He may also have met the painter John Hamilton Mortimer, who assisted in the gallery, and this could only have further advanced the ambitions of a boy already awakened to the great art of the classical period. 'The spirit said to him "Blake be an artist & nothing else. In this there is felicity." '[5]

But felicity is not necessarily to be obtained at once, and in the period of Blake's artistic training 'art' itself was being put to other uses. The original owner of the school in the Strand, William Shipley, had been a founder member of the Society for the Encouragement of Arts, Manufactures and Commerce; the title suggests a typically mid-eighteenth-century British refusal to make any distinctions between fine and applied art, but the Society itself represents the first real attempt to afford painting its proper place in a country which had never particularly valued it. It subsidised paintings on English historical subjects, and arranged the first truly public art exhibition in London in 1760 (window glass to the value of 13s 6d was broken by liveried servants and other common spectators). Nevertheless, the emphasis on the values of 'Commerce' was always there. Blake would have soon become aware that his own skills might one day need to be applied to 'such manufactures as require Fancy and Ornament'.[6] Examples were all around him, from textiles and wallpaper to vases and crockery; Henry Pars' sister taught at the school, but she also worked as an enamelist and engraver for Josiah Wedgwood's pottery. The visionary child could scarcely have known that, in later years, he would also be obliged to turn out designs for the Wedgwoods as if he were no more than a skilful artisan.

His father, an 'indulgent parent', purchased for him copies of 'the Gladiator, the Hercules, the Venus of Medicis', which indicates, if nothing else, that in this period radical dissent did not preclude any interest in more general culture.[7] We will find throughout Blake's life how early impressions lingered with him, and the forms of these sculptures studied in his childhood reappear in the paintings and engravings completed many years later. He had so strong a visual sense that he could never forget anything; so when Hercules Farnese emerges as Giant Despair in Blake's illustrations to Bunyan, or when Venus pudica turns into Eve within his illuminated Genesis as well as a figure from 'The Last Judgment', we are seeing the permanent shape of his imagination. His father also provided him with money to purchase old prints, and from a very early age Blake began to attend the sales and auction rooms of the capital. He also became well acquainted with the print shops that had existed in London since the sixteenth century (Pepys used to visit Faithorne's shop 'at the sign of The Ship, within Temple Bar'), although by Blake's time they had become emporia for curios of various kinds. Of course there were still engravings to be found in abundance – some carefully mounted and some loosely gathered in portfolios, some in volumes and some in albums, an enclosed artistic world in which the boy could momentarily dwell. John Boydell had a shop in Cheapside, while Fore's was at the corner of Sackville Street; there were the print shops of William Ryland and Mat Darley close by in the Strand (although the latter specialised in satires and caricatures), while down the road in King Street, Covent Garden, he could have attended the auctions at Patterson's or Hutchin's. The auction galleries were always open two or three days before a sale, when the fashionable or the interested could wander; there is an engraving by Rowlandson that depicts some collectors gathered around a long table while the prints are displayed by salesmen. Blake himself remembers, specifically, how the dealer 'Langford called him his little connoisseur; and often knocked down to him a cheap lot, with friendly precipitation';[8] it became possible for him to make threepenny bids for works that were then considered uninteresting or unfashionable, and as a result he began a collection, which in old age he would have to sell through poverty.

His own account of his acquaintance with the great engravings is clear enough: 'I am happy I cannot say that Rafael Ever was from my Earliest Childhood hidden from Me. I saw & I Knew immediately the difference between Rafael & Rubens',[9] and to his earliest biographer he mentioned 'Raphael and Michael Angelo, Martin Hemskerck and Albert Dürer, Julio Romano and the rest of the historic class'.[10] These are certainly exotic choices for a child, especially since they were considered to be hard, dry, almost 'Gothick', and quite out of the contemporary fashion. As his biographer goes on to say, 'His choice was for the most part contemned by his youthful companions, who were accustomed to laugh at what they called his mechanical taste.'[11] Such an early 'taste' is unusual enough, certainly, and has moved some biographers to question Blake's recollections: could he really have acquired so subtle and rare an interest in the masters of the High Renaissance and the Northern School, or was he merely fantasising about the genius of his younger self? But, since the verses of his childhood betray a knowledge of Ben Jonson as well as Edmund Spenser, there is every reason to believe that his precocity in literary matters extended towards art and sculpture; in a world of fluctuating perceptions, where visions and realities were strangely intermingled, there was perhaps even some coherence and strength to be found in the firm, determinate outlines of the artists whom he admired. As he said himself, 'Leave out this line and you leave out life itself; all is chaos again.'[12]

That is what he means when he distinguishes 'Rafael & Rubens'; Raphael represented the clear and distinct line, while Rubens employed the subtler shadings of mass and tone. Blake instinctively admired or needed the precise strong line of the engraver's burin and detested the effects of mezzotint, stipple, or aquatint. Of course he knew the work of Raphael through the engravings of Marcantonio

Raimondi, just as the heroic figures of Michelangelo were vouchsafed to him through the engravings of Adam Ghisi, which he endlessly copied; it was only through this medium that he could become closely acquainted with the great masters of Italy and the North. In the engravings of Bonasone and Raimondi he recognised all the power that comes from the confidence and purity of outline, and in the work of Ghisi after Michelangelo he learned the fine muscularity and heroic configurations of an art which approaches the condition of monumentality without ever losing its gracefulness. He saw the images of great angels bursting out of cloud, of Jupiter Pluvius with his arms outstretched, of the hooded Sibyl clutching a scroll, of young male nudes in gladiatorial attitudes, of heroic figures falling through infinite space; he knew the chaste outlines of Mantegna's 'Madonna and Child' as well as the visionary simplicity of Raphael's 'God Appearing to Isaac'. In these early engravings he first understood the line of visionary art, with the principal figures characteristically separate and apart: it was his own vision of himself, even from an early age, but here it was wonderfully exalted.

The engravings of Dürer also exerted a strange fascination over the child. It is not likely that he had seen that artist's title page for an edition of Theocritus's *Idylls* or his drawings in the margins of the Emperor Maximilian's prayer book, which bear a striking resemblance to some of the images in *Songs of Innocence*, but Blake would have understood the extraordinary subtlety and strength of Dürer's line, which achieves complex effects of light and space without ever losing the balance and drama of the composition. Here the line, the fine and regular line, the 'determinate and bounding form', the 'bounding outline', is everything.[13] Dürer once said, 'a good painter is full of figures within', by which he meant that it is not at all necessary to draw from nature; but there is also another significance that can be attached to the stray remark, which links Dürer with Raphael and all the other influences of Blake's youth. They share an intense spirituality or, rather, a visionary clarity, which is conceived within the strong and formal lines of the engraving; there is no 'colour', to use a word of the period that denotes painterly associations and tones, simply the vision of the artist powerfully expressed. It was the art that inspired him, and that moved him, for the rest of his life. He knew Dürer's rhinoceros, which became his own Behemoth; he knew 'Melancholia', from which he borrowed certain plangent motifs. Of the Northern masters he knew the elongated forms, and the drapery that falls upon them in angular folds; he saw the expressive and sometimes grotesque faces, the tapering limbs and the narrow fingers. There is one great fifteenth-century engraving, 'The Infant Christ and the Flower', which depicts the Saviour walking within a tulip as if he were about to enter the *Songs of Innocence*. But the first and finest engraving known to Blake's contemporaries is that of 'St Christopher Bearing the Infant Christ' of 1423; in its depiction of the saint and Saviour, it offers a striking resemblance to the figures upon the frontispiece of Blake's *Songs of Experience*. So began his true education, and we might remember here the words of George Gissing from another age: 'I gazed and gazed at them, with that fixed attention of a child which is half curiosity, half reverie, till every line of them was fixed in my mind . . .'[14]

In this period, then, he commenced 'an unabated study & practise'.[15] At the age of fourteen he kept a sketchbook in which he made his drawings, and he had already begun writing verses of extraordinary fluency in which he looks to Spenser and to Milton in the same way that he had looked upon Raphael or Dürer. Here, in the poetry of youth, he invokes 'the prince of love':

> He loves to sit and hear me sing,
>   Then, laughing, sports and plays with me;
> Then stretches out my golden wing,
>   And mocks my loss of liberty.[16]

There are also other influences which can be placed here, in an appropriate if not necessarily suggestive pattern. In his first year at the drawing school he had seen the vision of the angels in Peckham Rye, and it was also in this year that Robert Blake was born; this was his youngest brother, to whom he was unaffectedly attached, and, in later years, Robert was to become his companion as well as a docile and devoted disciple. By 1767 Blake had already started reading the verses of Thomas Chatterton in the *Town and Country Magazine*, and was so powerfully affected by their medieval vocabulary and cadence that he began to reproduce the same characteristics in his own verse; in this period, too, he saw George Stubbs's painting of a 'Tyger' exhibited by the Society of Artists along with works by the other eminent painters of the day.

But he did not become a painter. He became an engraver. At the end of his time at Pars' Drawing School he decided not to enter the recently established Royal Academy Schools (unlike another contemporary and son of a tradesman, Thomas Rowlandson) and, instead, was enrolled as an apprentice. It may have been partly an act of filial duty, as one of his first biographers explains in words which came from Blake or Blake's wife: 'His love of Art increasing, & the time of life having arrived, when it was deemed necessary to place him under some Tutor, a painter of Eminence was proposed & necessary applications were made, but from the huge premium required, he requested with his characteristic generosity that his Father would not on any account spend so much money on him; as he thought it would be an injustice to his brothers & sisters; he therefore himself proposed Engraving as being less expensive & sufficiently eligible for his future avocations.'[17] There seems no reason to doubt the story, and engraving was 'sufficiently eligible' to represent no overwhelming sacrifice on Blake's part.

This was a period when there was a renewed interest among English painters in the possibilities of engraving; the two artists Blake most admired, James Barry and John Hamilton Mortimer, were also engravers who transcribed their own extravagant, idealised and heroic images with the burin. Painters such as Benjamin West were beginning to appreciate the huge commercial potential in the reproduction of a single image, while dealers such as John Boydell were seeking out markets in Britain and Europe for what was becoming an English speciality. It was a burgeoning profession and although they might be classed as artisans rather than artists engravers could earn twice as much as any other skilled craftsmen in the period. The London Tradesman, as early as 1747, described the professions of engraving and etching as 'very profitable and are reckoned among the genteel trades'.[18] Blake's decision was not an unwise or unworldly one. In any event, all his love and understanding of art had come through the medium of engraving; why should he not learn to practise that which he revered? It was, in a sense, the perfect compromise; the young boy learned a trade, by which he could always live, and at the same time he was studying the lessons and possibilities of what was a newly revived art. If he were conventionally ambitious, there were reassuring examples: Hogarth had once been indentured to a silversmith, and Nathaniel Clarkson had been a coach painter. Blake was in no sense a 'Romantic' artist, like those of the next generation, who despised trade and who tended to withdraw from the urban turmoil of finance and competition; he was a lower-middle-class tradesman, a mystic intimately involved in the world of commerce and craft. In that sense he remained much closer to the people whom he wished to address in his work, and in that lifelong career of arduous labour perhaps there is something grander and more heroic than the lucubrations of the Lakeside poets.

There is a report that Blake and his father approached the fashionable stipple engraver William Ryland, to enquire about the chance of apprenticeship; Ryland was too expensive but, in any case, the boy raised his own objection. 'Father,' he said on leaving the studio in Russell Street, Covent Garden, 'I do not like the man's face: it looks as if he will live to be hanged!'[19] This would have been a strange example of precognition on Blake's part, since the celebrated Ryland was indeed hanged for forgery twelve years later; he also has the distinction of being the last man executed at Tyburn. But the story has all the marks of fantasy on someone's part, perhaps Blake's; at the time of the alleged incident, Ryland was already a bankrupt and hardly likely to appeal to such a sober and honest tradesman as James Blake. Many years later, Blake himself signally failed to predict a similar destiny for a much closer acquaintance: Thomas Griffiths Wainewright, whose strange life as an art critic and a poisoner provided Dickens and Wilde with suggestive plots, knew Blake well enough to extol the virtues of his unpublished *Jerusalem*. His career as a writer and murderer might have intrigued Blake, who declared that the 'enjoyments of Genius' were to be found 'among the fires of hell', but on no occasion does Wainewright seem to have been forewarned by Blake about his fate.[20]

So, on 4 August 1772, William Blake was apprenticed to a quite different engraver. There is a transcript of his indentures at Stationers' Hall, which reads, 'Wm Blake Son of James of Broad Street Carnaby Market to James Basire of Great Queen Street Lincolns Inn ffields. Engraver. seven years Cons[ideratio]n £52.10s – paid by his ffather.'[21] The use of the archaic 'ff' suggests the roots of this apprentice system in the medieval guilds: Blake undertook not to fornicate or to marry, not to game or dice, not to 'haunt Taverns, or Play houses'.[22] Basire, in turn, promised to instruct his new apprentice in the 'Art and Mystery' of his profession; he would also feed, clothe and protect the said apprentice for the term of seven years. Blake was entering a different kind of family; one in which he might be able to work out his own identity with less difficulty. They returned together to No. 31 Great Queen Street, where James Basire lived with his wife and children above his studio; the house was on the

north side, facing the Freemasons' Hall, and was built in the
seventeenth-century fashion. Here Blake shared a room with one
other apprentice – it was usual for guild members to have only two
apprentices in a given period – and for the next seven years his time
was at the disposal of his master. It was customary for apprentices to
work twelve hours a day, six days a week, and it may be that Blake
returned to his family home in Broad Street only on Sundays. There
were few holidays – merely Easter, Whitsuntide and Christmas –
although apprentices were often given their freedom on the eight
'hanging days' at Tyburn. So now Blake began the course which he
was to pursue, for better or for worse, for the rest of his life; 'during a
Period of Forty years,' he wrote in 1809, 'never suspended his
Labours on Copper for a single Day'.[23] 'Engraving is the profession I
was apprenticed to,' he told a correspondent ten years before, '&
Should never have attempted to live by any thing else.'[24] There
were occasions when his work could become a refuge from an
increasingly alien and antagonistic world, a space in which he could
patiently perform the familiar rituals of his youth, but in the end it
excluded him from recognition or reward. He could never have
realised, in these first days of learning and advancement, what a
long, arduous, isolated and heart-breaking labour it would eventually become.

It seems likely that Basire was recommended by Henry Pars,
Blake's old drawing master, since William Pars had already worked
with Basire on certain engravings of ruined antiquity. He came from
a family of engravers; he was forty-one when Blake joined him as a
fourteen-year-old apprentice, and was already working both for the
Society of Antiquaries and the Royal Society. He was a 'liberal-
minded' man of 'ingenuity and integrity', according to an obituary
notice, and there is no reason to doubt this posthumous praise.[25] He
had been highly regarded by Hogarth, and in that intermediary
connection between Hogarth and Blake we see evidence of a native
urban tradition; the character of Basire (and perhaps that of Blake)
may also be illuminated by Hogarth's remark that 'fine engraving
which requires chiefly vast patience, care and great practice is
scarcely ever attain but by men of a quiet turn of mind'.[26] Basire
has also been described as a 'kind master', and the evidence for this
must lie in the remarkable fact that for the seven years they were in
each other's company there is no record of any serious disagreement
between Basire and his passionate, often impetuous, apprentice.

The only extant portrait depicts him as an agreeable and thoughtful man, which might be said to match his character as an engraver.

The truth is that he was already considered to be slightly old-fashioned, which is no doubt why the Society of Antiquaries approved of him. One contemporary wrote rather disparagingly of 'the dry and monotonous manner of old Basire', by which he meant that the engraver eschewed the fashionable techniques of crayon or mezzotint and concentrated instead upon the art of correct outline and the precise delineation of form. It was an art of the past, an art partly derived from what Blake called 'the old English Portraits',[27] and not one designed to appeal to an age in which novelties, curiosities and 'improvement' were the catchwords of fashionable taste. But of course this powerful and severe style was precisely the one that appealed to Blake, who had himself discovered the virtues of Dürer, Raphael and Marcantonio. It was the art he wished to learn.

Basire's studio and workshop became Blake's home; he soon became accustomed to the smell of nut oil, varnish and lamp black from Germany as well as to the ink smeared across his hands and his face. For the next seven years – indeed for the rest of his life – he was surrounded by iron pots for the boiling of the oil, pans for warming the copper plates, tallow candles, racks of needles and gravers, fine linen cloths to strain the varnish, vessels for mixing the aqua fortis used in 'biting in' the plates, old rags for wiping the ink off the plates, pumice stones to polish the plates, feathers for smoothing the ground of varnish on the plates. Stacked around him were the sheets of fine paper, as well as the plates themselves, which were the thickness of a half-crown; there was the small leather cushion filled with sand, upon which he rested the plate while engraving, and the square wooden press with its table, rollers and woollen cloths. It was a dirty and malodorous workplace but it was one against which he never felt the slightest revulsion.

It was an arduous and difficult apprenticeship, even with a kind master. 'Use water and a grinding stone for polishing your plate, then go over it with a pumice stone, then again with a fine smooth stone and some water. Then go over it with charcoal, and remove any small strokes or scratching with a steel burnisher. Then clean it with stale bread or chalk. Smooth the varnish over the plate, just so. Take a great tallow candle with a short snuff, then apply the flame to the varnish as close as ever you can without touching the varnish with the snuff of the candle. Dry the plates on a fire, place your needle in firm wood of six inches or less, whet the needle with an oilstone and prepare for the graving. You must place the knob or ball of the handle of your graver in the hollow of your hand and, having extended your forefinger towards the point of your graver, laying it opposite to the edge that should cut the copper, place your other fingers on the side of your handle, and your thumb on the other side of the graver, in such sort that you may guide your graver flat and parallel with the plate.' The instruction continues – how to prepare the plates for the aqua fortis, now that the strokes have been made upon the 'ground', which is the varnish; how to cast the aqua fortis onto the plate, how to remove the varnish after the 'biting in' is completed, how to ink the plates, and then how to reproduce the image upon the paper. 'You turn the handle of the press gently and roundly, not by jolts and jogs.'[28] Hogarth had said that the greatest resource of an engraver was patience and, in the course of his apprenticeship with Basire, Blake learnt the virtues of discipline and precision. It bears repeating that he remained just such a workman all his life, mixing inks and varnishes, buying paper and copper plates, engaged in hard and continuous physical labour. Words were for him objects carved out of metal, and it could be said that the technical requirements of his trade – the need for strong outline, for example, and the importance of minute particulars – helped him to formulate an entire metaphysical system.

He had been trained to draw before he arrived at Great Queen Street, but his apprenticeship with Basire intensified that gift into a formal technique. Basire told him of a conversation he had once held with the French engraver Gravelot: 'De English may be very clever in deir own opinions but dey do not draw',[29] and Blake may have been echoing Basire's words when he declared, 'Engraving is Drawing on Copper & Nothing Else'.[30] Of course there are differences, and Blake learned how to reproduce tone or shading with hatching and cross-hatching, or with Basire's own favoured techniques of 'worm-line' and 'dot and lozenge'; but the core of Basire's instruction would have reinforced Blake's belief in the bounding outline and the 'Line of Beauty'.[31] Basire emphasised the importance of the burin, or graver, in the creation of clean furrows and regular contours, with the steady belief that the greatest engraver would also be the greatest simplifier.[32] It was the old style, known familiarly as 'The English School' and practised by such famous contemporary engravers as William Woollett and Robert Strange; but Basire was undoubtedly the most faithful exponent of it, and by employing reproductive techniques that went back to the seventeenth century he educated Blake in what the poet came to describe as 'the style of Alb Durers Hist[o]ries & the old Engravers'.[33]

With a fellow apprentice, James Parker, he was engaged on the general work of Basire's studio, which meant that, primarily, he was involved in various kinds of book illustration. It is hard at this late date to identify all the engravings for which he was responsible, but he would certainly have worked on Basire's standard commissions. There were the volumes of the *Philosophical Transactions* of the Royal Society, for example, which included illustrations of instruments, specimens and the general paraphernalia of science during the period. But if he became familiar with contemporary scientific development, he also found it possible to enter the past. He would have worked on *Archaeologia: Or Miscellaneous Tracts Relating to Antiquity*, published by the Society of Antiquaries, and thus been introduced to the more occluded passages of English history. Antiquarianism was already becoming an intense national passion (to be mocked by Goethe in *Faust*), and Blake became associated with a world of scholars and amateurs, which hunted for buried tombs, stone circles and rotten foundations, as well as medals, vases and heathen statuary. He was also well acquainted with another of Basire's projects, Jacob Bryant's *A New System, or, An Analysis of Ancient Mythology*; he mentions the book in later life, and it is generally supposed that he was responsible for its engraving of a 'moon ark', with a dove and rainbow, as well as various ancient stylistic motifs. These images became part of his imaginative world, to be reproduced in his own art at a later date, but at the time imagination had very little to do with it. His task was to copy as carefully and as accurately as possible; in one of his angry annotations to the *Discourses* of Sir Joshua Reynolds, he describes the effect such a training had upon him: 'If he means That Copying Correctly is a hindrance he is a Liar. for that is the only School to the Language of Art.'[34] He was taught, in the process, how to throw light directly upon objects, upon botanical specimens or the fragments of ruined stone, so that they floated in empty space without shadow. When we come to consider his own art, with its isolated figures cast against a generally abstract background, we may find further evidence of his early training.

Very little is known about his life in Great Queen Street. The neighbourhood was genteel, artistic without being bohemian;

Sheridan lived here towards the end of Blake's apprenticeship, while the delights of the Drury Lane and Covent Garden theatres were literally around the corner. If Blake did not go to the drama, he at least met a dramatist: he always remembered the occasion when Oliver Goldsmith 'walked into Basire's . . . The boy – as afterwards the artist was fond of telling – mightily admired the great author's finely marked head as he gazed up at it, and thought to himself how much he should like to have such a head when he grew to be a man.'[35] His wish was granted, and he acquired Goldsmith's round brow as well as certain cranial features associated by Gall 'with the qualities of ideality and belief in the miraculous'.[36] These characteristics were no doubt useful in conjunction with another of Blake's neighbours during this period, for immediately opposite Basire's house the Freemasons' Hall was being extended with a Freemasons' Tavern. This would not be of any great significance, were it not for the fact that Masonic emblems and motifs occur intermittently throughout Blake's work. Many of his friends were themselves Masons – indeed this particular group of Londoners bore affinities with the Dissenting tradition of his own family. The Freemasons had previously met at the Queen's Head in Great Queen Street on the first and third Monday of every month, but in 1775 the Freemasons' Hall was erected on a plot of ground on the other side of the street from Basire. They were, in other words, his most visible neighbours. The Freemasons' Tavern was added two or three years later, so Blake would have had ample opportunity to discover for himself the lore of certain people who believed that they had inherited a body of secret knowledge from before the Flood. He might also have been intrigued to hear that the central Masonic fable concerned the murder of Huram Abif, who oversaw the building of Solomon's Temple – at least because Huram was 'skilful . . . to grave any manner of graving'.[37]

One other story of engravers must be added here, interesting because it brings us once again into the workshop itself. Blake recalled how William Woollett, the English virtuoso in dry line and tonality, would visit Basire and embarrass him 'by laughing at Basires knife tools & ridiculing the Forms of Basires other Gravers till Basire was quite dashd & out of Conceit with what he himself knew but his Impudence had a Contrary Effect on me'.[38] The tenor of this is clear enough, as is the evidence of Blake's pugnacity and arrogance; he never forgot such a slight against himself, as well as against Basire, and at the end of his life he depicted one of these same derided 'knife tools' in an engraving from the Book of Job. It is there, above a palette and brushes, part of a scene that depicts the acceptance of Job's prayer by God. The graving tool is not necessarily out of place in such a sacred context, because Blake would also have learned from Basire that the art of engraving was known to the Hebrews and their Chaldean ancestors – and that it went further back to Zoroaster, to Mercurius Trismegistus and even to God himself, who engraved the tables of stone for Moses. From the Book of Job Blake would have known the words of the afflicted man, 'Oh that my words . . . were graven with an iron pen and lead in the rock for ever!'[39]

FIVE

Each Identity is Eternal

He stands upon an outcrop of rock along the English coast, lost in thought or vision, isolated and apart; he is looking steadfastly at the ground and, with his arms folded across a simple hooded shirt, there is such an air of intensity and brooding concentration about him that he might be a figure from a tomb-painting or a medieval Psalter. 'Joseph of Arimathea' was the earliest original work Blake completed in his apprentice years. This first engraving captures something of the strangeness of the early prints he so much admired, and although it copies the formal pictorial conventions of the period it has nothing whatever to do with the smoothness and picturesque gracefulness that were coming into fashion.

What was it, then, that drew Blake to this patriarchal figure? All his life he spoke of 'lost originals', as if he were reaching beyond his own civilisation to the simplicity and grandeur of a remote past, and with this image he was returning to the primary source of his inspiration. Joseph of Arimathea had fled from Judaea to England, bearing with him the blood of the Saviour in the Holy Grail; he was reputed to be the first to preach the gospel within these islands and, forty-three years after the crucifixion of Christ, he built the first Christian church at Glastonbury. He was, for Blake, the first Gothic architect and the direct progenitor of Westminster Abbey, which was soon to encompass and engross him. But Joseph of Arimathea had a further role in Protestant iconography. He was the founder of English Christianity, according to John Foxe, and was by implication associated with Arthur and Alfred; thus, by genealogical sleight of hand, he could be connected with Henry VIII and Elizabeth and, by association, with the new Protestant dispensation. In particular, Foxe could find in Joseph an idealised image of English evangelicalism, allowing him to neglect the role of Pope Gregory and the English mission of St Augustine in 597, which had been considered so important by Bede. Joseph could also be seen as an English prophet, therefore, just as Blake can be placed in that tradition of Dissenting prophets who comprised the alternative religious tradition of the sixteenth and early seventeenth centuries. It may also be worth remarking, in this context, that an entire culture of urban dissent and religious radicalism may be momentarily glimpsed in Blake's work of this kind. There was once an oral tradition, conveying beliefs and attitudes from generation to generation of Londoners, which is now quite lost – in the poems and images of Blake, however, we seem partially able to recall it before it slips once more into darkness.

Joseph of Arimathea was, in many respects, Blake's true ancestor. On an early proof of this first work, he wrote, 'Engraved when I was a beginner at Basires from a drawing by Salviati after Michael Angelo'. When he re-engraved the copper at a later date, he was more eloquent on the subject: 'JOSEPH of Arimathea among The Rocks of Albion Engraved by W Blake 1773 from an old Italian Drawing This is One of the Gothic Artists who Built the Cathedrals in what we call the Dark Ages Wandering about in sheep skins & goat skins of whom the World was not worthy such were the Christians in all Ages Michael Angelo Pinxit'. He was alluding here to prophecy as an integral part of Gothic art, since he was indirectly quoting certain lines from St Paul about those prophets who 'were stoned, they were sawn asunder, were tempted, were slain with the sword: they wandered about in sheepskins and goatskins; being destitute, afflicted, tormented; (Of whom the world was not worthy:) . . .'[1] The strident invocation of prophetic anguish in Blake's remarks owes much to his own sense of isolation in later life, but it need not all be the fruits of hindsight. In the poetry he was completing while still an apprentice he wrote, 'Liberty shall stand upon the cliffs of Albion', which is only a stone's throw from the 'Rocks of Albion';[2] the image itself also suggests that, even while Blake was young, his imagination was already captured by the antiquarian beliefs and theories that he discussed endlessly in his mature years.

The figure of the bearded hero, or prophet, is in part taken from an image of the Druid to be found in William Stukeley's *Stonehenge: A Temple Restored to the British Druids* – a further indication that his interest in British antiquity and in ancient religions was not confined to his engraving work for Basire. There may also be a more homely connection; Henry Pars' sister had just been depicting Joseph of Arimathea on some Wedgwood crockery for the Empress of Russia. But the principal pictorial source is, as Blake indicated, that of Michelangelo. The figure on Albion's shore is taken from a centurion to be seen in the foreground of 'The Crucifixion of St Peter' in the Pauline Chapel in Rome. It is in fact from an engraving by Beatrizet, not Salviati, but the important point is that Blake's eye was drawn to the sad, strange figure who stands apart from the scene: it was generally supposed to be Michelangelo's self-portrait, but Blake has captured that isolation and intensified it. He has placed the figure against a bleak background of sky and sea, and left him meditating among the rocks. It would be too easy to say that it is as much a portrait of Blake as of Joseph, but there is no doubt that the atmosphere of the engraving does coincide with some of the dramatically isolated and embattled voices that emerge in the poetry he was now writing.

It is not a great work by any means, but nevertheless it is suggestive. It bears all the marks of his early training, and provides various specimens of the engraving techniques he had just learned. He even uses the motif of the 'classical foot' (second toe more prominent than the big toe), which he was taught at the drawing school in the Strand. But, for an apprentice of sixteen, it is a notable achievement. Blake himself thought enough of it to keep the copper plate for the rest of his life – he re-engraved it some twenty years later, and was even making proofs as late as 1825. Here, then, is an image of all his youthful aspirations and ideals – the prophet, the Gothic artist, the heroic proportions out of Michelangelo, the vistas of remote antiquity, and, somewhere brooding within them, the figure of Blake himself. 'Joseph of Arimathea' marked the beginning of an artistic career that, happily, soon allowed him to meditate further upon 'the Gothic Artists who Built the Cathedrals'.

SIX

a Temple built by Albions Children

His education in what Nicholas Hawksmoor once called the hidden tradition of 'The English Gothick' proceeded indirectly, however, and almost fortuitously.[1] It seems to have begun with a quarrel or disagreement with his fellow apprentice, James Parker, the son of a corn-chandler from the parish of St Mary-le-Strand. Historically and characteristically London apprentices were known to be unruly and often violent: one of Blake's contemporaries remembered how they would often go out in gangs and 'clear the pavements' without the officers of the law daring to intervene.[2] The affair at Basire's was much less disruptive, at least according to the account which Blake gave to his first, informal biographer: 'Two years passed over smoothly enough, till two other apprentices were added to the establishment [this third apprentice was probably Basire's son, since there is no record of any other apprentice in this period], who completely destroyed its harmony. Blake, not chusing to take part with his master against his fellow apprentices, was sent out to make drawings. This circumstance he always mentions with gratitude to Basire, who said that he [Blake] was too simple and they too cunning.'[3] (There may have been some difficulty with Basire, however, since at a later date Blake placed his name in a notebook among certain artistic adversaries – but then he crossed it out.) It is likely that Basire wished to protect this nervous, impetuous boy and, in any case, he had a task that needed to be performed. Blake was 'sent out to make drawings' in Westminster Abbey. Basire had been commissioned to prepare engravings for the first volume of Richard Gough's *Sepulchral Monuments in Great Britain*, and had been asked specifically to record the tombs within that church. In this period he was preoccupied with some large historical engravings, and was consequently pressed for time, but it is still a tribute both to his sagacity and to Blake's conscientious abilities that he should allow the young apprentice freedom to labour on his own away from the workshop.

So William Blake began work in the vast and solitary church. He told Samuel Palmer that 'In Westminster Abbey were his earliest and most sacred recollections';[4] his reverence for the ancient tombs and monuments is akin to that of Thomas Chatterton for the old documents that he discovered in the muniment room of St Mary Redcliffe; for them both, so closely acquainted in spirit and genius, these relics of the dead had the force of revelation. Their work is impregnated with them, and it is as if they recognised part of their own selves when they encountered the evidence of past ages; indeed, in one of those examples of mutual comprehension, Chatterton had already written an essay in the *Town and Country Magazine* extolling the virtues of the tombs in the Abbey.

It was not then the bleak, if crowded, public place it has since become; Blake wandered among variously coloured waxworks of monarchs or dignitaries, among suits of armour, and among funereal effigies constructed out of plaster or of wood, which had once been painted as carefully as the waxworks. Of all the impressions that the Abbey made upon its visitors, the most immediate would have been of faded brightness and colour. The bosses and mouldings and vault ribs all bore traces of gilt and paint; the angels in the transepts had once been decorated, together with the doors and doorways. The illuminations in what Victor Hugo once called 'a book of stone' were also to be found in the stained glass of the old church, with their rich detail of vines and angels and prophetic figures in colours close to verdigris and rose carmethian. There were remnants of richly gilt wall paintings and panel paintings. There was for example the wall painting of Sebert, king of the East Angles and supposed founder of the Abbey in the early seventh century; he is standing upon a carpet of small flowers, his own narrow figure highly coloured in rose, dark green, purple, blue, red and white. It is generally considered that Blake's wonderful sense of colour – he ranks as one of the great colourists of the eighteenth century – is derived from illuminated medieval manuscripts which he may or may not have studied; but here, among the stained glass, the decorated walls, the marbles and mosaics of the Abbey, is a more immediate source of inspiration. In his epic poetry and in his descriptive prose, there are often visions of shining temples, of huge painted walls and giant statuary; what else would the Abbey have vouchsafed to him but the vision of some splendid original from the glorious days of England's past?

He once spoke of 'the wondrous architects of our cathedrals', but he first became acquainted with them here among the arches and pillars of the Abbey.[5] His apprentice work with Basire on the images of classical antiquity had already accustomed him to architectural detail, and so he recognised immediately the trefoil arches and the groins of the vaulting within the old church. He knew, and marked, the mouldings, the piers, the panels, the colonnades, the capitals and the bases, the stone roses, the sculpted foliage and the flagstones. Images of arches and ogees and canopies reappear throughout his subsequent art, springing directly from his time among the ancient monuments of the church, but there is also a more elusive and fugitive atmosphere that he recreates in much of his later work. He experienced the coolness and seclusion of 'masses of stone in orderd forms' in the nave and the ambulatories;[6] he knew the many rooms of intricate workmanship, the great doors, the narrow passages that seem to lead into the interior darkness of some labyrinth. It was an image of a stone world which Blake was to resurrect in his prophetic verse, at once forbidding, austere and inspiring. His art and poetry are filled with the images of steep steps and ancient doorways, of cloisters and arches and crypts that suggest dissolution and decay but which are also often seen as harbingers of a spiritual world still lying upon the surface of the earth.

His task was to draw the royal tombs clustered in the chapel of St Edward the Confessor, as well as some in the presbytery – there are preliminary drawings and engravings from the monuments of Edward III, Queen Philippa, Richard II and others. An early biographer states that Blake used to climb on top of the grey or black marble tombs, in order better to capture the solemn repose of their occupants, 'frequently standing on the monument, and viewing the figures from the top'.[7] In fact the oaken canopies are sometimes so low that even a boy of his diminutive stature would have had to crouch above the tombs, nose to nose with the brass and alabaster images of the dead. His drawings are very strongly defined, as stately and as austere as their originals, but there is a certain careful regularity about them that is not always pleasing. He was a copyist here, not an artist, although in the intense concentration upon head and shoulders there is an echo of James Barry's remarkable portrait of King Lear, which was exhibited at the Royal Academy in 1774. And yet for Blake these 'Gothic' memorials became the source and inspiration of his art: here, 'he found a treasure, which he knew how to value. He saw the simple and plain road to the style of art at which he aimed, unentangled in the intricate windings of modern practice.'[8] On the under part of the wooden canopy that extends over the tomb of Richard II was portrayed 'The Ancient of Days', 'a venerable old man . . . in a close garment, with his hand raised in the act of benediction'.[9] That image haunted Blake for the rest of his life, and on his deathbed he was working upon his own version of the great patriarch. Indeed the grave images of the dead lying upon Petworth stone, with their brass or copper drapery closely fitted around them, became the types for the monarchs and prophets of his art; they are close to the recumbent figures he liked to draw, and bear a striking resemblance to the 'visionary heads' that he completed in later life. In the poetry he was writing at this early time images of death and monumentality also recur: Fair Elenor 'stood, Like a dumb statue' and receives an image of 'Pale death',[10] while one of his prose pieces is entitled 'The Couch of Death'. There is a more suggestive parallel, however, since at the time he was crouched above the grey marble of Edward III's tomb he was writing a drama entitled 'King Edward the Third'; it was as if he was bringing him to life from the sepulchre and, in the strange alchemy of his imagination, also bringing him to life within himself.

He was always preoccupied with death, displaying it in a thousand heterogeneous images, but his is more than a representative example of the 'graveyard school' that was so fashionable in this period. At a later date he experimented with the idea of a series of drawings on the subject of death, and there may be a connection between his interest in the past and his interest in mortality – was there, perhaps, some sense in which he wished to lose himself in antiquity? Did he also, with all the nervous conflicts of his youth, sometimes wish to be dead? There is, of course, a more immediate and appropriate explanation. He experienced an intense collaboration with mortality, and with the remnants of the past, because in the chapels and cloisters of the Abbey he saw the legendary history of Britain revealed. For him it was as much a spiritual as a national or antiquarian revelation; he entered a communion with the dead, with the passage of the generations, and thereby was granted a vision of the world that never left him. It was a vision, in his own words, of 'the characters which compose all ages and nations: as one age falls, another rises, different to mortal sight, but to immortals only the same; for we see the same characters repeated again and again, in animals, vegetables, minerals, and in men; nothing new occurs in identical existence; Accident ever varies, Substance can never suffer change nor decay'.[11] And so it was that the religious impulses of his childhood were strengthened here, but in such a place and in such a fashion that they became permanently associated with images of history and of art.

There are two stories concerning his time in Westminster Abbey that should also be related. It seems that there were occasions when he was interrupted by the boys of Westminster School, who used the Abbey as a playground and skittle alley: '. . . one of them is said after having already tormented him to have got upon some pinnacle on a level with his Scaffold in order better to annoy him. In the Impetuosity of his anger, worn out with Interruption, he knocked him off & precipitated him to the ground, upon which he fell with terrific Violence.'[12] Blake is said to have complained to the Dean about the schoolboy's behaviour and, even though no notice of such an occurrence is to be found in the Abbey records, it does effectively convey the occasional violence of Blake's temper. But there is another incident of a more tranquil sort; it is reported that in the old church, with his mind 'simplified by Gothic forms & his Fancy imbued with the livid twilight of past days', he saw spirits.[13] 'The aisles and galleries of the old cathedral suddenly filled with a great procession of monks and priests, choristers and censer-bearers, and his entranced ear heard the chant of plain-song and chorale, while the vaulted roof trembled to the sound of organ music.'[14] There is an early sketch of a procession of monks, hooded and gowned, walking two by two; so it may be that he was already beginning to draw what he glimpsed in vision.

The faculty of 'eidetic hallucination' or second sight had not left him at the end of his childhood, therefore – although the dead re-emerged in a more tangible shape on 2 May 1774. On that day various antiquaries gathered in the Abbey around the tomb of Edward I in solemn expectation; the king had been embalmed, according to historical report, and it was decided that the great coffin should be unsealed in order to inspect the condition of the body. He lay in the same chapel where Blake had been working upon the tombs of the other monarchs, and the young apprentice was present on this spring day when the coffin was opened by Sir Joseph Ayloffe. The sepulchral wrappings and the *sudarium*, or face cloth, were removed to reveal the body of the king dead for more than four hundred and fifty years: his face 'was of a dark-brown, or chocolate colour, approaching to black; and so were the hands and fingers. The chin and lips were intire, but without any beard . . . Both the lips were prominent; the nose short, as if shrunk; but the apertures of the nostrils were visible . . . some globular substance, possibly the flesh part of the eye-balls, was moveable in their sockets under the envelope. Below the chin and under-jaw was lodged a quantity of black dust, which had neither smell nor coherence; but whether the same had been flesh, or spices, could not be ascertained.'[15] The entire operation took an hour, before the tomb was resealed, and within that period Blake stood with the antiquaries and made two quick sketches of the recumbent figure. He finished two more elaborate drawings later and wrote beneath them, 'The body of Edward ye 1st as it appeared on first opening the Coffin' and 'The body as it appeared when some of the vestments were remov'd'. In subsequent years Blake restored Edward I in quite another fashion, when he depicted the king as the vainglorious destroyer of the prophetic bards of Wales, but there may be a more immediate reference to that sepulchral business in the Abbey in his early poem *Tiriel*, where 'the king of rotten wood & of the bones of death' emerges as part of Blake's visionary world.[16]

Yet in the Abbey he had also found a treasure greater then the remains of the dead. There he had seen a more wonderful vision. He found in the 'Gothic' statuary and paintings of the Abbey – and in the great body of the church itself – what he ever afterwards called 'true Art', a sacred art, an art of vision rather than verisimilitude or proportion.[17] To Blake, Gothic art seemed to show heaven in the world, and the world in heaven; from his later reading he also came to believe that heaven longs to see itself in material form, while the world aspires to be reunited with its spiritual essence.

'I have a great ambition to know everything,' he wrote once; so it is not at all surprising that in these early years, tired by his apprentice work and troubled by the usual ardours of youth, he still sat down in the quiet hours of the evening and embarked upon a course of self-education as wide as it was various. He kept a notebook in which he experimented with his signature – as if he were about to engrave it upon a plate – and practised the invaluable art of 'mirror writing' or reverse writing. This of course allowed the engraved words, when printed, to read forwards in the customary fashion; but his habitual practice in writing backwards had a further significance for his own later art. It is perhaps not unreasonable that a man who can write fluently in both directions might be intrigued by the concepts of 'oppositions' and 'contraries'. He might even contemplate the nature of 'writing' itself.

We know that he was also an assiduous and sensitive reader because there are constant allusions to diverse authors even in the poetry he was writing during this period. He was reading Spenser, Shakespeare and Jonson; their poetry was not as fashionable then as it was later to become (Shakespeare's verse, and not simply his drama, was one of Blake's passions) and his evident fondness for the literature of the sixteenth and seventeenth centuries, rather than that of his own time, is of a piece with his interest in the 'old-fashioned' engravings of Dürer or Raimondi. His reverence for the past also emerged in his passion for the works of 'Ossian' and of Chatterton. The prose poems of Ossian were supposed to be the work of an ancient bard, a son of Finn from Scottish antiquity, when in fact they were the imaginative productions of an eighteenth-century clergyman named James Macpherson; there was a prolonged debate about their authenticity before Blake himself came across them, but he never entertained doubts of any kind. A man who declares, 'Ages are All Equal. But Genius is Always Above The Age',[18] is hardly likely to be concerned if a poem was written in the third century or the seventeenth century, as long as it became the agent of spiritual perception. In Ossian's work he discovered an extraordinary landscape of heaths and ghosts, of dreams and yews and misty hills. The themes were of battles lost and won, of youth destroyed and betrayed, all conveyed in the sublime cadence of presumed antiquity: 'Our youth is like the dream of the hunter on the hill of the heath . . . Her steps were the music of songs. He was the stolen sigh of her soul . . . The horn of Fingal was heard; the sons of woody Albion returned . . . No words come forth: they seize their spears. Each soul is rolled into itself . . . But thou thyself shall fail, one night, and leave thy blue path in heaven.' The ending of 'Oithona', a prose poem from which Blake borrowed for one of his own short epics, has genuine power: 'The brightness of the face of Gaul returned. But his sigh rose, at times, in the midst of friends; like blasts that shake their unfrequent wings after the stormy winds are laid!' A shadowy image of Blake's own epics emerges in 'Fingal': 'His face is like the beam of the setting moon. His robes are of the clouds of the hills. His eyes are two decaying flames.' Ossian's 'Songs of Selma' would also have influenced a young poet already steeped in the Bible and in antiquarian lore: 'Star of descending night! fair is thy light in the west! thou liftest thy unshorn head from thy cloud: thy steps are stately on the hill.' It is wonderfully sonorous, with a grandeur that inspired men as diverse as Goethe and Napoleon; it affected Blake profoundly, and the cadences of the Ossian prose poems effortlessly entered his own imaginative repertoire.[19]

Thomas Chatterton's medieval poetry, written under the name of Thomas Rowley, was also being condemned as a forgery and pastiche; but Blake knew that Chatterton had divined a truth and acquired the authority of the past in a manner unavailable to the orthodox scholars and fashionable critics of the period. As he wrote in the year before his death, when the spell of Chatterton's youthful genius might be expected to have disappeared, 'I Believe both Macpherson & Chatterton, that what they say is Ancient, Is so . . . I own myself an admirer of Ossian equally with any other Poet whatever Rowley & Chatterton also'.[20] Blake's own debt to Chatterton is extensive and profound; there are various references to him in his early writing, where he appears to be as much a rival as an inspiration, and Blake's youthful poetry is heavily influenced by the vocabulary and imagery of the 'Rowley' ballads. In these 'forged' poems the remote past becomes an arena of mystery and dread, heroism and conflict, seen with the solemn gaze of assumed antiquity:

> Strayt was I carry'd back to Tymes of yore
> Whylst the Poet swathed yet yn fleshlie Bedde
> And saw all Actyons whych han been before
> And saw the Scroll of Fate unravelled
> And when the fate mark'd Babe acome to Syghte
> I saw hym eager graspeynge after Lyghte.[21]

The full range of Chatterton's work, and his death at his own hand by arsenic poison in a garret room in Brooke Street off Holborn, was not fully known until the details were published in the the Gazetteer and then reviewed in the Gentleman's Magazine in 1777. But by 1778 he was, according to his best biographer, 'in people's mouths', and there can be little doubt that Blake consciously modelled himself upon him.[22] That is why he was writing poetry in Miltonic and Spenserian style, just as Chatterton had recreated the forms of medieval literature. Blake was also an avid reader of Bishop Percy's *Reliques of Ancient English Poetry*; his own copy survives, and shows intense study of the first seventy-four pages. His interest in antiquity could also be of a more prosaic nature, however, and he read Milton's *History of Britain* as well as *Samson Agonistes* and *Paradise Lost*. His own sense of the past follows that of Milton, albeit indirectly and with more genuine fervour, and it is probably no coincidence that in his earliest historical paintings he illustrates many of the episodes which are depicted in the *History* itself. He also used the immensely popular history of Rapin de Thoyras, which, in typically mid-eighteenth-century fashion, had been issued in instalments.

Blake's reverence for antiquity had mythological as well as religious connotations, however, and, like many brilliant autodidacts, he tended to favour recondite or esoteric systems of knowledge. He read Stukeley's *Abury* on the supposed Druid temples of that region, and Mallet's *Northern Antiquities* in which he learned that 'what particularly distinguishes the Celtic institutions from those of the Gothic or Teutonic nations is that remarkable air of Secrecy and Mystery with which the Druids concealed their doctrines from the Laity'.[23] 'Secrecy and Mystery' are also two of the principal elements in Jacob Bryant's *A New System, or, An Analysis of Ancient Mythology*, in which the author promises to 'give an account of the first ages, and of the great events, which happened in the infancy of the world'.[24] It is a somewhat confused work that affirms the existence of a giant race which had been dispersed over the globe, bearing with it memorials of an ancient faith, and there are chapters with such resonant titles as 'Of Temple Rites in the First Ages', 'Of the Migration and Dispersion of Nations', 'Of the Omphi, and of the Worship upon High Places'. It has already been suggested that Blake worked on some of the engravings for this sonorous treatise, and he can hardly fail to have been affected by the rest: they are characteristically forcible and distinct, while some of the images are bathed in chiaroscuro like some tokens of forgotten knowledge and a lost world. When Bryant writes that 'The mythology of Greece is a vast assemblage of obscure traditions, which have been transmitted from the earliest times. They were described in hieroglyphics and have been veiled in allegory', he might have been anticipating the cadence and substance of Blake's own prose.[25]

All his life Blake was entranced and persuaded by the idea of a deeply spiritual past, and he continually alluded to the possibility of ancient lore and arcane myths that could be employed to reveal previously hidden truths. It is part of his reverence for the mysteries of Gothic art that Westminster Abbey had instilled in him, but it is also connected to less distinct ideas; he became heavily influenced by beliefs in the lost continent of Atlantis, of which the British Isles were the only remnant, and in the existence of Druid priests or Welsh magicians. These were also very much the preoccupations of his period, when comparative mythology was often aligned with the wilder speculations of various prophetic sects; Blake's interest was, if idiosyncratic, at least comprehensive. Some scholars have suggested that he embarked upon a sustained course of reading, from Aylett Sammes to Richard Brothers, while others have inferred from the eclectic range of his references that he simply picked up pamphlets and scraps of learning when it suited him. Whatever their sources might be, however, we find in Blake's art and writing a vast compendium of eighteenth-century syncretist mythology. Of course some of his youthful study was of a more familiar kind, such as his readings in Bacon and in Locke. 'They mock Inspiration & Vision,' he wrote later, 'Inspiration & Vision was then & now is & I hope will always Remain my Element my Eternal Dwelling place. how can I then hear it Contemnd without returning Scorn for Scorn.'[26] That is why he was in the habit of writing polemical or caustic notes in the margin of these various texts, as if the young apprentice were engaged in a pitched battle with the unfortunate author: 'A Confession . . . Infernal Falshood . . . Nonsense . . . This is a Very Clever Sentence who wrote it God knows'.[27] It was an aspect of his adversarial nature but it was also a part of his genius: no one could have single-handedly created such an elaborate and distinctive mythology without a stubborn sense of uniqueness and self-certainty.

Other books were not treated as roughly. One year into his apprenticeship he purchased Annibale Carracci's volume of engravings *Historia del Testamento Vecchio*, and with a graver inscribed on it 'W Blake 1773'; he drew details from three of the engravings, and on the cover he fashioned an image of the sun bearing a human face. Another artistic mentor was Abbé Winckelmann, whose *Reflections on the Painting and the Sculpture of the Greeks* has the signature 'William Blake, Lincolns Inn' as if the owner were setting himself up as a gentleman rather than a workaday apprentice; all his life he embraced the fantasy of higher status. Winckelmann's treatise was one that confirmed many of Blake's own artistic sentiments, most notably in its encomium on Raphael as the prince of painting and the very type of the artistic genius. He would have understood Winckelmann's praise of outline and enthusiasm for allegory, and was no doubt interested to discover that the 'most eminent prerogative' of painting is 'the representation of invisible, past and future things'.[28] Winckelmann extolled the simplicity and grandeur of classical art, and Blake's earliest engraving, 'Joseph of Arimathea', might almost have been executed in obedience to the German theorist's instructions to begin 'with one figure strongly fancied and masterly executed'.[29]

The nature of ideal beauty and artistic imitation was also a theme taken up by Winckelmann, which in turn reflected upon Blake's own practice at this time. He was learning to be a copyist by profession, in engraving the work of others, but he was also 'imitating' or reproducing figures from Michelangelo as well as cadences from Spenser and Shakespeare. It is a subject to which he must have given much thought, therefore, and it is one of the central elements within the poetry that he was now writing at the house in Great Queen Street. There is a phrase in an essay by the eighteenth-century poet James Thomson which serves as the best possible introduction to Blake's youthful verse: 'let poetry once more be restored to her ancient truth and purity'.[30] It is the spirit with which Blake approached engraving, and it is the theme which he announces in an address to the poetic muse:

> How have you left the antient love
> That bards of old enjoy'd in you!
> The languid strings do scarcely move!
> The sound is forc'd, the notes are few![31]

There are no forced sounds in these poems, 'the production of untutored youth, commenced in his twelfth, and occasionally resumed by the author till his twentieth year', but, rather, an extraordinary rush of association and remembrance.[32] Blake's early poetry is saturated with the cadences and imagery of the Bible, so that there are times when you might think that the anonymous author of 'The Song of Solomon' had been reborn in the eighteenth century. But there are also insistent recollections of Spenser, of Shakespeare, of Milton, as if the youthful Blake already felt himself to be a part of their visionary company. If he was restoring the lineaments of the past in his tomb drawings, there is a yet more wonderful resurrection as the dead speak through Blake's own voice:

> Let thy west wind sleep on
> The lake; speak silence with thy glimmering eyes,
> And wash the dusk with silver.[33]

This is not necessarily a poetry of private mood or self-expression –
these are *Poetical Sketches*, to give the title appended to them some
years later, but a competent draughtsman would have known that a
sketch need not be provisional or incomplete. And, just as it would be
absurd to expect a painting or engraving directly to express the
'feelings' of the artist, it would be quite wrong to approach Blake's
poetry with a Romantic belief that he is engaged in an act of
confessional lyricism or brooding introversion. To some extent, like
an engraver, he is subdued by his craft. But he also already knew that
he belonged to something larger than his own self. There may be an
occasional personal allusion; there is a continual attention to death,
for example, while envy and sexual jealousy seem to have been two of
the spurs towards creativity in his case. One phrase is repeated twice
because Blake liked either the sound or the sense of it: 'lord of thyself,
thou then art lord of all'.[34] In his attachment to fables of the past, or
to imaginary landscapes, there may also be some need to create an
alternative world in which he might hide or lose himself. But these
are essentially poems of dramatic narration or thematic argument.
Nineteenth-century critics noted the range of Blake's prosodic
experimentation – it was part of his instinctive attitude towards any
kind of authority that he never could approach an inherited or
familiar form without wishing to change it – but his technical
accomplishment is only an aspect of his more general intellectual
bravura. The poems are marked by dialectical argument and
continually touched by irony, while the invocations of earlier writers
are often so exact as to come close to parody. Blake once declared that
'the productions of our youth and of our maturer age are equal in all
essential points' and even in these youthful verses he is beginning to
create a landscape of visionary figures;[35] they are not personifications
or abstractions in the orthodox eighteenth-century manner, but
forces of human or divine will that have as much reality as the 'Elenor'
or the 'Gwin' of the ballads which he so skilfully adapts. This is not
the poetry of a melancholy or self-absorbed youth, but the first flight
of a spirited and exalted imagination. In his dramatic fragment on
King Edward III, loosely based upon a Shakespearian model, he
declares that the 'pure soul' will '. . . cut a path into the heaven of
glory, / Leaving a track of light for men to wonder at.'[36]

There is no doubt that Blake sought for 'glory' of some kind even now. That is why, in the 'holiday hours' of his apprenticeship, he was already engaged in some rather conventionally executed drawings and watercolours that were to form a series entitled 'The History of England'.[37] 'They were selected from a great number of historical compositions,' as one contemporary put it, 'the fruits of his fancy. He continued making designs for his own amusement whenever he could steal a moment from the routine of business.'[38] Among them were 'The Penance of Jane Shore' as well as 'The Landing of Brutus in England' and 'The Making of Magna Charta', all of which might have come from Milton's *History*. He was being very ambitious indeed, because he was attaching himself to the most recent and most advanced artistic movement of his time; in his childhood the Society of Arts had set up an annual prize for 'the best original Historical Picture' from the British past,[39] in a deliberate attempt to create a national school of painting that might rival those of classical antiquity or of the great European nations. (The radical politician and demagogue John Wilkes proposed the establishment of a national gallery in 1777.) Joshua Reynolds had suggested that 'Historical Painting ought to be called Poetical',[40] since it was intended to display 'intellectual grandeur . . . heroic virtue . . . philosophical wisdom'.[41] This was the tradition to which the young Blake now attached himself and, in future years, he would choose subjects from the medieval or mythological past with the same freedom as Mortimer, Barry and Romney. But he was not an artist, not yet, and all the force of nature and circumstance now determined his course for him. On finishing his apprenticeship with Basire, he did not join the Stationers' Guild as the first step towards becoming a professional engraver. Instead he applied to be enrolled in the Royal Academy Schools. He was still a nervous and excitable young man – qualities he retained all his life – and there is a suggestion that on occasion he endured abdominal pain as a result of his anxieties. He wanted to be artist and poet; he wanted to triumph; and, as he said at a later date, 'Excess in Youth is Necessary to Life'.[42]

SEVEN

We do not want either Greek or Roman Models

T he Royal Academy Schools were situated in Old Somerset House, off the Strand. Tuition was free and some twenty-five aspiring scholars were chosen each year by a formal system; a month before he completed his apprenticeship Blake submitted a drawing to the members of the Academy, and at the same time was obliged to provide a testimonial from an established artist. He had been working on various historical compositions for some time, no doubt with a view to producing one for this occasion, but the name of his sponsor has not survived. It was probably one of the artists who frequented Basire's studio but it might have been James Barry himself: what would have been more natural for a young man, so in love with an idealised and grandiloquent art, than to approach the contemporary master of that style? Since Barry did some work for Stuart's and Revett's *The Antiquities of Athens*, upon which Blake was also engaged, the possibility of their being acquainted at this early date is reasonably strong. His submission was approved, at any rate, and in August 1779, he was admitted as a probationer for three months. In that period he was obliged to work in the Antique School, or Plaister Academy, where he was asked to produce a complete and technically accurate anatomical drawing of a human figure. It sounds like a school exercise of the most mechanical sort, but at least it would test Blake's skills as a draughtsman. He was successful; on 8 October of that year he was enrolled as 'Blake William – 21 Yrs 28th last Novr. Engr.', and given an ivory ticket of admission for a period of six years.[1] Although he paid no fees, he was asked to provide his own materials.

He was entering an institution that had, in the eleven years since its foundation, become the most prominent artistic body in the country. It had been formed under the patronage of George III, after a series of internecine squabbles between the three existing societies of artists in a city which scarcely noticed their existence – it was not until the 1760s that there were art galleries or exhibitions of any kind, and if the patriot Hogarth had not founded the St Martin's Lane Academy there would have been very little interest in the possibility of a national school of art. But the Royal Academy now had high artistic aims and, in the words of its President, Sir Joshua Reynolds, the purpose of its teaching was to instil the notions of 'ideal beauty' and 'intellectual dignity';[2] that is why any taint of commerce or trade was considered unbecoming and, although Blake was admitted as an 'Engr.', professional engravers themselves were not allowed to become Academicians. As one acerbic contemporary put it, 'the Royal Academy was founded, consisting of members who had agreed to withdraw themselves from various clubs, not only to be more select as to talent, but perfectly correct as to gentlemanly conduct'.[3] But whatever the political and social motives of the Academy may have been, the aesthetic ones of its Schools were clear enough – their purpose was to train scholars in the ideals of classical art, to instil in them a true talent for drawing and its allied skills, and to promote the idea of a national school of historical painting. England could then become another Greece or Rome, and the empire that had already been established in India and Canada could be extended into the realm of what were called 'the fine arts'.

It was considered a noble undertaking and there is no evidence that Blake was in any way opposed to it, although he did eventually come to believe that Empire followed Art rather than the reverse. Someone trained in the spiritual nationalism of Westminster Abbey would not have balked at the idea of England's artistic greatness. Indeed the record suggests that, despite his later attacks upon Sir Joshua Reynolds, he was an assiduous and dedicated student. He began his instruction in the Antique School under the direction of the Keeper and Deputy Librarian, George Michael Moser. He was seventy-four years old when Blake first came under his care; one report has it that in the Academy 'all noise and tumult immediately ceased on his appearance',[4] but another contemporary records how the students tormented him by imitating the cries of cats, playing leap-frog and 'pelting one another with modeller's clay and crusts of bread'.[5] The Schools were about to move to new premises, but when Blake first joined he worked in the old plaster room, which was cluttered with

58 · BLAKE ·

heads, busts, friezes and fragments of statuary; copies of the great
works of antiquity were mounted on pedestals and rolled around on
casters to catch the changing light. It was not uncommon for young
scholars to break the hand of the Fawn or the fingers of Apollo, but
the pieces were promptly glued back together. There is an engraving
by Edward Burney of the scene, with Moser leaning over the drawing
of a young pupil who sports a pigtail. The students sit upon wooden
boxes, and rest their portfolios and port-crayons upon a rail: one can
almost enter the scene and tread upon the wooden floor, see the light
catch the cast of Apollo Belvedere coloured in oils, smell the
mustiness of the clothes, and hear the murmured words of Moser. The
cast of Cincinnatus can also clearly be seen in the engraving and part
of Blake's student drawing of that figure survives still, together with
certain heads and nudes that have also been attributed to him; they
show a careful if hesitant hand, striving for mastery over the classical
outline. He has drawn the lower legs and feet of Cincinnatus in a
half-hearted fashion, however, and his attitude to the tasks now set
for him may well be reflected in one of his later poems:

> Portions of life; similitudes
> Of a foot, or a hand, or a head.[6]

Towards the end of his first year the Academy and its Schools
moved to their much more spacious premises in the New Somerset
House. Now it could proclaim its status as a national institution
established on an Athenian model; when Blake came through the
entrance to the right of the Strand he walked into a hall lined with
famous statuary, including 'Hercules' and 'Two Centaurs' as well as
'Apollo Belvedere'. This was an interior quite different from that of
Westminster Abbey, and all his life Blake emphasised the disparity
between classical and Gothic art. He mounted the staircase, passing
various figures and busts, until he came to the first landing, where
Cipriani had painted an allegory of 'Arts and Sciences'. The library
was situated on this floor, its ceiling decorated by Reynolds and
depicting 'Theory' seated upon clouds. Here Blake could pursue
classical art, in the standard school texts of the period – Bishop's
Statues was one, '. . . a book which is in every young Artist's hand'
according to Reynolds,[7] in which Blake would have seen illustrations
of the Laocoön and a series of engravings from Michelangelo by
Vasari. Other Academy favourites were the Antiquities of Sir William
Hamilton, Antiquity Explained and Preserved in Sculpture by Bernard de

Montfaucon, Eckhel's *Antique Gems*, and *Polymetis* by Joseph Spence; these volumes were at the centre of Blake's orthodox and classical education. His early training at Pars' and Basire's was here reinforced by the study of the outlines of antique gems and friezes, vases and medallions, which embodied all the grace, restraint and decorum that were aspects of the classical ideal.

The new Antique Gallery, less cluttered and more grandiose than the old, was on the same floor as the library; but, after he had proved his proficiency to the satisfaction of Moser, Blake was allowed to move down to the Life Gallery on the ground floor. Here, a male or female nude was placed in an appropriate sculptural attitude, perhaps even imitating the pose of the statuary in the entrance hall beyond; the model stood upright, or sat upon a cushion, in front of a semicircle of students. The classes began in the late afternoon, so that the Academy scholars could earn their living during the day, and, according to the rules of the Academy, 'While the Visitor is setting the Model, the Students shall draw Lots for their Places . . . As soon as any Student, hath done Drawing or Modeling, he shall put out his Candles, and while Drawing or Modeling, he shall be careful to keep them under the Bells.'[8] Some life studies of Blake have survived, but the practice was not altogether to his taste. He once told a friend that in Westminster Abbey 'he early imbibed the pure & spiritual character of the female expression & form';[9] once he had found art, he had no taste for nature. In fact he found life drawing 'hateful' and of 'looking more like death, or smelling of mortality'.[10] Blake himself wrote, at a later date, that 'As to a modern Man stripped from his load of cloathing, he is like a dead corpse.'[11] There is no need to speculate about the nature of his inhibitions here, although it is paradoxical that a young man who would soon be proclaiming the virtues of sexual energy should also be disgusted by the physical medium of its transmission. But it may simply be that his distaste was fostered by William Hunter's disquisitions on anatomy in the Lecture Room on the first floor – here, it is reported, he would sometimes display the corpses of criminals recently executed at Tyburn. But Blake learned something from these naked exercises: he learnt the musculature of the human form, and in a work such as 'Nebuchadnezzar' his Academy training is seen to best advantage.

Painting and Anatomy were two of the courses available for study at the Academy, the others being Perspective and Architecture. There were four professors who lectured on these disciplines, as well as various 'Visitors' who coached the aspiring artists. The teaching insisted upon an implicit obedience to the 'Rules of Art, as established by the practice of the great MASTERS',[12] and students contended among themselves over 'who shall have the purest and most correct outline, who shall dispose his drapery in the most graceful folds, which shall give the most grace and dignity to the human figure'.[13] The forms of the pursuit of art were 'Invention, Composition, Expression, Colouring and Drapery',[14] the art of fresco and the art of oil, and from the great masters the young Blake was asked to learn 'how the masses of light are disposed . . . how artfully some parts are lost in the ground, others boldly relieved',[15] how 'the principal figure should be immediately distinguished at the first glance of the eye' and how objects 'must be disposed in large masses and groups properly varied and contrasted'.[16]

Joshua Reynolds himself was, according to Oliver Goldsmith, 'gentle, complying and bland', an artist whose fashionable taste and orthodox aesthetic would have meant little, or nothing, to Blake.[17] In the first address or 'discourse' to the students that Blake heard in the new Lecture Room, Reynolds extolled the idea of 'general beauty' and the pursuit of 'general truth',[18] while going on to say that 'we perceive by sense, we combine by fancy, and distinguish by reason . . . the beauty of which we are in quest is general and intellectual'.[19] The address lasted only ten minutes or so but, as Reynolds's serene and mellifluous voice filled the room, it would have been quite long enough for Blake. His later annotations to Reynolds are filled with indignation and disgust, but the source of his anger can be located in these student days. He was also scathing about Reynolds's professions of humility; indeed Blake always considered humility to be a form of hypocrisy, an attitude that throws an interesting light on his own temperament.

REYNOLDS: I felt my ignorance, and stood abashed.

BLAKE: A Liar he never was Abashed in his Life & never felt his Ignorance.

REYNOLDS: I consoled myself by remarking that these ready inventors, are

extremely apt to acquiesce in *imperfection*.

BLAKE: Villainy a Lie.

REYNOLDS: But this disposition to abstractions . . . is the great glory of the human mind.

BLAKE: To Generalize is to be an Idiot To Particularize is the Alone Distinction of Merit – General Knowledges are those Knowledges that Idiots possess.

REYNOLDS: The great use in copying, if it be at all useful, should seem to be in learning to colour.

BLAKE: Contemptible.

REYNOLDS: But as mere enthusiasm will carry you but a little way . . .

BLAKE: Damn the Fool, Mere Enthusiasm is the All in All![20]

Blake remembered two moments in the company of the great and famous President:

REYNOLDS: Well, Mr Blake, I hear you despise our art of oil painting.

BLAKE: No, Sir Joshua, I don't despise it; but I like fresco better.[21]

This is an interesting remark, given that Reynolds's oils were the fashion of the day, but perhaps at this late date it needs further elucidation: 'fresco' was the term used for the productions of the great masters of water-based paint and tempera, rather than oil, who worked within the ideal outlines and contours of spiritual form. The purity and radiance of Fra Angelico's painting may stand as a sufficient example. Oil was a later and more sensuous medium, which, according to Blake at least, was too fluid and indeterminate: 'Oil was not used except by blundering ignorance, till after Vandyke's time . . .'[22] Eventually Blake came to believe that single-handedly he had revived the art of fresco painting. It has been suggested that he disliked oil painting simply because he was not proficient at it. But this is to mistake his own commitment to quite another kind of art: in the two years before he joined the Royal Academy Schools his imagination had been established upon the recognition of pure outline and clearly defined form. His understanding of art, as well as his belief in his own artistic gift, rested upon the certainties of the engraving and the 'Gothic' style. Oil was too blurred, too muddy, too indistinct. We must imagine a young man coming to the Schools with a vigorous and no doubt outspoken attachment to a style that was shared only by a few radical painters of the day. It was not 'old-fashioned' – it formed part of the heroic art of Mortimer or Barry – but it was unfashionable.

Another anecdote suggests an even less gracious encounter with the President of the Royal Academy. A friend remembered 'his talking to me of Reynolds. He became furious at what the latter had dared to say of his early works. When a very young man he had called on Reynolds to show him some designs, and had been recommended to work with less extravagance and more simplicity, and to correct his drawing. This Blake seemed to regard as an affront never to be forgotten. He was very indignant when he spoke of it.'[23] Of course it is exactly the sort of remark Reynolds could have been expected to make; more interesting is Blake's continuing indignation at a comment volunteered many years before. It is like his memory of being 'threatened' with a beating by his father, where the stray remarks of those in authority over him are turned into permanent mementoes of humiliation or fear; and, as a result, he could become very angry indeed.

But the reverse side of such sensitivity, and anger, is a kind of obstinacy or extravagant self-confidence. Another story from his time at the Royal Academy suggests how little respect he held for the opinions of even his oldest masters. In one of his angry annotations to Reynolds, made over twenty years after he left the Schools, his mind went back to that time: 'I was once looking over the Prints from Rafael & Michael Angelo. in the Library of the Royal Academy Moser came to me & said You should not Study these old Hard Stiff & Dry Unfinishd Works of Art, Stay a little & I will shew you what you should Study. He then went & took down Le Bruns & Rubens's Galleries How I did secretly Rage. I also spoke my Mind I said to Moser, These things that you call Finishd are not Even Begun how can they then, be Finishd? The Man who does not know The Beginning, never can know the End of Art.'[24] There may be an element of hindsight in such a quick riposte, and Blake's 'memories' are not always to be fully trusted, but a true picture of the man is to be found here: 'How I did secretly Rage.' It sounds like a line from one of his lyric poems and suggests once again that anger which was a real, formidable and permanent aspect of his personality.

There was one teacher at the Royal Academy whom Blake did admire, and when James Barry was appointed Professor of Painting in 1782 Blake listened to his lectures with great attention – we know this because at a later date he reasserted some of Barry's theories and themes in his own writing. Barry was for him the single most important English painter; there was a time when he planned to write an epic poem in three books entitled simply *Barry* and he continually deferred to him as an artist unjustly neglected by the contemporary world. Barry's paintings had a marked effect upon Blake's understanding of the heroic style: his grave or monumental figures were characteristically placed in situations of grandiloquent passion, as if neoclassicism had been irradiated by the wild energy of his imagination. He adored the *terribilità* of Michelangelo and the pure outlines of Raphael with the same fervour as Blake; he revered Milton as the prophetic outcast of England, in the same manner as Blake, and interpreted that poet's work with his own idealised figures. (It is significant that it was in this period that Blake himself began work on a series of illustrations for *Paradise Lost.*) Barry also engraved his own works in a manner that would have strongly affected the younger man – he did not follow the prettifying tendencies of the age but struck out boldly on the copper to reproduce the definite outlines and extravagant foreshortening of his paintings. He was dedicated to the idea of historical painting and to the idea of a national school, but not in the anodyne and formal manner of Sir Joshua Reynolds – 'History painting and sculpture,' he said, '. . . are the tests by which the national character will be tried in after-ages', and for him it became a private if eventually self-destructive crusade.[25] For six years he was engaged in a cycle of historical paintings within the interior of the Royal Society of Arts, and received very little recompense. As Blake put it in another of his peremptory memories jotted in the margin of Reynolds's *Discourses*: 'Who will Dare to Say that [Fine] Polite Art is Encouraged, or Either Wished or Tolerated in a Nation where The Society for the Encouragement of Art. Sufferd Barry to Give them, his Labour for Nothing . . . Barry told me that while he Did that Work – he Lived on Bread & Apples.'[26] He did not add that the older painter had seen visions, too, in a London which seems to have been filled with visionaries. Barry had a sad end; he was expelled as Professor of Painting because he attacked a 'cabal' at the Royal Academy itself – 'attacking the Academy's administration of its funds & denouncing private combinations & jealousies,' as one contemporary put it.[27] He became a solitary, and lived in a ruined house at No. 36 Castle Street East, by Cavendish Square, where the local children would torment him by stuffing dead rats through the letterbox and throwing stones at his already broken windows. Eventually he succumbed to a terrible paranoia, and believed that the Fellows of the Royal Academy were attempting to murder him.

But that is to move too far ahead, and to miss him lecturing in the

Assembly Room of the Royal Academy Schools with the young Blake in his audience. Here he speculated on a great Oriental art that had emerged long before that of the Greeks and Romans; he envisioned 'the golden statue, sixty cubits high, of Nebuchadnezzar', and stated his belief in the relics of a lost art that had flourished before the Great Deluge.[28] Blake's imagination had already turned in this direction as part of his reverence for the mysteries of the remote past, but now he had found someone within the Schools who confirmed his own sense of life.

Perhaps the most important influences, however, came from his contemporaries – many of them blessed with talent, one or two touched by genius, whose subsequent lives and works were to play a large part in Blake's own history. Thomas Stothard had joined the Royal Academy Schools two years before Blake; he had been apprentice to a silk pattern maker in Spitalfields for seven years and, under the patronage of Samuel Rogers and Josiah Wedgwood, was eventually to become one of the most skilful and fashionable artists of the day. He was an amiable and gentle young man – once 'a delicate child', according to his daughter-in-law, who had developed 'a quiet and docile spirit'.[29] They met in Blake's first year at the Schools, when Stothard was already trying to establish himself as a professional artist (the hours of tuition being such that a student could pursue his own work in the morning and early afternoon), but they had more in common than shared ambition. The young Stothard revered Dürer and Raphael, while at the same time he wished to attach himself to a school of national historical painting. That is why he had a pronounced affection for Gothic antiquity, and very much admired the 'Monumental Effigies' of the Middle Ages – in particular he used to mention the tomb of Queen Eleanor in Westminster Abbey that Blake had already delineated.[30] In the year that he and Blake first met, 1779, Stothard was also illustrating the poems of Ossian. It is easy to see, then, how the two young men would have been instinctively drawn to one another; there would be terrible quarrels in later life, when Blake would accuse Stothard of being 'jealous' of him and assert his superior genius,[31] but in these first years they became close artistic companions.

It was Stothard who, that same year, introduced Blake to John Flaxman, although Flaxman himself was not a student at the Schools. He was the son of a plaster-cast maker in New Street, by Covent Garden, and had grown up among the models and casts that his father made or repaired: the shop had little figures in its window which were much admired by the children of the area, and Mr Flaxman's workmen were well known to the local tavern-keepers. Flaxman himself was 'a puny, ailing little boy' with a slight curvature of the spine;[32] he used to sit on a small chair behind the counter and read his Latin primers, but his central gift was artistic. He is in fact one of the paradoxes of cultural history; he became the single most influential English artist of his day, a sculptor whose name was known all over Europe, but he is now almost entirely forgotten except by scholars and art historians. There is an additional irony of course in that his companion, William Blake, remained quite unknown in his lifetime. Flaxman had started working for Josiah Wedgwood even before he met Blake; like his father he was adept at modelling, and he began fashioning samples for the industrialist's range of pottery and crockery. Blake may even have seen him at work since Wedgwood's London shop was in Portland Place, by Greek Street and Soho Square, only a few yards from Blake's family home in Broad Street. Flaxman was very successful in what was a delicate task, and there is a report of his being vain in his early years; it was probably not vanity, however, but the exhilaration of knowing that, however infirm he had been, he could make his own way in the world. His actual temperament seems to have been a sober one; he had a profound sense of duty and responsibility, but was sometimes mocked by his contemporaries (by whom he was known as 'Little Flaxman, the Sculptor') for 'his fixity of ideas, his imaginative poverty, his tendency to lapse into the sentimental or melodramatic'.[33] He was even a collector of the watch-rate, by which householders paid a fixed sum for a neighbourhood constable, and one observer reported, 'I have often seen him, with an ink-bottle in his button-hole, collecting the rate.'[34]

He was a loyal friend, and remained a firm if sometimes bewildered and frustrated supporter of Blake for many years. No friendship with Blake was ever easy, and sometimes Blake turned on him with accusations of hypocrisy and double-dealing; which is why there was a perceptible cooling of their relationship in later years when Flaxman, like most others, simply grew tired of the poet's erratic behaviour. But although Flaxman considered him 'wild', he never accepted the general opinion that he was mad:[35] he knew him too well to come to any such conclusion and, as Blake himself admitted in a conciliatory letter, he also knew how 'to forgive Nervous Fear'.[36]

In these first years, they found that they had much in common. Flaxman venerated Gothic art and, despite an insistent tendency towards neoclassicism in his later career, he remarked on the tombs of Westminster Abbey that they were 'specimens of the magnificence of such works of the age . . . which forcibly direct the attention and turn the thoughts not only to other ages, but to other states of existence'.[37] His literary tastes were also very similar to those of Blake; he executed several drawings from the verses of Chatterton, and even designed a memorial for the dead poet, which was exhibited at the Royal Academy the year after Blake joined. Here, then, was another kindred spirit.

So Blake was never isolated in these years, despite the impression he gives in his own retrospective notes, where he emphasises his freedom from influences of any kind; he was in fact part of a little club or community with shared interests. They were all sons of London tradesmen, all in love with the Gothic past, all reading Chatterton and Ossian with profound interest. In a larger perspective it might be said they were part of a generation that rediscovered the English strain of moral seriousness and earnest spirituality after some of the more febrile speculations of their sceptical and deistical predecessors; but, in the world of the Academy by the Strand, it is more important to recognise that these were young men who shared a sensitivity towards sacred art that was not common among their older teachers who were more concerned with the classical ideals of the mid-eighteenth century. That is why Blake had such difficulty with Cincinnatus, while delighting in the tombs of the great dead.

Two other contemporaries must be introduced here, if only to suggest the larger eighteenth-century world around Blake. James Gillray entered the Royal Academy Schools in the spring of 1778, as an engraver, and Thomas Rowlandson was admitted in the winter of 1772. Blake would have just missed Rowlandson, although he may already have noticed his history paintings at the annual exhibitions, but he would certainly have encountered Gillray. There is no record of any friendship, however, despite the fact that they shared a similar background – Gillray had been born in Chelsea, of Dissenting parents, and after a course of self-education was apprenticed for seven years to a writing-engraver in Holborn. The coincidences are remarkable enough, and it is intriguing to consider the possibility of young Gillray and young Blake sitting side by side drawing a model in a life class. Who would copy from whom? But the connection does not necessarily end there. Gillray was a remarkable artist, and in the extravagance of his baroque imagination there is at least a passing resemblance to the painted visions of William Blake. Both created their own private mythology from the raw material of the world, and there are several occasions when Blake borrowed a motif or image from his contemporary's cartoons. Eventually Gillray went mad and was locked in an upstairs apartment of a printseller while under the delusion that he was Rubens. He died, apparently after throwing himself out of a window, at a time when Blake lived in the deepest obscurity and was himself condemned as insane.

Blake's acquaintance was not confined to his contemporaries at the Academy however, and, in an obituary notice of John Flaxman, some mention is made of other youthful companions: '. . . in his early life he [Flaxman] was in the habit of frequently passing his evenings in drawing and designing in the company of that excellent painter Mr Stothard, Mr Blake, the engraver (lately deceased), so remarkable for the eccentricity of his opinions and his designs, Mr George Cumberland, and Mr Sharp.'[38] Blake had met George Cumberland in his first year at the Schools; he was a clerk in the Royal Exchange Assurance Company, but he was also an amateur artist and aesthetician. He was later to write a number of books, among them 'verse-tales' and some not undistinguished artistic treatises; and already in his youth he was a collector of early Italian prints and shared Blake's belief in 'the inestimable value of chaste outline'.[39] Here, again, are certain affinities. William Sharp was some seven or eight years older than the others, and was already a skilful professional engraver whose elaborate and refined style had become unmistakable. He was also an enthusiast, in the seventeenth-century sense, and his spiritual pilgrimage through the years testifies to the extraordinarily rarefied religious atmosphere of the times. He was first a Theosophist but then converted to Swedenborgianism; he was also a mesmerist and physiognomist, at a time when both were aspects of radical London culture. But, more importantly, he became a devotee of the two great religious prophets of the period, Richard Brothers and Joanna Southcott. The particular doctrines of 'the Prophet of the Lost Tribe' and the 'the Woman Clothed with the Sun' will be discussed later, when they directly touch upon Blake's own millennial beliefs, but they may be noted here as the culmination of one Dissenting tradition.

There is one other set of attitudes that linked Stothard with

Cumberland, and Sharp with Flaxman – and thus directly to Blake.
At this time they were all committed political radicals. Sharp,
Cumberland and Stothard joined the Society for Constitutional
Information. Sharp engraved a libertarian banner that Stothard had
designed with the title 'A Declaration of Rights'. George Cumberland
wrote an ode in praise of the radical agitator Horne Tooke, and
himself became the object of attention from government spies. 'No
news,' he once wrote to a friend, 'save that Great Britain is hanging
the Irish, hunting the Maroons, feeding the Vendée, and establishing
the human flesh trade.'[40] They had all become acquainted at a time
when Old Corruption fouled the air, and a fierce radicalism
characterised the politics of London. England was at war with
America but that conflict, prosecuted by Lord North and George III,
was unpopular – the Corporation of London opposed it, the old
Dissenters opposed it, the Wilkeite radicals opposed it and the
merchants opposed it. It was a time when a poet known to Blake could
ask, in a work entitled The Desolation of America, 'Are Britain and her
crimes so little known?',[41] although the numerous twopenny newspapers of the period made sure that their readers were well enough
acquainted with them. England was also at war with France, and
there was a threat of rebellion in Ireland; the government was being
accused of financial corruption, while food riots occurred sporadically
in the streets of London. These were the conditions in which the
political radicalism of Blake's friends was being fostered, and the
ardour of youth was exacerbated by a general urban political culture
that considered the king and the king's government to be obtuse,
uncertain and wretchedly incompetent. Blake is said to have
professed himself always 'a "Liberty Boy", a faithful "Son of Liberty";
and would jokingly urge in self-defence that the shape of his head
made him a republican'.[42] No doubt he learned that lesson from the
physiognomical Sharp. In fact he had worked within a radical milieu
all his life; his parents were of old city stock characterised by its
republican attitudes and, even while he was an apprentice, he had
worked on engravings for the radical Memoirs of Thomas Hollis. He
had been accustomed to the movement of urban politics since
childhood, from the mobs who for a while controlled London with
the cry 'Wilkes and Liberty!' to the supporters of the 'Sons of Liberty'
then attacking British soldiers in the United States. Radicalism could
take various forms, however, from the middle-class revolutionaries
(who at a slightly later date would include Wordsworth and

Coleridge) to the urban debating clubs and the 'underground' societies practising or preaching their own forms of subversion.

The nature of Blake's radicalism was perhaps not clear even to Blake himself; it would have been a natural and almost instinctive stance, which would require neither apology nor explanation. But the fact that he never joined any particular group or society suggests that his was, from the beginning, an internal politics both self-willed and self-created. In later life he managed to combine an intense visionary belief in brotherhood and the human community with that robust and almost anarchic individualism so characteristic of London artisans during this period. It is likely in these first years, however, that his radicalism was an aspect of his own imaginative and brooding temperament; it helped to afford him an identity, and thus assuage his fears of the world, at the same time as it complemented his own visionary experiences.

The generally dangerous and uncertain nature of the times can be shown in an anecdote from these years, when Stothard and Blake were enjoying a drawing expedition up the Medway. They had stopped upon the shore and were making pencil sketches of the scene when 'they were suddenly surprised by the appearance of some soldiers, who very unceremoniously made them prisoners, under the suspicion of being spies for the French government'.[43] They were detained in a tent, made out of their own sails, with an armed guard to superintend them until members of the Royal Academy could be found to verify their story. There is a small pen-and-ink drawing made by Stothard of their confinement, which shows a young man looking disconsolately upon the waters of the Medway. Once they had regained their freedom 'they spent a merry hour with the commanding officer', but Blake's predisposition towards anxiety could not have made the experience a particularly happy one.[44]

There was danger in London, too, and the revolutionary spirit of the capital at this time manifested itself in days of rioting and what Gibbon called 'dark and diabolical fanaticism'.[45] Blake was caught up in the general madness, and the images of fire and havoc that pervade his poetry may spring in part from the terrible destruction of the city which he witnessed as a young man. It began with a parliamentary Bill designed to relieve Roman Catholics of certain ancient penalties and disabilities; it was then that Lord George Gordon and his Protestant Association set up a cry of 'No Popery!', which left 'every man, woman and child in the streets panic struck, the atmosphere red as blood with the ascending fires'.[46] On Friday 2 June 1780, at around midnight, the rampaging mobs invaded Broad Street and Golden Square; the Bavarian Chapel and the house of the Bavarian ambassador were put to the torch and pillaged, while there was a pitched battle between the mob and militia in Broad Street itself. There is an engraving of the scene, by James Heath after Francis Wheatley, which shows houses being plundered among pillars of smoke, the drunken staggering in disarray, bloody fighting on the ground amid fires while some of the injured are dragged away – 'Howlings & hissings, shrieks & groans, & voices of despair' no more than a few yards from Blake's own house.[47] Soon the ostensible aim of the rioters was lost in the general confusion and slaughter; it was as if all the anger of the London mob, restless for so long under the yoke of King and Parliament, had found a terrible fruition. On the Tuesday evening, 6 June, Blake was walking down Long Acre towards the shop of his old master in Great Queen Street when suddenly he was swept up by a wave of advancing rioters who rushed down Holborn towards the Old Bailey and Newgate Prison. On this occasion the mob consisted of the more disruptive elements in London – apprentices, servants and even criminals joined in the general pillage. Then, outside the barred entrance of Newgate prison, Blake witnessed those scenes of burning and devastation that are so vividly depicted in Charles Dickens's *Barnaby Rudge* – the huge gates were attacked with pickaxes and sledgehammers, and soon the entire prison was enveloped in flames. The prisoners shrieked and screamed, because they were in imminent danger of being burned alive, until the rioters clambered over the walls and literally tore off the roof above their heads. They were dragged out, or crawled, from the prison, their fetters clinking on their legs before they reached blacksmiths in the vicinity. The cry went up as they poured out of the prison, screaming and blaspheming, 'A clear way! A clear run!'[48] George Crabbe was another poet who witnessed the scene, and described the rioters 'rolled in black smoke mixed with sudden bursts of fire – like Milton's infernals who were as familiar with flame as with each other'.[49] When the house of a vintner by Fetter Lane was put to the torch, the mob lay in the gutter and drank the streams of burning spirit until they expired. It is reported that Blake was 'forced to go along in the very front rank' and witness the destruction of Newgate, but he is not likely to have been 'forced' the entire distance.[50] Other observers, such as Crabbe, seem to have been able to move around of their own accord. It is much more likely that he went along with the mob willingly, perhaps impulsively, and, when he saw the fire and heard the screaming, he stayed out of sheer panic or overwhelming curiosity. He was fortunate, however, in not being recognised by any of the soldiery once the disturbances were crushed in the following week: he might have been hanged, and in the days after the riot had been quelled he would have seen many young men of his own age strung up at the scenes of their supposed crimes.

There are two drawings he completed in this year, which he later engraved with the title 'Albion Rose'. They show two views of a young man with his arms outstretched in a gesture of liberation – it is an idealised figure in a classical pose, but there is such a look of exaltation upon his face that it has been related to the sense of energy and liberation that the Gordon Riots may or may not have induced in Blake. There was in particular a handbill entitled The Scourge that depicted the mob as 'persevering and being united in One Man against the infernal designs of the Ministry'. But such an association is not likely. Even his most radical friends, such as George Cumberland, reacted with horror to the spectacle of the city in a state of incendiary revolution, and there is no reason to suppose that Blake felt differently about the fires and the deaths. A far more likely image of the Gordon Riots may be found in such paintings of death and destruction as 'Fire', 'Pestilence' and 'A Breach in a City', to which he returned with such frequency that they might represent some primal scene. 'Albion Rose' looks more like a study connected with his work in the Academy Schools – suggested pictorial sources for the image have ranged from Agrippa's Of Occult Philosophy to Scamozzi's Archiettura, from the precepts of Vitruvius to the curves of a Roman bronze found at Herculaneum, even though in Blake's hand the classical motif has been transfused with an intense spiritual energy. It may be related to his new sense of freedom after completing his apprenticeship, or to general youthful exuberance, or to the recognition of his own great powers.

Already he was showing signs of proficiency that had not been immediately apparent in his early sketches from the antique. That is because he was now working within the broad context of the new English school of painting, with its emphasis upon the historical and literary subjects which he revered. There are watercolours of Brutus, of Edward III, of Earl Goodwin, of Jane Shore as well as sketches of a more indeterminate nature – some of them may have been intended as engravings, or as studies for exhibition works, or even perhaps as frescoes. Queen Emma walks across red-hot ploughshares in order to prove herself innocent of her son's murder, while the courtiers look on in dismay or consternation; Earl Goodwin falls dead from the table after being struck down by divine displeasure; Jane Shore walks in sad and demure penance across the nave of St Paul's. He exhibited his initial work, 'The Death of Earl Goodwin', only eight months after joining the Royal Academy Schools; this confident first step testifies to his ambition at such an early stage and, even though his watercolour was confined to the Academy's Ante-Room (the best room was given over to oils), he was no doubt pleased by George Cumberland's notice in the *Morning Chronicle and London Advertiser* that it was of 'good design, and much character'.[51] It is generally suggested that Blake soon wearied of the Royal Academy and ceased to attend its classes, but there is no evidence to support this. He may well have tired of its conventions and traditions – in various essays George Cumberland was to attack the Academy for its 'languid and cold assistance' of the Arts, and no doubt he received this information from his friend.[52] But Blake continued to offer his work for exhibition at the Academy and, of all his contemporaries, he was by far the most successful in that endeavour.

Of course historical subjects were popular in the mid-eighteenth century – in 1763 Robert Edge Pine received a hundred-guinea prize for his painting of Canute, while in the same year Mortimer completed his own version of Queen Emma's humiliation. There were in addition many plays with ancient English settings – John Brown's *Athelstan*, Richard Glover's *Boadicea* and Thomas Arne's *Alfred* among them. Certain works were very close to Blake's particular themes. 'The Ballad of Jane Shore', for example, was in Percy's *Reliques*, while Rowe's play *Jane Shore* was extraordinarily successful (with Garrick playing Lord Hastings). In a sense, then, Blake was touching upon the popular or folkloric roots of his subjects – all of which were dismissed as 'fiction' by the historians of the period. Earl Goodwin is not supposed to have choked on a morsel of food as a sign of divine displeasure, and Eleanor is not likely to have sucked the poison from her husband's dagger wound. But Blake chose to depict these subjects precisely because they were part of the fabulous and mythological history of the country; he was not concerned with literal truth but with the spiritual realities that these legends contained. It was the legacy of the boy who had worked among the dead in Westminster Abbey.

He was at the same time following the artistic programme of a Barry or a Mortimer in illustrating subjects from Shakespeare, Milton and the Bible. It is what any ambitious young painter would do but, although they are generally well composed and show great fluency of a conventional kind, they display certain idiosyncrasies; small traces of his mature vision can be glimpsed, just as certain phrases from his later epic poetry can be found in his first *Poetical Sketches*. It is as if the process of growth for Blake was one of stripping away the various levels of conventional perception and composition to find his own starker figures beneath. In his illustrations to Milton and the Bible, for example, two of his enduring interests are to be seen – that of elemental conflict in the swirling activity of the Milton drawings, and that of the stony law-giver in the statuesque stillness and verticality of his Old Testament work. (There may also be a connection between Blake's art of expressive gesture, in works such as 'Abraham and Isaac' or 'Saul and the Ghost of Samuel', and the eighteenth-century tradition of biblical operas and oratorios; Handel's *Samson* or *Joseph and His Brethren* could have had some affect upon Blake's handling of the same subjects, and we will see how the structure of the opera and oratorio eventually affected his own understanding of poetic form.) He seems already to have projected his vision in terms of series, each part of which illustrates a moment of dramatic encounter; that is why a later sequence of poems such as *Songs of Innocence* can be intimately related to his first use of painting as a medium.

In these early drawings and sketches, a characteristic Blakean scenario has already become evident; it is that of an isolated figure with upraised arms in an attitude of fear or reverence. The compositions are dramatic, on occasions evincing a certain stiffness, and even at this stage there are clear signs of Blake's interest in formal and hieratic design – an interest that springs from his training as an engraver and his understanding of Gothic art. His work rarely has a private or intimate character – there is nothing like Turner's brooding intensity, which seems to bear the marks of the artist's mind – because it is an art on display, an art designed to elicit a particular affect. It is essentially a public exercise, in other words, and throughout his life Blake continued to think of himself as a public artist. His art is to be associated with Barry or Mortimer, not with Constable or Turner, just as he is better understood in the company of James Thomson or Edward Young rather than that of Wordsworth or Coleridge.

He exhibited no work at the Academy for three years after 'The

Death of Earl Goodwin', since in that period he began work as a professional engraver. He was living in the family house at Broad Street while studying at the Schools, and it was necessary for him to earn a living and help to support his parents. His first commercial work was completed in August 1780, less than a year after he had joined the Academy; it was after a design by Stothard on a Shakespearian theme, and is the earliest example of what would become a close collaboration between the two men over the next few years. He was to engrave a good deal of Stothard's work, including scenes for editions of Chaucer and Ariosto as well as illustrations for well-known works of fiction in the *Novelist's Magazine* – the ninth volume, for example, contained 'Sentimental Journey, Gulliver's Travels, David Simple, Sir Lancelot Greaves, The Peruvian Princess and Jonathan Wild' all printed in double columns with full-page engravings. He worked on Ritson's *Collection of English Songs* and on a volume that, more than any other, gives a sense of the general culture through which Blake then moved. Entitled *The Wit's Magazine, or, Library of Momus, being a Compleat Repository of Mirth, Humour, and Entertainment*, it was a monthly periodical that included essays such as 'The Errors of the Press', tales such as 'The Story of the Bleeding Finger', poems such as 'The Sweeper', as well as puzzles and anecdotes of an anodyne nature. Blake was asked to engrave illustrations to poems in rhyming couplets such as 'Tythe in Kind; or The Sow's Revenge', which he did in a deliberately rough and populist chapbook style. It says something about the nature of his relationship with Stothard and other artists, however, that he was implicitly the subsidiary part of the creative process. This was always to be his position in the world of commerce and printselling. Over the next few years he finished some fifty-seven commercial engravings; he copied fencers for *Fencing Familiarized* and little children for *An Introduction to Mensuration*, he engraved sylvan scenes for Ritson's *Songs* and a rotunda for *An Introduction to Natural Philosophy*. But his most intensive early commercial work was for various editions of the Bible, where the influence of Raphael upon his style is appropriately strong. By these means he could return to the world of biblical allegory and spiritual reality that he had known since childhood, and was even given the opportunity of designing one of his own plates. Nevertheless his commercial work was mere methodical routine. He knew all the techniques from his days with Basire and although he often produced work of fluency and grace his practice is never really more than competent.

Yet this was the trade to which he would be always bound. There were advantages to it, since he could never have survived upon his art alone, but he had entered a life of continual labour in which he was forced to work within strictly defined limits and to carefully formulated rules. Truly he was 'The labourer of ages in the Valleys of Despair!'[53] He completed some 580 plates within his lifetime, all of which had to be produced by a faithful and sometimes even simple-minded literalism. If we think of hatching and cross-hatching as a form of net or web that defines an object, then we may be able to hear in Blake's verse something of his weariness at the drudgery of his professional life: 'I have taught pale artifice to spread his nets upon the morning / My heavens are brass my earth is iron . . .'[54] And so Blake laboured over the metal plates, scratching in the regularised lines with his 'iron pen', using compass and rule to mark the outlines of his work, subduing himself to the shallow product of another's imagination:

> None could break the Web, no wings of fire.
>
> So twisted the cords, & so knotted
> The meshes: twisted like to the human brain[55]

In his later life he was known only as an engraver, a journeyman with wild notions and a propensity for writing unintelligible verse. He laboured for his bread, eccentric, dirty and obscure. He was part of the first great period of commercialism and mass manufacture in English history, and he was one of its first casualties.

EIGHT

My Eyes are always upon thee

I t is one of the most poignant relationships in literary history. William Blake had gone to stay with relatives of his father in Battersea, amongst the fields and market gardens of that parish, when he met Catherine Boucher. He was recovering from an unhappy courtship of a girl who had allowed him to 'keep company' with her, but had rejected the idea of marriage; when he had complained about her acquaintance with other men, she turned on him with the laconic question: 'Are you a fool?' 'That,' he used to say in later life, 'cured me of jealousy.'[1] In fact it would have been a foolish complaint from a less idealistic young man, since it was a period of open sexuality and public licentiousness. Erotic prints and books such as *Aristotle's Master-piece* were freely on sale, even to children, in print shops such as Roach's in Russell Court;[2] and at a contemporary exhibition of waxworks was displayed a penis 'injected to the state of erection'.[3] One working man recalled 'the immorality, the grossness, the obscenity, the drunkenness, the dirtiness and even the depravity of the middling and even of a large portion of the better sort of tradesman . . . want of chastity in the girls was common'.[4] The prostitutes of Charing Cross would take their customers 'behind the wall' for twopence, and young girls would often sell themselves for small amounts if they were in need of funds. 'The manner in which many of the drunken filthy young prostitutes behaved is not describable,' the same contemporary reported, 'nor would it be believed were it described.'[5] Blake was not untouched by the general licence and would in his lifetime complete many drawings of erotic fantasies or scenes.

Nevertheless he expected undivided attention and loyalty, which by great good fortune he found at Battersea. According to Catherine Boucher's own account, as relayed through a friend and patron of her later years, Blake was visiting her parents' house when he related the story of his unkind lover. Catherine expressed her sympathy, at which point Blake asked her direct:

'Do you pity me?'

'Yes indeed I do.'

'Then I love you.'[6]

It is reminiscent of Othello's lines upon Desdemona – 'She lov'd me for the dangers I had pass'd / And I lov'd her that she did pity them' – but the results were a little more successful. In fact, as soon as Blake had entered the room Catherine had 'instantly recognised her future partner' and 'was so near fainting that she left his presence until she had recovered'.[7] It was a union established in just a moment of time, and we are almost led to believe the ancient theory that man and woman are two halves waiting to be reunited – yet how strange that Blake should ask for 'pity' as a condition of his love. It demonstrates lack of confidence, perhaps, but in his impulsiveness there is also a curious childishness or child-likeness; it is as if he always felt the need to be defended and protected. We also come close here to a sorrowful and suffering aspect of his character, which he tried very hard to conceal: 'You know that it is my way to make the best of everything,' he told his brother.[8] But he was pitied by those who knew him. 'Poor Blake' was their constant refrain since they saw in him a man in the grip of nervous anxiety and prey to delusions or hallucinations, which would come close to destroying his career and his life. There was one person who never doubted him, however, who protected and comforted him, who would sit beside him quietly 'to calm the turbulence of his thoughts' while he worked.[9]

They were both in their early twenties when they met. She was a pretty girl with brown hair and large dark eyes; there is a pencil drawing of her by Blake that shows a fine and delicate face. After their first interview was over, he determined to marry her; he gave himself a year to earn enough money to provide for her, and so set himself up as a commercial engraver in his father's house. In July of 1782 he moved to Battersea, and stayed with his relatives for the four weeks required to become a resident of the parish; he declared himself 'Gentleman' in the Marriage Bond, which was then an unusual description for a working engraver. On 18 August 1782, they were married in the church of St Mary; Blake pressed his signature down very hard in the register, while his wife inscribed simply an 'X', which implies that she was either illiterate or unskilled at handwriting. She came from a poor family, and was one of many children; her father was a market gardener whose fortunes had declined, in a period when people were frequently and swiftly 'ruin'd' or 'destroyed', 'fallen to decay' or 'forced to break'. So it was by no means a marriage of convenience. It must, after all, have been a marriage of love.

They moved as lodgers to a tailor's house in Green Street by the southeast corner of Leicester Fields (or Leicester Square, as it was rapidly becoming); Sir Joshua Reynolds lived in the square itself, but there was a much more interesting monument in the vicinity. It was in Green Street that Charles Dickens found the original 'Old Curiosity Shop'. They remained here until the death of Blake's father, two years later, while Blake continued his trade as an engraver and attended (perhaps infrequently) the Royal Academy Schools. Early biographers have alluded to occasional argument and discord in the first years of the marriage, although this would hardly be unusual in the life of any young couple. In particular, Catherine Blake has been found guilty of 'jealousy' towards Blake's friends as well as harbouring a more general discontent with her husband's opinions on sexual matters. Whether his opinions or fancies were ever given physical expression, however, is quite another matter. Certainly he took a radical libertarian view of such issues – even at the end of his life he declared that wives ought to be shared 'in common',[10] and some of his early poetry contains passionate encomia on the virtues of free love: 'I'll lie beside thee on a bank & view their wanton play / In lovely copulation bliss on bliss . . .'[11]

But there is another, and more complicated, aspect of his eroticism. At a later stage in this history we will discover his interest in the practices of sexual magic, when, according to George Cumberland, he was 'dim'd with superstition',[12] and in his last years he was still promulgating some very esoteric ideas about sexual androgyny. Yet in his poetry there are also images of fear and revulsion; the horror of the female (together with the horror of passivity and softness) is forcefully expressed, while the dread of female power and female domination becomes a constant refrain. There are powerful hymns to sexuality, as opening the gate into eternity and inspiration, but their power is of a rhetorical and often impersonal kind. And here probably lies the heart of the mystery. There is no evidence that Blake was ever unfaithful to his wife; there is no reason to believe that Blake ever practised homosexuality, despite the presence of homo-erotic art in his illustrated books; there is no plausible excuse for the conjecture, made by some biographers, that he tried to bring a second 'wife' into the home in accordance with Swedenborgian religious precepts. His depictions of sexuality are idealised, almost abstract, and they seem to have remained for him a matter of the mind rather than of the flesh. But this is not to suggest that his was an excessively cerebral attitude; quite the opposite. He *saw* what he imagined, but, perhaps more importantly, his consciousness was such a powerful force – so naked and so susceptible – that all the repressed or unacknowledged erotic potentialities of his period seem to gather there. No other person in that century realised, for example, that warfare can be seen as a form of repressed sexuality:

> I am drunk with unsatiated love
> I must rush again to War: for the Virgin has frownd &
> refusd[13]

or that phallocentric sexuality may be linked to inhibition and religious guilt:

> Embraces are Cominglings: from the Head even to the Feet;
> And not a pompous High Priest entering by a Secret Place.[14]

These are astonishing insights, not revealed until the late nineteenth century, to Freud, and they suggest Blake's extraordinary powers of intuition and divination. Is it any wonder that he was rejected by his own time? There are also more private intuitions, of which he may never have been wholly aware. Catherine was the name of Blake's mother and sister, so there are powerful reminiscences at work when Blake created his vision of Cathedron; it is the place where human bodies are woven upon shining looms. And in the name itself, the consonance between *Catherine* and *cathedral*, those two places where Blake might lose himself, we see also the haberdasher's *thread* and the *dread* of the procreating female.

Catherine admitted that she did not always understand her husband's writings, 'though she was sure they had a meaning, and a fine one', but throughout their life together she remained a docile and compliant wife.[15] '*Reach me my things*,' was his familiar demand to her when he saw his visions.[16] Indeed Blake held relatively orthodox views about the status of men and women: 'let the men do their duty &

the women will be such wonders, the female . . . lives from the light of the male'.[17] There is no reason to believe that Catherine Blake dissented from this opinion. He called her 'beloved', and they were separated for only two or three weeks over a period of forty-five years; it was a childless marriage (it is a curious fact that none of Blake's siblings had children), although perhaps in a sense the true children were themselves. It also became a quiet and introverted union from which the world was excluded. Catherine was his 'helpmate' in his tasks, and learned how to use a printing press and colour his proofs, but she was also his protector. She was an impressionable woman, and soon expressed all of her husband's ideas with the same forcefulness as he did; but she also made his clothes, provided food even in the midst of penury, sang to him, prayed with him, ministered to him. In turn it was he who lit the fire, and put on the kettle, before Catherine awoke in the morning. On his deathbed he drew a portrait of her, saying, 'you have ever been an angel to me'; after his death he returned to her in vision and they sat quietly conversing together.[18]

There are few anecdotes of their early life. It is known that they used to go on long walks into the fields beyond London, sometimes journeying twenty miles before returning home. And there are two recorded instances of Blake's temper being directed against her.

'The money is going, Mr Blake.'

'Oh, damn the money!'[19]

This is not a serious incident, perhaps, but there was a much more significant explosion of anger in these first years. It concerned his youngest brother, Robert, who was a frequent visitor to Green Street. There had been some kind of argument between him and Catherine, in which she said something to the young brother that annoyed Blake. 'Kneel down and beg Robert's pardon directly,' he told her, 'or you never see my face again!' She thought it 'very hard' to kneel in front of a boy, especially when she believed she was not at fault, but she complied and apologised. 'Robert, I beg your pardon, I am in the wrong.' At which Robert himself was gracious enough to dissent. 'Young woman, you lie! I am in the wrong.'[20]

The story was no doubt improved by Catherine's telling of it, but it does suggest that in this period Blake thought at least as highly of Robert Blake as he did of his own wife. He did not particularly mind being separated from the rest of his family – it seems that Catherine Blake did not 'get on' with her sister-in-law – but he remained close to his youngest brother. Robert was fourteen when the Blakes moved to

Green Street but was already Blake's 'affectionate companion' who shared his interests and enthusiasms.[21] Blake trained Robert in the art of draughtsmanship from a very early age; he would draw figures that his brother would faithfully copy, and there are occasions when they would compete by drawing each other's profiles. A sketchbook survives, with the inscription 'Robert Blake's Book, 1777', which includes their painstaking drawings of lips, eyes, noses, arms and faces. There is even a dog or two to lighten the anatomical detail. Although in fact Robert was not as good a draughtsman as his older brother, he was skilled enough to be admitted to the Royal Academy Schools a few months before the wedding in Battersea. He had by that time also adopted his brother's artistic preoccupations. Some drawings have been preserved which depict strange religious ceremonies from antiquity, as well as ominous figures in attitudes of threat or supplication. This was the mythological reality that Blake himself was now beginning to create, as if his early reading of the Bible and his fascination for the Gothic or antique had been combined to create his own legend of the world.

Another notebook has survived from these early days; Robert used it as a portfolio, and it includes his drawings of Druid ceremonies and mythological scenes from British history. But the little book had an interesting career: such was the love that Blake bore for his brother that he kept it by him for the rest of his life, preserving Robert's own work while using the spare pages for drawings and verses of his own. It was into this notebook that he placed his most private, and sometimes most angry, thoughts; it is the book in which he wrote drafts for his *Songs of Experience*, and for the bitter public addresses of his later years. It served both as a memento and as an inspiration, and as a result the presence of Robert Blake never wholly left his life.

There is one sketch by Robert that also had an enduring legacy. It is of several ancient men huddled together in fear upon a cliff, or rock, as they watch a light or fire in the sky above them. It has been entitled 'The Approach of Doom', and the composition of the terrified figures was so striking that Blake made an engraving of it soon afterwards; indeed he continued to use the image in later work. The origin of the 'Doom' itself has remained obscure, however, although the most likely interpretation must be the arrival of 'The Great Fiery Meteor' over London in the summer of 1783. Blake was well acquainted with the night sky and stars, using the movement of the constellations as a backdrop for his epic dramas, but he needed no special knowledge to

understand the power of this scene on a summer night. The fiery
meteor was in fact a fireball; it was seen at 9.16 p.m., according to the
many published reports of the phenomenon, and lasted some thirty
seconds. It was the size of a full moon, but bluish in colour with an
orange tail of flame sweeping behind it; it was so bright that it lit up
the streets of London, casting shadows as it went across the sky and
making a noise like that of thunder. This strange bolide above the
eighteenth-century city seems to resemble the glowing moons and
suns of Blake's painting, but it also has more nebulous connotations.
Some observers said that it resembled a spear being hurled across the
heavens, and in this period the Perseid meteor showers were known as
'the tears of St Laurence' or his 'fiery tears' as he was martyred on the
gridiron. Here are Blake's lines from 'The Tyger':

> When the stars threw down their spears
> And water'd heaven with their tears.

We may see them, then, in Green Street – William Blake, with his
wife and younger brother. Engravings covered the walls of their
lodgings, just as they would in all of the Blake residences, no doubt
accompanied by drawings and watercolours of his own. But it would
be wrong to imagine them, in this period, as isolated from the general
life of the world. They were visited by Thomas Stothard, George
Cumberland, John Flaxman and Blake's fellow apprentice from Basire
days, James Parker. Flaxman also took various opportunities to
introduce Blake to his own friends and patrons; at this time he had a
very shrewd idea of Blake's skill, or genius, and wished it to be known
as widely as possible.

That is how Blake entered, for a while, the artistic circle of the
Reverend Anthony Stephen Mathew and his wife, Harriet, in
Rathbone Place. He was the minister for the newly built Percy Chapel
in Charlotte Street, a few yards from his house, but he had known
Flaxman for some years; there is a report that he found the infirm little
boy teaching himself Latin behind his father's counter, but it is more
likely that he became a general patron and tutor to the promising
young artist. Harriet Mathew was a 'Blue-stocking' in the jargon of
the day, along with the very much more famous Mrs Montagu, Mrs
Vesey and Mrs Carter – all 'delectable in the Blue way', as Fanny
Burney put it. The Mathews' house in Rathbone Place had been
decorated by Flaxman in the style of the ancients, with sculpted
figures made out of sand and putty; the windows had been painted to

imitate stained glass and the furniture had also been designed in antique fashion. Mrs Mathew was a relatively minor patron of artists and composers but, in this rarefied setting, over green tea and lemonade, they discussed matters concerning 'the Sage, the Poet, or Historian'.[22] It seems an unlikely environment for Blake, but there is a witness who saw him there: 'At that lady's most agreeable conversaziones I first met the late William Blake, the artist, to whom she and Mr Flaxman had been truly kind. There I have often heard him read and sing several of his poems. He was listened to by the company with profound silence, and allowed by most of the visitors to possess original and extraordinary merit.'[23] The notion of Blake singing his poetry may seem unusual, but it has the air of authenticity: he was known to sing songs in later life, and he was always susceptible to the simple popular melodies of his time. (He was not particularly affected by more formal or symphonic music.) Indeed during this period he was composing a prose sketch in which a young man sings one of the Songs of Innocence to a small gathering – 'After this they all sat silent for a quarter of an hour'.[24]

But, after the silence, what then? Boswell remembered one scrap of Mrs Mathew's conversation: 'Marriage,' she said, 'must have its Bass, tenor, treble, that is esteem, affection, passion.'[25] He also mentions a popular song that was sung at one of her gatherings, 'Like Parrot, call the Doctor'. There may even have been what was called 'general conversation':

'It is a fine day.'
'A glorious day.'
'How do you?'
'Pretty well, I thank you. You look better.'
'Yes, sir. I now eat suppers and wear a double-flannel jacket.'
'What noise is that?'
'Oh, never mind it. It is only the sneezing of a cat.'

And Blake entertained the assembled company. He may have sung the poetry he composed in his youth, or he may have chanted one of the Songs of Innocence he was writing in the period, but it is important only that the performance of his poetry was even then part of his London inheritance. He had already engraved for Ritson's Collection of English Songs, and was well aware of the tradition of drinking songs, ancient ballads and miscellaneous love songs. It was an aspect of the general urban interest in ballads and popular music, performed in tea-gardens and tavern-grounds (Blake would have heard them on his rambles to the Jews-harp-house and the Green Man); he would have sung his own poems in the manner of the tunes from Vauxhall, or from the night cellars and the tavern concerts featuring such London poets as Bob Summers the 'Singing Cobbler' or Dick Bowyer the comic songster. If he considered himself to be another Chatterton, he was one from Broad Street and not from Bristol.

Flaxman seems to have considered his friend in a similar light because, in the year after the Blakes' marriage, he materially helped Blake to a first publication. It is a nondescript volume, with the pages hand-stitched between blue-grey covers, and is entitled simply 'POETICAL SKETCHES By W.B.' He had written the earliest of these poems when he was twelve years old but he had thought so highly of his apprentice work that he had kept it by him, in fair copy, for at least ten years. There is also the strong possibility that those line-engravings from the period that have already been described, 'Albion Rose' and 'The Approach of Doom', were meant to illustrate passages from the verses. This in turn would suggest that, even from his earliest days, he wished to combine the two arts in which he was already proficient. The little book was printed by a friend of his old master Basire, and was stocked by Flaxman's aunt, who owned a print shop in the Strand. Blake amended printing errors, while both he and Flaxman sent copies to interested parties. He was presenting copies to his friends twenty-five years later and at his death he still had a pile of unstitched pages.

The poetical evenings with the Mathews did not last, however, and a contemporary observer remarked that 'in consequence of his unbending deportment, or what his adherents are pleased to call his manly firmness of opinion, which certainly was not at all times considered pleasing by everyone, his visits were not so frequent'.[26] This is delicately, if ironically, put; the truth was that Blake often offended people with his manner and conversation. 'Always be ready to speak your mind,' he wrote once,[27] and in his mythic poetry Los, the representative of the creative imagination, speaks out to similar effect: 'I have no time for seeming; and little arts of compliment'.[28] It can fairly be said that Blake is describing himself here, and in the accounts of his general conversation there are often suggestions that he could be deliberately wild and contrary, nervous or sarcastic, according to mood. Some of his reported phrases have a fierce ring to them – 'It is false!', 'That is a lie!', 'Mark this', 'False!' – but there were times when he was simply definite and outspoken. 'As fine as possible,

sir,' he is remembered saying of one work, 'it is not permitted to man
to do better.'[29] He could also be elliptical, but sometimes outrageous.
Swinburne describes reactions of 'horror and pity' to his speech, but
there would also have been a large element of incomprehension.[30]
One of the great truths of the age, after all, was the belief in
conversation as a means of acquiring right principles -- what
Reynolds, in his seventh lecture to the Royal Academy, called 'the
conversation of learned and ingenious men, which is the best of all
substitutes for those who have not the means or opportunities of deep
study'.[31] It is the belief that lies behind the vogue for debating clubs
and coffee-house societies during this period, and encompasses the
idea of civilised values and public truth, of knowledge acquired
through social intercourse and dialogue. But Blake would have none
of it. His was a privately gained and more esoteric knowledge, which
could never be imparted in the kind of liberal and rational
conversation that Reynolds extolled. In that sense Blake stood apart
from the mores of his age, and as a result he never became a member of
any group or sect or club. He prided himself on his self-sufficiency,
and his 'unbending deportment' was such that he was to spend much
of his life in self-imposed isolation. '*This Quid*,' one of his characters
remarks in the satire on intellectual society he was now writing,
'*always spoils good company in this manner & its a shame*.'[32] So he left the
Mathews to their green tea and lemonade.

That is also why attempts to place him within the 'Johnson circle'
in these early years have not proved altogether successful. Joseph
Johnson was the first publisher to commission Blake as a copy-
engraver, and at this time he was his single most important patron.
He was described by Joseph Priestley as 'the most active, punctual &
intelligent, as well as the most honest man in the trade'.[33] He had
been raised as a Baptist but had moved towards Unitarianism, and his
Dissenting background influenced many of the volumes that he
published and sold; his interests were in religous, educational and
medical material rather than poetry or fiction, and his politics were of
a radical persuasion. He was the model of a liberal Dissenter,
interested in the details of scientific and industrial progress while at
the same time supporting the cause of religious toleration. He gave
weekly dinner parties above his shop at No. 72 St Paul's Churchyard,
arranged for a Tuesday or Sunday and beginning at four in the
afternoon. The food seems to have been plain enough – a standard
meal comprised boiled fish, roast meat, vegetables and rice pudding –

but his guests came for the company and the conversation. In the period when Blake was first employed by Johnson, these guests included Joseph Priestley, Henry Fuseli and Mrs Barbauld; at a slightly later date he entertained Tom Paine, Mary Wollstonecraft and William Godwin. It has often been suggested that Blake was an intimate member of this radical circle, and he himself seems to have boasted of some acquaintance with Tom Paine. (There is a report that he warned the pamphleteer to leave the country at the height of the Jacobin scares of the 1790s.) In fact the evidence suggests that Blake only ever attended one of these dinners, and his presumed friendship with these Unitarian dissenters and radicals is a matter of pure speculation. It would have been a much more informal and passing arrangement, established upon the duties and coincidences of the day.

So Blake did not join clubs or circles and, for similar reasons of temperament, he rarely became attached to ideas or suggestions other than those that he formulated for himself. But he was immensely receptive to beliefs which might confirm his own sense of life, and in this period he became acquainted with a particular kind of Neoplatonism promulgated by a young man named Thomas Taylor. Taylor resembled Blake in one respect at least – he was one of those extraordinary Londoners who, self-taught, reach out towards the past and seek the truths of ancient knowledge. He was born near Bunhill Fields, the son of a Dissenting stay-maker, and from an early age earned his living as a bank clerk; he first became interested in mathematics, and from a study of that discipline he became absorbed in Platonism. In the evenings, after his return from the bank, he taught himself Greek and read the classical authors. He was a strident opponent of Newton and what he called 'the philosophy in vogue', by which he meant 'Materialism' or Science;[34] unlike the nineteenth and twentieth centuries, this was not a period when science was considered to be an inevitable or even necessary way of investigating and understanding the world. Curiously enough Taylor came to relate the pursuit of science to 'the lucre of traffic and merchandise';[35] this was precisely the complaint that Blake made against the fashionable artists and engravers of the day, quite apart from his own attacks upon Newtonian science, and it suggests that there was among certain people a growing distrust for the industrialisation and commercialisation of English society. It is an important context in which to understand the true nature of Blake's life.

Taylor's own experiments were of a more ideal order than those of the natural scientists: he tried to explain the principle of perpetual light with certain 'Everlasting Lamps' stuffed with phosphorus, but he managed only to set fire to the lecture room. That lecture was held in the Freemasons' Tavern, opposite the house where Blake had once been an apprentice – a small coincidence, perhaps, but it emphasises the extent to which Blake's London was a compact and intimate place. It was at this time (whether before or after the conflagration among the Freemasons is not clear) that George Cumberland 'rescued' Taylor from his banking duties and, with a small subsidy, afforded him the opportunity of writing and lecturing. The first series of public lectures he ever gave were held at the house of John Flaxman and so, with Cumberland and Flaxman now numbered among his friends, could Blake have been far behind?

In fact at one stage Taylor attempted to teach Blake mathematics but, as a relative of one of Taylor's patrons later explained, they 'got as far as the 5th propositn. which proves that any two angles at the base of an isoceles triangle must be equal. Taylor was going thro' the demonstration, but was interrupted by Blake, exclaiming "ah never mind that – what's the use of going to prove it, why I see with my eyes that it is so, & do not require any proof to make it clearer." '[36] No doubt it was this education that Blake recalled when

> ... others move
> In intricate ways biquadrate. Trapeziums Rhombs Rhomboids
> Paralellograms. triple & quadruple. polygonic
> In their amazing hard subdued course in the vast deep[37]

But there were probably enough similarities in their backgrounds (Taylor a year younger than Blake) for them to be able to surmount such disagreements. There is one reported conversation between them which suggests that they understood one another rather well:

BLAKE: Pray, Mr Taylor, did you ever find yourself, as it were, standing close beside the vast and luminous orb of the moon?

TAYLOR: Not that I remember, Mr Blake: did you ever?

BLAKE: Yes, frequently; and I have felt an almost irresistible desire to throw myself into it headlong.

TAYLOR: I think, Mr Blake, you had better not; for if you were to do so, you most probably would never come out of it again.[38]

This may have been elaborated in the telling, but the substance seems quite authentic; in a later poem Blake described how he 'flung myself . . . directly into the body of the sun'.[39] And, since he shows himself thoroughly familiar with the basic tenets of Taylor's Neoplatonism, there is no reason to doubt the general supposition that he attended the twelve lectures given by the young man at Flaxman's house in Wardour Street. It is hard to believe that Blake ever accepted 'pure' Platonism, complete with its doctrines of Ideas and Forms; indeed among the volumes of 'wisdom shallow' he once depicted Plato's De Anima Immortalitate as well as works by Locke and Aristotle. But it is very likely that he accepted, with enthusiasm, Taylor's belief that there was a body of ancient knowledge or prisca sapientia that had been conveyed through the ages of the world by such revered figures as Orpheus, Hermes Trismegistus, Zoroaster and of course Plato himself. It was the knowledge enshrined in the cabbala, and in the ancient myths already vouchsafed to Blake through the pages of Bryant and others -- as one London prophet declared in Signs of Times or a Voice to Babylon, 'Pythagoras and Plato borrowed of the ancient Church of God'.[40] The great names of Paracelsus and Boehme may also be mentioned in this context, although their part in Blake's spiritual history will be explored later; it is more appropriate here to return to Taylor's words in Wardour Street.

In his first treatise, Concerning the Beautiful, he declared, 'having now closed the corporeal eye, we must stir up and assume a purer eye within, which all men possess, but which is alone used by a few'.[41] This is something Blake would have understood in a special sense. Taylor announced that 'Every one, therefore, must become divine, and of godlike beauty, before he can gaze upon a god, and the beautiful itself.'[42] This is standard alchemical doctrine, and suggests how close Taylor's Neoplatonism came to occult magic and to the whole array of spiritual dissent which marked Blake's period. Blake never believed with Taylor that 'incorporeal forms or ideas resident in a divine intellect are the paradigms or models of every thing which has a perpetual subsistence according to nature',[43] but he was much more ready to accept 'that man is a microcosm, comprehending in himself partially every thing which the world contains divinely and totally'.[44] In his eclectic assumption of Taylor's Neoplatonism, in fact, we can observe the movement of Blake's mind; he picked up separate ideas, or fragments of knowledge, as he needed them. He was a synthesiser and a systematiser, like so many of his generation, but it was his own synthesis designed to establish his own system of belief. He was likely to adopt an item he had read in a periodical or pamphlet with the same frequency that he borrowed notions from Swedenborg or Paracelsus. He was, above everything else, an artist and not an orthodox 'thinker': he was attracted to images or phrases as a means of interpretation, and never espoused a complete or coherently organised body of knowledge. He agreed with some of Taylor's most general principles, for example, but he never accepted any particular interpretation of them. Taylor himself went on to become Secretary to the Society for the Encouragement of Arts, Manufactures and Commerce and remained what was called 'pagan'. On his deathbed he was told that a comet had appeared in the evening sky. 'Then I shall die; I was born with it, and shall die with it.'[45]

These are some of the friends and acquaintances of Blake's early years, then: Taylor, Flaxman, Cumberland, Johnson, Mrs Mathew, the Reverend A. S. Mathew, Stothard, all of them 'happy Islanders' in the eighteenth-century city.[46] At least that is the name he gave his contemporaries in a satirical burlesque that he wrote in 1784 and 1785. In this prose piece, posthumously entitled 'An Island in the Moon' by Blake's first proper editors, W. B. Yeats and E. J. Ellis, we are in the world of Rathbone Place or Wardour Street or St Paul's Churchyard in the company of Blue-stockings and antiquarians, philosophers and artists, all of them discussing Voltaire and Chatterton, the latest experiments with the microscope or the most recent developments in printing. The narrative is written in a legible, even elegant, hand on a series of narrow foolscap sheets; there are occasional corrections but it looks as if Blake was copying from some unknown original. The use of different inks suggests that he took up the writing on eight separate occasions, and a line is drawn at the end of each chapter; on one end-sheet he practised the mirror-writing of his name, as well as some specimens of copperplate script, interspersed among drawings of horses, lambs and lions. Within the text itself there are some early references to Chatterton, the idol of the day, and some late allusions to balloon hats, the fashion of the hour. It was a topical piece of humour; moon-ballets and moon-burlesques were common, and there were often political or social satires with titles such as 'Expedition to the Moon' or 'A Voyage to the Moon'. But Blake's is not a generalised satire on the Swiftian model; it stays too close to his own world for that, and in this sharp burlesque we hear the people talking to one another as if they were in the next room: 'then said Quid I think that Homer is bombast & Shakespeare is too wild

. . . Chatterton never writ those poems. a parcel of fools going to Bristol – if I was to go Id find it out in a minute . . . If I dont knock them all up next year in the Exhibition Ill be hangd . . . my Cousin Gibble Gabble says that I am like nobody else I might as well be in a Nunnery There they go in Post chaises & Stages to Vauxhall & Ranelagh And I hardly know what a coach is . . . Aradobo said that the boys in the street sing something very pritty & funny [about London O no] about Matches'.[47]

And so it goes on, with this continuous stream of speech and dialogue being interrupted by ballads, street cries, popular songs and nursery rhymes. Much ingenuity has been spent in trying to determine who Aradobo, Suction, Quid and the others may be; but it is important only that Blake is taking a fiercely ironic attitude towards his friends and contemporaries. Cumberland is here, as well as Stothard and Flaxman. But the work was not intended for publication, and has all the marks of that caustic private humour in which Blake often engaged; he could sometimes be whimsical, or mildly ironic, but the general tone is one of angry sarcasm and rivalry. And yet in this somewhat strained society the Islanders sing words that would eventually appear in Blake's *Songs of Innocence*:

O what a multitude they seemd, these flowers of London town
Seated in companies they sit with radiance all their own
The hum of multitudes were there but multitudes of lambs
Thousands of little girls & boys raising their innocent hands.[48]

Then in a different ink, and perhaps some days later, he added the line we have noted before: 'After this they all sat silent for a quarter of an hour'. In an atmosphere of argument, backbiting and general social futility, he has placed one of his most resounding lyrics. The difficulty here is one that re-emerges throughout Blake's work. Is he being ironic or is he being serious? The truth is that he was generally both, and an underlying note of dramatic raillery and sarcastic scepticism must never be discounted in even his most apparently 'serious' or 'lyrical' poetry.

The actual form of 'An Island in the Moon' has some relevance here. It is in the manner of a burlesque of a peculiarly London type – 'after-pieces' or 'comic lectures' that included songs and dialogues were one of the features of popular entertainment in tavern grounds, pleasure gardens, the 'long rooms' of saloons and theatres. Foote performed 'Tea at the Haymarket', while Stevens gave his 'Lectures

on Heads'; at Marybone Gardens the comedian did 'a sketch of the
Times in a variety of Caricatures, accompanied with a whimsical and
satirical Dissertation on each Character', with names such as Mr
Fiddle Stick, Mrs Artichoke and Mr Small Coal.[49] These sketches
were often accompanied by the songs and tunes of the day, since
popular music was enjoying a marked revival in collections such as
Tom d'Urfey's *Pills to Purge Melancholy*. It was a peculiarly urban art,
emerging from the energy and variety of the city, and one that Blake
instinctively employed – he called himself 'English Blake', and
appropriately so, but he might also be known as 'London Blake'.[50] He
left the city only once, and most of his life was spent in the same small
area bounded by the Strand, Holborn and Oxford Street. He did not
need to travel any further because he saw, literally *saw*, Eternity
there. But these conditions helped to shape the kind of artist he
became: he was a Cockney visionary, and takes his place with Turner
and Dickens as one of the great artists of London. If we consider the
possibility of a unique urban sensibility, it will be one intimately
connected with 'An Island in the Moon' and Blake's subsequent
poetry – it embodies an art that is preoccupied by light and darkness in
a city that is built in the shadows of money and power, an art
entranced by the scenic and spectacular in a city that is filled with the
energetic display of people and institutions. Blake tends instinctively
towards those great London forms, spectacle and melodrama, and is
often preoccupied with the movement of crowds and assemblies; he
has a sense of energy and splendour, of ritual and display, which may
have little to do with the exigencies of the individual moral life. But if
Blake understood the energy and variety of London, he was
continually aware of its symbolic existence through time: in his epic
poetry, and the vast concourse of figures who flow through it, we find
the pity and mystery of existence in a city he described as 'a Human
awful wonder of God!'[51]

Yet infinite London can be seen only within mundane London,
and 'An Island in the Moon' is wholly concerned with the life around
Blake in the 1780s. He manages to mention half the events and
sensations of the day – the performing monkey Jacko was to be seen at
Astley's theatre in Lambeth; Vincent Lunardi ascended in a balloon
from Moorfields, and the famous vehicle was later exhibited at the
Pantheon in Oxford Street; a Handel Festival was held in
Westminster Abbey; scientists were lecturing on phlogiston, or the
principle of inflammability, while exhibitions of the microscope and

its slides were very popular; Toby, 'the Learned Pig' with his red waistcoat, caused great public excitement; the French transvestite Chevalier d'Eon had moved to Golden Square and gave parties dressed as a fashionable eighteenth-century woman – 'all the Women envy your abilities my dear they hate people who are of higher abilities than their nasty filthy Selves but do you outface them & then Strangers will see you have an opinion – now I think we should do as much good as we can when we are at Mr Femality's do you snap & take me up'.[52] 'Mr Femality', with all these other sights and events, emerges in Blake's early prose. Reading his satire is in many respects like looking at contemporaneous prints of London, where the details are always ingenious and suggestive. If we look at images of London life from between 1780 and 1800 we see a lost city restored – a woman filling her kettle at the neighbourhood pump, the washing hanging out from poles, the labourers sitting down with their tankards of porter, the birdcages and pots of flowers on the windowsills, the shabby man standing on a corner with a sign in his hat saying 'Out of Employ', a man carrying a plate of pickled cucumber on his head while another sells toy windmills, the dogs, the cripples, the boys with hoops. There, on the walls, are signs and handbills – 'Vauxhall Opera' and 'Park Fair' pasted alongside handwritten slogans such as 'Joanna Southcott', 'Murder Jews' and the ubiquitous 'Christ is God'. This was the city of William Blake, and it was here that his extraordinary myth slowly began to form.

Rossetti once discovered a handwritten list that Blake had made, 'giving a few details about names of Gods in different mythologies. The spelling is very bad and must belong to Blake's youth.'[53] Already Blake was concerned with the lineaments of the legendary world, and in his first extant manuscripts he begins to create his own cosmogony. Drafts of two prose poems survive, written on both sides of the paper, inscribed in differently coloured inks at different times with occasional additions in pencil, and ending with a terminal flourish of the quill pen – 'These are the Gods which Came from fear. for Gods like these. nor male nor female are but Single Pregnate or if they list together mingling bring forth mighty powrs.'[54] These words were written in the period he was still associated with the Royal Academy and had begun to earn his living as an engraver; it is no accident, therefore, that in these same years his art began to acquire its distinctive features.

He had started exhibiting again. In 1784, 'A Breach in a City' and

'War Unchained' were to be seen in the Exhibition Room of Sculpture and Drawings at the Royal Academy, and in the following year 'The Bard, from Gray' was hanging between other artists' depictions of 'The Prophet Elijah, Bringing to the Widow Her Recovered Child' and 'The Birth of Adonis from Ovid'. Flaxman and Stothard were also exhibiting this year, but Blake had excelled himself: not only had 'The Bard, from Gray' been accepted but he was also allowed to display three watercolours from the life of Joseph carefully placed within rosewood frames. Joseph was a popular prophet among artists of the period – the influential and successful Benjamin West completed three paintings on the subject – and there is no doubt that Blake was trying to appeal to a certain fashionable taste or market. That is why his paintings at the Royal Academy bear all the marks of the heroic style derived from the contemporary school of history painting. It is an art of idealised figures and grand gestures united in the spacious rhythms of the composition, an elevated art that emphasises formality and expressiveness as well as a kind of grave intensity. But Blake's art was more than a generalised image of neoclassicism; in 'A Breach in a City' and 'War Unchained' there are traces of his preoccupation with death, mortality and apocalypse, while in the smaller drawings and pen sketches of the period he concentrates upon emblems and allegories of the spiritual life. In one series he portrays Christ as the 'good farmer' and 'lord of the harvest', while there are separate drawings of holy books and angelic instructors, which share, with his poetry, an intense concentration upon moments of an expressive drama in a generally idealised landscape. They are nothing like his 'life' drawings at the Royal Academy or the grandly heroic figures of his historical painting –here, in these less finished works, he is attempting to delineate the permanent, spiritual image of the human form. That is why his rough pencil sketches are often very fine, when, in a few hastily drawn lines, he manages to catch the spirit on the wing. But another quality is now beginning to emerge when, in the same period, he finished two pen sketches of 'The Complaint of Job' and 'The Death of Ezekiel's Wife'. These are finely controlled works, in which grave and monumental figures dominate the composition in attitudes of imploring worship, but they are also bathed in an extraordinary luminescence. The light within Blake's paintings and watercolours is often the most immediately noticeable characteristic; it represents the light of understanding, the light of eternity suffused through material reality, but it was an artistic and painterly discovery before it became part of his myth.

> In Great Eternity, every particular Form gives forth or Emanates
> Its own peculiar Light, & the Form is the Divine Vision
> And the Light is his Garment This is Jerusalem in every Man.[55]

The artistic world that he had begun to create was of prophets and bards, of biblical and mythical figures from a sublime past who have the power of revelation and who generally stand alone against the world – Job and Ezekiel are the very types of such visionaries, while 'The Bard, from Gray' is perched upon a lonely eminence. In the 'Joseph' series, too, we find the figure of the prophetic outcast who has been rejected by his own family. A further, and unwelcome, connotation was contributed by the Daily Universal Register, which characterised that bardic figure as 'like some lunatic, just escaped from the incurable cell of Bedlam'.[56] Of course it would be wrong to suggest that Blake's paintings are solely or even primarily motivated by autobiographical impulses – all of his themes were employed by other artists – but it seems that he was drawn to the image of visionaries isolated in a world that did not understand them.

He was, on the face of it, doing rather well. He was exhibiting at the Royal Academy and was a relatively successful engraver who had recently managed to earn eighty pounds for a work entitled 'The Fall of Rosamund'. He was also composing lyrics, and had started upon a longer poem. He was a skilful and ambitious artist, whom Romney is supposed to have compared with Michelangelo. But, despite this success, strains and difficulties were beginning to appear in his life. For reasons unknown he stopped working with his friend Stothard, and in retrospect he accused Flaxman of 'blasting my character as an Artist' at this time.[57] This is unlikely, but he might have been patronising in a way that deeply offended so sensitive a man as Blake; when Flaxman sent a copy of his friend's Poetical Sketches to the poet William Hayley, he remarked that 'his education will plead sufficient excuse to your liberal mind for the defects of his work' and in the same letter he went on to say that Blake's fortunes as an engraver were 'not extraordinary'.[58] It may also have been in this period that Blake began to acquire a reputation for being dilatory, if a letter of complaint from an irate author to Joseph Johnson is anything to go by;[59] perhaps as a consequence, he did very little commercial engraving over the next few years. So he was withdrawing from his immediate circle of friends, as well as from his old habits of work.

At this same time he also suffered a disappointment that materially affected his artistic prospects. One of his early patrons, a wealthy young collector and aesthetic traveller by the name of John Hawkins, was, according to Flaxman, 'endeavouring to raise a subscription to send him [Blake] to finish (*his*) studies in Rome'.[60] It would have been a remarkable opportunity for Blake – to see the works of Raphael and Michelangelo, which he so much admired, to understand them beyond the narrow confines of reproductive engraving, and to appreciate something of the culture from which they came. But it did not happen; the subscription failed. Flaxman himself travelled to Italy with his wife under the patronage of Josiah Wedgwood, stayed there for seven years, and came back famous; Blake remained in his native country all of his life, and never experienced fame of any kind. At a later date we will see that the more obscure he grew the more grandiloquent and insistent he became. That is why, in his epic poems, England becomes the holy land, the seat of the ancient patriarchs and the home of the chosen race; for it was here, too, that he experienced his own spiritual reawakening.

NINE

The Ocean of Business

His father died in the summer of 1784, and was buried in the Dissenters' graveyard at Bunhill Fields. Blake hardly ever mentioned him again – unless it is permissible to include a poem about a lost boy that appeared in 'An Island in the Moon': 'O father father where are you going'.[1] It is not at all clear what, if anything, James Blake meant to a son whose actions characteristically moved from wilful independence to extreme dependency. The death was not unexpected, since he had been ailing for some time and had given up control of his hosiery business to a relative; no doubt plans had already been made to divide the father's legacy. The eldest son, also James, took over the shop and ran it with the help of his mother; the business flourished, and within a few years James erected stone pillars outside the shop as a token of respectability. Another son, John, established a bakery in a house opposite the family home. Blake himself moved with Catherine from Green Street to No. 27 Broad Street, next door to his mother and brother; they were all now within a few yards of one another, and the proximity demonstrates how closely knit his family remained. And, like the faithful son of any tradesman, Blake now also established a business: he bought a wooden rolling press for forty pounds and, with his quondam fellow apprentice James Parker, he set up a print shop. Parker was seven years older than Blake but, no doubt because of the passionate advocacy of his colleague, he was also an enthusiast for Ossian and British antiquity in general.

The Parkers and the Blakes lived above their shop, and the two men already had a clear idea of their respective contributions to the business – Parker excelled at mezzotint, where Blake was the master of line engraving. But since very few engravings were actually issued under their imprint, it is clear that their main occupation was the selling, rather than the reproduction, of prints. Yet the wooden press itself was the best investment Blake ever managed – it saved the expense of having a neighbourhood print shop make proofs, at a typical cost of threepence per sheet, but, more importantly, it allowed him to work and experiment for himself. It was, in any event, a good time to start such a business. Print selling was one of the fastest growing trades in London (there were fourteen in 1785, and fifty-three by 1802), and under the influence of entrepreneurs such as John Boydell it had established a lucrative export trade. Mezzotint, Parker's speciality, was even described as '*la manière anglaise*'. The end of the war with France and with America materially affected the prosperity of the country and, with Pitt now securely in power, 'Parker and Blake' might be sanguine about their prospects. Two years later a visitor declared that the English were 'pampered by a redundance of meat & money',[2] while a more vitriolic home-grown observer reported, 'The spirit of luxury rages here with greater violence than ever . . . the great articles of trade in the metropolis are superfluities, mock-plate, toys, perfumery, millinery, prints and music.'[3] 'Prints' here is, of course, the operative word.

It was, in Blake's case, a bid for independence. Previously he had worked for others, with booksellers and print shops as commercial mediators, but over the next five years he finished only six commissioned engravings. Now he could work for himself. Yet was it, in a sense, a kind of defeat? His contemporaries had begun to flourish as artists but Blake had turned his back on that and, like his father, had become a shopkeeper and tradesman who sat behind the counter waiting for customers. Flaxman was to live in Rome, among the splendours of classical antiquity, while Blake was back with his family in Broad Street. The revelations of Westminster Abbey and the aspirations of the young historical painter at the Royal Academy had now retreated some way into the distance. It ought to be remembered, also, that on one level William Blake must have seemed a very ordinary person to those who encountered him. That is why so few people bothered to keep his letters and why he came to be regarded, if at all, as a harmless tradesman with some strange ideas. Flaxman's words bear repeating, if only because he ought to have known him best and understood his art: 'his education will plead sufficient excuse to your liberal mind for the defects of his work'. So Blake sat in the shop – normal hours were from six in the morning until nine in the evening – and attempted to continue with his 'work' in the night hours.

James Parker and his wife were sharing the first-floor apartment with Blake and Catherine; it was not unusual for a small family to live in a single room, but it was not easy. No doubt that is why the Blakes moved to a house in Poland Street the year after the business was opened – perhaps 'Parker and Blake' had already earned enough money to make such a move possible; in any case, there is no reason to believe that they had in any sense decided to part company. Poland Street was around the corner, and it is unlikely that Blake would wish to set up a rival business in such close proximity. Certainly he lived here until 1790, and during that period issued engravings from the work of Richard Cosway and Henry Fuseli. It was a little more fashionable than Broad Street, and the Blakes had much more space: No. 28 Poland Street was a narrow house of four storeys and a basement, with a single front and back room on each floor. Their neighbours included printers and dress-makers; the entrance to the local workhouse was across the street, and there were lodging houses and coffee houses nearby. Also at this time, Thomas Rowlandson was resident at No. 50 Poland Street, while, a few yards down from Blake's house, 'The Ancient Order of the Druids' had been established in an ale-house. It would have been a convivial society, not a religious assembly, in a room with stuffed leather benches, mahogany tables and tallow candles – meat at fourpence, bread at one half-penny and a pint of porter for seven farthings – but it does suggest the kind of atmosphere in which Blake acquired his own sense of England. When he painted 'The Bard, from Gray' he was drawing upon a new antiquarianism, both popular and scholarly, which was actively rewriting British history – from Cooke's *The Patriarchal and Druidical Religion* to Stukeley's *Stonehenge: A Temple Restored to the British Druids*. Welsh 'bards' met on Primrose Hill (there was supposed to be a tribe of Welsh-speaking Indians descended from lost patriarchs) and parodies of 'Druid' literature were already appearing. But there was a more portentous aspect to this extraordinary interest in 'Ancient Britons': their inheritance was claimed by Freemasons, by students of the cabbala and by political radicals. This was the religious and historical reawakening in which Blake participated.

But his own close and earnest study of spiritual matters was preceded, as is so often the case, by private loss. His young brother,

Robert, was struck by a fatal illness, probably consumption. He was nineteen years old, and although he could have continued with his studies at the Royal Academy he no doubt 'helped' in the print shop next door to the family house. Blake tended almost single-handedly to the young man as he lay dying, in the first days of February 1787: 'Mr Blake told me that he sat up for a whole fortnight with his brother Robert during his last illness & upon his going to bed which he did as soon as Robert died he slept for three days and nights. Mrs Blake confirmed this.'[4] These are the words of John Linnell, who became acquainted with him many years after the event. But we may see here one of Blake's many deathbed scenes, in which the dying man lies with his head propped upon a pillow; beside him sits the grieving companion, sometimes watchful and sometimes with bowed head. But Linnell does not repeat what a friend and contemporary of Robert remembered: Blake 'beheld him in his visions' and 'At the last solemn moment, the visionary eyes beheld the released spirit ascend heavenward through the matter-of-fact ceiling "clapping its hands for joy" – a truly Blake-like detail.'[5] That same image of liberation is seen in some of Blake's engravings, where the freed human form hovers above the dead figure or is accompanied by angels towards the sky. There is also a phrase in Blake's then unpublished poetry that seems like a memory of that revelation in Broad Street, when Urizen '. . . rose up from his couch / On wings of tenfold joy clapping his hands'.[6] And so the soul or form of his young brother left the dead body, exultant; he had returned to the eternal world, where he still remained visible. '[W]ith his spirit I converse daily & hourly in the Spirit,' Blake once wrote, '& See him in my remembrance in the regions of my Imagination. I hear his advice & even now write from his Dictate.'[7] He stated this some thirteen years after the experience of Robert's death and there is a suggestion here, highly significant to the biographer, that to contemplate the dead is also to hold communion with them.

He slept for three days and nights, as if he were going through a rite of passage. Then he awoke. In that same year, we have the record of his close study and annotation of Emmanuel Swedenborg's writings – Swedenborg being, in particular, the great theologian and philosopher of the age who believed that the spirits of the dead rose from the body and reassumed physical form in another world. He was the philosopher who could give substance to Blake's visions, in other words, and reaffirm Blake's own instinctive sense of life and death.

Flaxman may have introduced him to Swedenborg's works; the sculptor had already become a convinced follower, and in his wonderful funereal monuments he would depict the physical form of the dead rising from the mortal body just as Swedenborg had expressed it.

It was not unusual in this period for artists to espouse strange or unorthodox faiths. William Sharp had joined the Theosophical Society, which was the forerunner of the Swedenborgian New Church. The painter Cosway, who had once taught Blake at Pars' Drawing School in the Strand and for whom Blake now worked, was also a Swedenborgian and a Freemason; he was a practising occultist who saw visions, too, and drew from them. (This did not preclude his dressing fashionably, and for a time in the 1770s he was known as the Macaroni Painter or Billy Dimple.) Cosway was also adept in magical practices and rituals, which he performed at his house in Stratford Place, and in later years Blake was close to Cosway in many respects. Philippe De Loutherbourg, the great scenic designer whose 'Eidophusikon' was the theatrical sensation of the day, was also a Swedenborgian and Freemason; the constant alignment between these two strands of radical dissent suggests just how powerful the movement of unorthodox belief had become in the late eighteenth century; De Loutherbourg was also a practising mesmerist or 'magnetic healer', and his house in Hammersmith Terrace was crowded on 'healing days' with those searching for a cure.

These were artists who became convinced Swedenborgians but among the fifty people who attended the first meetings at New Court in the Middle Temple, designed to promote the writings of the Swedish theologian, there was a watch-maker, an engraver, a bookseller, an artist-jeweller, a silversmith and an engineer. Such people represented the urban radicalism of the period among the trading classes – exactly the class to which Blake belonged – but it was a radicalism imbued with spiritual and millenarian impulses. Then, on 13 April 1789, Blake and his wife attended a general conference of the New Jerusalem Church at the Swedenborgian chapel in Great East Cheap; it lasted five days and there were some sixty or seventy participants, filing through a portal that had inscribed upon it 'NOW IT IS ALLOWABLE' – words that Swedenborg had once seen in a vision. After the meetings were over they all dined together at a tavern around the corner in Abchurch Lane – the presence of Blake at such a gathering is significant in that it marks the only occasion when

he attached himself to a group or congregation of any kind. Indeed
the fact that he had begun to read Swedenborg two years earlier
suggests that, for some time, he was profoundly committed to the
precepts of the New Church.

He might even have seen Emmanuel Swedenborg in the streets of
London. The philosopher lived in the city at the end of his life, and in
March 1772 died in a lodging house near Clerkenwell at precisely the
time he had anticipated. He had been an engineer and scientist of
great distinction – he published books on mineralogy, astronomy and
anatomy – until he had a vision of Jesus on the night of 6 April 1744.
Here, then, is the first clue to Blake's attachment to the New Church.
Swedenborg was a visionary who conversed with angels and spirits.
Blake continued to 'see' his own visions – there is every reason to
believe that this faculty was enlarged in his later life – but now he had
encountered the writings of a man who declared, 'I have spoken with
many spirits . . . it has been my destiny to live for years in company
with spirits . . . I have conversed about this with the angels . . . I
have often been permitted to see the atmosphere of falsehood which
exhales from hell'; Swedenborg even describes 'a certain state that is
midway between sleeping and waking . . . [where] spirits have been
seen to the very life, and have been heard . . .'[8] This was precisely
Blake's own experience, and now he was reading a contemporary
philosopher who gave his visions corroboration and meaning; it
meant that he was blessed. All the evidence suggests, then, that he
began reading Swedenborg very carefully after the death of Robert –
after he had seen his brother's spirit leaping from the body – and it
may again have been John Flaxman who directed Blake's attention to
Swedenborg's belief that 'immediately on the Death of the material
body, (which will never be re-assumed), man rises again as to his
spiritual or substantial body, wherein he existeth in perfect human
form'.[9] It is one of Swedenborg's most remarkable doctrines, since it
suggests that the spiritual form takes human shape and that heaven or
hell are extensions of our human desires and capacities.

This in itself may not be enough to explain Blake's association with
the New Church. His annotations to Swedenborgian writings are
actually more concerned with elucidating philosophical maxims than
in understanding the details of spiritual topography. His notes are
written clearly in pencil, with an occasional 'Mark this' in the
margins; their most interesting aspect, however, is the ease and
lucidity with which even the most pregnant remark has been

transcribed. They look like fair copies from an early draft but they are simply the annotations he made as he read on; they prove, if nothing else, what an instinctively intelligent man he was. In almost every case, too, Blake is concerned to press Swedenborg's beliefs into the framework of his own concerns; he was not a disinterested enquirer after truth but, rather, a self-taught artist who wished to bolster and amplify his own beliefs with any material that came to hand. In particular, he introduced the concept of 'Poetic Genius' as he wrote his notes in the margin, all the time bringing the focus back to himself and his own potential for spiritual expression.

He had come across a rich mine in Swedenborg because, on one level, the teachings contained in *Arcana Coelestia*, or *Heaven and Hell*, are a synthesis of occult and alchemical doctrine placed in the Christian context of redemption. Blake had encountered such doctrines before, but here they were given a formal and systematic status which lent them a certain impersonal authenticity. Swedenborg, like Bryant and the other syncretists whom Blake had read, believed that there were ancient truths to be revealed – as one of his followers put it, that which 'has for many Ages been lost to the World. The Egyptian Hieroglyphics, the Greek and Roman Mythology, and the Modern Freemasonry being the last remnants of it. The honourable Emanuel Swedenborg [is] the wonderful Restorer of this long lost Secret.'[10] And what was this secret?

It is the opening of the gate. It is the sure knowledge that nature and the material world are the vessels of eternity. It concerns the 'Alchymical Furnace' in which the spiritual world is revealed and is intimately related to Swedenborg's doctrine of 'correspondences', through which each material form reflects or contains its spiritual source by exhibiting 'a Three-fold Sense, namely, Celestial, Spiritual, and Natural . . . in each sense it is Divine Truth, accommodated respectively to the angels of the three heavens, and also to men on earth'.[11] That is why it is possible to see eternity in a grain of sand. It was a persuasive doctrine for an artist such as Blake, because it is established upon vision rather than the mathematical notations of Newton or the abstract calculations of Locke. An artist who admired the heroic figures of Michelangelo, and who agreed with Winckelmann that the beauty of the human form is an emblem of the Supreme Being, would also have very little difficulty with the cabbalistic strains in Swedenborg's thought. For Swedenborg, too, believed in the Grand Man or the Heavenly Man: 'God is very Man.

In all the heavens there is no other idea of God than that of a Man; the Reason is, because Heaven in the Whole, and in Part, is in Form as Man. By Reason that God is a Man, All Angels and Spirits are Men in a perfect Form.'[12] These were very powerful ideas for an artist who had spent a lifetime observing and drawing the human form, whether in the tomb monuments of Westminster Abbey or in the fluent outlines of Mantegna's engravings.

They were also part of the political and spiritual radicalism that was in the centre of London – the chapel in Great East Cheap had become a meeting place for a small group of people who were quite outside the current dispensation. Some of them practised mesmerism or sexual magic, some were Freemasons or Jacobite sympathisers, some were cabbalists or occultists, but all of them believed in the primacy of the spiritual world. They were often considered eccentric or mad, as remnants of a murky superstitious past or as small tradesmen with absurd ideas quite above their station in life. Indeed there is something cloistered and credulous about their panoply of beliefs – their enthusiasm was certainly considered to be vulgar and even crude by more high-minded Dissenters such as Joseph Johnson and Dr Priestley – but, during his years as a shopkeeper, this was the world in which Blake felt most at home. Eventually he turned against Swedenborg and the New Church, in the way he abjured all those who might have influenced him or affected him, but much of his art and poetry of the period is suffused with a spirituality that can have only one immediate source:

> Then every man of every clime,
> That prays in his distress,
> Prays to the human form divine
> Love Mercy Pity Peace.[13]

It would be wrong to assume, however, that all of Blake's acquaintance were radicals or occultists of various kinds. Indeed it might be said that the most important relationship he formed in these years was with a quite different and very distinctive person. Flaxman and his wife left for Rome in 1787 but, as Blake put it later, 'When Flaxman was taken to Italy, Fuseli was given to me for a season.'[14] As it turned out, the gift of Henry Fuseli could not have been more timely. He was of Swiss descent; he had been born in Zurich in 1741, so he was middle-aged when Blake came to know him. He was already famous --particularly after one of his most extravagant paintings, 'The

Nightmare', captured the latent fantasies and horrors of the age. He was an essayist and cultural historian, too, and it was his translation of Winckelmann that Blake had once studied. He was widely travelled, and although he had only finally settled in London in 1780 he seemed to know everyone there, from Thomas Coutts to Joseph Johnson and John Flaxman. Goethe had met him some years before and had told Herder, 'What fire and fury the man has in him!'[15] Blake put his own approbation in more Cockney terms: 'The only Man that eer I knew / Who did not make me almost spew'.[16]

They had a certain amount in common, despite the difference in their backgrounds. Fuseli had grown up in a family steeped in religion, art and literature; from childhood he was an admirer of Milton and Shakespeare, and was ordained as a Zwinglian minister before undertaking a series of European travels in pursuit of art and philosophy. He could quote much of the Bible from memory throughout his life and, despite his inclination towards profanity and blasphemy, the sacred narrative often reduced him to tears. Like Blake, he admired the lachrymose 'graveyard poets' of the mid-eighteenth century. He was a writer as well as a painter, and composed poetry for most of his life; he joins Turner and Blake as one of the artist-poets of the era. He considered himself to be a history painter and, again like Blake, detested drawing from life – 'Nature puts me out' is probably his most quoted remark. He continually extolled the genius of Michelangelo and Raphael; he pursued the virtues of form and outline, while attacking colour as an 'insidious foundation' to true art.[17] Fuseli was a painter who depicted the human figure in various extravagant, heroic or erotic gestures; he took the *terribilità* of Michelangelo to fantastic heights, a mannerist who conveyed 'enormous passion' in a splendidly artificial and overtly theatrical style.[18] He was in many respects, therefore, very close to Blake. Fuseli adored the theatre, and we might imagine the two men visiting Drury Lane or Covent Garden to see the latest scenic spectacles or the most recent experiments in stage lighting – two short, intense men entering the brightly lit caverns of city entertainment. It casts a novel 'light', at least, upon some of Blake's more spectacular tableaux.

We know, without the benefit of such speculation, that Blake and Fuseli became acquainted with each other in the 1780s. They must have met through Johnson or Flaxman, although they would already have known each other by sight – Fuseli moved to No. 1 Broad Street in 1781 and remained there for seven years. He was not easily missed, either; he was five feet two inches in height and 'creaked about in top boots';[19] his hair was pure white, having been blanched by a fever in Italy, and he kept it neatly powdered to match the elegance of his dress. But his manner and general conversation were most remarkable. Like some short people he could be strident and domineering; he could also be conceited and not a little sensitive about his reputation. He was never willingly eclipsed in company and his conversation, according to William Hazlitt, was 'striking and extravagant . . . he deals in paradoxes and caricatures'.[20] He also dealt in oaths and imprecations, and was well known for being able to swear in nine languages. There is a conversation, recorded in the papers of one of Blake's later acquaintances:

FLAXMAN: How do you get on with Fuseli? I can't stand his foul-mouthed swearing. Does he swear at you?

BLAKE: He does.

FLAXMAN: And what do you do?

BLAKE: What do I do? Why – I swear again! and he says astonished 'vy, Blake, you are svaring' but he leaves off himself![21]

Fuseli was also known for his wit, or sarcasm, which was all the more pronounced for being couched in a strong Swiss-German accent. Blake one day showed him a painting or drawing he had just completed:

FUSELI: Now someone has told you this is very fine.

BLAKE: Yes. The Virgin Mary appeared to me, and told me it was very fine. What can you say to that?

FUSELI: Say? Why nothing – only her ladyship has not an immaculate taste.[22]

There are many other anecdotes, the majority of them from the time when Fuseli was a Member of the Royal Academy. The students loved him, although he could be severe. On inspecting one young man's drawing he remarked, 'It is bad; take it into the fields and shoot it, that's a good boy.' When he was told that the boat he depicted in 'The Miracle of the Loaves and Fishes' was too small, he replied, 'That's part of the miracle.' When he voted for Mrs Lloyd rather than the honoured Benjamin West as President of the Royal Academy, he is said to have remarked, 'Is not one old woman as good as another?'[23] He could also be acerbic about contemporary painters; after talking to some of them he remarked to a friend, 'I feel humble, as if I were one of them.' Blake responded to Fuseli's sarcasm and acerbity, almost to the point of mimicry, because they were precisely the attributes that he possessed. He was in certain respects a volatile and even incomplete person because he was continually changing as an artist; one might compare him with Keats, who, in the words of Oscar Wilde, displayed 'passionate wilfulness' and 'fine inconsistence'.[24] The connection must not be stretched too far, however, since Blake knew himself that 'all Genius varies'. That is why Blake also admired Fuseli's more significant qualities. He seems to have been the only contemporary artist whose 'superiority' Blake ever acknowledged, at least according to Fuseli himself,[25] and he is certainly recorded as saying that it would take two centuries for Fuseli's art to be appreciated properly. By which, of course, he also meant his own.

Fuseli's opinions of Blake are more ambiguous. He is not known to have admired, or even been acquainted with, his poetry; his favourite contemporary authors were Cowper and Gray, and Blake is never mentioned. His art seems to have elicited a more encouraging response. One of Blake's younger friends remarked, in later life, that 'Fuseli and Flaxman were in the habit of declaring with unwonted emphasis that "the time would come" when the finest [of Blake's works] "would be as much sought after and treasured in the portfolios" of men discerning in art "as those of Michaelangelo now".'[26] Fuseli is also said to have admitted that 'Blake is d— good to steal from!',[27] and there is the account of his seeing one of his friend's designs and saying, 'Blake, I shall invent that myself.'[28] These stories may have come from Blake, in his old age, but that is not necessarily a reason to doubt them; in any case, Blake just as often borrowed images and compositional devices from Fuseli.

The principal reason for their association, in the 1780s, was simply that Fuseli required a good engraver. His work had been butchered in France, and he needed a competent draughtsman to prepare a frontispiece to his translation of Lavater's *Aphorisms on Man*, which Johnson was about to publish. The two men worked together very successfully; Fuseli gave Blake a somewhat rough sketch and Blake transformed it into a noble composition of the inspired writer, which, strangely enough, bears a resemblance to a later portrait of Blake himself. It was a labour of love for both of them – Fuseli was an intimate friend of Lavater, while Blake so admired the maxims that in his own copy of the book he inscribed his signature next to Lavater's name and drew a heart to encompass both of them. This may have been in part because Lavater was a convinced Swedenborgian, but there was a more general sympathy that Blake expressed in some spirited notes in the margins of the volume. He had been sent an unbound copy of the book by Johnson, as soon as it was printed, and he immediately began to annotate it in pen. There are ink blots where he has turned over a page in haste.

These annotations have been described as 'gold-dust' by his mid-Victorian biographer, Alexander Gilchrist, for the insight they provide into Blake's beliefs and character in this period.[29] They offer nothing like a complete portrait, of course, but they do give evidence of his formidable confidence and conviction in scribbled asides, which are alternately enthusiastic and impulsive: 'all life is holy', '*love is life*', 'O that men would see immortal moments O that man would converse with God'. It is clear from these jottings that he had already formed something close to a philosophy or theology of his own, and he alludes to 'A vision of the Eternal Now' in which past and future are consumed, and defends the role of 'True superstitition' in the pursuit of faith. This is close to Swedenborg, but there are also annotations that seem all his own work: 'Active Evil,' he wrote, 'is better than Passive Good.' This is the first occasion on which he mentions 'evil', but for him it remained a heretical concept introduced by the wicked god of this world; it was, if anything, merely a state through which men and women passed without necessarily being damaged or affected. Blake understood that, essentially, everything that lives is holy. There are occasions, too, when he marks passages from Lavater that seem attributable to his own life. He underlines the phrase 'every genius, every hero, is a prophet' and triply underlines 'The greater that which you can hide, the greater yourself'. He knew that, purposefully or accidentally, he had already concealed much of his own 'genius' from the world, which is undoubtedly why he could be very aggressive towards others. He even noted confidently that 'Severity of judgment is a great virtue'; he obeyed his own maxim with such remarks as 'I hate crawlers', 'damn Sneerers', 'damn him', 'I cannot love my enemy for my enemy is not man but beast & devil if I have any'. On hypocrites and dissemblers, he exclaims 'Ah rogue I could be thy hangman' and 'a dog get a stick to him'. He could, then, be extremely belligerent, but the general tone is one of spiritual enthusiasm matched by an awareness of his own abilities and aspirations.[30]

Fuseli had some idea of Blake's talent as an engraver, at least, and they worked together on a number of designs over the next few years. But the relationship could not have been easy; they never were with Blake, especially when he was forced into a subordinate role, and by 1803 Fuseli had dispensed with his services altogether. Blake never turned on him, as he did on Stothard and Flaxman, but in contemplation of Fuseli's artistic career he would have found many opportunities for self-appraisal and self-doubt. It was not simply that Fuseli passed effortlessly through the artistic establishment – he was Associate Member, then Member, then Professor of Painting, at the Royal Academy – but, rather, that he was given scope and occasion for his genius to flourish. He had begun writing for Joseph Johnson's *Analytical Review*, for example, an opportunity that Blake was never afforded. More significantly, Fuseli was invited to become part of the most important artistic enterprise of the period.

In 1786, the year after Blake's move to Poland Street, John and Josiah Boydell conceived a grand scheme to rescue national history painting and make a fortune at the same time. The Boydells, uncle and nephew, established what became known as the 'Shakespeare Gallery'; the famous artists of the day would be invited to paint scenes from Shakespeare's works, which in 1789 were hung in an especially built gallery at No. 52 Pall Mall, while the best engravers would produce a portfolio of prints from these works that could be purchased by subscription. The great artists and engravers of the day were asked to contribute – with the single most obvious exception of William Blake. His reactions to this humiliating rebuff are not recorded, although his later comments on the pernicious role of commerce in the arts suggests that the memory or disappointment lingered for many years. It meant that he was being left behind again, while friends or colleagues such as Flaxman and Fuseli prospered. In the next century he declared that 'the Neglect of my own Powers' by patrons and employers would be 'Execrated in future Ages',[31] and he also remembered 'Having spent the Vigour of my Youth & Genius under the Oppression of Sir Joshua & his Gang of Cunning Hired Knaves Without Employment'.[32] So he was left in a corner to pursue his own work without the aid or encouragement of anyone on earth, except his wife; a less gifted artist, without such faith in his own genius, might have yielded to circumstances in despair. But Blake had the stubborn obstinacy of his class, as well as the confidence of genius, and he maintained his own path. 'I thank God,' he wrote later, 'that I courageously pursued my course through darkness.'[33]

In his otherwise spirited annotations to Lavater, there had also been one or two more homely jottings, such as his admission that 'I seldom carry money in my pockets they are generally full of paper'.[34] It was the paper he used for sketching, and for scribbling down scraps of poetry, as he worked behind the counter in Poland Street. There is a drawing he made at this time, a parody of Gillray's 'The Morning After Marriage', which has always been supposed to show Blake and his wife rising from sleep. Blake is sitting on the edge of the bed, putting on his stockings, while Catherine, wearing a mob-cap, lies beside him. The bed has no curtain, and the only furniture depicted is a simple dressing-table and mirror; it might be a study of what in the next century came to be called plain living and high thinking. The drawing was made in his brother's notebook, which he preserved, after Robert's untimely death, as a continual reminder of his living spiritual presence; he kept it by him until the end of his life and was writing 'The Everlasting Gospel' on its faded pages as late as 1818.

In Poland Street, however, he began to use it for some carefully composed emblem drawings, small sketches in which visual motifs are given an allegorical or typological significance. He entitled the series 'Ideas of Good & Evil', in large pencilled letters, and began by drawing a traveller with a staff in his hand, which he called 'Thus the traveller hasteth in the Evening'; it became one of his most cherished and continually repeated figures, like some form of self-image, and it was followed on succeeding pages by depictions of sickness and fatality, of floating spirits and figures upon clouds, as if the experience of Robert's death had indeed infused the notebook. But in the margins Blake has also doodled some more mundane scenes, which he might have glimpsed out of the window in Poland Street – a man urinating against a wall, a boy and a dog looking at each other intently, a monstrous figure swooping down from the skies like some harbinger of moral decay.

At the same time as he was drawing 'Ideas of Good & Evil', he was completing the sequence of poems eventually entitled *Songs of Innocence* – at this stage, for him, 'Songs' and 'Ideas' demanded separate expression. He was also working on a longer poem; he made a fair copy in small flowing handwriting, and then bound it in a blue-grey cover with the legend 'Tiriel/MS. by Mr Blake'. The poem continues for fifteen pages, with a final section added at a later date; there is no real attempt at punctuation and each line is transcribed as if it were an exhalation of breath. There are a few revisions and when Blake deletes a passage he scratches vertical lines across it just as he would cancel an image on one of his copper plates. It may have been written as an experiment, but it is more likely that he made such a copy with a view to publication – and what could have been more natural than to show it to his employer, Joseph Johnson, as an illustrated book of a highly embellished kind? The poem remained unpublished, however, like most of Blake's literary work.

Tiriel itself is set in a mythical landscape, and concerns the wanderings of an aged king who curses his family and begins a self-imposed exile in a dead world that he has in part created. It sounds as if it might have come out of Shakespeare or Sophocles, but the elements of Blake's unique mythology have already begun to emerge. It is the primeval world of Bryant and of Stukeley, which he had glimpsed within engravings of stones and broken pillars; some of the names come from the kind of magical texts he could have borrowed from his fellow Swedenborgians; and for the first time he makes use of the septenarius, or seven beat line, which he was to employ in his later prophecies:

> Why is one law given to the lion & the patient Ox
> And why men bound beneath the heavens in a reptile form
> A worm of sixty winters creeping on the dusky ground.[35]

The images of death and 'pestilence', so vividly depicted in his paintings of the period, are also present here; but already there is a more complicated allegory running beneath that Miltonic 'sublime' tone which is itself the poetic equivalent of history painting. *Tiriel* is a fable of familial blindness and foolishness – father against sons, brother against brother, a family dispersed and alienated – which concludes with Blake's belief in the spiritual, rather than the natural, man. It is an interesting performance, but it also marks a further stage in his artistic development: for the first time he had clearly decided to illustrate his own poetry, and he completed twelve pen and wash drawings to accompany the narrative. They are conceived in the heroic style, stemming in part from his admiration for Barry and Romney, but they are far more finely composed and modelled than the neoclassical works he had been exhibiting at the Royal Academy; once he starts working from his own invention, rather than from the repertoire of stock motifs, he becomes inspired. They look as if they might have been intended for engraving (in the event, like the poem itself, they remained unpublished) and already Blake has mastered effects of luminosity that are more generally to be seen in prints than in drawings. His continual experience of working upon copper, from the days of his apprenticeship, meant that it had become for him the ideal or image of the creative process. It also contained moral connotations: he was later to say that error had to be given definite form before it could be cast out, and in this emphasis upon clearly outlined expression can be seen the effects of his own commercial training. But he had not yet found a way of resolving certain technical difficulties. The illustrations for *Tiriel* did not quite match the text, and could have been only awkwardly placed beside it. Clearly, Blake wanted to combine his two great gifts, for painting and for poetry, but there seemed to be no appropriate medium in which to do so. If he were to integrate his skills, and thus his vision, he would need to create a new kind of book altogether. Astonishingly, in Poland Street, this is what he managed to do.

Many of his works begin with a visitation, of a bard or muse or angel who inspires the poet and dictates the words of his song; it is, for Blake, a way of emphasising the divine source of all art. But it was also the way in which he understood the important events of his own life, and it would be possible to write his biography in the style of a medieval hagiography like that of St Guthlac or St Wilfrid. They ordered their lives in terms of apparitions and spiritual messages, too, because they were convinced of their mission upon the earth. When, in the introduction to *Songs of Innocence*, the piper is requested to 'Pipe a song about a Lamb . . . Piper pipe that song again', Blake comes close to a similar epiphany in the life of Caedmon, the first English poet; a spiritual messenger came in a dream to him, in AD 680, and requested him to 'sing me a song . . . you shall sing to me'.[36] So are the lives of the poets connected, and our English music is sustained by visions.

In particular, Blake always claimed that the secrets of his new technique of engraving were vouchsafed to him in a vision. His dead brother Robert revealed them to him. The first account came from a contemporary: 'Blake, after deeply perplexing himself as to the mode of accomplishing the publication of his illustrated songs without their being subject to the expense of letter-press, his brother Robert stood before him in one of his visionary imaginations, and so decidedly directed him in the way in which he ought to proceed, that he immediately followed his advice.'[37] One biographer takes up the story: 'On his rising in the morning, Mrs Blake went out with half-a-crown, all the money they had in the world, and of that laid out 1s 10d on the simple materials necessary for setting in practice the new revelation.'[38] The circumstantial detail, and the accuracy of the costs involved, suggest that this is close to the truth. Robert may have come to him in a dream, or he may have been running over in his head one of the conversations they had once had about such matters – or it may be that, in thinking of him and using his notebook, he actually *saw* and *heard* him again. The consequence was, in any event, that he adopted the technique of 'relief etching'. It was not entirely a new process – variants of it had been employed for three centuries, in which the letter or image was raised from the surrounding metal rather than being etched or engraved into it. It stands up in 'relief' against the flat plain of the copper plate, to be inked and printed. But Blake took the practice a significant stage further. In an age that encouraged the alignment of poetry and painting as an aesthetic whole, and in which illustrated books of various kinds were enormously popular, he hit upon a method of creating words and images in a single operation. He put his artistic training to exemplary use, and found a way of painting rather than engraving the copper plate.

He had been engaged, previously, in his regular commercial work; in fact he was at this time involved in his most elaborate and probably most lucrative commission, with an engraving after Hogarth of the third act of *The Beggar's Opera*. It is a most skilful and resourceful piece of work, which emphasises that he could have continued as one of the best copy-engravers of his day, in the tradition which Hogarth had himself maintained. But he decided not to do so. He wished to experiment with his new technique and, while working on Lavater's *Essays on Physiognomy* at this time, he chose his own profile to illustrate that philosopher's description of the 'forehead . . . of a thinker who embraces a vast field'.[39] He has also covered the profile with a dense web of hatching and cross-hatching, as if to emphasise the defects inherent in conventional copy-engraving. But he could now break free and, with 'relief etching', enter a 'vast field' of his own invention. This is how he did it.

He worked directly upon the copper plate as if it were a sketch pad. It is likely that his first purpose had been to execute engravings with

the same freedom and inventiveness as drawings; the deployment of
actual words upon the surface of the plate may have marked a second
and decisive stage.[40] His first step was to cut out plates from a large
sheet of copper, using a hammer and chisel, and to prepare the
surface for his labours upon it. Then he made out a rough design
with white or red chalk and, with that as his guide, he used a
camel-hair brush to paint the words and images upon the plate with
a mixture of salad oil and candle-grease. This mixture resisted the
aqua fortis (of vinegar, salt armoniack, baysalt and vert de griz
purchased from the local druggist), which bit into the surrounding
plate for three or four hours – this was normally achieved in two
stages, so Blake could check upon the progress of the operation.
After that time the words and images stood up, and stood out, as
part of one coherent design. There were technical complications
that Blake, a very practical and intelligent craftsman, managed to
overcome – the most important being that he wrote the words
backwards with his quill, so that when the image was printed in
reverse they would be the correct way round. He used various
instruments to lend variety to his designs – among them quills,
brushes of various thickness, as well as his own stock of engraving
tools. After the plate was 'bitten in', to a depth of approximately
one-tenth of a millimetre, he used a conventional printer's ball of
cloth to ink or black the plate with burnt walnut oil or burnt linseed
oil; the plate was then gently printed on Whatman paper. Once the
design had been produced Blake gave the paper a preliminary 'wash'
with glue and water, before hand-painting the words and images
with a 'size colour' or 'distemper' made out of water, colour pigment
and carpenter's glue. As a result of the hand-colouring, too, every
page of every 'illuminated book' is unique. The variety within copies
may have been the product of chance or technical necessity, of
course, rather than the result of deliberate design or invention; he
would, for example, have printed the same pages successively
(perhaps in different coloured inks) to create several copies of the
same edition of one book. There would then have been differences
in alignment and ink quality as well as colour. At each stage of the
process, however, he was engaged in spontaneous composition –
from the moment he painted the words and drawings upon the
copper, to the moment he coloured the freshly printed page. There
was no need to make preliminary drafts or designs, because the
actual process of composition was the most important. One can see

him bent over the plate, with his engraver's lamp and magnifying lenses, rapidly writing his verses backward with the quill:

> I must Create a System, or be enslav'd by another Mans
> I will not Reason & Compare: my business is to Create.[41]

The first months of this novel technique were ones of trial and experiment; there is a small relief etching of an estuary and he used one of his brother's drawings, 'The Approach of Doom', to attempt various styles of the new process with acid-resistant inks or varnishes. Indeed, it may have been while working on this design that he hit upon the method; this might explain his belief (if explanation is needed) that Robert had truly inspired him. It has already been suggested that his first aim with 'relief etching' was simply to render prints as close as possible to drawings, thus tapping into the burgeoning market among connoisseurs for fashionably engraved works.[42] As soon as he had perfected it, however, other advantages became obvious. Now he could produce and print his own books upon his own press, without the aid of such entrepreneurs or middle-men as Josiah Boydell and Joseph Johnson. It was also a cheaper process than conventional letterpress and he claimed in a prospectus five years later that this 'method of Printing both Letter-press and Engraving in a style more ornamental, uniform, and grand, than any before discovered . . . produces works at less than one fourth of the expense'.[43] Towards the end of 'An Island in the Moon' there is a description of a printing method very similar to his own: 'Then said he I would have all the writing Engraved instead of Printed & at every other leaf a high finishd print all in three Volumes folio, & sell them a hundred pounds a piece. they would Print off two thousand then said she whoever will not have them will be ignorant fools & will not deserve to live.'[44] As this passage suggests, he was not entirely unaware of commercial considerations. All his life he was both tradesman and artist, quite unlike his Romantic successors, whose experience of the industrial revolution turned them irrevocably against commerce. There were times when he believed that he was about to make his fortune – it was his destiny to be wrong on each occasion – and in this same prospectus he declared, 'the Author is sure of his reward'. But the 'reward' was also of a higher and nobler kind. Blake had invented a method that allowed him to deploy the full range of his genius for painting, poetry and engraving; by combining these several arts he managed to create a wholly new kind of art that proclaimed the unity of human vision. 'But first the notion that man has a body distinct from his soul, is to be expunged; this I shall do, by printing in the infernal method, by corrosives, which in Hell are salutary and medicinal, melting apparent surfaces away, and displaying the infinite which was hid.'[45]

At the end of his life he declared that he created his 'Original Stereotype' in 1788,[46] and the work which has best claim to that title is a little series of words and images that are known as 'All Religions are One' and 'There is No Natural Religion'. They are related to the emblems he had been drawing in his brother's notebook, but these are of a much more explicitly spiritual and metaphysical content. A crouched figure draws a triangle on the ground with a pair of compasses, while above him are the words 'He who sees the Infinite in all things sees God. He who sees the Ratio only sees himself only.' A recumbent figure, in a state of trance or ecstasy, is surmounted by 'Therefore God becomes as we are, that we may be as he is'.[47] These are small and deliberately simplified works, in the style of the chapbooks and handbills he would have known as a youth, and the earliest of them have been hand-coloured in only the most limited way; but Blake never forgot or abandoned them. In fact he was printing them from the original copper plate some twenty years later, and there was a stock of unbound sheets found in his lodgings after his death. They represented, after all, one of his defining moments; he had produced, for the first time, a complete statement in which words and images are unified. Perhaps that is why 'All Religions are One' is preoccupied with the theme that 'the Poetic Genius is the true Man' who creates the conditions for spiritual knowledge and awakening. It is precisely what Blake had done or, as he puts it here, 'As none by traveling over known lands can find out the unknown. So from already acquired knowledge Man could not acquire more. therefore an universal Poetic Genius exists.' Above this aphorism he has once more drawn the solitary traveller with a staff in hand, so much like an image of Blake himself on his own difficult journey, while the first plate shows a prophet figure gesturing towards the motto 'The Voice of one crying in the Wilderness'.[48] He now considered himself to be a prophet as well as a poet, in other words, and this early work emphasises his affection for the didactic, as well as the lyrical, mode – or, rather, that he saw no necessary distinction between them. He wanted to combine them, just as he could now combine words and images; indeed his newly invented form now changed the nature of his expression. It had enlarged his range; with relief etching, the words inscribed like those of God upon the tables of the law, Blake could acquire a new role.

He went on with fresh confidence to a much larger 'illuminated book', as these volumes of relief etching are generally known: *Thel* is a poem of some 130 lines and seven coloured plates printed on one side of the paper only. It is a much more sumptuous work than its predecessor, with the earliest copies hand-coloured in mild greens and luminous pinks or blues. It concerns the descent of the trembling young soul into the world of matter, and as such Blake has picked up elements of Thomas Taylor's Neoplatonism as well as Swedenborgian doctrine and some alchemical terminology. Everything upon the earth has a spiritual correspondence, and the world itself is inspired with the breath of divine humanity. But then what is this 'fall' that leads us into the dark?

> Why fade these children of the spring? born but to smile & fall.
> Ah! Thel is like a watry bow. and like a parting cloud.
> Like a reflection in a glass. like shadows in the water.
> Like dreams of infants. like a smile upon an infants face,
> Like the doves voice, like transient day, like music in the air.[49]

The importance of *Thel*, then, is not its variegated origin but Blake's attempt to create an autonomous myth for his own period. Certain elements of that myth, as well as certain recurring images, had already appeared in 'There is No Natural Religion'. He takes it one stage further here, with the beginnings of a system of truths that draws upon all the old sources of wisdom he revered; more importantly they are explicitly created to oppose prevailing contemporary belief in mechanical nature and deistical knowledge. It could be said that he was giving an eighteenth-century shape to ancient mysteries, and is to be seen as part of the impulse that had already carried him towards the visionary allegories of historical painting. He had already adopted the images of biblical painting, also, and so here he redeploys the cadences of the 'Song of Solomon' in the movement of *Thel*:

> Why should the mistress of the vales of Har, utter a sigh.
> She ceasd & smild in tears, then sat down in her silver shrine.
> Thel answerd. O thou little virgin of the peaceful valley.
> Giving to those that cannot crave, the voiceless, the o'ertired.
> Thy breath doth nourish the innocent lamb, he smells thy milky
>   garments.[50]

He has taken the 'vales of Har' from his unpublished poem *Tiriel*, and one of his mythological personages now appears -- 'Luvah', the principle of sexual energy, is the first of Blake's pantheon to emerge in his poetry. Just as he had managed to create his own method of composition, so now he felt compelled to create his own system – he took material from various other philosophies where it suited him, as we have seen, but he needed his own language to encompass all that he felt obliged to say. Thus he became the first English poet since Edmund Spenser single-handedly to create his own mythological reality. He had learned from the Elizabethan poet how to depict high powers in love or combat – how much he must have loved, for example, the second book of *The Faerie Queene*, in which the history of ancient Britain is followed by an account of 'Faery', and in which the biblical conceit of Mammon's underground caves is succeeded by the description of a sacred castle. Here is the English allegorical tradition, all compact, and Blake became the poet who maintained it.

Sixteen copies of *Thel* survive, for the most part preserved in the rare-book rooms of various university libraries in England and America; since each copy is unique and unreproducible by conventional mechanical means, it can now be read only in facsimile or as 'pure' poetry printed without its accompanying imagery. This is rather like seeing an engraving of the Apollo Belvedere or the Hercules Farnese without ever being able to see the real object, but it is the inevitable consequence of Blake's own methods. He produced at least six early copies, and gave an example of each to George Cumberland and Thomas Stothard; it is possible that he bound other copies in the usual blue-grey wrappers and distributed them to fellow Swedenborgians as a kind of tract, while keeping a stock at the print shop in Poland Street for more casual readers, but the evidence for this is hypothetical. Certainly he printed and sold copies at a later date – there are some found on paper with an 1815 watermark ·· and it is best to imagine Blake with the copper plates of his books always ready for reprinting when the occasion warranted the expense. Nothing was ever forgotten or abandoned, but remained in the continual present of his creative labours. The poem itself was never given a fixed and immutable form, either, since the nature of his reproductive techniques did not permit the uniformity of conventional print and design. Extra plates were added at another stage, and the later copies of *Thel* merge text and illustration into a more highly embellished and decorated ensemble.

Of all his illuminated books, however, the one most frequently reproduced was *Songs of Innocence*. It followed soon after *Thel*, but it is a more elaborate and skilful production; he might have hoped to make his fortune out of it and, with its pastel shades and its images of children and nurses, it looks as typically Georgian as a Wedgwood tea-set or a Hepplewhite library chair. It has all the signs of being written and designed for children, with 'happy songs / Every child may joy to hear',[51] and there can be little doubt that Blake was trying to capitalise on the growing market for such literature in his period. Goody Two Shoes, Tommy Trip and Mother Goose were already very popular, while such volumes as *Trifles for Children* and *A Present for a Little Boy* were now handsomely presented in a style quite different from the chapbooks and rude woodcuts of a less enlightened era. He could take various pastoral images from these works and, in similar fashion, he borrowed the movement of the ballads, hymns and nursery rhymes that were all in the air around him. He was trying to use a conventional and marketable form for his own purposes.

He produced the little book with the help of his wife. Even at this stage it is possible that Catherine helped him to colour the relief-etched prints once they had come off the press, and there is no doubt that she stabbed holes in the finished pages, and stitched and bound them within their covers. The first batch of copies were printed in a conventional recto-verso book format, and the whole operation must have taken about a week. At printing sessions in succeeding years he would change the format so that the images appeared on one page only, and did not face each other, while at a much later date he began to draw borders around the poems. Blake issued *Songs of Innocence* separately until the last years of his life – the price rose from five shillings in 1793 to three guineas in 1818 – but no two copies ever contain the poems in the same order. One of the salient technical effects of Blake's method was the necessary uniqueness of each individual copy, as we have seen, and he later used his methods as a way of justifying his art against the general trend towards standardisation and mechanical conformity in printmaking or bookselling. Colour changes can also be marked; in some of the early copies 'The Little Black Boy' is painted pure white, while in later ones he becomes dark brown or black. There is one more general movement of colour that can be traced, since it is also part of the movement of taste in the period from which even Blake was not wholly immune. In the early copies he employed 'Georgian' pastel shades of blue and yellow or brown, but later copies are much more richly and brilliantly coloured with the liberal use of intense purples and dark greens as well as gold leaf. These are clearly related to the illuminated manuscripts of the medieval period, which Blake had every chance of seeing, and in his last years it was as if he was moving back to the first sources of his inspiration in the Gothic spirit hovering within Westminster Abbey. He had moved from poetry back to art.

On its first appearance, however, *Songs of Innocence* was not an overwhelming success. He kept a small stock, but since he preserved the original copper plates he could always print a new edition. Yet only twenty-five copies of this particular work are known to have survived, which suggests that the general opinion was much like that of a contemporary: 'The whole of these plates are coloured in imitation of fresco. The poetry of these songs is wild, irregular, and highly mystical, but of no great degree of elegance or excellence.'[52] The finished production certainly had none of the high-toned 'elegance' of the aquatints or mezzotints in the better anthologies, and the poems themselves were only tenuously connected with the children's verse of the period. Some of the songs had already appeared in 'An Island in the Moon', where they had been given a satirical context quite different from the celebration of 'Innocence', and others were concerned with social and topical matters that had no place in the usual fairy tales or moral fables imbibed by the young. 'Holy Thursday' is a celebration of the charity children who attended an annual service of thanksgiving in St Paul's Cathedral, but it also has sorrowful connotations of constriction and convention:

> Twas on a Holy Thursday their innocent faces clean
> The children walking two & two in red & blue & green
> Grey headed beadles walkd before with wands as white as snow
> Till into the high dome of Pauls they like Thames waters flow[53]

while 'The Little Black Boy' adverts to the English trade in slaves:

> My mother bore me in the southern wild,
> And I am black, but O! my soul is white;
> White as an angel is the English child:
> But I am black as if bereav'd of light.[54]

These are often poems with an argumentative or satirical intent, and they are emphatically not expressions of lyrical feeling or the spontaneous overflowing of emotion in the conventional 'romantic' mode. That is why the *Songs* aspire to be as formal and as impersonal as the folk ballads and nursery rhymes from which Blake borrowed; he could thereby dramatise the spiritual significance, as well as the possible deficiencies, of 'Innocence' itself. 'Unorganizd Innocence, An Impossibility,' he wrote in one of the margins of his later poems. 'Innocence dwells with Wisdom but never with Ignorance.'[55] He had also read Swedenborg on the same theme and knew that 'In particular, cattle and their young correspond to the affections of the natural mind, sheep and lambs to the affections of the spiritual mind, while winged creatures, according to their species, correspond to the intellectual things of either mind.'[56] In *Songs of Innocence* the lambs graze upon the cropped grass beneath the images, and birds soar among the etched words.

The dramatic perspectives and continual allusiveness of these lyrics has meant that they have been endlessly interpreted and re-interpreted, but one important truth is sometimes missed in that critical process. These are not poems as the 'Lyrical Ballads' are poems: these are discrete works of art in which the words are only one element in a unified design. They are art-objects that 'mean' something in the way a picture 'means' something in any given period. In the late eighteenth century, for example, a painting 'meant' an interpretation of its predecessors and of the tradition in which it placed itself; its principal purpose was to reinterpret familiar subjects in an impressive or timely manner. That is why, in *Songs*, the components of Renaissance emblems, biblical themes and the pastoral imagery from Elizabethan poetry are combined in the single focus of Blake's intense vision. But the truth is that they could only have been written by an artist who believed himself to be a spiritual poet; the associations here are all with medieval illuminations, with stained glass, with bardic prophecy, with the cadences of the Bible and popular hymns.

Yet they were not quite right for the age – 'wild' and 'mystical', with an old-fashioned Gothic appearance that was not acceptable to connoisseurs. They seem to us now to express all the energy and confidence of a poet who has at last found his way forward; *Songs of Innocence* has the obliquity of 'An Island in the Moon', the spirituality of *Thel*, the dramatic directness of *Tiriel* and the melodic control of the *Poetical Sketches*, all working together to form a complete and coherent statement. And yet Blake's contemporaries were partly right: there is something 'wild' about these highly compressed and concentrated lyrics. At first glance they might have seemed aspects of amenable pastoralism (he even deliberately copied Stothard's soft style in a few images) but there is an intensity in the words and the designs that sets them apart from the more agreeable work of his contemporaries. The verse is part of the design, the design part of the verse, in an extraordinarily condensed and almost ritualistic way; the visual completeness, the insistent metres, the impersonal skill of the calligraphy, turn these poems into achieved works of art that seem to resist conventional interpretation. The sense of energy and intensity within such taut bounds leads also to an awareness of possible loss of control and disequilibrium; that is why the tight metres and formal concentration of the poems seem actively to exclude the reader and the world. Blake protects the deepest sources of his inspiration very carefully, and there is always a suggestion of distance and even parody within even the most apparently 'naïve' lyrics; they resemble the man himself, who could be cryptic or maddeningly oblique when he felt himself to be challenged. And then perhaps we can see once again Blake himself, this small man pacing through the streets of the city, keeping his own counsel, seeing his own visions. And what, in turn, may we still see or imagine?

TEN

And so he was quiet

The Chimney Sweeper

When my mother died I was very young,
And my father sold me while yet my tongue,
Could scarcely cry weep weep weep weep.
So your chimneys I sweep & in soot I sleep.

Theres little Tom Dacre, who cried when his head
That curl'd like a lambs back, was shav'd, so I said.
Hush Tom never mind it, for when your head's bare,
You know that the soot cannot spoil your white hair.

And so he was quiet, & that very night,
As Tom was a sleeping he had such a sight,
That thousands of sweepers Dick, Joe, Ned & Jack
Were all of them lock'd up in coffins of black,

And by came an Angel who had a bright key,
And he open'd the coffins & set them all free.
Then down a green plain leaping laughing they run
And wash in a river and shine in the Sun.

Then naked & white, all their bags left behind,
They rise upon clouds, and sport in the wind.
And the Angel told Tom if he'd be a good boy,
He'd have God for his father & never want joy.

And so Tom awoke and we rose in the dark
And got with our bags & our brushes to work.
Tho' the morning was cold, Tom was happy & warm,
So if all do their duty, they need not fear harm.

On the first of May each year a holiday was granted to the young chimney sweeps of London, known as 'climbing boys' or 'lilly-whites'; for the rest of the year they were engaged in 'calling the streets', from the dark hours before dawn until midday, but on this one festival they were permitted to celebrate. Their faces were 'whitened with meal, their heads covered with high periwigs powdered as white snow, and their clothes bedaubed with paper lace'.[1] Southey saw a later version of this festival: 'their clothes seemed as if they had been dragged through the chimney, as indeed had been the case, and these sooty habiliments were bedecked with pieces of foil, and with ribbons of all gay characters, flying like streamers in every direction as they whisked around: their sooty faces were reddened with rose-pink, and in the middle of each cheek was a patch of gold leaf, the hair was frizzed out, and as white as powder could make it, and they wore an old hat cocked for the occasion, and in like manner ornamented with ribbons, and foil, and flowers'.[2] They also banged their brushes and climbing tools as they paraded through the city. They were the lords of misrule and for that day had become white, and clean, and even beautiful.

How the people laughed – and perhaps even the little boys themselves were for a while able to forget the conditions of their wretched existence. They were generally sold between the age of four and seven; they either left the poorhouse in batches, or were individually bartered by their parents, who would accept between twenty and thirty shillings for their seven-year 'apprenticeship'. There was a great need for their services in London, where the flues were characteristically narrow or twisted so that they easily became constricted. The average size of these vents was something like seven inches square, and the small child was prodded or pushed into the even smaller spaces within; sometimes they were encouraged with poles, or pricked with pins, or scorched with fire to make them climb with more enthusiasm. Of course many died of suffocation, while others grew deformed; many others suffered from what were known as 'sooty warts', or cancer of the scrotum. One social reformer described a typical climbing boy towards the end of his career: 'He is now twelve years of age, a cripple on crutches, hardly three feet seven inches in stature . . . His hair felt like a hog's bristles, and his head like a warm cinder . . . He repeats the Lord's prayer . . .'[3] They finished their work at noon, at which time they were turned upon the streets – all of them in rags (some of them, it seems, without any clothing at all), all of them unwashed, poor, hungry. It is really no wonder that they were typically classified with beggars and with vagrants, considered to be criminals and making up 'the greatest nursery for Tyburn of any trade in England'.[4] They could also be employed in the more theatrical of radical rituals, where a chimney sweep might be employed to 'behead' a king or magistrate.

But there were other associations: the actual practice of their trade, as they entered small dark places, had undoubted sexual connotations; chimney sweeps were often hired to kiss the bride at wedding ceremonies, as an emblem of potency, and no doubt the young vagrants on the streets became an easy prey to those who lusted after them. It was an element of their being that Swedenborg had intuitively understood; in *Concerning the Earths in our Solar System* he described 'Spirits whom they call Sweepers of Chimnies, because they appear in like Garments, and likewise with sooty Faces . . . [they are] among those who constitute the province of the Seminal Vessels in the Grand Man or Heaven . . . for in these Vessels the Semen is collected . . . thus what is reserved within may serve for the Conception or the Impregnation of the Ovulum; hence also that the seminal Matter hath a strong Tendency and as it were a burning Desire to put itself off.'[5] The 'burning' here is reminiscent of the child sweep whose head felt like 'a warm cinder'. This is a potent mixture indeed, of sex and dirt and criminality and desire embodied within the very young; it is no wonder that it had to be turned into an annual farce that Southey could dismiss as a 'spectacle' by which he was 'amused'. It was a power that had to be controlled and diminished: at the Mechanic Theatre, or Androides, in Norfolk Street there was a miniature automaton of a boy who entered the house, climbed the chimney, cried out 'Sweep! Sweep!' and then came out with a full load of soot.

What, then, does William Blake make of this human trade? The engraved images that surround the poem are of the small chimney sweeps being awoken from their coffins by the Saviour; but they are very finely and tentatively delineated at the bottom of the page, and they seem threatened or overpowered by the words above them. Perhaps there is an explanation for this sense of threat in the poem itself. On one level it might be Blake's own testament, with its desire for a spiritual genealogy – 'God for a father' – and its muted yearning for death as vouchsafed in dream or vision. It is clear enough that Tom Dacre will soon die during the course of his work – God will indeed become his father 'if he'd be a good boy' and climb the chimneys; it almost seems as if Tom has willingly and joyfully embraced his fate. It is a poem of death, then, but one that ends with a line that might have come from Watts or Wesley: 'So if all do their duty, they need not fear harm.' We know that Blake once wrote 'Innocence dwells with Wisdom but never with Ignorance', yet what does he affirm here but the placebos and aphorisms of ignorance? What is 'duty' in a situation such as this? It has been suggested that this closing line is in sharp contrast to the rest of the poem but in fact it maintains precisely the same note; the innocence of the speaker, and of Tom himself, is a destructive and ignorant innocence because it actively complies both with the horrors of the climbing trade and of the society that accepts it without thought. It is the 'Unorganizd Innocence' that can persuade a deformed or dying sweep that he is happy, after all, while confirming the credulous or the sanctimonious in their belief that 'duty' is all that needs to be, or can be, done. Blake has dramatised a 'State' or an attitude without in the least acceding to it; then, in the companion poem within *Songs of Experience* that shares the same title, he emphasises his disgust:

> And because I am happy, & dance & sing,
> They think they have done me no injury:
> And are gone to praise God & his Priest & King
> Who make up a heaven of our misery.[6]

Once more we see the two realms of his poetry, like those two worlds of earth and eternity or time and vision in which he lived. 'Never mind it' was, as we have seen, a commonplace phrase of his period; the river in which the young sweeps wash is a reference to the New River in Islington, where the apprentices could bathe on Sunday mornings; Tom Dacre may be named after Lady Dacre's almshouses near James Street; in 1788, during the period 'The Chimney Sweeper' was being composed, an Act to alleviate their conditions of employment was brought before parliament. So the poem is filled with the sights and sounds of London. But these in turn are transformed by Blake's visionary imagination and, at a further level of interpretation, the plight of the chimney sweep becomes the plight of all humankind trapped in their mortal bodies and longing to be free. In the same passage upon chimney sweeps in Swedenborg's treatise, he describes how they are prepared for Heaven by being 'stripped of their own Garments, and are clothed with new shining Raiment, and become Angels'. The blackened and sooty body of the young child becomes an emblem of the body itself, the coffin carried with us everywhere. In the spiritual universe of William Blake, Lamentations may become Revelation, for 'We are called by his name'.[7]

ELEVEN

From Lambeth We began our Foundations

In the last months of 1790, William and Catherine Blake moved from Poland Street across the river to the Surrey shore and Lambeth. His address now was 'Mr Blake Engraver, Hercules Buildings, Westminster Bridge'. He had realised, while he worked upon his relief etchings, that the establishment in Soho was too small for his needs – at last in Lambeth, he said later, 'I had a whole House to range in'.[1] No. 13 Hercules Buildings was a terraced house of three storeys and a basement, containing nine or ten rooms, some of them with marble fireplaces and panelled walls. For the first time in his life he possessed a garden; there was a large fenced one at the back, which contained a vine and a fig tree, and there was also a smaller one at the front – 'a garden mild' or even 'the Garden of Love', as he expressed it in the poems he was writing now.[2] Multitudes of marigolds were seen there in later years, and so together with all the vines and fig trees that appear in the gardens of Blake's poetry we may add 'the bright Marygold of Leutha's vale'.[3] A literary enthusiast, in 1912, remembered being shown 'William Blake's "painting room" (a panelled room) which, to the best of my knowledge, was on the ground floor back, looking on to the then spacious and beautiful garden, where the luxurious vine was still to be seen nestling round the open casement'.[4] There has been a great deal of scholarly controversy over that vine, with some authorities asserting that Mrs Blake pruned and nourished it so there was 'ripe fruit hanging in rich clusters', while others assert that Blake forbade the vine to be touched and that there was as a result 'a luxuriant crop of leaves, and plenty of infinitesimal grapes which never ripened'.[5] On such occasions the symbolic dimension of the episode becomes of paramount importance, and we have either the exuberant and fruitful poet or the untamed visionary who never 'pruned' his verses. One story can be laid to rest, however. It has sometimes been claimed that the painter Romney gave Blake the plant; but such a gesture would not have been necessary. At that time Lambeth was well known for its vines and vineyards.

Hercules Buildings was named after the classical hero only indirectly. It was a new development, built in Blake's lifetime by Philip Astley; Astley was the manager of the 'Royal Saloon' or, later, 'Ampitheatre of the Arts' in Westminster Bridge Road, and he had named the new houses after the strong man in his circus. On the bill, the year after the Blakes had moved to Lambeth, was 'Sleight of Hand, Comic Dancing, Rossignol's Imitation of Birds, the Dancing Dogs, the Polander's Tricks on Chairs, and a Grand Display of Fireworks'. The Blakes' house was situated on an area known as Lambeth Marsh, which when they first arrived still retained at least part of its rural appearance. It was close to the Lambeth workhouse and asylum, while Lambeth Palace itself was surrounded by alleys and courts, which were a sanctuary for debtors. Nevertheless, the Blakes could still look out across open fields towards the river; down the street were village green and charity school in the old style. Like any marsh, too, it was an area of ponds, ditches and rivulets, where the Cockney sportsmen shot at birds and where the elusive 'will-o'-the-wisp' could be seen. There were breweries and 'tenter-grounds' for the bleaching and drying of clothes, which used the clean running water of the region, while in the fields there was the famous 'Lactarium', established by a lady who called herself Lactaria; she purveyed milk and syllabubs and would 'accommodate no disorderly people'.[6]

From his upstairs window Blake could have seen the wherries, fishing boats and sailing ships upon the Thames, while the river bank had over the centuries become the site of coal wharves and timber yards. Even as they moved to the area, however, it was changing. The construction of Westminster and Blackfriars bridges meant that it was open to vastly increased traffic from the cities of London or Westminster, and new roads had been constructed across the fields. Pennant's *Perambulation of London* acclaimed the urbanisation of Lambeth Marsh, just as any of Blake's contemporaries would have done: 'Most of this tract is become firm land, and covered with most useful buildings even to the edge of the river.' Soon the area had a stone manufactory and a wine factory, potteries and dye-works, lime

William Blake One who is very much delighted with being in good Company

January 16 1826

Born 28 Novr 1757 in London & has died several times since

Blake's autograph exploding into energy in William Upcott's album.

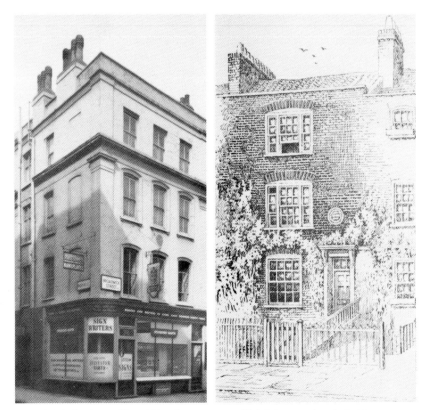

Blake's first house, No. 28 Broad Street, where God appeared in an upstairs window.

Blake's house in Lambeth, No. 13 Hercules Buildings, where he sat naked with his wife in the garden.

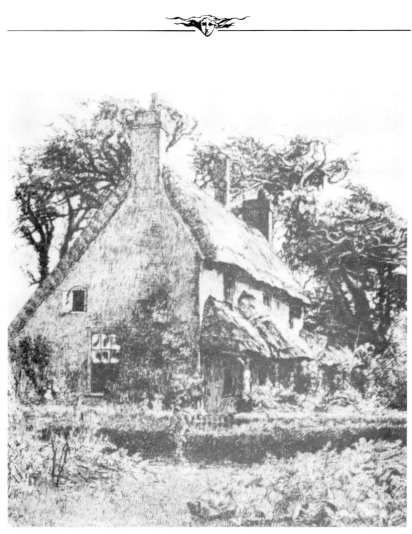

The cottage at Felpham, which Blake considered the dwelling of immortals.

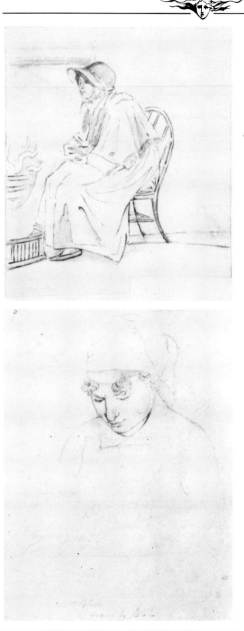

A drawing of Catherine Blake, c. 1785, displaying here something of that patience and 'stillness' which were invaluable to her husband.

A sketch of Catherine Blake, by Blake himself, early in the nineteenth century. Here too the beauty and patient labour shine through the poverty.

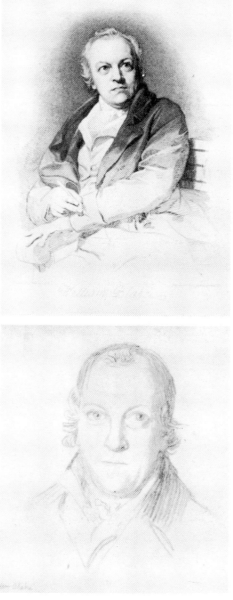

An etching taken from Thomas Phillips's portrait of Blake. Blake explained, as he sat to him, that he had been visited by an archangel; this may account for the rapt look which the painter imparts to him.

A sketch of Blake by his fellow artist John Flaxman. Here we see the lineaments of the London tradesman.

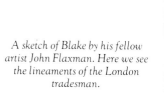

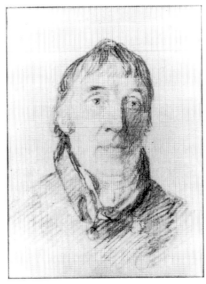

These were the friends of Blake's youth, artists and engravers who shared his love of the Gothic and the ancient style.

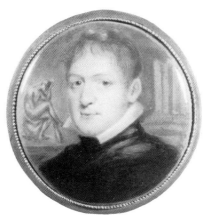

Thomas Stothard

George Cumberland

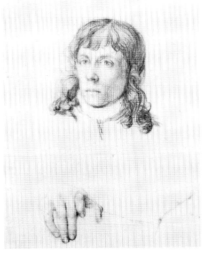

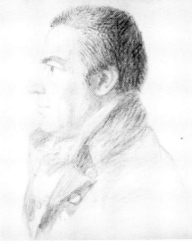

John Flaxman

James Parker

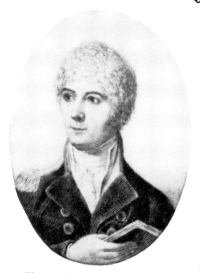

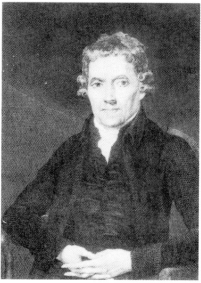

Thomas Butts – in many respects a typical late eighteenth-century gentleman, but one sensitive and resourceful enough to support the 'mad' poet.

Joseph Johnson, Blake's first, and best, publisher.

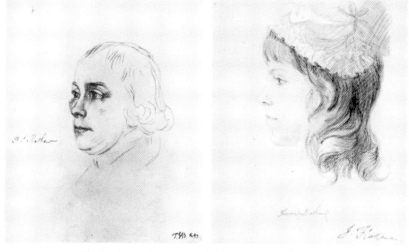

The Mathews, clergyman and 'blue-stocking', who invited Blake to their tea-parties.

A scene, supposedly that of Blake and his wife, taken from the Notebook. The tentative title for a series of poems appears above them.

kilns and blacking factories; Blake and his wife lived in Lambeth for ten years, and by the time they left in 1800 it was already acquiring the characteristics of a peculiarly repellent urban slum with wretchedly built and undrained houses. 'Beth-el' was in Hebrew the name for a sacred place, as Blake would have known from Genesis, but this place of the Lamb was soon degraded. And then there came Bethlem itself, when the madhouse was moved to Lambeth from Moorfields in 1815.

Yet this area became the ground or circumstance of some of Blake's greatest writing; it was the landscape in which his imagination continued to flourish and, as a result, he refers to it more often than to any other London region: 'From Lambeth / We began our Foundations; lovely Lambeth!'[7] These 'Foundations' were his great works, because

There is a Grain of Sand in Lambeth that Satan cannot find
Nor can his Watch Fiends find it: tis translucent & has many Angles.[8]

It lies between Westminster Bridge Road and Lambeth Road, where Blake had his dwelling and where he found a gate into the translucent world of vision. The area around him then becomes invested with spiritual significance, and the lowliest tavern or hospital charged with the light of eternity:

Begining at Jerusalems Inner Court, Lambeth ruin'd and given
To the detestable Gods of Priam, to Apollo: and at the Asylum
Given to Hercules, who labour in Tirzahs Looms for bread.[9]

We can name these abodes of Blake's Lambeth: the Apollo Gardens, together with the Flora Tea Gardens and the Temple of Flora (Priam's classical gods), were the decayed resorts of the neighbourhood. The Flora Tea Gardens were in the fields opposite Hercules Buildings, with entertainments of music and fireworks as well as painted benches and boxes for its customers; it closed in 1796 when its proprietor was sent to the nearby King's Bench Prison for keeping a disorderly house. Apollo Gardens were across the New Road, a few yards from Blake's house, another dilapidated place of pleasure for the new urban residents of Lambeth and beyond. Lambeth Marsh was in any case widely known as a centre of makeshift entertainment, with such taverns as the Adam-and-Eve, the Canterbury, the Pineapple and the Dog and Duck (which, in the charmingly haphazard character of the period, also housed a school for the indigent blind). It was generally considered a louche and even disreputable quarter; radical insurrectionaries were hunted down in the area and the French transvestite spy, Chevalier d'Eon, moved here from Golden Square.

So 'Apollo' can be recognised among the 'Gods of Priam', but what is the 'Asylum Given to Hercules' where they labour at the looms? Around the corner from Hercules Buildings was the Lambeth Asylum for Girls; it was designed to harbour two hundred of them, between the ages of seven and fourteen, largely to save them from prostitution (at that age they were known as 'chicken whores') and to train them for the new manufactories or for domestic service. There is a picture of them, by Thomas Rowlandson and Auguste-Charles Pugin, sitting down to a meal at two long tables in an undecorated stone hallway. They sang as they worked at their looms, but essentially they were regarded as the material for cheap labour. 'Lambeth mourns calling Jerusalem. she weeps & looks abroad'.[10]

There are two other relics of old Lambeth which may be glimpsed in Blake's poetry, although many critics would deny the possibility of such overt physical reductionism. Nevertheless, the parallels are suggestive. In the 1780s, just before Blake moved to Hercules Buildings, a group of subscribers built a Dissenting chapel on the junction of Blackfriars Road for the followers of Rowland Hill; then, in 1793, the South Lambeth Chapel was built on the South Lambeth Road. Blake wrote 'The Garden of Love' after he had moved to Lambeth:

> And saw what I never had seen:
> A Chapel was built in the midst . . .
> And the gates of this Chapel were shut,
> And Thou shalt not. writ over the door.[11]

The two South London chapels are not the occasion for this lyric, but they may at least provide one context for it. Blake was the poet of eternity, but he was also the poet of late eighteenth-century London. And what could provide a more suitable emblem of that city than the famous automated Albion Mill? It had been built along the Blackfriars Road, a short distance north of Hercules Buildings; it was the first great factory in London, designed by John Rennie to run upon steam-engines and supposed to produce some six thousand bushels of flour a week. It was one of the 'sights' of the metropolis, which Erasmus Darwin described as 'a grand and successful effort of human art'.[12] But in March 1791, just after Blake had moved to

Lambeth, it was burnt down – some believe it to have been arson, and the rejoicing millers on Blackfriars Bridge made no secret of their feelings. 'Success to the mills of ALBION', one placard was inscribed, 'but no Albion Mills'. The factory was destroyed, and remained as a black ruined shell until 1809 – Blake passed it every time he walked into the City, with the hills of Highgate and Hampstead in the distant smoky air.

> And did the Countenance Divine,
> Shine forth upon our clouded hills?
> And was Jerusalem builded here,
> Among these dark Satanic Mills?[13]

TWELVE

the crushing Wheels

Satan himself is the 'Miller of Eternity' and 'Prince of the Starry Wheels' that grind out material reality in the same fashion as the mill on the Blackfriars Road.[1] These are the mills that entrance the scientist and the empirical philosopher who, on looking through the microscope or telescope, see fixed mechanism everywhere.

> O Satan my youngest born, art thou not Prince of the Starry Hosts
> And of the Wheels of Heaven, to turn the Mills day & night?
> Art thou not Newtons Pantocrator weaving the Woof of Locke
> To Mortals thy Mills seem every thing . . .[2]

Tom Paine compared the universe to a mill, while Blake continued to insist, 'He who sees the Ratio only sees himself only.'[3] It is the sin of the philosopher or deist to believe that everything is created in the image of their own deluded perceptions. Theirs is a world of wheels, or orbits, of particles, points and lines. These are the 'crushing Wheels' that create 'Stern Philosophy' and 'knead the bread of knowledge'.[4] It is the philosophy of Locke and Bacon, blotting out the light of divinity and inspiration. Blake knew well enough how Samson ground 'Eyeless in Gaza at the mill with slaves'. It is the creation of the material universe, and all the panoply of stars and soils that are emblems of our fallen state and objects of our divided perceptions:

> These are the starry voids of night & the depths & caverns of earth
> These Mills are oceans, clouds & waters ungovernable in their fury.[5]

The mills also create 'Sexual texture', and the woes springing from the separation of the sexes.[6] They are connected to the distaffs and spindles with which the Female Will weaves the shapes of physical illusion, or spins the finite body; in her fallen state Jerusalem also sits at the mill: 'She sat at the Mills, her hair unbound her feet naked / Cut with the flints . . .'[7] Yet, as is often the case in Blake's writing, his own vision is strangely implicated with the great oral myths of the past. The primary god was known as 'Zeus the Miller', while both Greek and Eastern astronomers saw the cosmos itself turning like a millstone, grinding out time, separating earth from heaven. In Norse myth, too, the mill is believed to be the progenitor of mankind – of which there is also a vague echo in Robert Burns's 'John Barleycorn'. As one study of mythology puts it, 'the mill-tree is also the world axis'.[8]

So it is that the mills are made up of the 'Wheel of Religion' and of 'the dark Preacher of Death'.[9] They are sustained by the enormous wheels of the libraries and of learning by rote, 'which in the mill was Aristotles Analytics', circular, ever revolving.[10] The first factories in England were also known as 'mills', so there is a connection between enslaved perception and industrial production. There were the wheels of the engraving press, also, as well as the mills and furnaces of London, all around him, as he walks down Blackfriars Road, comprising the 'vast machinery' of the fallen universe.

THIRTEEN

Jerusalems Inner Court

Blake had moved to Lambeth because he needed more room – it was in any case cheaper to rent a house in Hercules Buildings than in Poland Street. He needed space and time to concentrate upon those new techniques of relief etching that seemed to offer such great rewards; he realised, like anyone educated in a trade, that he would have to work consistently and continuously if he were to be a success. But it was not just public and commercial reputation that he courted; the possibilities that these new methods had revealed to him, and the sense of inspired achievement which they had already afforded him, meant that he had set his own course in a new direction. Even now he was equating 'Poetic genius' with the 'Spirit of Prophecy'. And so, in Lambeth, he entered the most productive period of his life.

Of course he was obliged to carry on his trade. But he ended his partnership with James Parker – Parker himself continued trading in Broad Street, beside Blake's family, and made a speciality of engraving after the drawings and paintings of John Flaxman. Blake's confidence in his ability to support himself was well-justified; he was engaged in a number of engraving projects during the Lambeth years, which provided him with a decent income. There was even a period at Hercules Buildings when they were able to afford a servant, 'but finding (as Mrs Blake declared & as everyone else knows) the more service the more Inconvenience, she like all sensible women, who are possessed of industry & health & only moderate means, relinquished this incessant Tax upon domestic comfort'.[1] Without a servant, however, the house was sometimes unguarded; and on one occasion thieves broke in and 'carried away Plate to the Value of 60 Pounds &

clothes to the amount of 40 more'.[2] At Lambeth, then, Blake was not
reduced to the poverty he would experience later in his life – although
it is possible that the 'Plate' mentioned here might not be silver but
'plates' of copper for engraving.

He was sometimes called 'Mr Johnson's engraver', since most of his
commissions were still undertaken for the books published by Joseph
Johnson in St Paul's Churchyard. Some of these are of no particular
significance, although Blake's engraving of four urinary tract stones
for James Earle's *Practical Observations on the Operation for the Stone*
have at least the merit of oddity. But there were other assignments of a
more substantial nature, the most important being for Fuseli. They
continued to work very closely in this period, in ways that
demonstrate theirs was more than a simple relationship between artist
and engraver. Boydell's 'Shakespeare Gallery' seemed about to
become a great success, and there are sketches from the plays in
Blake's notebook, which suggest that he may have hoped to
participate in it. But no such offer was made, as we have seen, and
instead he worked upon another grand project. Joseph Johnson came
up with the complementary plan of a 'Milton Gallery' – William
Cowper would edit the text of Milton's poetry while Fuseli would
complete various illustrative paintings, which in turn would be
engraved by Blake and two others. But Cowper succumbed once more
to insanity and all the terrors of assumed damnation – he would
become for Blake the type of the 'mad poet' whom he both pitied and
celebrated – and so the project was shelved. Fuseli saw other
possibilities in the venture, however, and decided to arrange his own
'Gallery of the Miltonic Sublime'; forty paintings were eventually
exhibited in the old Academy Room in Pall Mall. 'I never read
Milton, but I will,' one idiotic visitor told Fuseli. 'I advise you not to,'
the painter replied, 'for you will find it a damned tough job.'[3] Fuseli
had already asked Blake to engrave two works for the gallery, but they
were either never completed or have failed to survive; in his
notebooks, though, Blake made a series of sketches from episodes in
Paradise Lost and there is even a very accomplished pen and wash
drawing, 'The House of Death', taken from the eleventh book of that
poem. All of this implies that he was working closely with Fuseli on
Miltonic themes and motifs, and there is no doubt that the painter
gave his engraver wide latitude in formal composition.

In this period, for example, they worked together on illustrations
for Erasmus Darwin's *The Botanic Garden* – Blake took a sketch by

Fuseli of the 'Fertilization of Egypt' and brilliantly intensified it so it contains all the majesty and horror that he associated with early civilisation. For the same project he also engraved the then celebrated Portland, or Barberini, Vase; he would have worked from one of Wedgwood's copies (the vase itself was exhibited at the salesroom in Greek Street), and was no doubt aware of the controversy over the scenes represented in the various compartments of that illustrious object. It was not clear whether they depicted episodes from the life of Adonis, or the re-enactment of the Eleusinian mysteries, but Blake knew of one important aspect of the classical debate – much scholarly work had been devoted to establishing the sexual and, in particular, phallic component of ancient religious ritual. He had already done some sketches of Bacchic rites, and we have only to remember the emphasis upon sexual magic among certain Swedenborgians to realise how powerful this strain of religious belief might remain. It was not necessarily confined to Swedenborgians, however, and one of Blake's most elaborate engravings is derived from an overtly erotic drawing by Fuseli; entitled 'Falsa ad Coelum Mittunt Insomnia Manes', it depicts slightly obscured female genitalia as well as explicit phallic symbols. Of course Fuseli is well known to have completed many erotic studies, with the same obsessiveness if not quite in the same manner as Blake, and the survival of this print suggests that their collaboration strayed beyond the conventional bounds of 'Fine Art'. Indeed the first prints that Blake produced for sale after he had moved to Lambeth, 'Zephyrus and Flora' and 'Callisto', have been described by one authority as exhibiting a 'fey eroticism'.[4] Is it straining credulity too far to believe that Blake may once have been happy to stock and sell prints of an even less 'fey' nature? Certainly he depicted bizarre sexual encounters for the rest of his life and, as he once told George Cumberland, 'Enjoyment & not Abstinence is the food of Intellect'.[5]

It has often been suggested that Blake, when illustrating Darwin's *The Botanic Garden*, was heavily influenced by its imagery and theme; that is why, of all his commercial undertakings, this project has received the most analysis. There is certainly a great deal of erotic imagery devoted to 'The Loves of Plants', and Blake did re-employ some of the motifs he first engraved here, but it is hard to believe that he was very much affected by a poem designed 'to inlist Imagination under the banner of Science'.[6] He had the eclectic instincts of the autodidact, however, and he could have acquired a wide knowledge of contemporary science from Darwin's somewhat turgid couplets. The footnotes alone cover such subjects as geology and biology, the production of iron and the power of magnetism, the formation of the star clusters and the nature of salt crystals, pumps and steam-engines, volcanoes and electricity. But another engraving after Fuseli would also have opened his eyes to a quite different world of knowledge, if he had not explored it already, when in December 1791 the *Conjuror's Magazine* reproduced one of his prints from Lavater's *Physiognomy*. He may not have been particularly interested in the methods 'To prevent dogs barking at you in the night-time' and 'To be sure of winning a wager', but he was well aware of the repertoire of beliefs that the *Conjuror's Magazine* represented. The journal contains references to the 'Intelligence of Tiriel' and the 'Intelligences of Bne Seraphim', for example, so perhaps the opening of Blake's poem *Thel* should be noted: 'The daughters of Mne Seraphim led round their sunny flocks.'[7] In this 'Magical and Physiognomical Mirror', also, Sweden-borg is mentioned in a list of 'eminent Conjurors' and the fact that Lavater's work is reproduced here suggests how close Blake was to those 'secret societies' of magical exponents that advertised at the back of the magazine. When we see him in Lambeth, working in his panelled room, dabbling in magical terminology and engraving erotic prints, we come across a more human and recognisable Blake than the inspired prophet and lonely genius of twentieth-century legend.

But he was not confined to engraving after the work of Fuseli. Johnson also commissioned him to illustrate a somewhat gruesome children's book entitled *Elements of Morality for the Use of Children with an Introductory Address to Parents*, which contains the tale of a child lost in a wood that has suggestive parallels with a poem Blake was soon to write; it often seems that he was spurred into creating contrary or antagonistic lyrics by dislike of something he had read or seen. It was an element of his essentially pugnacious nature. Johnson also asked him to work with a retired soldier and adventurer, John Gabriel Stedman, who had written his memoirs in *Narrative, of a Five Years' Expedition, against the Revolted Negroes of Surinam*. The nature of that book can more usefully be described closer to the time of its publication, when it materially affected Blake's views both of slavery and of women, and at this stage only Stedman's comment in his journal for 1 December 1791 need be quoted: 'I wrote to the Engraver Blake to thank him twice for his excellent work but never received any answer.'[8] It is one of the most persistent complaints about him. A month earlier John Flaxman's wife had written from Rome to her sister-in-law, 'pray call on Mr Blake & beg of him to answer your Brother's Letter directly'.[9] No such 'answer' is recorded. This tardiness was not confined to letters, and there is evidence to suggest that he was not always a very reliable workman: he had been asked to provide new plates for the third volume of Stuart's and Revett's The Antiquities of Athens, after the designs of his old schoolmaster's brother, William Pars, and the request elicited his first surviving response. 'Mr Blake's Compts to Mr Reveley,' he wrote, 'tho full of work (as Mr R said he should be by then [tho] the plates were put in hand) he is glad to embrace the offer of engraving such beautiful things & will do what he can by the end of January.'[10] In fact he did not produce the required work until April. He did not finish the copper plates for Elements of Morality in time for the first edition, which was published without the intended illustrations, and it seems that his delay in producing the engravings of the Portland Vase may also have affected the publication of The Botanic Garden.

He might have been 'full of work', but this pattern of dilatoriness persisted through his life. He may just have been very slow, or he may have been preoccupied with his own creative endeavours, but it is also possible that, in his own words, 'my Abstract folly hurries me often away while I am at work, carrying me over Mountains & Valleys, which are not Real, in a Land of Abstraction where Spectres of the Dead wander'.[11] This has generally been taken to mean that he was pursuing some aesthetic ideal as he laboured over his copper plates, or that he was simply daydreaming, but he is actually much more specific. He finds himself in an abstract land where he sees the spectres of the dead – he was, in other words, haunted or beset by those visions he had experienced since childhood. Were we to employ the psychological terminology of spontaneous eidetic imagery, we would conclude that he was now suffering from an almost clinical condition: he was seeing visions continually, and they were actively preventing him from getting on with his daily work. These were the 'Spectres of the Dead' – his dead brother, the dead monarchs he had drawn in Westminster Abbey, the spirits and angels that he was always sketching in his notebooks. At a later stage we will hear him talking to Michelangelo or to the Angel Gabriel, and watch him summoning the ghost of a flea. He saw them in front of him, neither real nor unreal. He knew precisely what he saw, and with the sturdy obstinacy of his London stock he refused to be bullied or dissuaded. Is it any wonder, then, that he should have turned to Swedenborg or to occult literature and radical spiritual groups? They could at least account for the phenomena, even justify them, and free him from the taint of madness. Is it surprising, either, that he should testify to his great love for the writings of St Teresa? In a natural and graphic style she recounted her visions of the dead, which were also continual, and explained, 'There is nothing we can do about them; we cannot see more or less of them at will, and we can neither call them up nor banish them by our own efforts.'[12] In 1560 she saw the hands of the Lord, 'the beauty of which was so great as to be indescribable'.[13] She had seen the Divine Humanity of Jesus, just as Blake had, 'in very great beauty and majesty';[14] she also spoke often with the dead and of one departed friar she wrote, 'Since his death it has been the Lord's great pleasure that I should have more intercourse with him than I had during his life and that he should advise me on many subjects.'[15] The unaffected and graceful tone of her descriptions is very much like that of Blake, or Swedenborg, or any other true visionary. To read St Teresa is to understand something of the mystery of William Blake.

Yet his slowness and lack of punctuality, even as he saw his visions, did cost him employment; he was advertised to work on Bowyer's edition of Hume's *History of England*, for example, but he never completed any of its plates. There were other ways of earning money, and there are persistent reports that he 'took in' pupils during this period. It is not unlikely, and he certainly worked as a part-time tutor at a later date, although it is not at all clear who his students were. Flaxman may have recommended him to his own pupils on his departure for Italy and Fuseli, who became a full Member of the Royal Academy in 1790, could also have steered his students towards Lambeth; but the most direct description concerns pupils 'of high rank'. The report comes from Frederick Tatham, who was closely acquainted with the Blakes in later life, but it throws an intriguing light upon Blake himself: 'About this time he taught Drawing & was engaged for that purpose by some families of high rank . . . after his lessons he got into conversation with his pupils, & was found so entertaining & pleasant, possessing such novel thoughts & such eccentric notions, together with such jocose hilarity and amiable demeanour, that he frequently found himself asked to stay to dinner, & spend the Evening in the same interesting & lively manner, in which he had consumed the morning.' But then there came a change, as Tatham goes on to report: 'He was recommended & nearly obtained an Appointment to teach Drawing to the Royal Family. Blake stood aghast . . . because he would have been drawn into a class of Society, superior to his previous pursuits & habits; he would have been expected to live in comparative respectability, not to say splendour, a mode of life, as he thought, derogatory to the simplicity of his designs & deportment . . . His friends ridiculed & blamed him by turns but Blake found an Excuse by resigning all his other pupils.'[16] This is a very curious anecdote – it is possible to see Blake visiting the houses of rich London pupils, portfolio under his arm, and the image of his 'jocose hilarity and amiable demeanour' is a corrective to those who are content to treat him more solemnly, but the idea of his being recommended to the Royal Family strains credulity. The circum-stantial detail of this account strongly suggests that it came from Blake or possibly from his wife, but it sounds as if a very minor episode has been elaborated and embellished for effect. It is probable that one of his 'high-rank' employers mentioned the possibility of teaching the Royal Family in passing and that Blake, with his usual nervous weakness, was thrown into a state of general anxiety at the prospect. How can I refuse the Royal Family? I will have to cease to teach altogether. I cannot manage this situation. I will have to withdraw from this kind of society. This is at least as likely as Tatham's bland report. Blake was a wonderful fabulist and, in much later life, may well have provided a more coherent narrative of a panic-struck decision.

All the while he was using his dead brother's notebook. He had for the moment given up any painterly ambitions – he did not exhibit at the Royal Academy at all for fourteen years – because he was too absorbed in the possibilities of his new creative techniques. It is given to very few artists, after all, to invent their own medium. He was filling the notebook with a series of emblems to which he added verses from Milton, Dryden and others as a form of commentary; he was interested in conveying the spiritual significance of the great poets, while the drawings themselves are characteristically concerned with death and with the grave. There is in fact a private obsessiveness about these deathbed scenes that suggests he had not fully recovered from the effect of his younger brother's own demise. Two years after his move to Lambeth, his mother died at the age of seventy and followed her husband to the graveyard of Bunhill Fields; as with his father, Blake rarely spoke of her, and seems only to have thought of Robert. He was an idealised version of his younger self, dead in his youth with all his glory still around him. And, secretly, did Blake wish to follow him out of a world which scarcely noticed him? In his art and poetry, the human world is often one of sorrow and of war while the spiritual world is interfused with energy and power.

But within the emblems there are associations other than those of death. This was primarily an artistic exercise; it was a visual equivalent of *Songs of Innocence* and, like that collection, it takes its place in a long tradition of emblem books and chapbooks. There is a drawing here of an aged man on a crutch being led by a child; it is the image he would eventually choose to illustrate one of his most famous poems, 'London', as has already been suggested, and no doubt he invented it under the (perhaps unconscious) influence of Zechariah: 'There shall yet old men and old women dwell in the streets of Jerusalem, and every man with his staff in his hand for very age. And the streets of the city shall be full of boys and girls playing in the streets thereof.'[17] It is sometimes suggested that he worked or wrote with his Bible open in front of him, checking the references; but he had been so closely acquainted with the book from earliest childhood that his imagination would quite naturally take the form first intimated by its powerful prophetic verses. He remained, to the end of his life, a biblical artist and poet who also considered himself to be a prophet. But the sketch of the old man and the child was only partly a biblical emblem, since it also belongs to a history of expression that is now lost to us; it conveyed earlier images of patriarchs and children, of Tiresias and Oedipus, of the great blind poets of the past, all quite accessible and comprehensible to the citizens of eighteenth-century London.

He began drawing the emblems in 1787, and completed the last of them in the first month of 1793. At that point he decided to print and publish the best of them as a kind of child's primer. There were sixty-four in the notebook but he employed only seventeen; as always in his revisions of this period, his instinct was towards reduction and compression. So he traced out the emblems he wished to use before engraving them upon the copper, and by May he had completed a small series of images entitled 'For Children: The Gates of Paradise'. He also inscribed, on the title page, 'Published by W Blake N° 13 Hercules Buildings Lambeth and J. Johnson St Pauls' Church Yard'.[18] It seems likely that Johnson displayed the book in his shop but the stock could not have been great – only five copies survive, and at least two of them were given by Blake to Henry Fuseli and George Cumberland. He wrapped the coppers in cloth for future use and at a much later date took them out, redesigned the series, and gave it a new title – 'For the Sexes: The Gates of Paradise'. He was still working upon it in the last year of his life, which again suggests how closely he mantained and protected the original sources of his inspiration. On the occasion of this first publication, however, after he had inscribed 'For Children: The Gates of Paradise', he sketched the title page of a different volume altogether; it was called 'For Children: The Gates of Hell'. And this in turn leads us to another of his contraries and oppositions. No sooner had he finished *Songs of Innocence* than he began work upon *Songs of Experience*.

The process of composition is, for once, easy to describe. He had carried on drawing emblems in his brother's notebook until he had almost reached the last page; then in the autumn of 1792, around the time of his mother's death, he simply turned the book upside down and, working from the back, began to write out drafts of various lyric poems. The first of them look like fair copies, and by the end of the year he had filled fourteen pages with fifty-eight complete or incomplete poems. Out of these carefully transcribed verses came *Songs of Experience*. On the first page of the notebook, composed in two columns as if they were part of an eighteenth-century Bible, there are poems that variously begin 'A flower was offerd to me', 'I told my love I told my love', 'Love seeketh not itself to please', 'I laid me down upon a bank', 'I went to the garden of love', 'I saw a chapel all of gold'. On another page the first draft of 'London' is above the first draft of 'Tyger', so that the two most celebrated of Blake's poems can be seen emerging together into the world. Yet the disenchanted solitary who observes 'Marks of weakness, marks of woe'[19] is very different from the exultant questioner who asks 'Did he who made the Lamb make thee?'[20] These are not pure lyrics emanating from one voice but dramatisations of various mental states and attitudes – or, perhaps, dramatisations of the various selves that inhabited Blake. Poets such as Ezra Pound and W. B. Yeats have described the 'masks' that they employed as a creative medium, 'casting off complete masks of the self in each poem';[21] if this reference seems anachronistic, then we may turn for illumination to an artistic form which Blake knew well. In the Handel operas of this period, each separate aria by the same singer reveals a different sentiment or mood, 'presenting every emotion in isolation, unmixed, pure, and leaving it to the listener to form an impression of the character as a whole'.[22] This is not some arcane literary theory, but the very stuff of fashionable and popular entertainment in London at this time. The songs of Robert Burns could also be cited, which again are dramatic utterances from the mouths of various selves or speakers. But there is a difference in intent – Blake's insistence upon tight rhymes and forms is a way of suggesting the limits of the medium he is employing, in exactly the same way as he emphasised the hatching and cross-hatching of his conventional commercial engravings. This gives his lyrics the power of direct statement, while allowing a dramatic withdrawal from the perceived sentiments of the poetic 'voice'.

He originally conceived *Songs of Experience* as direct satires of *Songs of Innocence*, poem for poem, but in the process he found more general possibilities of expression. At first he printed both of the *Songs* as separate series, but then linked them together with a new title page, 'Songs Of Innocence and Of Experience Shewing the Two Contrary States of the Human Soul'. These are opposites in more than one sense, however, since many of the *Songs of Experience* are etched upon the other side of the copper plates for *Innocence*. Two contrary states could be held, as an object, in the hand. It was of course a way of saving copper, and therefore money, but it also indicates Blake's very practical and material handling of his vision. There are contraries and oppositions at every turn – not only is *Experience* etched on the back of *Innocence*, but Blake used a different calligraphy and a different method of printing colour. There may even have been copies of the combined volumes in which *Experience* preceded *Innocence*. The technical process is also of extraordinary importance, because Blake was actually writing *backwards* upon the copper on the *back* of the poems he was partly satirising. He was sculpting words as if they were as much images of his ideas as the illustrations beside them; he was seeing words as discrete objects, not as transparent signifiers of meaning. They are objects to be looked at, upon which much care has been lavished, and at some point they cease simply to be the medium for lyric expression and become as materially based as any other copper image. But in this process of being formed, they become resistant to conventional interpretation; they do not float off the page in the manner of innumerable poetic volumes, with the words residing somewhere between the poet and the reader, but remain firmly based in the splendid isolation of a unique art-object. 'Two Contrary States of the Human Soul' are fixed upon a few millimetres of copper plate.

There would be a good case, then, for claiming that Blake's

technical experiences as an engraver preceded and fashioned his own particular vision. For that, too, is irradiated by contraries and oppositions – love and hate, expansion and contraction, opaqueness and translucence, reason and energy, attraction and repulsion, these are the poles of his world, where 'Without Contraries is no progression'.[23] He establishes pairs and couples within his poetry and his art; his painted objects are often placed in symmetry with each other, just as his epic verse is heavily imbued with parallelism and antithesis. In his greatest work he creates giant forms that contain his own contradictory impulses and private oppositions; he establishes a 'bounding line' of art or poetry that does not unite contraries but allows them to exist in harmony beside each other. There is wisdom to be acquired in continual activity and mental strife. In that sense the works become almost an idealised version of Blake himself, and in these *Songs* he becomes both writer and artist, satirist and lyricist, poet and prophet. W. H. Auden once said that 'Truth is Catholic, but the search for it is Protestant', and in these words we can see part of Blake's pilgrimage upon the earth.[24] He was creating words as objects, intimately related to the Catholic and sacramental sense of the 'Word' and 'the Word made flesh'; it represents a universe of emblematic discourse established upon the signatures and correspondences of the material and spiritual worlds. But his search for it is through the practical labour and arduous struggle that are the marks of the Protestant conscience. Now it is time to face the tiger.

FOURTEEN

eyes of fury

I t is perhaps the most famous of Blake's lyrics, sung by his more enlightened contemporaries and chanted by schoolchildren in the twentieth century as if it were a secular hymn.

> Tyger Tyger, burning bright,
> In the forests of the night;
> What immortal hand or eye,
> Could frame thy fearful symmetry?
>
> In what distant deeps or skies.
> Burnt the fire of thine eyes?
> On what wings dare he aspire?
> What the hand, dare sieze the fire?
>
> And what shoulder, & what art,
> Could twist the sinews of thy heart?
> And when thy heart began to beat,
> What dread hand? & what dread feet?
>
> What the hammer? what the chain,
> In what furnace was thy brain?
> What the anvil? what dread grasp,
> Dare its deadly terrors clasp!
>
> When the stars threw down their spears
> And water'd heaven with their tears:
> Did he smile his work to see?
> Did he who made the Lamb make thee?
>
> Tyger Tyger burning bright,
> In the forests of the night:

> What immortal hand or eye,
> Dare frame thy fearful symmetry?

He wrote out the first three stanzas fluently enough, as if they had been echoing within his head and needed only to be transcribed in the notebook; perhaps he had already jotted them down on one of the scraps of paper he kept in his pocket. Then he began the fourth verse:

> Could fetch it from the furnace deep
> And in the horrid ribs dare steep
> In the well of sanguine woe[1]

He stopped, perhaps not able to find a rhyme for 'woe' or disliking the phrase itself, and tried another couplet:

> In what clay & in what mould
> Were thy eyes of fury rolld

But he was dwelling too long upon the more grotesque attributes of the beast, and he deleted this entire stanza with vertical strokes of ink. He continued with what became the fourth and sixth stanzas, but then turned the page and tried to create a different effect altogether:

> Burnt in distant deeps or skies
> The cruel fire of thine eyes
> Could heart descend or wings aspire
> What the hand dare sieze the fire

It was an attempt to reach the sublime, but it carried on too insistently the cadence and therefore the meaning of the preceding verses. So he crossed out the stanza with three lines and began again:

> And did he laugh his work to see
> What the shoulder what the knee
> Did he who made the lamb make thee
> When the stars threw down their spears
> And waterd heaven with their tears

With the sudden brilliance of these last two lines, in which astronomical observation and mythological lore are compressed, he knew he had found the right opening for the verse: he carefully numbered them '1' and '2', crossed out 'What the shoulder what the knee', and numbered the last remaining lines '3' and '4'. Then he went back over the entire draft and numbered the stanzas with the order in which they now appear. At one point, in another fair copy, he seems ready to omit the second and fourth stanzas; but he relented, and the poem was finally relief etched on the back of 'The Voice of the Ancient Bard'. He also etched and colour-printed the image of a tiger, which, in the context, is ludicrously comic; it has all the expressiveness of a stuffed toy, with a silly grin upon its face, and can perhaps be seen as an ironic foil to the dramatic invocation of the poetic voice. It might, however, be simply an example of his inability to depict anything other than the human form.

Few poems have been scrutinised so closely or so frequently, but the critics have produced such a bewildering confusion of explanations that the tiger might just as well be grinning at them. It may be appropriate, then, to step back and consider 'The Tyger' from another vantage; if we were in Swedenborgian fashion to find 'correspond-ences' or 'signatures' of the poem in the world that Blake knew, then we may find ourselves at least a little closer to the origins of its power. He could have seen tigers in London at any time in various private menageries – there were two at the Tower of London, 'fierce and savage beyond measure';[2] and when the Blakes lived in Green Street a tiger was being exhibited around the corner in Leicester House. As a child he had seen images of tigers -- Stubbs's painting of one was exhibited in the same building as Pars' Drawing School when Blake was a pupil there. One of Barry's heroic paintings for the Society of Arts had as its commentary 'The Priest divine was fabled to assuage / The Tyger's fierceness, and the Lion's Rage', while, in a more homely setting than the assembly room in Adelphi, the tiger was a favourite motif in 'oriental' textiles of the period.

More important childhood associations are necessarily at work here, also, since his close acquaintance with the Bible would have familiarised him with all the images of wrath and fear, wild beasts and forests: 'Will a lion roar in the forest, when he hath no prey?'[3] And of course Blake knew the sublime interrogations of the Lord to Job: 'Out of his mouth go burning lamps, and sparks of fire leap out . . . His breath kindleth coals, and a flame goeth out of his mouth.'[4] The natural history of the period would have confirmed this particular range of animal imagery, in which the sublime and the terrible are uniquely mingled. The tiger was consistently described as a ravening and ferocious beast, 'perpetually thirsting for blood . . . He has no instinct but perpetual rage, a blind and undistinguishing ferocity . . . He roars at the sight of everything that lives.'[5] There were also numerous engravings to complement this description – in Thomas

Bewick's *A General History of Quadrupeds*, in Thomas Boreman's *Description of Three Hundred Animals*, and in the *Encyclopaedia Britannica*. But there were also engravings in books upon which he himself had worked; there is a head of a spotted tiger in Lavater's *Physiognomy*, and there is an engraving of 'Bacchus with his Tyger' in Stuart and Revett's *The Antiquities of Athens*. The Bacchic tiger also cuts a rather ludicrous figure, and some memory of it may have helped to form Blake's own image – the association with Bacchus would in any case have been suggestive and, in late eighteenth-century studies of phallic worship and priapic rituals, the tiger was connected with fire and with the destruction that must inevitably precede creation. Blake was already working on Stedman's *Narrative of Surinam*, and would have read of the 'tyger cat . . . with its eyes emitting flashes like lightning' and the 'red tyger . . . its eyes prominent and sparkling like stars'.[6] That stellar range and depth was already spread across the heavens, since a constellation of nineteen stars discovered by Helvetius was known as 'The Tyger'. Such a potent range of associations must surely play some part in a poem which itself mixes the stars and the fury, the forests and the destruction, in so intense and elliptical a way. There is also a private association that is fully expressed in one of Blake's later and longer poems:

They erected the furnaces, they formd the anvils of gold beaten in mills
Where winter beats incessant, fixing them firm on their base
The bellows began to blow & the Lions of Urizen stood round the
   anvil . . .
The tygers of wrath called the horses of instruction from their mangers.[7]

From the forests of the night is derived the dark charcoal that is used to forge the iron for Blake's copper plates, on which he inscribes the tiger – the anvils of gold are like the orange stripes on the tiger's flanks, a combined image of creation and destruction. Once more Blake is celebrating all the material processes involved in the creation of the tiger, the creation of the word upon the copper plate by means of varnish and acid, and the creation of the beast itself out of the dark forest. In the sixth plate of *Jerusalem* he depicts Los, the Poetic Imagination, at work with the hammer and the anvil in his perpetual labour over the furious brightness of his forge. The powerful concentration of the poem radiates, also, from Blake's repetition of 'night'/'bright' and all the associated phonemes of 'eye', 'thine', 'aspire', 'fire', and 'tyger' itself – as if in the paradox of the opposition and identity of 'night' and 'bright' all the contraries of the poem can be formally resolved.

There are also more immediate connotations. Even as Blake worked upon the poem the revolutionaries of France were being branded in the image of a ravening beast – after the Paris massacres of September 1792, an English statesman declared, 'One might as well think of establishing a republic of tigers in some forest of Africa',[8] and there were newspaper references to 'the tribunal of tigers'.[9] At a later date, Marat's eyes were said to resemble 'those of the *tyger cat*'.[10] A whole cluster of significant associations can be seen to form around Blake's conception of the wild beast, so haunting in its imagery and so disturbing in its invocation of both rage and celebration. The stars of the heaven and the words of the Bible, the destructive instinct of natural creation and the wrath of God, the forces of social revolution and the images of ancient cults, are here forged together with the tools that Blake depicts in the sixth plate of *Jerusalem*. There is another force, too, that is carried within the poem. It is the force of Jacob Boehme, whose extraordinary writings are part of Blake's spiritual inheritance – 'Heaven is in hell, and hell is in heaven, and nevertheless there is neither of them revealed to the other . . . Thus the angels do not see the darkness; they see only the light of divine power; but the devils see only the darkness of the wrath of God.'[11] These are dark words indeed, but for Blake they shone a light into the heart of his visionary world. In those words is part of the mystery of the tiger, conceived in Lambeth Marsh.

FIFTEEN

---

walking among the fires

B lake was very clear about his spiritual ancestors. He told John
Flaxman that 'Paracelsus & Behmen appeared to me', but their
arrival meant that he turned away from Swedenborg.[1]
'Swedenborgs writings are a recapitulation of all superficial opinions,
and an analysis of the more sublime, but no further. Have now
another plain fact: Any man of mechanical talents may from the
writings of Paracelsus or Jacob Behmen, produce ten thousand
volumes of equal value with Swedenborg's.'[2] It is true that the
writings of Paracelsus and of Boehme (Behmen) do seem to come from
a purer spring of spiritual revelation than those of Swedenborg, but
there may also have been external reasons for Blake's change of heart.
He may have been influenced by Fuseli or Johnson, for example, who
had consistently attacked Swedenborg and the New Church in the
Analytical Review. That Church itself was becoming more ritualised
and institutionalised – it began ordaining ministers, and eventually
prescribing their robes of worship – and therefore far less radical. The
influence of the occultists, mesmerists and magicians was replaced by
that of conservative Church leaders who pledged their faith to 'the
Constitution and Government of their country' as opposed to the
'principles of infidelity and democracy'.[3] The slow processes of
organised religion began to unfold; in particular, the ministers of the
New Church now attached less importance to the energetic life of
charity and began to emphasise the duty of avoiding sinfulness. This
renunciation of the original spirit of the Church, so notably present in
the sign above the portal in Great Eastcheap, 'Now it is Allowable',
also repudiated all of Blake's instinctive beliefs: he began to annotate
Swedenborg's *Divine Providence*, published in 1790, and denounced

him for 'Lies & Priestcraft', 'Cursed Folly!' and, most seriously, 'Predestination'.[4]

So he turned to the writings of Paracelsus and of Boehme. They were widely known and readily available: the bookshops that sold the revelations of Emmanuel Swedenborg also stocked their works; and Blake's acquaintance Cosway even owned one of Boehme's original manuscripts. There were also many tracts and pamphlets that provided summaries of their teaching; in fact it sometimes seems that late eighteenth-century London was awash with mysticism and millenarian yearnings, complementing its appetite for commerce and power. It would not have been hard for him, then, to learn as much as he wished of these two visionaries. And, if he meditated upon their lives, he would have found suggestive parables of his own 'Holy Word' in previous centuries. Paracelsus, the itinerant scholar and physician born in the late fifteenth century, placed no faith in orthodox learning and the established authorities. Jacob Boehme, the cobbler from Upper Lusatia born towards the close of the sixteenth century (it is suggestive that both of these visionaries, like Blake, should emerge in the transition between two centuries), saw a vision of light in a pewter dish and from that time began to formulate his extraordinary body of mystical teachings. Both of them were denounced and reviled as fanatics, drunkards and impostors; both of them were forced to wander from city to city, in search of work and bread; both of them were considered coarse and vulgar to more orthodox believers, but, as Paracelsus put it, 'I am a rough man born in a rough country . . . what seems silk in my eyes may be but homespun to you.'[5] Paracelsus and Boehme both believed that they were rediscovering ancient sources of wisdom – what Boehme called the teachings of 'wise heathens'[6] – and within the context of a Christian spirituality they reasserted the significance of alchemical and cabbalistic knowledge. And, in the process, they both repudiated the supremacy of logic and of reason while concentrating upon the visual signs and emblems of the divine presence within the world. There can be little doubt that Blake considered himself to be an inheritor of their legacy.

No one who reads Paracelsus can remain unaffected by him and an artist such as Blake, slowly coming to believe in his own prophetic and spiritual mission, could only have been exalted and exhilarated by the celebration of the imagination in his writings. 'I know of no other Christianity and of no other Gospel,' Blake later wrote, 'than the liberty both of body & mind to exercise the Divine Arts of the

Imagination.'[7] This is the central truth of Paracelsus, who declared that 'Imagination is like the sun. The sun has a light which is not tangible; but which, nevertheless, may set a house on fire.'[8] The great truth of the universe lies within the human imagination; it is the source, the sun, and those who understand its powers are the lords of all created things. The world of Paracelsus is filled by spirit, with the elements of mercury, salt and sulphur as its trinity of dwelling places, and in his extraordinarily successful treatment of disease he considered the body as a form or definition of the soul itself. Of course Blake need not necessarily have learnt this from Paracelsus; he could have found it within his own heart.

The especial mystery revealed by the fifteenth-century visionary came in his belief that 'Man is compacted of all bodies and created things'.[9] So 'it is a great truth, which you should seriously consider, that there is nothing in heaven or upon the earth which does not also exist in man, and God who is in heaven exists also in man, and the two are but One . . . Man is a sun and a moon and a heaven filled with stars; the world is a man and the light of the sun and the stars is his body . . . The human body is vapour materialized by sunshine mixed with the life of the stars. Four elements are in the world, and man consists out of four, and that which exists visibly in man exists invisibly in the ether pervading the world.'[10] The poetic imagination, as Blake now began to understand it through the work of Paracelsus, can discern the spiritual outline of all created things because it contains them; with the spirit reborn, the poet may see with the eyes of eternity into himself and thus into the universe. That is why Blake is able to equate the 'Poetic Genius' with the 'Spirit of Prophecy',[11] and why in the last months of his life he proclaimed 'The Imagination which Liveth for Ever'.[12] But it would be unwise to be too systematic about such arcane matters. The influence of Paracelsus lay not in the introduction of certain specific principles but in a kind of reawakening. It is as if Blake had looked up at the night sky and seen another constellation among the ones he already knew; perhaps he did not need to look up at all since, as he learned from Paracelsus, the constellations were already within his own self. An art historian once suggested that, for all the attention Blake paid to the outer world, he 'could almost have been blind';[13] one of the great emblems of the spiritual life is of course the visionary who sees with closed eyes.

There is an engraving that Blake declared to be 'very beautiful. "Mich: Angelo co^d not have done better".'[14] It is a frontispiece to the translated works of Jacob Boehme, whom Blake called 'a divinely inspired man',[15] and shows the figures of man and woman; each figure has several flaps which can be opened up to reveal fresh images beneath, and these human forms are shown to contain heaven and hell, and all the stars, within themselves. It is a depiction of the 'One Man', 'Universal Man', or 'Cosmogonic Man' that was so influential among the mystics and philosophers of the late eighteenth century. It is always the same great theme, the *mysterium magnum*, and Boehme elaborated upon it in one of his most celebrated aphorisms: 'He to whom time is the same as eternity, and eternity the same as time, is free of all adversity.'[16] It is a motto placed in the English edition of Boehme's works, which might also have as its epigraph his contention that 'Our whole doctrine is nothing else but an instruction to show how man may create a kingdom of light within himself . . . He in whom this spring of divine power flows, carries within himself the divine image and the celestial substantiality. In him is Jesus born from the Virgin, and he will not die in eternity.'[17] Boehme's mystical system, expounded in many volumes, is one of the great triumphs of human thought. It is sometimes believed that it was too complex for Blake to master, but that is to underrate his sheer technical intelligence: he knew how to manipulate, and thus to understand, systems. Certainly he was well acquainted with Boehme, and one of his contemporaries wrote, 'I have possessed books well thumbed and dirtied by his graving hands . . . [among them] a large collection of works of the mystical writers, Jacob Behmen, Swedenborg, and others.'[18]

His was not a unique or solitary enthusiasm. The works of Boehme had been highly influential during all the religious disputations of the mid-sixteenth century, particularly within the radical sects at that time, and one educationalist wished to establish two colleges specifically to study and promulgate his doctrines; he was also generally believed to be the prime spirit behind the Quakers. In Blake's own lifetime there was a chapel of Behmenists in Bow Lane, and in the religious literature of the period we find references to the 'poor people who love Jacob Behmen'.[19] Six Methodists were actually expelled from their church for preaching his doctrines.

These are not simple, however, and they are not always easy to comprehend on first reading; but at least the spiritual context of Boehme's intensely concentrated thought can be understood without undue difficulty. He traced the presence of the divine spirit within all created things, in words that are profoundly reminiscent of Blake himself: 'If thou conceivest a small minute Circle, as small as a Grain of Mustard-seed, yet the Heart of God is wholly and perfectly therein: and if thou are born in God, then there is, in thyself, (in the Circle of thy Life), the whole Heart of God undivided . . .'[20] Boehme then established an elaborate mystical or ontological system to account for the nature of the material world and, in particular, postulated the existence of seven 'source spirits', which in a cycle or spiral of interaction perpetually create the cosmos. The details are subtle and intricate, but the essential point is that a continual cycle of striving and becoming is activated by desire or will, which is 'the fire-will' and the 'flaming world'. Its contrary or counter-force is 'Abyss', the 'dark world', and its moment of fulfilment into being is found in the 'lightning flash'; everything must emerge from that 'Abyss', which is the ground of God for 'The wrath and the anger, together with the abyss of hell, stand in the centre of the Father.'[21] God wishes to be aware of himself, and thus the cosmos is created in an act of eternally renewed will and desire. In the same way the sevenfold spiritual properties of the world are engaged in continual dialectical activity, and the striving of these various qualities enters the very nature of creation itself – 'Man must be at war with himself,' Boehme wrote, 'if he wishes to be a heavenly citizen . . . fighting must be the watchword, not with tongue and sword, but with mind and spirit, and not to give over.'[22] Thus we find in Blake:

> I will not cease from Mental Fight,
> Nor shall my Sword sleep in my hand:
> Till we have built Jerusalem,
> In Englands green & pleasant Land.[23]

So we have in Boehme a great and holy revelation of the wheel of life, the flaming wheel, or wheel of fire, which is the emblem of will creating desire and motion, the properties of matter longing to see themselves in material form and yet aspiring to be reunited as one with their spiritual essence. Everything comes into being through conflict. It is easy to see why Blake should be impressed by such a view of the world and of eternity: in his writing, too, we find the simultaneous desire to project himself and also to hide from the evidence of that projection. He might not have wanted to come too close to himself, in case he did not care for what he found there. He may have recognised that the sources of his greatness lay in sufferings long forgotten or in childhood fears long buried. That is why he felt the pressing need to express himself and yet at the same time to frame doubts about the nature of that expression by making it ambiguous, satirical or impersonal.

Certainly that is the style which he adopted in the first prophetic book he completed in Hercules Buildings. *The Marriage of Heaven and Hell* is not explicitly entitled a 'prophecy', as are the later Lambeth productions, and even within the canon of Blake's work it remains something of a puzzle. It opens and closes with poetry, but the rest of the text is composed of proverbs, short descriptive narratives, observations, arguments and parodies; it also contains some of Blake's most intensely conceived and richly coloured illustrations. It is closest in form and satirical intent to 'An Island in the Moon', but with a more didactic purpose and 'sublime' prophetic style – a form of the urban and popular literature that Blake so frequently copied. And it is significant that he did not add his name to the title page – it might have been a pamphlet, or a primer, or a catchbook, or a collection of proverbs. In fact it is all four at once and only the extraordinary intensity of its artistry might prevent it from being sold in the streets like any other political or religious broadside.

Many critics have noticed how intimately *The Marriage of Heaven and Hell* is related to Blake's movement from Swedenborg towards Boehme and Paracelsus, but it is important to note the populist (almost folk) form that he chooses to use. His background remained that of the London artisan and radical, and he understood the works of Paracelsus and Boehme in terms of that particular antinomian tradition; he adopted an attitude of mind, in other words, rather than a coherent set of principles or beliefs. He did not swallow them whole, but, as always, picked those ideas and concepts that particularly appealed to him – concepts and ideas which he lost no time in displaying with a flourish, even though there are occasions when he does not seem to have thoroughly assimilated them. He never had any faith in orthodox powers or authorities, whether in the shape of George III or John Locke, but at the same time he always considered himself to be neglected and underrated. The works of Paracelsus and of Boehme lent moral authority to this perilous position, by confirming that the outcast could also be the visionary and that there was quite another way of looking at the world. That is why *The Marriage of Heaven and Hell* contains some of his most powerful epigrams – 'The road of excess leads to the palace of wisdom', 'The cut worm forgives the plow', 'He whose face gives no light, shall never become a star', 'Eternity is in love with the productions of time', 'The tygers of wrath are wiser than the horses of instruction', 'Sooner murder an infant in its cradle than nurse unacted desires'.[24] But it is important to remember that Blake never sustained one attitude or tone for very long; in the *Marriage* he can be both strident and mocking, playful and serious, continually veering from theme to theme as if he did not want to settle upon any specific point. 'I then asked Ezekiel. why he eat dung, & lay so long on his right & left side? he answerd. the desire of raising other men into a perception of the infinite.'[25]

There is no doubt that the *Marriage* represents Blake's most serious attack upon Swedenborg and Swedenborgians, for reasons that have already been discussed, and he is happy to parody the more solemn aspects of Swedenborg's revelations. He uses the Swedish theologian's device of the 'Memorable Fancy', for example, to convey some very scandalous conversations with angels, while at the same time explaining that he treats the Bible in its 'infernal . . . sense' rather than Swedenborg's tamer 'internal sense'.[26] But there is also a larger spirit to the work, which gives it a powerfully bracing and astringent tone – it is a celebration of energy, of impulsive virtue, and of sexuality. 'Energy is Eternal Delight,' he proclaims,[27] and in the last words of the final 'Song of Liberty' he adds a grace-note to that perception, 'For every thing that lives is Holy'.[28] Samuel Palmer remembered Blake explaining to him at a later date that there were certain passages in the *Marriage* that 'would at once exclude the work from every drawing-room table in England', but that suggests only that Blake was not particularly interested in drawing-room tables.[29] It is the work of an angry, exalted young man who feels the truth of his own sexual and creative energies. It also displays his confidence and ambition, because here for the first time he establishes himself in the role of artist-prophet: 'I have also: The Bible of Hell: which the world shall have whether they will or no. One Law for the Lion & Ox is Oppression.'[30] It is of the greatest importance, too, that in this particular context he also celebrates his new methods of printing with an allegorical account of the etching and creating of copper plates; he surely believed he had invented a form that would redeem the work of the individual craftsman, in a society that was turning towards commercial mechanisation and specialisation. He was beginning to affirm his own status as the poet-prophet of the late eighteenth century.

The earliest of the nine known copies of the *Marriage* is lightly and delicately coloured in yellow, pale orange, pink and green; it conveys that mood of growth and optimism which was so much part of his work in the period. Another copy, printed two or three years later, has intense reds and browns, dark blues and blacks; it looks as if it had been created as an individual work of art, where the earlier copy seems to spring from a more open sense of an audience. There are already traces of those obscurities and difficulties that would so injure the reputation of his great prophetic works in later years, but it is clear that here he revelled in some almost playful sense of 'mystery' and 'secrecy' as part of his sublime prophetic role. He was expecting an audience, however, and would not willingly forsake one. It was part of the creative self-confidence that ensured Blake's years in Lambeth were so productive. In one copy, above the words 'a new heaven is begun', he has painted in blue letters '1790', the date of his removal to Lambeth.

There are several anecdotes of this period that throw a suggestive light upon his behaviour. Perhaps the most notorious of them was recounted by one of his closest friends and patrons: 'One story in particular he [Thomas Butts] was fond of telling . . . At the end of the little garden in Hercules Buildings there was a summer-house. Mr. Butts calling one day found Mr. and Mrs. Blake sitting in this summer-house, freed from "those troublesome disguises" which have prevailed since the Fall. "Come in!" cried Blake; "it's only Adam and Eve, you know!" Husband and wife had been reciting passages from *Paradise Lost*, in character, and the garden of Hercules Buildings had to represent the Garden of Eden; a little to the scandal of wondering neighbours, on more than one occasion.'[31] This is not simply gossip – Thomas Butts was a sober and respectable individual, a government employee who became Blake's most significant patron, and he is highly unlikely to have invented or even conceived of such a story. Most nineteenth- and twentieth-century commentators have dismissed the possibility of the Blakes parading naked in their back garden as an irrelevant fancy, but that is because they did not understand the religious radicalism with which Blake was at least marginally involved. Alexander Gilchrist, the biographer who had the benefit of questioning Blake's surviving contemporaries, recorded that he 'thought that the Gymnosophists of India, the ancient Britons, and others of whom History tells, who went naked, were, in this wise, wiser than the rest of mankind – pure and wise – and it would be as well if the world could be as they'.[32] This corresponds with Blake's known interest in primitive beliefs, but there were other influences all around him from the old sectarian faiths. The Ranters were believed 'to preach stark naked many blasphemies',[33] and the Adamites went naked in order to practise 'promiscuous sexual intercourse'.[34] The Quakers went 'naked for a sign', in accordance with the twentieth chapter of Isaiah, and antinomians in general considered nudity as a representation of primeval innocence before the Fall as well as an emblem for the 'naked truths' of the gospel. Swedenborg's own interest in sexual magic was related to his belief that 'nakedness corresponds to innocence'.[35] There was also the contemporary doctrine of Nareism, in more intellectual circles, which associated the practice of nudity with the liberation of female sexuality. There is nothing peculiar, then, in Blake's adoption of this radical belief; again we must think of him locating a doctrine here, and an image there, all the time trying to find material to bolster his unique and idiosyncratic vision.

Another Lambeth story shows him in the sympathetic and conventional role that his early biographers preferred. 'A young man passed his House daily whose avocations seemed to lead him backward & forward to some place of study, carrying a Portfolio under his Arm. He looked interesting & eager, but sickly. After some time Blake sent Mrs Blake to call the young man in; he came & he told them, that he was studying the Arts. Blake from this took a high interest in him & gave him every instruction possible.' Unfortunately the young man's 'sickly' appearance was indicative of some fatal disorder: 'his illness was long & his sufferings were great during which time Mrs Blake or Blake never omitted visiting him daily & administering medicine, money, or Wine & every other requisite until death relieved their adopted of all earthly care & pain. Every attention, every parental tenderness, was exhibited by the charitable pair.'[36] The story comes from Frederick Tatham, who knew them both, and there is no reason to question its general authenticity. There is something touching, too, about the childless couple who were ready to give such nurturing parental care to the impoverished young man.

But there was also, and always, Blake's anger at the world. 'Blake was standing at one of his Windows, which looked into Astley's premises . . . & saw a Boy hobbling along with a log to his foot such an one as is put on a Horse or Ass to prevent their straying . . . Blakes blood boiled & his indignation surpassed his forebearance, he sallied forth, & demanded in no very quiescent terms that the Boy should be loosed & that no Englishman should be subjected to those miseries, which he thought were inexcusable even towards a Slave.'[37] Astley's house was in a courtyard behind Hercules Buildings, and so the story has at least the merit of topographical accuracy. It seems that Philip Astley, on hearing of his neighbour's conduct, rushed around to Blake and demanded 'by what authority he dare come athwart his method of jurisdiction; to which Blake replied with such warmth, that blows were very nearly the consequence'.[38] In fact the argument was satisfactorily resolved, but one other anecdote emphasises the extent to which Blake identified with the victims of his period. 'Seeing once, somewhere about St Giles's, a wife knocked about by some husband or other violent person, in the open street,' Blake fell upon him 'with such counter violence of reckless and raging rebuke . . . that he recoiled and collapsed'. The offending husband or lover is supposed to have told a bystander that he thought 'the very devil himself had flown upon him in defence of the woman; such Tartarean overflow of execration and objurgation had issued from the mouth of her champion'.[39] Such public punishments and fights, as those affecting the boy in Lambeth and the woman in St Giles, were frequent in the streets of London; there are stories of foreigners cruelly bated, of animals beaten to death, of expeditious vengeance meted out to thieves or pickpockets, of public whippings by the city authorities. These events were generally encouraged by the gaping populace, and Blake's formidable distaste for them is uncharacteristic of his contemporaries. It emphasises how keenly he felt the forces of social oppression, and how swiftly he reacted against public manifestations of the violence that he sensed within himself.

Are we then to believe the story, which he may even have promulgated himself, that he played some symbolic part in the revolutionary Jacobin fervour of the early 1790s? 'Blake was himself an ardent member of the New School, a vehement republican and sympathiser with the Revolution, hater and contemner of kings and king-craft . . . he courageously donned the famous symbol of liberty and equality – the *bonnet rouge* – in open day, and philosophically walked the streets with the same on his head. He is said to have been the only one of the set who had the courage to make that public profession of faith.'[40] If by 'set' this biographer means such friends and acquaintances as Johnson or Cumberland, then he was wrong to

claim that Blake was alone in his public commitment. It was the very
spirit of their lives in this period, and, as a result, for them and
perhaps for Blake himself it became a time of frustration, disappointment and even danger. From the spring of 1788 until the spring of the
following year, 'the levelling spirit' had been abroad;[41] it was a period
when Court and Government were lampooned in the window of
every London print shop, with 'corrupt and inflammatory prints and
publications in the cheapest form'.[42] The first stirrings of the
Revolution in France were greeted with delight by that broad
spectrum of Dissenters, Foxite Whigs, radicals and artisans who saw
here the seeds of a great transformation; by the middle of July 1789,
news had been received of the Fall of the Bastille and Fox proclaimed
it as 'how much the greatest event . . . that ever happened in the
world! and how much the best!'[43] In the *Annual Register* for this year
William Godwin wrote, 'From hence we are to date a long series of
years, in which France and the whole human race are to enter into
possession of their liberties.'[44] Blake had placed 'A Song of Liberty' as
the conclusion to *The Marriage of Heaven and Hell*: 'The fire, the fire,
is falling! Look up! look up! O citizen of London. enlarge thy
countenance . . . Spurning the clouds written with curses, stamps the
stony law to dust, loosing the eternal horses from the dens of night,
crying Empire is no more! and now the lion & wolf shall cease.'[45]

So we may move on to the hot spring of 1792 – the temperature had
reached 82 degrees by the middle of March – and in that unseasonable
warmth there was a kind of fever or madness in the London air. The
radical London Corresponding Society was established and began to
work closely with the revived Society for Constitutional Information;
the Friends of the People were organised in March, in direct and
enthusiastic response to the second part of Tom Paine's *Rights of Man*,
published the month before. There were clubs and societies,
convening in taverns or arranging meetings in the squares or greens of
London. The hair of the Jacobin sympathisers was being worn short,
without powder, and their clothes had been drastically simplified to
welcome the new age. The turbulence in France had now reached a
point where the mobs invaded the Tuileries and the power of the
monarch was suspended; in his notebook Blake began a poem
commemorating the stages in Louis XVI's inevitable decline. But he
made no effort to publish it. In May 1792 a Royal Proclamation was
issued against 'divers wicked and seditious writings', and throughout
the spring and summer English and Prussian troops were barracked

around London.[46] This served to exacerbate radical feeling, and in October a contemporary observer reported, 'Nothing . . . can be more evident than the growth of popular feeling in favour of the Revolution, and democratic clubs and societies are starting upon all sides.'[47] At a dinner of the Revolution Society in November the 'Marseillaise' was sung, and on the walls of markets could be seen the chalked signs of 'Liberty and Equality!' But then, in the depths of winter, the urban fever began to abate. The arrest of the French monarch and the first Jacobin terrors of September had begun to alarm the more conservative or nationalistic elements among the Dissenters and radicals; the government also found that it could use the growing horrors of the Revolution as a way of inflaming the Francophobia of the London populace. There were voices prophesying war and invasion, and by the end of the year the general sentiment of the country had moved towards Pitt's decision to confront the new French government.

Blake is to be imagined, then, wandering through the streets in his *bonnet rouge* during those hot spring days, only to remove it (so his biographer says) when he first heard news of the Jacobin massacres of the autumn. Yet by that time he had written a poem set along those same streets when, at the height of revolutionary enthusiasm, he had clearly expressed his own convictions.

> I wander thro each dirty street
> Near where the dirty Thames does flow
> And see in every face I meet
> Marks of weakness marks of woe
>
> In every cry of every man
> In every voice of every child
> In every voice in every ban
> The german forged links I hear
>
> But most the chimney sweepers cry
> Blackens oer the churches walls
> And the hapless soldiers sigh
> Runs in blood down palace walls[48]

Here we come close to the heart of that anxious and turbulent year; in this first draft of 'London' he had written 'german forged links' because he could see around him the Hessian and Hanoverian mercenaries imported by the King to withstand a French invasion or (more likely) to maintain public order in the event of mob rule like that of the Wilkeite or Gordon Rioters a few years before. Then Blake changed it to 'mind-forg'd manacles' because 'manacles', like 'chartered', was one of the radical code words of the period that was directed at the oppression of the authorities. That is why 'each dirty street' was changed to 'each charter'd street', and behind the word one can hear the echoes of Tom Paine's *Rights of Man*, when he insisted that 'Every chartered town is an aristocratical monopoly in itself.'[49] Some pages later, Paine adds a remark about the English government that might also have found a place in Blake's 'London': 'It is a market where every man has his price, and where corruption is common traffic.'[50] The 'youthful Harlots curse', added in a later version of the poem, is an echo of that corruption, at a time when the city had fifty thousand prostitutes. And where in Paine's own text will be found the explanation for 'the hapless soldiers sigh'? 'All the monarchical governments are military. War is their trade, plunder and revenue their objects.'[51] During the summer of 1792 young English soldiers were sent out on manoeuvres, which prompted a report in *The Times* of 2 August that 'We never beheld troops suffer more'.[52] On the palace walls were written the slogans of the revolutionary sympathisers: 'No coach tax. Damn Pitt! Damn the Duke of Richmond! *No King!*'[53]

Where is Blake among these slogans? There is no doubt that his closest associations were with people who held advanced republican views. Many of his fellow engravers, such as William Sharp, were of that type. Perhaps engravers were radicals precisely because of their profession; they knew that the reality of symbols and images was made, not given. Blake's work for Joseph Johnson, in particular, meant that he was acquainted with a group who actively campaigned for what was known as 'innovation' in all areas of English life. Johnson had commissioned him, for example, to engrave illustrations for some rather feeble children's stories by Mary Wollstonecraft; they are interesting only because they represent one of the few occasions when he actually designed his own commercial work, and there is visible in them the strong vertical line that was so crucial to his art. So the chances are that he would have known her and would have read her *Vindication of the Rights of Woman*, which was published a year later. But the extent of Johnson's radical friendship was very large. In particular, he published, and admired, Joseph Priestley, whose republican enthusiasms were loudly and publicly expressed – Priestley's house in Birmingham was ransacked by a 'patriot' mob in 1791. In fact it has been calculated that Johnson published some thirteen books in defence of the French Revolution between 1789 and 1791, and his *Analytical Review* continually pressed the case for republican reform.[54] In 1792 he issued Joel Barlow's *Advice to the Privileged Orders*, which was an attack upon monarchy and a defence of revolutionary principles in the face of Edmund Burke's critique. He also published an abridged version of Tom Paine's *Rights of Man* and, for most of 1791 and 1792, he was an essential part of the radical group that was attached to Paine's English campaign. Blake's friend and associate Fuseli was also part of the same group. Fuseli repeated an anecdote to his own biographer that emphasises the close association in this period between artists, engravers and political reformers: 'Paine was an excellent mechanic,' he said; 'when Sharp was about to engrave my picture of "The Contest of Satan, Sin and Death" he employed a carpenter to construct a roller to raise or fall it at pleasure; in this, after several ineffectual attempts, he did not succeed to the expectations of Sharp, who mentioned the circumstance in the hearing of Paine; he instantly offered his services, and soon accomplished all, and indeed more than the engraver had anticipated.'[55] There is an added significance to be found in this collaboration between Paine, Sharp and Fuseli since the painting in question was designed to be part of the 'Milton Gallery', fostered by Johnson as an implicitly social and political project under the aegis of the great blind republican himself.

So we have a small group well known to each other and bound by both artistic and political ties – Henry Fuseli, Mary Wollstonecraft, Tom Paine, Joel Barlow, Joseph Priestley, to be joined by others such as Horne Tooke and William Godwin, all of them eventually excoriated as atheists and traitors by such periodicals as the *Anti-Jacobin*. It would be tempting, then, to place Blake firmly in their midst – even to consider them as in some way his natural audience. But this may not be altogether appropriate, since in many respects he was utterly unlike them. If points of religion had been brought up, for example, there would have been manifest differences: 'Himself [Blake] a heretic among the orthodox, here among the infidels he was a saint and staunchly defended Christianity – the spirit of it – against these strangely assorted disputants.'[56] His friend in later life, Tatham, adds substance to the suggestion: 'In one of their conversations, Paine said that religion was a law & a tye to all able minds. Blake on the other hand said what he was always asserting, that the religion of Jesus, was a perfect law of Liberty.'[57] Paine also dismissed Isaiah, as 'one continual incoherent rant', and, since Blake had celebrated the glory of that prophet in *The Marriage of Heaven and Hell*, it is unlikely that they would have agreed on the subject of the Old Testament.[58] Paine was also a political philosopher who denied the efficacy or significance of historical tradition in a way that Blake, the child of antiquity and Westminster Abbey, would have found deeply offensive. In the same way he could hardly have been an enthusiast for the works of Joseph Priestley, whose materialism and pre-destinarianism were utterly opposed to everything Blake considered holy. Nor can he have been very impressed by Mary Wollstonecraft's belief in 'the law of reason' and 'Rational religion'.[59] In many important respects, therefore, he fundamentally differed from their principles and their beliefs, and it would be wrong to see him as in any sense part of this little group of radicals who met above Johnson's shop in St Paul's Churchyard; his encounters with them were probably brief and sporadic and, for their part, they would have seen only a journeyman engraver of eccentric views.

There is another aspect of his isolation, however. The evidence of his work suggests he already had an overwhelming sense of his unique prophetic mission, even if it was one that no one else seemed to notice or understand. That is why, when considering the general question of his political beliefs, one should not be surprised to encounter contradiction or inconsistency. He was opinionated and contrary, ready to form judgments under the momentary spur of irritation and express forcible sentiments from the desire to be vexatious or playful. That is how he managed to retain his belief in his own uniqueness, while at the same time exercising his sense of humour, which ought to be considered more often and more carefully by his occasionally solemn commentators:

> A ha To Doctor Johnson
> Said Scipio Africanus
> Lift up my Roman Petticoatt
> And kiss my Roman Anus[60]

So he had paraded his red bonnet, and then snatched it off his head. But on later occasions, according to Samuel Palmer, he 'repeatedly expressed his belief that there was more civil liberty under the Papal government than any other sovereignty';[61] others have considered him variously a Shakespearian populist, a Platonist, an anarchist, a Christian reactionary, or a quietist. We can be certain only that he never bothered to vote, and that his most elaborate statement about organised or doctrinal politics took the form of wholesale rejection: 'I am really sorry to see my Countrymen trouble themselves about Politics. If Men were Wise the Most arbitrary Princes could not hurt them If they are not Wise the Freest Government is compelld to be a Tyrrany   Princes appear to me to be Fools Houses of Commons & Houses of Lords appear to me to be fools they seem to me to be something Else besides Human Life.'[62] This entry, scribbled in the margins of his notebook, proclaims what one would expect from an artist and inventive craftsman; he believed only in the efficacy of individual virtue or enlightenment, and he displays not the slightest interest in any particular political or social philosophy. He could never have accepted the uniformity of *bien pensant* opinion demonstrated by Priestley or Wollstonecraft any more than he could have joined, with fellow engravers and artists, the radical Society for Constitutional Information.

But his comparative isolation made him more vulnerable, and he described in a letter to Flaxman how the calamitous events of the period provoked in him 'Nervous Fear'.[63] 'No King!' had been the slogan daubed upon the wall of the Privy Garden – and soon there was to be no king, at least in France. In the first month of 1793 Louis was executed, and a few weeks later there started a war between England and France that was to endure for the next twenty years. It was Blake's fate to produce his most extraordinary and elaborate works in a period when 'War and politics absorb every faculty',[64] and when, as he explained in the same letter to Flaxman, the shadow of great events continually disturbed him:

> . . . terrors appear'd in the Heaven above
> And in Hell beneath, & a mighty & awful change threatened the Earth.
> The American War began. All its dark horrors passed before my face
> Across the Atlantic to France. Then the French Revolution commenc'd in thick clouds,
> And My Angels have told me that seeing such visions I could not subsist on the Earth . . .[65]

His first reaction to these dark visions appears in sixteen pages of typeset verse that were never published. Grandly entitled 'THE FRENCH REVOLUTION. A POEM, IN SEVEN BOOKS', it is priced at one shilling, gives Joseph Johnson as the publisher, and goes on to state that 'The remaining Books of this Poem are finished, and will be published in their Order.'[66] That these other books have not survived, and were possibly never written, does not detract from the scale of Blake's ambition. He planned to write an epic poem, almost of Miltonic breadth, on a public and contemporary theme; it is clear that at this stage, despite his enthusiasm for his new medium and new engraving techniques, he had not abandoned his more conventional literary aspirations. Relief etching was just one of his marketable skills, albeit the most significant. He still wanted, or expected, to be an established poet. No doubt Johnson was happy to encourage him, especially since he was intent upon a theme of such topical interest. Long poems about current events were not unusual – there had already been several devoted to the American Revolution – and a reasonable sale might be expected.

The surviving first book indicates that Blake was prepared to write a considerably heightened version of contemporary political epic. The narrative is largely concerned with the debate between king and nobles in the early stages of the Revolution, and he has deliberately modelled it upon the assembly of Satan and his legions in the second book of *Paradise Lost*. Thus he is able to give epic cadence and dignity to current events:

> At length, trembling, the vision sighing, in a low voice, like the voice
>   of the grasshopper whisper'd:
> My groaning is heard in the abbeys, and God, so long worshipp'd,
>   departs as a lamp
> Without oil.[67]

The story itself compresses the events of weeks into days, changes the scene from Versailles to Paris, invents new characters and confuses old ones, and as a result it is a genuinely original achievement. Where most political poems aped the diction of Dryden or Thomson, Blake has tapped into a strange mixture of Miltonic cadence and Gothic fantasy; he employs imagery culled from contemporary political pamphlets and from Shakespearian drama, from Ossian as well as the Old Testament. In the great history paintings of the period there was an attempt to place contemporary events within the context of heroic myth – Benjamin West's 'The Death of Wolfe' is probably the most famous example – and in his own way Blake was trying to create a new epic style out of the resources of the English literary tradition. In the process there emerges the authentic Blakean note, as the events of the world become material for a visionary history and giant forms inhabit a desolate landscape: 'The enormous dead, lift up their pale fires . . .'[68]

But it was never published, and remained only as a set of uncorrected page proofs that he stored away. It was a fascinating exercise, yet in its incomplete state it remains only an exercise. Several explanations have been advanced to account for its failure to appear in volume form. It has been suggested that Joseph Johnson took fright, for example, and refused to publish anything of an even remotely seditious nature; this is implausible, since he continued to publish and advertise tracts of a far more radical and polemical kind. It is more likely that, along with everybody else, he failed to appreciate Blake's poetry; he looked it over, once it had been set, and decided that it would not do. There is of course also the possibility that Blake himself was unhappy with what he had written and, after consultations with Johnson, decided to withdraw it. Perhaps he realised that he could not continue with such an elevated style for another six books, or perhaps he just lost interest in the project at this stage. There is, however, one other, more complex and intriguing, explanation – that Blake, cursed by his 'Nervous Fear', decided himself to withdraw it in the neurotic suspicion that he might be prosecuted, or persecuted, by the state authorities. The chances of any such action were remote, especially since the poem has not the slightest element of conventional sedition, but the possibility that Blake withdrew his own poem in nervous panic is strengthened by his anxiety over the next work he completed. He engraved a poem entitled *America* and then, at a late stage, removed all references to George III or to government ministers. The vulnerable side of his single-minded independence is to be found in his fear of being threatened or attacked.

The failure to publish *The French Revolution* had permanent results of a kind that Blake could not have anticipated. It marked the last opportunity he ever received of publishing his work in conventional form, and therefore the last occasion when he might have acquired a substantial audience. He liberated himself from commercial considerations, by printing and promoting all of his own subsequent work, but at the cost of forfeiting a public. His independence meant that he could preserve his vision beyond all taint – and that integrity is an essential aspect of his genius – but it also encouraged him to withdraw from the world of common discourse. Although these consequences were not immediately apparent, over the years his range of reference and allusion became more private and more confined. Out of his isolation he created a great myth, but it was one that was never vouchsafed to his contemporaries and one that, even now, is generally neglected or misunderstood. Blake's life is in that sense a parable of the artist who avoids the market place, where all others come to buy and sell; he preserved himself inviolate, but his freedom became a form of solitude. He worked for himself, and he listened only to himself; in the process he lost any ability to judge his own work. He had the capacity to become a great public and religious poet but, instead, he turned in upon himself and gained neither influence nor reputation. His great predecessor Milton had declared, 'I cannot praise a fugitive and cloister'd vertue, unexercis'd & unbreath'd, that never sallies out and sees her adversary, but slinks out of the race, where that immortall garland is to be run for, not without dust and heat.'[69] Blake eventually eschewed the 'heat' of any public voice or role; but, as a result, it is as if he were another Milton raging in a darkened room.

The true nature of his artistic career did not become clear until many years later, however, and at this stage he continued to think of himself as a poet and artist with a public prophetic mission. After the withdrawal of *The French Revolution* he simply went on with a renewed determination to be heard; but now he decided to do so in his own way, beyond the jurisdiction of even the most sympathetic publisher. He once again went back to the relief techniques he had employed for *The Marriage of Heaven and Hell* and *Songs of Innocence*, since he seems to have believed that his new medium was destined to cater to a popular market. The *Marriage* had been in the style of the chapbook or primer and *Songs* in the style of the children's book; now, in his next work, he followed the contemporary vogue for pamphlets invoking political and spiritual apocalypse. He inscribed 'Prophecy' twice, on the title page and on the frontispiece, with the second example embellished with a soaring figure, birds ascending, budding wheat and flourishing lilies. The book is called *America* and Blake's confident declaration of a prophetic role is matched by his decision to make it twice as large as any of its predecessors – its eighteen pages measure nine inches by six and a half.

The story of *America* is simple enough, since it concerns the rebellion of the thirteen American colonies and the inexpert British response; George Washington and 'The Guardian Prince of Albion' are engaged in a cosmic conflict extending over plains of despair and the lost regions of Atlantis, deserts of stone and forests of affliction. It is a mighty cataclysm in which we can hear the voice of 'Bostons Angel' crying aloud in the night:

> What God is he, writes laws of peace, & clothes himself in a tempest
> What pitying Angel lusts for tears, and fans himself with sighs
> What crawling villain preaches abstinence & wraps himself
> In fat of lambs? no more I follow, no more obedience pay.[70]

For Blake the entire conflict becomes part of a larger impulse towards spiritual rebirth and revelation; so at this point he is trying to create a popular prophecy with his own set of mythic characters. Here for the first time appears Orc, who together with Urthona and Urizen will soon comprise the complex system of action and impulse that makes up Blake's mature vision. For the moment, however, their roles remain simple – Orc, the principle of energy and rebellion, stands against Urizen, who is tyrant, priest and lawgiver. The nature of Blake's myth will be explored later, when it comes close to its full development, but in this early period he was simply trying to write a popular narrative of an Ossianic and heroic kind. The names are strangely resonant – Enitharmon, Urthona, Vala – because they fulfilled his preoccupation with ancient learning and the truths of older faiths. But he takes an almost boyish delight in the invention of this strange world, through which he can oppose all the rational orthodoxies of the day while emphasising the uniqueness of his relief engravings. It could be said that, in one sense, the medium created the myth. Or that, rather, they are both aspects of Blake's singular vision.

There are some early drawings in his notebook that became part of the completed work; as so often with Blake, he sketched figures and only afterwards devised a verbal meaning for them. There are also extant proof sheets of *America* that show Blake revising his verse after engraving it; 'flames' has been changed, in pencil, to 'damp mists', and 'Around St James glow the fires' becomes 'Around St James chill and heavy'. Then at a later date he cancelled the entire plate simply because it makes a reference to 'the King'. But it is in *America* that, for the first time, his images acquire their central importance. They take up entire pages of the book, and hardly illustrate the text at all; they form a separate sequence and might have been a portfolio of late eighteenth-century cartoons to be sold at a print shop in the Strand.

Certainly they belong in the same world as Gillray, with the words floating in the middle of the page beside distorted human figures. On one proof sheet he has written a note to himself, 'Angels to be very small as small as the letters that they may not interfere with the subject at bottom which is to be a stormy sky & rain separated from the angels by Clouds'. Yet his images are immeasurably more radiant and spectacular than any other artist of his period – a huge winged figure bowed in despair upon a broken wall; an old man hastening into the darkness through a stone portal; a nude youth sitting beside a skull and looking expectantly towards the sky; a bearded patriarch extending his arms before some clouds. All these can be seen already as characteristically Blakean: the heroic or terrible figures of Michelangelo have fallen into an abyss. Their gestures also owe something to Gothic drama, and to pantomime, as if Blake had seen the performances of the young Grimaldi. But the steady concentration and intensity with which they are conceived make them authentic inhabitants of that visionary myth that he was even now constructing. Though he has imparted to them the solemn air of ancient imagery, he has somehow also been able to place these exalted figures within the context of the political print and the topical spiritual pamphlet; once again the force of his genius broke through contemporary forms of expression to create something much more rare and strange.

But this was not achieved without difficulty and even despair. In the first copy of *America* he erased four lines so they would not be printed:

> The stern Bard ceas'd, asham'd of his own song; enrag'd he swung
> His harp aloft sounding, then dash'd its shining frame against
> A ruin'd pillar in glittring fragments; silent he turn'd away,
> And wander'd down among the vales of Kent in sick & drear
> lamentings.[71]

Are we to see him wandering disconsolate along Lambeth Road and the New Road (now the New Kent Road) by the tenter-grounds? It is not an unlikely image. In a relief etching, dated 5 June 1793, he depicts a hysterical king between two warriors with the title 'Our End is come'; but that title seems to have more than a political significance for, in the previous month, he had written in large pencilled letters in his notebook, 'I say I shant live five years And if I live one it will be a Wonder'.[72] The atmosphere of war and general political repression, even then gathering momentum, seems severely to have affected his sense of personal safety. There were also consequences for his own understanding of his art. He may have read that passage in Mary Wollstonecraft's *Vindication* in which she notes, 'Dr Priestley has remarked, in the preface to his biographical chart, that the majority of great men have lived beyond forty-five.'[73] In this year, 1793, Blake was thirty-six years old. Did he already see the prospects for greatness slipping away?

SIXTEEN

The Bible of Hell

Blake was wrong in his prediction; he lived far beyond the five years he had decreed for himself, and only four months after he had written that solemn note he issued a more public document. It was essentially a bookseller's catalogue, in which he listed a variety of recent works. No doubt he had spare stock on his hands that he wished to sell, but in his prospectus for it he also made the kind of extravagant claims that amused or annoyed the contemporaries who chanced upon them: 'Mr. Blake's powers of invention very early engaged the attention of many persons of eminence and fortune; by whose means he has been regularly enabled to bring before the Public works (he is not afraid to say) of equal magnitude and consequence with the productions of any age or country.'[1] He also extolls his new technique of relief etching, 'which combines the Painter and the Poet . . . [and] exceeds in elegance all former methods' and will now allow 'the Man of Genius' to publish his own works.[2] It was not the last time he would make such assertions and throughout his life, in the face of disinterest and neglect, he would compare himself with Michelangelo and with Raphael; obviously there is an element of wilfulness and self-assertiveness here, which would become all the more pronounced as he grew more isolated, but at this stage in his career there is no reason to doubt his ambition or his belief in his own powers of capturing 'public attention'.[3] Certainly he was astute enough not to alienate it altogether and, in the list of works for sale, he included two large engravings 'highly finished' in the orthodox and fashionable manner.[4] One of these was 'Edward and Elinor'; it is over twice the price of Songs of Innocence at 10s 6d, but, more importantly, it seems to be a version of an untraced watercolour completed fourteen years before. The second of the 'historical engravings', 'Job', remains a constant image throughout Blake's work, and one of the salient aspects of his artistic life is the extent to which he returned to the same themes and figures. This may also have been an aspect of his ordinary behaviour in the world, and one contemporary noted that in conversation he tended to repeat himself, 'which must in time become tiresome'.[5] There was another subject listed in his catalogue that also advances some of his earliest preoccupations; he entitled it 'The History of England', a small book of engravings that acted as a complement to 'The Gates of Paradise' and that provided a series of historical scenes for children. No copies of this work have survived, but there is a handwritten list of subjects at the back of Blake's notebook that suggests his range of reference; he begins with 'Giants ancient inhabitants of England' and ends with three that suggest the radical tone of his prospectus, 'The Cruelties used by Kings & Priests . . . A prospect of Liberty . . . A Cloud'.[6] It is unlikely that any reference to 'Kings' or 'Liberty' appeared in published form, and Blake no doubt contented himself with such allegorical subjects as 'Edwin & Morcar stirring up the Londoners to resist W the Conqr' or 'The Penance of Jane Shore'.[7] He employed themes dating from his earliest watercolours, which he had decided to rework for this historical series, and once again he can be seen making a deliberate decision to systematise and to order his previously scattered conceptions. It is the instinct of the fabulist or mythologist who wishes to create a comprehensive pattern or narrative out of apparently unconnected materials.

But it is also likely that in the spring of this year he had seen the first exhibition of Old Masters ever held in London – the paintings, mainly Dutch and Flemish, came from the collection of the Duc d'Orléans and were being shown at the Royal Academy's old rooms in Pall Mall. Perhaps Blake's first sight of certain great masters rekindled his old ambition to be a historical painter on the grand scale and, although he would not exhibit at the Royal Academy for another six years, the comprehensive list of works for sale in his catalogue suggests that he was eager for public approbation. The 'Illuminated Books' were designed to provide that, from *The Book of Thel* priced at 3s to *America* priced at 10s 6d. He had also completed some more conventional intaglio etchings, with the lines cut into the copper in the orthodox manner, but these were not included in the catalogue because of their implicit political references. 'Albion Rose', 'Our End is Come' and 'Lucifer and the Pope in Hell' are clearly designed to attack the authoritarianism of state and religious power, while 'Albion' himself rises from the nets of traditional perception as if he were indeed some free spirit of energy and revolt. These three works could even be seen as political cartoons of a familiar late eighteenth-century kind, wrought to a pitch of intensity beyond the reach of anyone but Gillray, and it is likely that they were originally meant to be included in such 'Prophecies' as *Europe* or *America* before Blake's 'Nervous Fear' dictated otherwise. In any event they remained unpublished for the moment, and over the next few years he would experiment with them as a way of refining his own craft.

There is one other work listed in Blake's catalogue which, at 7s 6d, was the same price as *The Marriage of Heaven and Hell* and was in certain respects related to it – 'Visions of the Daughters of Albion, in Illuminated Printing. Folio, with 8 designs'.[8] The title itself suggests the presence of Blake's continually forming myth – here, for the first time, he alludes to those 'Visions' with which he had been acquainted for so long – but, as always, the defining context for this latest work comes from the world in which he lived and acted. He had, for example, been working for some time, in a somewhat desultory fashion, on the engravings for John Gabriel Stedman's *Narrative of Surinam*, from which an element of Blake's tiger might have emerged. He despatched the first batch of illustrations for this book in December 1792 and a second batch a year later, precisely the period in which *Visions of the Daughters of Albion* was composed. One of the lines in that poem, devoted to the liberty of love, is delivered by a monstrous figure of authority – 'Stampt with my signet are the swarthy children of the sun'[9] – and in one of Blake's engravings for Stedman's account a slave is shown with the initials 'J G S' stamped upon his right breast. In fact Blake executed some of the more gruesome of the book's illustrations, including the 'Flagellation of a Female Samboe Slave', 'The Execution of Breaking on the Rack' and 'A Negro hung alive by the Ribs to a Gallows'. They are powerful images indeed, with the dense cross-hatching on the bodies of the slaves intensifying the effect of their tortured figures against an unengraved background. But Stedman's narrative was more than a compilation of horrors, and in particular he described his relationship with a fifteen-year-old mulatto slave named Joanna. Her mother sold her to him (although this is not mentioned in the published narrative), they went through a form of marriage and, although Joanna remained a slave, they managed to maintain what seems to have been a loving relationship. A child was born but Stedman left the island four years later; so mother and son were left behind on what was an increasingly barbarous and violent island. She died six years later, by which time Stedman had remarried and retired to Devon.

It was here that he wrote his memoirs and began to form an acquaintance with his engraver in Lambeth. His friendship with Blake flourished, even as it soured with his publisher; Stedman called Johnson a 'Jacobin scoundrel' and one 'who I would now not Save from the gallows',[10] and the fact that Blake maintained his friendship with him suggests difficulties in his own relationship with Johnson. It will later become clear that he was not altogether impressed by him. But there were also aspects of Stedman's life that must have awakened some sympathy in Blake – Stedman had wanted to be a painter, but his apparently violent and impetuous temperament did not make him a suitable subject for tuition. His desire for artistic excellence was in any case thwarted by his need to earn a living, and he had become a soldier. He also seems to have had the faculty of second sight, at least according to Fuseli, who reported that Stedman had once seen a fairy on his way to dinner with Johnson in St Paul's Churchyard. In one of his diary entries, Stedman recorded, 'Saw a Mermaid'[11] – although this is less likely to be the fabulous creature herself than a curiosity exhibited at one of the fairs or taverns, like the stuffed mermaid displayed at the Turk's Coffee House in St James's Street some years later. But the resemblance to Blake might be thought to end there: Stedman was also a staunch monarchist, an anti-Jacobin and, despite his own experiences in Surinam, a supporter of slavery if not necessarily the British slave trade itself. He was also a man whose views were loudly expressed, and it is peculiar that a man who could damn Joseph Johnson as a 'Jacobin' found himself so at ease in Blake's company that on two occasions he stayed with the Blakes in Hercules Buildings. This suggests that Blake kept his own counsel, or perhaps even agreed with some of Stedman's opinions: it has already become clear that he had no real sympathy with the deistical and materialist beliefs of Tom Paine's 'set'. Stedman also seems to have considered Blake a sober man of affairs, since he entrusted him with his business dealings on his return to Devon. As some kind of recompense he presented Mrs Blake with a blue sugar cup, and sent them a Tiverton goose at Christmas.

This friendship throws an interesting light upon Blake. Stedman's letters and diaries demonstrate that he himself could be very belligerent (he might also be called a 'character' or an 'eccentric' but in this period, as foreign observers testify, half the population of England could be similarly described), but in his combination of thwarted artistic ambition and nervous awkwardness may lie the seeds of Blake's sympathy for him. Here was a man who railed against publishers and booksellers and seems, from his own account, to have been quite alienated from the conventions of the late eighteenth-century world. So they dined together, and Stedman was given a bed when he needed to stay in London. We also learn from Stedman's diary that at some point 'Blake was mob'd and robbd' – by which he meant that Blake was set upon by a group of 'Ruffians', perhaps in the increasingly dangerous lanes around Lambeth Marsh.[12] 'I'll have this!' was often their facetious cry.

So Blake worked on the engravings for Stedman's book intermittently over a period of years. There was much to interest Blake in that narrative, particularly because in the sad fate of Joanna there could be found two of the most pressing issues of 'liberty' or 'innovation' that animated the social debates of the late eighteenth century. Mary Wollstonecraft's A Vindication of the Rights of Woman had already provoked wide controversy (including a sarcastic reply by Blake's old mathematics teacher, Thomas Taylor, entitled A Vindication of the Rights of Brutes), while the public argument over Britain's continuing involvement in the slave trade was loud and prolonged. But for Blake the inferior position of women, and the servitude of the Africans, were part of a much wider perception of enslavement – in his newly published and advertised Visions of the Daughters of Albion he repeats a phrase that he had used before, 'for every thing that lives is holy!'[13]

This poem, touched by images from Stedman and Wollstonecraft, is concerned with the expression of energy and sexual liberty; it has no parallel in the poetry of the eighteenth century:

The moment of desire! the moment of desire! The virgin
That pines for man; shall awaken her womb to enormous joys
In the secret shadows of her chamber; the youth shut up from
The lustful joy. shall forget to generate. & create an amorous image
In the shadows of his curtains and in the folds of his silent pillow.[14]

The narrative is simple enough: Oothoon is raped by Bromion, and in her violated state is rejected by her betrothed, Theotormon; the story is highly reminiscent of Ossian's more purple passages and in fact Blake seems to have taken his names from Oithona, Tonthormod and Brumo, whom Ossian had already created in a fable of thwarted love not unlike *Visions*. But the story here is important only as the context for Blake's extraordinary invocation of energy and desire as comprising the soul of the world; he inscribed a motto on the title page, 'The Eye sees more than the Heart knows', and in the context of an argument about the nature of human perception he continues the exploration of sexual freedom that he had begun as early as his *Poetical Sketches*. Now he has acquired the pure bardic voice, however, and from his memories of Milton, Shakespeare, the Bible and all the eighteenth-century imitations of epic he creates an extraordinary poetry:

> I cry arise O Theotormon for the village dog
> Barks at the breaking day. the nightingale has done lamenting.
> The lark does rustle in the ripe corn, and the Eagle returns
> From nightly prey, and lifts his golden beak to the pure east;
> Shaking the dust from his immortal pinions to awake
> The sun that sleeps too long.[15]

That is why the poem can become a powerful and perceptive assault upon sexual repression as one element of the general restriction of human consciousness. Blake sees the connection between the slaves of Surinam and the women of England, between commerce and sexual brutality, between Lockean theories of sensation and religious orthodoxy, all filaments in the web of the materialist mercantile world:

> They told me that the night & day were all that I could see;
> They told me that I had five senses to inclose me up.
> And they inclos'd my infinite brain into a narrow circle.
> And sunk my heart into the Abyss, a red round globe hot burning . . .[16]

The frontispiece shows Bromion and Oothoon bound back to back in the mouth of a cavern while Theotormon is crouched behind them with his head bowed; the sun glows above them like the great eye of the heavens. In other 'illuminations', the daughters of Albion sit huddled in despair. A naked man whips himself with thongs while a woman looks away. A manacled girl hovers over a male figure crouched in despair. Once again, both in text and design, Blake has taken the heroic or classical figures so familiar to an eighteenth-century audience and set them down in his own spiritual (sometimes theatrical) space. His is an astonishingly comprehensive vision, in which the deep wells of the English antinomian tradition are seen to contain the purity of ancient truth, but it is perhaps not surprising that his contemporaries quite failed to understand it. Blake coloured his earliest copies of the poem in characteristic Georgian pastels – pale blues, violets and mauves – but even this homage to pictorial conventions cannot disguise the true originality of *Visions of the Daughters of Albion*. It seems to assault the senses, while at the same time revising all orthodox assumptions about perception itself. So it was dismissed, or taken up by a few collectors for its 'Gothic' charm.

If at this stage Blake suffered from any sense of neglect or disparagement by his contemporaries, however, it served only to spur him forward. That is why he had issued his own catalogue, in the hope of extensive sales (which did not occur), and why he now made a conscious attempt to organise and systematise his own mythic world. It had begun in an instinctive way, with his almost boyish enthusiasm for creating an alternative imaginary reality – he once said of a young child's efforts to invent a magic region that he had 'that greatest of all blessings, a strong imagination, a clear idea, and a determinate vision of things in his own mind'.[17] In fact the six-year-old boy had made up his own country called 'Allestone', and it seems clear that Blake was motivated by a similar impulse when he first created Los, Orc and Urizen. But his myth took hold of him and, with that combination of stubbornness and obsessiveness that was so much a mark of his character, he began to deepen and elaborate it until it became an enormously complicated, and in certain respects incomprehensible, *summa theologica*. He had said in *The Marriage of Heaven and Hell*, 'I have also: The Bible of Hell: which the world shall have whether they will or no',[18] which is uncompromising enough in the face of public apathy, and Dante Gabriel Rossetti was the first to find among Blake's extant papers a sheet that had a drawing on one side and on the other a projected title: 'The Bible of Hell, in Nocturnal Visions collected. Vol 1 Lambeth'. Here lies the origin of what may be called the Lambeth prophecies, in which Blake deliberately copied the numbered chapters and verses of the Bible to create an alternative testament. In three separate works, *The Book of Urizen, The Book of Ahania* and *The Book of Los*, he wrote his own Genesis and Exodus.

It was a bold undertaking but not, in the climate of the time, an inexplicable one. Indeed his ambitious attempt to rewrite the

Scriptures was materially assisted by the fact that, in this period, the Bible was itself being studied as a form of literature. It could even be said that the actual model of Blake's creative processes, in which one layer of his myth is overlaid upon another and in which the same events or themes are continually described from slightly different perspectives, springs from his recognition that the Bible had been formed in precisely the same way: all the biblical research of the period, much of it discussed in Johnson's *Analytical Review*, was concerned with understanding the various layers and stages of composition. When Blake came to fashion his own myth of origins in *The Book of Urizen*, he already knew that Genesis was considered to be the work of several hands and the collation of several myths. But there was a more compelling reason for the Bible to be considered a literary, as well as a sacred, object – in a series of important lectures in the mid-century, and in subsequent published volumes, Bishop Robert Lowth first explained the particular and peculiar nature of Hebrew poetry. He introduced the term 'parallelism' to explain in part the rhythmic structure and distinctive cadence of the biblical narrative, and at the same time managed to confirm the idea of a primitive and fervent bardic force behind the sublime utterances of the prophets; Lowth himself translated Isaiah as a prose poem, which bears striking similarities to the work of Ossian and, indeed, to that of Blake's own prophetic books. One theologian of the period declared that God 'taught poetry first to the Hebrews, and the Hebrews to mankind in general',[19] and Bishop Percy published his own version of the 'Song of Solomon' a year before he issued *Reliques of Ancient English Poetry*. Here then is the context for the passionate hymns of the Wesleys, for the spiritual odes and ballads designed for children, for Burke's *A Philosophical Enquiry into the Sublime and Beautiful* as well as its eighteenth-century counterparts, for the biblical oratorios by Handel and by Arne, for Cowper's *Olney Hymns* and Smart's *Jubilate Agno*. And here, also, is the setting for Blake's own achievement. It would be too facile to say that he composed the *Songs of Innocence* under the direct influence of the Wesleyan hymns, or that he fashioned the poetry of the prophetic books after a reading of Lowth's *Isaiah*; but the rediscovery and reinterpretation of the Bible in his period does at least set the context for his own understanding both of his poetic inspiration and of his prophetic mission. Why, then, should he not issue his own 'Bible of Hell'?

He was, however, in competition with other prophets in this era of war and revolution; as one contemporary put it, 'times of calamity are peculiarly fertile in visions and prognostications, predictions and prophecies'.[20] One of the most vociferous exponents of such matters was Richard Brothers, who, in the year that Blake composed *The Book of Urizen*, published his own biblical redaction, *A Revealed Knowledge of the Prophecies and Times*, in which he attacked king and empire, while prophesying that British designs against the French would fail. He was the same age as Blake and, believing himself to be the Slain Lamb of Revelation, attracted rather more disciples. He was in fact the first 'British Israelite', who proclaimed that a large proportion of the English race were descended from the Jews and decided that he would be the one to lead them back to the Holy Land for the coming apocalypse. It is easy now to dismiss such popular prophets but it ought to be remembered that, in tone and attitude, Blake was closer to Richard Brothers than he was to Tom Paine or Mary Wollstonecraft. He would have been particularly interested in Brothers' fate, therefore. Arrested after the publication of his 'Prophecy' and tried for treason, Brothers was consigned to a madhouse in the spring of 1795. Eventually he was released and wrote *A Description of Jerusalem*, at the same time that Blake was composing his own *Jerusalem*.

Of course it would be foolish to make any direct comparisons between these two London visionaries, the most striking disparity being that Blake was a writer and artist of genius. He also possessed a sense of humour and a capacity for astringent irony, with which Brothers does not seem to have been blessed, and this is nowhere more evident than in the first book of his own 'Bible of Hell'. He originally entitled it 'The First Book Of Urizen', although some of the seven known copies have the 'First' removed, and it is clear that he considered himself at the beginning of some great enterprise. It is plausible to assume that in this period, having thoroughly mastered his techniques of relief etching and printing, he believed his task was to write one great epic poem; but, as so often in his artistic career, the first grand ambitions were quickly abandoned or forgotten. *The Book of Urizen* instead provides an introduction to Blake's mythological world.

It is on one level a parody of Genesis, in which Creation itself is seen as a giant fall from bliss and the God worshipped in this world as a most cruel demon.

> Eternals I hear your call gladly,
> Dictate swift winged words, & fear not
> To unfold your dark visions of torment.[21]

There is an element of 'spoofing' here, as it was called on the stage, since Blake deliberately adopts a portentous and solemn tone to mock some of the more absurd petitions of eighteenth-century poetry, but there are indeed 'dark visions' to be revealed. His myth of creation may owe something to Plato or to Boehme, to Plotinus or the Gnostics, but the spirit that animates it is all his own. His visions had already afforded him access to a reality in which the Newtonian concepts of space and time, let alone Lockean concepts of sensation, need not apply. And in *Urizen* he states his belief that the dimensions of material existence are a prison from which we must escape and that the human senses are a degraded and pitiful residue of eternal powers:

> Six days they shrunk up from existence
> And on the seventh day they rested
> And they bless'd the seventh day, in sick hope:
> And forgot their eternal life.[22]

The story here is of Urizen, 'the dark power' cold and abstracted, who is wrenched from 'the Eternals' and in his desperate desire 'for a joy without pain' and a 'solid without fluctuation' begins to form this universe that we inhabit;[23] Los, in pity for his earnest quest after permanence and unity, labours to give him a definite and finite form. Thus time, and space, are created. Yet Blake did not rest with the description of this elaborate cosmogony. It is the great strength of his single-handed attempt to create his own myth that, in the process of naming characters and describing individual episodes, he was able to explore the nature of reality in ways not available to his contemporaries with their more orthodox vocabulary. It could be said, in fact, that his decision to establish his myth was a way of strengthening and deepening that sense of a visionary world which he had possessed since childhood. He had broken open the conventional doors of perception and, through the space he had created, he could now see further than anyone else:

> They began to weave curtains of darkness
> They erected large pillars round the Void
> With golden hooks fastend in the pillars
> With infinite labour the Eternals
> A woof wove, and called it Science.[24]

In this emerging universe of opaqueness and division there issues 'the first female form' and, when man copulates with this divided image of his greatness, inevitably springs the line of finite generations with the first 'birth of the Human shadow'.[25] Out of his sorrows Urizen weaves a 'Web dark & cold', in its elaboration like the poor human brain, 'And all calld it, The Net of Religion'.[26] He measures out the abyss with rule and compass, creating shape and number, and from his dark visions spring all the woes of this world in which science and religion, commerce and politics, sexuality and repression, are intermingled:

> One command, one joy, one desire,
> One curse, one weight, one measure
> One King, one God, one Law.[27]

You do not have to go far through the polemical pamphlets of the period to realise that *Urizen* could be seen as part of the strident political debates of the 1790s – one anti-republican poem of the period celebrates the Britons' 'Good God, their old Laws, their Old King' in an inversion of Blake's satanic trinity.[28] But Blake used the biblical style and cadence of this poem precisely to indicate that time is only a corrupted aspect of eternity. The world of George III, or the French Revolution, or Tom Paine, had to be assimilated with his own absorbing visions of another world.

If they were absorbing, they were on occasions self-absorbed. He turned his visionary eye inwards and, with a self-consciousness as intense and elaborate as that of Milton, he saw his life as a revelation of eternity. He had a unique sense of his own mission and destiny, but it was one continually accompanied by anxiety, distrust, and fear of punishment – as the contemporary accounts of his behaviour suggest, he was always extraordinarily sensitive and susceptible. For much of his life he remained self-enclosed, withdrawn, self-willed, secretive, distant, detached from ordinary affairs. It is not necessarily a coincidence, then, that Blake should describe Urizen as 'Self-closd, all-repelling':[29]

> Dark revolving in silent activity:
> Unseen in tormenting passions.[30]

Perhaps it is fanciful to see here the image of Blake, labouring and brooding over his silent work, but it is curious nonetheless that he describes Urizen as engaged in precisely that activity:

> Here alone I in books formd of metals
> Have written the secrets of wisdom.[31]

There is some cause, then, for recognising Urizen as an aspect of Blake that the poet has seen parading in dumb show before him. There are occasions, in fact, when it is fruitful to read his illuminated poems as the story of a collection of various selves, each one struggling for mastery. This intimate and instinctive association also accounts for some of the more difficult passages in his poetry, where the drama between his epic combatants is what we might now call a 'psychological' drama between different modes of human consciousness. In the very act of creating books that few people would ever read, in conditions of isolation and neglect, Blake continues an endless debate with himself about the true nature of perception and expression. And as he works upon the first book of his 'Bible of Hell' he confronts Urizen with Los – the god of rationality and narrowed perception is to be redeemed by this figure, who represents the power of the creative imagination and the worth of continual artistic labour.

Something was happening to Blake's art at the same time. In place of the defined forms and careful figuration of the earliest examples of his relief etching, he now introduces freer and more indeterminate elements. He begins to apply paint to the copper plate itself and then print it directly upon paper, so that the texture and improvised shape of the paint becomes an important part of the images he depicts. Urizen broods over his books of brass with outstretched hands; Los howls in torment among flames; a huge globe of blood, like a planet, emerges from his bowed head; Urizen is crouched in despair beneath great rocks; an ancient man is floating upwards through water, and in one copy Blake had added upon the back in brown ink:

> I labour upwards into
> futurity
> Blake[32]

They are extraordinary images, conveying a sense of weight and compression, which is heightened by the thick textures of the applied paint; the figures seem to be struggling to liberate themselves from the confines in which they are crushed by paint, and metal, and print. One can sense behind them, too, the power and momentum of Blake's own creative instinct as he pushed and pummelled his images into shape. No two copies are alike, and in some he has inexplicably allowed certain pages to be repeated or lost without particular reason

– inexplicable, that is, until one remembers that the important aspect of his myth and his poetry is the concentration of his own presence within the work. This is a made object, a unique artefact beyond the dispensations of the print world; he celebrates that quality in his depiction of Los contending against Urizen, but he also presents it within the actual nature and process of his work. One early copy of *Urizen*, now known as 'Copy D', has been laden with thick crepuscular colours – some of them conveying an extraordinary dark intensity of black flame and green rocks, while others burst out in incandescent red, lavender and blue. It is often forgotten that Blake is one of the most extraordinary colourists of his period.

He used the back of the copper plates he had first employed on *The Marriage of Heaven and Hell*, but there are also traces of other images beneath the thick colours of *Urizen*. Of course it is cheaper and more convenient to use the same copper twice, but we see here also the play of Blake's mind; just as the protagonists are seen characteristically lifting their arms apart and breaking rocks or books into two, continually dividing material objects as they themselves are divided into various faculties, so also Blake consistently breaks things into two, makes pairs and copies, just as he was trained always to make copies when he was an engraver's apprentice. Through force of skill and training it became a psychological and physiological habit that informs his whole myth. There is another aspect of his early training to be seen in *The Book of Urizen*: he was happy to change or remove plates on instinct, but in one copy he discarded an image that had not been successfully aligned on the paper. It is as if that kind of visual and technical consistency was more important to him than verbal or thematic continuity, and suggests once more the material basis for all his art.

He had written 'I labour upwards into futurity', and his hand-written prophecy – wholly accurate, as it has turned out – resembles a story from this period of his life in Lambeth. While carrying home a picture he had stopped to rest at a tavern, when, according to his later account to a friend, 'the angel Gabriel touched him on the shoulder and said, Blake, wherefore art thou here? Go to, thou shouldst not be tired. he arose and went on unwearied.'[33] So he laboured on and, despite his failure to secure many commissions for *Urizen*, he continued his 'Bible of Hell' with two further books – *The Book of Ahania* and *The Book of Los*. They were printed on the back of each other but only one copy exists, which suggests that he either lost, damaged or erased the plates. The poems are much shorter than their predecessors, and more conventionally etched in intaglio. *Ahania* and *Los* continue the saga of Urizen; he contends with Los and with a mythical figure called Fuzon, while at the same time Blake documents the formation of our mortal part out of these vast wars in the heaven. The first chapter of *Ahania* begins with a challenge to the dominance of the god of reason and the horizon:

> Shall we worship this Demon of smoke,
> Said Fuzon, this abstract non-entity
> This cloudy God seated on waters
> Now seen, now obscur'd; King of sorrow?[34]

But *The Book of Los* ends with the petrifaction of Urizen and the creation of the material universe:

> Till his Brain in a rock, & his Heart
> In a fleshy slough formed four rivers
> Obscuring the immense Orb of fire
> Flowing down into night: till a Form
> Was completed, a Human Illusion
> In darkness and deep clouds involvd.
>
> The End of the
> Book of LOS[35]

This is powerful poetry and, despite the relative brevity and simplicity of the two Books, there is nothing makeshift about Blake's continuation of his narrative. The same elements are repeated or, rather, the same moment – that moment of human origin – is recreated and reinvented again and again in an endless plangent lament. It is the moment of the 'Human Illusion', with all its woes of sexual division and jealousy, of science and religion. Yet Blake returns to that moment because, for him, it is also the occasion of self-expression and thus of self-creation when, in a sense, he becomes part of his own myth. It is the impulse or the instinct of the autodidact who, in the process of recreating history, recreates both himself and the idea of sacred poetry.

There is always that element of irony or humour in Blake, however, which prompts him to pile horror upon horror in an almost gleeful manner; he takes a delight in terror, and often exploits it in an exaggerated or theatrical way. Of course this was also an aspect of other verse in the period, but Blake's attitude has a more popular source. It is known that he read Gothic fiction, and even copied out some lines from Ann Radcliffe's bestseller of 1794, *The Mysteries of Udolpho*, onto the back of one of his prints; one of the few paintings by Catherine Blake depicts Agnes from Matthew Lewis's Gothic extravaganza of 1796, *The Monk*. It is also likely that Blake knew of the Gothic dramas presented in the patent theatres of late eighteenth-century London, since there are occasions when the action of his prophetic books is close to the standard dramaturgy of those productions; fabulous villains such as Abomalique and Sanguino are not so far from Blake's Ijim and Ololon, while a preface to one volume of Gothic drama invokes 'Gigantic Forms, and visionary Gleams of Light'.[36] So a connection does exist. It may not appeal to those critics who would prefer Blake to be influenced only by the most literary or intellectual sources; but there can be little doubt that he was drawn to the popular Gothic melodramas of his day and borrowed some of their tricks. He was a Londoner, affected by all forms of London drama and London literature just as he was influenced by topical pamphlets, popular prints and broadside ballads. A contemporary comparison might be made with the modern comics devoted to 'science fantasy', and genre fiction in general – the Gothic element persists there in the illustrations of gigantic villains and superhuman heroes, all of them placed in abstract landscapes not unlike those of Blake himself. And when in *Ahania* he piles on the Gothic effects – 'Hopeless! abhorrd! a death-shadow, / Unseen, unbodied, unknown' – we are close to the overwrought language of contemporary fantasy with its death stars and dark forces.[37] Of course it would be unwise to press the comparison too far, since there is a qualitative difference between Blake's illuminated books and the comics of the late twentieth century. But there is a resemblance, at least, which springs in part from the sense of alienation or exclusion from the conventional literary establishment that many writers of fantasy experience; modern writers of fantasy tend also to be political radicals with an urban sensibility not untouched by an interest in the occult. They might be seen, then, as sharing part of Blake's consciousness. But before we ask what is so twentieth-century about Blake, we might consider what remains eighteenth-century about ourselves.

It is sometimes believed that he moved from the public prophecies of *America* and *The French Revolution* to the biblical allusiveness of *The Book of Urizen* as a way of dissociating himself from the fervid political climate of the period. He would have had every right to do so, even despite his tendency to nervous anxiety, because the atmosphere of the 1790s was not at all conducive to the prophetic or polemical examination of political affairs. To have lived in London, at the time of the war with France and the approach to that 'Great Terror' of 1795, which marked the climacteric of the Revolution, was to live in an atmosphere of continual suspicion, espionage and intrigue; many of Blake's acquaintance, such as Thomas Holcroft and William Sharp, were arrested or questioned. There were treason trials and transportations, while the threat of execution was stayed only by juries who refused to condemn their countrymen for their opinions. At time of crisis mobs of 'patriots' could be relied upon to wreak swift vengeance on anyone considered to be a Jacobin or anti-monarchist, but the actual London populace – faced with unemployment and shortages of bread as the French war continued – were far less amenable to the usual state slogans. 'On the day the King went to open the parliament,' one contemporary observed of the autumn of 1795, 'the crowd which was immense, Hissed and groaned and called out No Pitt – No War – Peace Peace, Bread Bread.'[38] Habeas Corpus had been suspended in the spring of 1794 but now two acts were passed against 'treasonable and seditious Practices' as well as 'Seditious Meetings and Assemblies'. These laws, flawed and uncertain though they were in execution, effectively marked the end of organised radicalism in London. In the spring of 1797 Blake dined with his publisher, Joseph Johnson, in the company of Fuseli among others; in the following year Johnson was arrested for selling a seditious pamphlet attacking an anti-radical tract entitled *An Apology for the Bible*, and was sentenced to six months' imprisonment in the King's Bench Prison near Blake's house in Lambeth. In the same year Blake furiously annotated a similar tract but added, at the beginning, 'To defend the Bible in this year 1798 would cost a man his life The Beast & the Whore rule without controls . . . I have been commanded from Hell not to print this as it is what our Enemies wish'.[39] It was not printed but, more to the point, there is no evidence that he ever again attached himself to any formal or informal political cause.

There were also more pressing considerations in the period. 'As poor Blake will not be out of need of money . . .' a young patron and connoisseur remarked,[40] and there is no doubt that in the period he was working upon the 'Bible of Hell' and other illuminated prophecies he was receiving far fewer commissions from artists and booksellers. He may have been preoccupied with his own work, and particularly with his new experiments in direct colour printing from the copper plates, but this is unlikely. In fact it seems that he had to rely largely upon the recommendation of friends, and there is no evidence that he turned down serious offers from any quarter. There now begins to emerge in his life a pattern that could do nothing but dismay and discourage him. While he remained a journeyman engraver, dabbling in what most of his contemporaries considered to be primitive experiments, his closest friends and acquaintances began to gain the success and reputation that were always denied to him; yet, at the same time, he was forced to rely upon the influence of those same friends to acquire work. It is not surprising, then, to read reports of his anger and bitterness; he knew that he was greater than any of them, and yet he was forced to toil in their shadow and sometimes at their behest.

Richard Cosway, recently appointed a Royal Academician, was eager to find him work. And in 1794 Stothard, his contemporary from the days at the Royal Academy Schools, himself became a Royal Academician. In that same year Flaxman returned after seven years in Italy to find himself a London celebrity: his very particular outline work, based upon the finest and clearest delineation of figure, started something close to a European fashion. He and Blake resumed their companionship, although Flaxman was shocked by the change in Catherine's appearance – he 'never saw a woman so much altered', which suggests at least that the years in Poland Street and Hercules Buildings had not necessarily been idyllic ones.[41] But Flaxman recommended Blake to potential employers and, according to contemporary sources, asked him to re-engrave some of his outlines from Homer's *Odyssey*, which had (appropriately enough) been lost at sea. George Cumberland had also returned from an aesthetic sojourn in Italy and he, too, began to find work for Blake's graver. He helped him to receive a further commission for Stuart and Revett's *The Antiquities of Athens*, and he asked him to engrave six of the plates in his own *Thoughts on Outline*. In fact he considered Blake's artistry to be very high indeed, and remarked in the text that his engraving work was 'a compliment from a man of his extraordinary genius and abilities, the highest, I believe, I shall ever receive'.[42] Blake returned the compliment in a letter apologising for his dilatoriness and absent-mindedness in engraving the plates: 'Go on. Go on. Such works as yours Nature & Providence, the Eternal Parents, demand from their children.'[43] This note is written in a large and firm hand, as if it had been transcribed from a draft, and is signed 'Will Blake'. So we can guess that he was addressed as 'Will' by his intimates, at least when they were not calling him 'poor Blake' behind his back.

It is a mark of his susceptibility to others, in fact, that, on the return of Cumberland and Flaxman from Italy with their respective portfolios, his own interest in classical antiquity seems to have quickened. He even went so far as to say, to one correspondent, that his desire was 'to renew the lost Art of the Greeks'[44] and spoke with approbation of 'Greek workmanship'.[45] It was in this period that classical statuary was being shipped in large quantities from Greece and Italy, but Blake was not alluding to the usual neoclassical ideals which he had learned at the Royal Academy; he was aligning himself with an art that, in Cumberland's words, had nothing whatever to do with 'the clumsy patronage of traders'[46] or with the standards of the Royal Academy itself with its 'tyrants of the trade, with their fierce contours'.[47] In espousing Greek art he was emphasising the importance of ideal form and imaginative composition, in opposition to the tame art patronised by the Academy; but he was also ascribing a more mighty social and spiritual purpose to art itself. In an essay written three years before *Thoughts on Outline*, George Cumberland, no doubt under the direct influence and advice of Blake, had suggested that Greek art itself derived in part from earlier 'Hindoo compositions'.[48] Charles Wilkins's translation of *Bhagvat Geeta* had appeared in 1785, and through the latter part of the century there was much interest and speculation about the nature of Indian religious art and Brahmin belief. The central point is, however, that Blake was continually attracted to a grave and ceremonial art, an art close to that of biblical prose in its use of ritual forms and non-naturalistic figures. That is why he was intrigued by Flaxman's linear and almost abstract representations of primeval scenes, which were described by one contemporary as 'a mixture of the Antique and the Gothic'.[49] In his own poetry he attempted to evoke the occluded origins of language in bardic and prophetic sources; in his art he was engaged in a similar pursuit of the eternal forms of sacred antiquity. That is why he could not rest with the myth of creation he had espoused in his 'Bible of Hell'. He had finished the last two books of that work quickly enough; it is as if he wanted to complete the verbal and poetic rendition of his myth before concentrating upon, and intensifying, his purely visual art.

He had been experimenting with colour printing in a variety of ways. He had begun putting colours on relief-etched copper plates, and then printing out the results in the press or with the pressure of his hand. The colour was mixed with size or gum, not water, and the impressions upon the paper are noticeable for the thick, variegated and mottled texture of the paint; it was a method that emphasised mass and surface, and its extraordinary novelty emphasises Blake's technical and practical dexterity. In their house in Lambeth he and his wife worked assiduously together; she was the 'devil' in charge of the press work, including both the paper and the printing, while Blake busied himself over the inking of the plates. She might also have drawn attention to his mistakes: in one plate he had drawn only six legs upon a spider before correcting his error. They coloured the subsequent books together, with Catherine taking Blake's first copy as her model; it is even possible for scholars to determine which were coloured by her and which by her husband:

And first he drew a line upon the walls of shining heaven
And Enitharmon tincturd it with beams of blushing love
It remained permanent a lovely form inspird divinely human . . .[50]

They had to work very rapidly on the 'colour-printed' pages because the paint dried fast, and it is appropriate to think of them as a 'team' or 'unit' who managed to keep up a very high standard of production. Once Blake had started to experiment with this new method, he began to test its possibilities. He had used coloured printing on relief-etched plates with *Urizen*, and the two other testaments from hell, but then in his subsequent illuminated books of this period he took the process a stage further and painted his colours upon smooth unetched plates. The results are to be seen in perhaps the two most extraordinary illuminated books that he ever created – *Europe* and *The Song of Los*.

Both are related to the books that preceded them, but the mythic and verbal characteristics of the narratives are less immediately striking than their pictorial aspects. Blake's imagination had been fired by his new technique, and it cannot help but dominate his invention now. *Europe* itself is perhaps the most wonderful of all the illuminated books. It was etched on the back of *America*, with which it was also sometimes bound, but certain pages have been entirely colour printed; Blake worked directly upon the plate with his brush and colours before pressing it down upon the paper. After the paper had been printed he added more colour with a brush, and then with a pen emphasised outlines and forms where necessary: it was intensely concentrated work, applying layers of paint to the images, deepening and strengthening the textures, solidifying the masses so that the pages of the poem are thickly encrusted objects of art in which blazes of colour break out like fires or flares in the darkness. Indeed it could be said that the images of *Europe* carry the burden of the 'prophecy', as he had once more called it, with the extraordinary figures and tableaux like some narrative of the fallen world. A malevolent figure, holding a knife, waits within a cave to strike at a hopeful traveller; there is clear reference to the images of contemporary political cartoons here, and in particular to Gillray, but there is also a more general sense that Blake is introducing a world in which no human joy or optimism can flourish. Three bald-headed figures, looking very much like the sculptures of the mad by Caius Cibber that adorned the entrance of Bethlem Hospital, fall in tormented wrestling through an infinite abyss. In a scene of plague, the bellman, in dark costume, passes three people who lie stricken with the pestilence. In a scene of famine a dead baby lies before a boiling pot, and seems about to be thrown into it by two hungry despairing women. These are images of torment and horror, which can plausibly be related to Blake's imaginative recreation of London at a time of war and famine – in that sense the association with political cartoons is no doubt intended – but the visionary intensity of his work comes from other sources. There is a serpent on the title page, mottled and writhing like some creature of primitive mythology, and it is related to the central perception of *Europe* itself – concerned, as it is, with the enslavement of man to the circles of fallen consciousness as well as the monstrous forms of commerce and organised religion.

> Thought chang'd the infinite to a serpent; that which pitieth:
> To a devouring flame; and man fled from its face and hid
> In forests of night . . .
> Then was the serpent temple form'd, image of infinite
> Shut up in finite revolutions, and man became an Angel;
> Heaven a mighty circle turning; God a tyrant crown'd.[51]

Indeed the visionary images may, themselves, be visions. Perhaps the most famous of those in *Europe* is that of an ancient man kneeling down from a lighted orb, measuring the abyss below him with a pair of compasses. It is called 'The Ancient of Days', and Blake had once seen him. A contemporary wrote that the 'splendid grandeur' of this figure was inspired by 'the vision which he declared hovered at the top of his staircase'.[52] On that same staircase, he had also seen something else. 'Did you ever see a ghost?' a friend asked him. 'Never but once,' he replied. An early biographer takes up the story: 'Standing one evening at his garden-door in Lambeth, and chancing to look up, he saw a horrible grim figure, "scaly, speckled, very awful" stalking down stairs towards him. More frightened than ever before or after, he took to his heels, and ran out of the house.'[53] That ghostly visitant may have played some part in his later conception of 'The Ghost of a Flea', which is similarly scaled and speckled, but it is interesting how Blake makes a definite distinction between this singular 'ghost' and his usual 'visions'; he once declared that ghosts appeared only to unimaginative people, which suggests that he believed his visions to be in part shaped by the powers of his own imagination. They were 'mental', without the physical presence of ghosts; when he described one of them to an inquisitive lady he tapped his forehead to reveal its source. He understood that they came from 'Here, madam'.[54]

Certainly he thought enough of 'The Ancient of Days' to issue it as a separate work, and in fact many of the illustrations to Europe have a life independent from the poetic narrative of oppression and revolution; the poetry is always there, some of it very fine, but his attention to the written text has now changed. He is repeating, and elaborating upon, the elements of his myth but he prefers to remain at a level of lucid generalisation that allows for any number of Gothic touches. It is significant, in this respect, that in one edition of the poem George Cumberland has transcribed in hand (no doubt under the direction of Blake himself) several quotations from Bysshe's Art of English Poetry that are connected with the popular 'graveyard school' of eighteenth-century English verse. It is possible, within Europe at least, to see Blake's own lines in the same light.

He and Catherine printed several copies of Europe, over a few days, before using colour printing in an even more elaborate way upon The Song of Los. Its title page seems to have been colour painted without any previous etching or engraving, so for the first time Blake creates words by simply painting them in reverse on unmarked copper. The book itself is vividly, almost luridly, coloured with some of his most heavily decorated images; its frontispiece depicts an old man kneeling before an altar like a giant book of stone, in the act of worshipping a dark sun. This is a landscape in which Boehme's concept of the fire world, Swedenborg's description of the dead sun of the natural world, and contemporary beliefs in the turbulence of periodic stars, are all closely aligned with his use of colour, texture and surface mass. *The Song of Los* also marks the culmination of the first stage of Blake's illuminated books, and is the last of the prophecies to be published from Lambeth; the poem begins with a survey of the primeval faiths inherited by the generations of fallen men, and ends with a celebration of excess and sexuality in a world where '. . . the Churches: Hospitals: Castles: Palaces: / Like nets & gins & traps to catch the joys of Eternity . . .'[55] The culmination of his mythological system, then, is here associated with the most resourceful use of his colour printing method for the illuminated prophecies; myth and medium are not separated, therefore, but operate within the same sphere of artistic activity. That is why the last of the Lambeth prophecies led to what is arguably the greatest sequence of painted works which he ever created.

It was a natural step. The method of painting colour upon a copper plate, and then printing it directly upon paper, need not be confined to his illuminated books. It could be a means of creating paintings, with the added advantage that he could produce more than one copy of the same image by simply repeating the procedure. Twelve such works are known to exist, each of them in three very different impressions, and among these are Blake's most famous images. They are arranged in pairs, in compliance with his obsession for reversals and 'contraries'. So it is that 'Newton' is associated with 'Nebuchadnezzar' – in one painting the scientist sits upon a rock and contemplates the figure that he has drawn with his compasses, while in the other the mad king looks up in horror from the grass he has been eating. Sometimes Blake varied the method by which he created these works. A contemporary in whom he and his wife confided gave the following account: 'Blake . . . took a common thick millboard and drew, in some strong ink or colour, his design upon it strong and thick . . . he painted roughly and quickly, so that no colour would have time to dry. He then took a print of that on paper, and this impression he coloured up in water-colours, repainting his outline on the millboard when he wanted to take another print. This plan he had recourse to, because he could vary slightly each impression; and each having a sort of accidental look, he could branch out so as to make each one different. The accidental look they had was very enticing.'[56] The same informant recalled that the paintings 'gave the sort of impression you will get by taking the impression of anything wet.'[57] Blake could also add heavier colours in order to lend mass to the images, and there were times when he scratched roughly through the paint to make white lines like rain falling over his figures. It is as if he were actively trying to subvert the flatness of his compositions by thickening and varying the surface itself; like early Italian frescoes or medieval illuminated manuscripts, they exist within no pictorial illusion of volumetric space. It was a physical mode that perfectly complements an art which depicts the fallen world of material process. Consider Newton and Nebuchadnezzar, both, as Blake supposed, grown mad with unbelief. Each figure is symmetrically poised and balanced within the flat plane of the composition; there is an intensity and concentration here that are in part aspects of their own obsessive activities, but that are also intimately related to Blake's own vision. In all of these colour prints there is an extraordinary sense of formal control, as if the figures themselves were imitating the boundaries of the millboard or the copper plate; but, again, Blake's deliberate roughness with the painted texture, and his love of the 'accidental', suggests his desire somehow to liberate himself from the closely organised restraint of his actual compositions. It is another aspect of his contrary nature.

The same quality of figural restraint is explicit in the other paintings – in 'God Judging Adam' and 'Satan Exulting Over Eve', in 'The House of Death' and 'Pity'. In all of them figures are starkly defined against a barren landscape, arrested in moments of pathos or fear; it is an art of gesture, codified, with feeling conveyed by line and posture. These are not painterly works; if we were to redeploy the terminology of the period, which Blake himself would have known and used, we would note that there is no liquid softness, no glow of colour, no flowing liberty and freedom. Instead he employs what was known as a hard manner of great force and brilliancy, which, as a result of early training with the engraver's burin, would also have been described as old, or dry, or cold. It is an explicit art, designed to impress rather than to delight or persuade; it is the work of a visionary who understands precisely what he means to convey, both in attitude and conception. That is why he is able to delineate energy, terror and exultation with such conviction; but his painted works are never restful or intimate, and they rarely convey tenderness. At most they manage pathos or resignation, but the more amiable or elusive aspects of human feeling are never registered.

At least one set of these twelve colour prints was sold by Catherine Blake after her husband's death, so he had not necessarily completed them with any particular purchaser in mind; he was simply impelled to do them, and they represent the finest artistic statement of Blake's Lambeth visions. It was an art of his own creation in every sense, and it remains his most distinctive contribution to eighteenth-century English painting. But he put them away, with the unsold copies of his illuminated books, and some ten years later repainted and reprinted them. He had now resigned himself to relatively small sales of his work, but there was a certain reassurance and sense of worth to be found in keeping the plates or proofs in close proximity. One of the merits of working outside the conventional network of print shops and booksellers is that he never suffered the experience of being 'taken up' and then forgotten, of having an immense success proved to be only temporary: he had his work around him always, and could entertain the possibility of future success or renown. The 'development' of his art becomes, in this context, a very complicated process; the salient fact about his artistic career is his willingness to reissue earlier works with the same facility as he invented new ones.

In the period of the colour prints, for example, he reprinted selections of his art that have become known as the 'small' and 'large' books of designs. One 'small' book was especially commissioned by Ozias Humphry, a miniature-painter and close friend of Flaxman who became something of a 'collector' of Blake's work – it is described by a contemporary as 'a small quarto volume of twenty-three engravings of various shapes and sizes, coloured as before, some of which are of extraordinary effect and beauty'.[58] Among them are colour-printed pages from *Urizen* and *Thel*, as well as other prophecies, and it is significant that Blake wished to include material from his earliest illuminated book. Similarly, in the 'large' book of designs, he included colour-printed versions of some of his earliest engravings; one of them, 'Albion Rose', had first been executed fifteen years before. This is hardly surprising for an artist who proclaimed that 'Vision or Imagination is a Representation of what Eternally Exists',[59] and his studio itself resembled that visionary city of art where all is 'Permanent, & not lost not lost nor vanishd, & every little act, / Word, work, & wish, that has existed, all remaining still'.[60]

Blake described the project, almost twenty years later, as 'Those I printed for Mr Humphry are a selection from the different Books of such as could be Printed without the Writing, tho' to the Loss of some of the best things. For they when Printed perfect accompany Poetical Personifications & Acts, without which Poems they never could have been Executed.'[61] It is one of his few extant comments on the nature of his illuminated books, and suggests the close relation which he still made between the poetry and design. This does not necessarily imply that he took an orthodox attitude towards the combination of poetry and painting – 'Poetical Painting' was the name that Joshua Reynolds gave to historical painting, after all, and the notion of *ut pictura poesis* was one of the aesthetic commonplaces of the age. There were illustrated epics long before those of Blake (*Paradise Lost* being the standard text for engravers and painters of every kind), but for him the connection between poetry and painting was a much more intense and serious one. He saw them as aspects of the same vision, which must be reunited in order to raise the perceptions of fallen man. He made the connection explicitly when he wrote, 'as Poetry admits not a Letter that is Insignificant so Painting admits not a Grain of Sand or a Blade of Grass [Insignificant]'.[62] He was concerned to evoke the sense of the sacred within both arts, at a time when the pressures of specialisation and commercialisation were reducing both to the status of a standardised and secularised activity. The great sin, during this period of industrial revolution, lay in the forces of separation and exclusion.

One contemporary has recorded how 'He worked at literature and art at the same time, keeping the manuscript beside him and adding to it, at intervals, while the graver continued its task almost without intermission', and in a sense both activities can be seen to interanimate each other in a most striking manner.[63] His verse is often concerned with pictorial values and with the creation of tableaux – 'see' and 'behold', 'dark' and 'bright' are among his most used words – while his painting often depicts the nature of what were then called 'mental states'. He frequently uses terms from engraving to elucidate his own philosophy – the doctrine of 'States' is predicated upon the various stages of the copper plate, while such words as 'lake', 'grave' and 'opacity' have for him a network of associations and resemblances. He was inspired equally by Milton and by Dürer, by Shakespeare and by Raphael, while his ideas often first came to him in the shape of images or scenes. There are even occasions when a painting, such as that now known as 'Los and Orc' (in which a naked human figure looks down in horror at a boy chained to a rock), inspires an entire plot or narrative. There are thematic connections of a more general kind, also; his biblical paintings complement a poetry that is pervaded by the cadence and imagery of the Bible, while his historical paintings are the natural equivalent to his poetic adaptations of Milton or of Shakespeare. It is significant, in this context, that he generally portrayed Shakespeare's ghosts as a complement to his own spiritual creations. Both poetry and painting are on an epic scale, and both forms have been influenced by the theatre of the period; there is a drawing by him of 'Richard III and the Ghosts' that is directly taken from a stage tableau. The scenery of the prophetic books is not so far from the scenic displays of De Loutherbourg at Drury Lane, while we have already seen how the language of the verse bears a resemblance to late eighteenth-century Gothic drama.

But this in turn raises a larger question. There are times, both in his art and in his poetry, where Blake seems to prefer the clarity of a vivid surface without any underlying context of meaning. It is as if a bright light were shining beneath the poetry and the painting, lending them great vibrancy and outline but without any real feeling of depth. His poetry is often one of declaration and assertion, just as his art resides upon the pictorial plane; much of his creative activity takes place on the immediate surface and there are occasions when an image, or a verse, seems to have no concerted or established 'sense' – with the proviso of course that this indeterminacy, this missing signification, is often part of a work's power. It is like the oblique character of the man himself, who, according to one interlocutor, made assertions without bothering himself with argument or debate; his work shares that same denotative brilliance, but sometimes at the expense of bewildering those who encounter it. This may have been one of the reasons why he detested oil painting, which can never attain that kind of formal clarity, and it may also be connected with the absence of any real subtlety of passion or feeling in his work. He instinctively disliked Rembrandt's oils and chiaroscuro – 'Smears & Dawbs' was his generic term for such work – partly because in that artist's painting much emphasis is placed upon the complexities of characterisation and the intricacies of feeling.[64] Blake never bothered himself with such things, except in the most formal and emblematic way.

Critics and semiologists have uncovered much more complicated associations between Blake's poetry and art – Roman Jakobson wrote that the play of couplets in Blake's lyrics resembled 'the converging lines of a background in a pictorial perspective',[65] while another linguist has decribed how his 'nouns and gerunds supply the colour of all action while the verbs [have] epic simplicity and sublimity'.[66] One literary critic has, in addition, described Blake's poetry as one of continual process in which elements of a 'grand simplicity' are 'foregrounded from the indefinite mass'.[67] This might be a description of 'Newton' or 'The Ancient of Days', and it emphasises a truth that Blake himself understood very well – 'Every Eye Sees differently As the Eye – Such the Object'.[68]

He put away 'Newton' with the other colour prints and in this same year, 1795, he produced a uniform set of all his illuminated books on larger, folio-sized, paper. He knew that this stage of his artistic life was over, and by reprinting the entire canon he was completing the work of eight years with a flourish. He had believed that his new method of relief etching, or illuminated printing, would prove successful with the public who bought prints and illustrated books; but in fact he had found his sales limited to connoisseurs and to other artists. Any hope of financial independence had also disappeared. The works had not proved a failure – otherwise he would not have wished to reprint them in a special edition – but he had learned over the years to lower his expectations of any immediate renown or commercial reward. He did reprint his books, when he needed to replenish his stock or when he received a large commission, but he never returned to the intensive methods of colour printing he had developed. Over the next few years he would revert to more conventional techniques, and earn his living by working for others. A chapter had come to an end.

SEVENTEEN

Newtons sleep

A naked man sits upon a rock and, with outstretched hand, measures the arc and triangle of a mathematical diagram outlined upon a scroll. A white cloak is draped across his left shoulder, like some 'wintry mantle' of 'aged Snow'.[1] He is looking downward with great intentness, head bowed in meditation, and he has become part of the rock itself. In one version of this colour print Newton seems to be sitting on the sea bed, the waters of materialism around him and above him: he might be the remnant of Eternal Man roused to sluggish activity like the polypus at his feet.

> The Corse of Albion lay on the Rock the sea of Time & Space
> Beat round the Rock in mighty waves & as a Polypus
> That vegetates beneath the Sea the limbs of Man vegetated
> In monstrous forms of Death a Human polypus of Death[2]

'Time & Space' are to be seen as existing apart from the vast machinery of the Newtonian universe, but in their abstract form they may overwhelm us like the ocean. Then we would surely drown in the material world. In another version Newton seems to be sitting within a cave, like that of Plato's in which only the shadows of the ideal world can be seen; in that darkness the senses are narrowed, and perception itself a form of darkness. He is trapped within the confinement of his own calculations. Whether cave or sea bed, then, Newton is surrounded by emblems of the fallen world: moss, lichen, and pitted rock, 'vegetated / Beneath your land of shadows'.[3]

In one copy of the painting Blake has inscribed 'NEWTON' upon the surface of the rock itself to suggest the identity between the great scientist and the stony world that he has helped to create. And what of the diagram which Newton is contemplating? It might have come from his own *Opticks* since it bears a striking resemblance to some of the illustrations in the first book of that work, in which he speculates upon the nature of light itself as it passes through the prism: 'To separate from one another the heterogeneous Rays of compound Light . . . The Sine of Incidence of every Ray considered apart, is to its Sine of Refraction in a given Ratio.'[4] White light, which is for Blake the image of the spirit, has become part of a mathematical equation; the diagram itself is an emblem of separation and division, which for Blake, as we have read, are the origins of the great sin. It is the Ratio, the generalisation, the use of abstract reason, 'Mathematic Proportion' that is the negation of 'Living Proportion'.[5] To which Blake answers, 'May God us keep / From Single vision & Newtons sleep!'[6]

At the beginning of *Europe* Blake asks a little spirit, 'Then tell me, what is the material world, and is it dead?' He is promptly shown another world or, rather, a true image of this one in which dwells 'each eternal flower' and where 'every particle of dust breathes forth its joy'.[7] It is that same world where 'particles bright' are 'jewels of Light' and where each 'particle' is also 'Human formd'.[8] It is the direct answer to Newton's physics in which particles are 'hard and solid', the opaque atoms of the material world, dead, inert, 'Petrifying all the Human Imagination into rock & sand'.[9] It is the rock and sand where Newton sits. It is his universe of concentric orbs, with the spheres and shells revolving about each other in mechanical movement and governed by the immutable laws of the inverse square and the fluxional calculus. It is the system, the vast machinery of order and uniformity, the 'Newtonian Voids' of causal necessity and inert force;[10] it is technology, industrial production, and the moral law. Thus, in Newton's sleep, 'his eternal life / Like a dream was obliterated'.[11] Blake has used the image before; the figure crouched in a cave or in water is one of his most persistent, since it represents the shrunken or submerged state of fallen man. The form itself may owe something to the engraving of Abias by Ghisi after Michelangelo, an engraving that Blake once copied. But the fall also takes place within the human body – the rock upon which Newton sits bears a passing resemblance to an illustration that Blake engraved for a medical treatise on stones of the urinary tract.

'Newton' is one of Blake's most powerful works; within the random accretions of paint and inked line he has delivered his own ingenious and instinctive response to the scientist's trust in system and uniformity. The textures here are roughly and variously articulated; there are no indistinguishable atoms or intermeasurable elements of Newton's fluxional calculus but the free play of one man's visonary lines. Space and time are not separate entities, to be attached by the rules of perspective, since in this painting the lineaments of the human body are the image of the mental state. Everything here denies the significance of Newton's theoretical enquiries, and it stands as the single most important symbol of a popular tradition that derided Newtonianism as an aberration and a heresy. The *Conjuror's Magazine*, which had printed one of Blake's engravings, suggested that the ghost of the scientist 'may keep his nonsense of vacuum and attraction out of the way'.[12] Even at the end of his life Blake is reported to have 'incidentally denied *causation*'.[13] 'I know too well,' he wrote five months before his death, 'that a great majority of Englishmen are fond of The Indefinite which they Measure by Newton's Doctrine of the Fluxions of an Atom, A Thing that does not Exist.'[14]

Yet there is a grandeur about this painting, which suggests the sacred monumentality of Michelangelo's own figures. The power of the image may come from another source, also, since it has sometimes been suggested that the face of Newton here is like some idealised image of Blake's own youthful or eternal countenance. It ought to be remembered that science and literature were not so far apart as they have since become, and there is no reason to believe that Blake thought of Newton as a very different kind of writer from himself. Indeed there is an intensity about this image that suggests he recognised the creative importance of the scientist's vision. He could have known little or nothing about Newton's alchemical and occult interests, but clearly he understood his capacities as a myth-maker and a systematiser. That accounts for the power and authority that surround the presence of Newton; he seems almost to become an alternative image of Orc, who within Blake's pantheon was the representative of liberation and revolutionary desire. In such a reading it would be possible to see the image of the triangle upon the scroll as the alchemical symbol for Fire. Perhaps also, in this contemplative figure, there is some suggestion of the obsession and isolation that were part of Blake's own experience. Once again, in the ambiguity of the image as well as of the word, we approach the mystery of Blake's own nature.

EIGHTEEN

Go on & on

Blake had been reading an edition of Edward Young's *Night Thoughts*, which he had agreed to illustrate, and had come to a passage in which the poet asks 'who can paint an angel?' Blake closed the book, according to his own account, and spoke aloud.

BLAKE: Aye! Who can paint an angel?

VOICE: Michael Angelo could.

He looked about the room but noticed nothing 'save a greater light than usual'.

BLAKE: And how do *you* know?

VOICE: I *know*, for I sat to him: I am the arch-angel Gabriel.

BLAKE: Oho! You are, are you? I must have better assurance than that of a wandering voice; you may be an evil spirit – there are such in the land.

VOICE: You shall have good assurance. Can an evil spirit do this?

Blake 'looked whence the voice came, and was then aware of a shining shape, with bright wings, who diffused much light. "As I looked, the shape dilated more and more: he waved his hands; the roof of my study opened; he ascended into heaven; he stood in the sun, and beckoning to me, moved the universe. An angel of evil could not have *done that* – it was the arch-angel Gabriel." '[1]

So in the study of his house in Lambeth, Blake saw an angel stand in the sun and move the universe. It is like the vision of some medieval saint or anchorite. This spiritual conversation was later reported by another artist, Thomas Phillips, but it is entirely consistent with Blake's usual remarks on the subject of his visions. It is also the sort of conversation that effectively prevented him from moving upward in the social or artistic world. In this period it seems that discreet enquiries were being made about Blake's suitability as a member of the Royal Academy, and the 'fixer' of these matters, Joseph Farington, had several conversations on the subject of Blake's competence as an artist. His illuminated books were owned by a few collectors, and it is likely that Ozias Humphry showed Farington the small book of designs which Blake had printed for him. An entry in Farington's diary for 19 February 1796 sets the scene: 'West, Cosway & Humphry spoke warmly in favour of the designs of Blake the Engraver, as works of extraordinary genius and imagination – Smirke differed in opinion, from what He had seen, and so do I.'[2] A later conversation, also reported by Farington, was less polite: 'We supped together and had laughable conversation. Blakes eccentric designs were mentioned. Stothard supported his claims to Genius, but allowed He had been misled to extravagance in his art, & He knew by whom.' He was referring here to the influence of Fuseli upon Blake. 'Hoppner ridiculed the absurdity of his designs, and said nothing could be more easy to produce such. – They were like the conceits of a drunken fellow or a madman. "Represent a man sitting on the moon, and pissing the Sun out – that would be a whim of as much merit." '[3] So there is talk of madness, and the image of the man pissing on the sun is an appropriate late eighteenth-century secular variant on Blake's vision of the angel Gabriel standing within it. Another of Farington's diary entries makes a similar point: 'Fuseli called on me last night & sat till 12 oClock. He mentioned Blake, the Engraver, whose genius & invention have been much spoken of. Fuseli has known him several years, and thinks He has a great deal of invention, but that "fancy is the end, and not a means in his designs". he does not employ it to give novelty and decoration to regular conceptions; but the whole of his aim is to produce singular shapes & odd combinations. he is abt 38 or 40 years of age, and married a maid servant, who has imbibed something of his singularity. They live together without a servant at a very small expence . . . Fuseli says, Blake has something of madness abt him.'[4] If Blake were ever canvassed as a possible member of the Royal Academy, then such conversations would have ruined his chance. He was singular, probably a little mad. He had even married a servant. When he spoke of his angels, also, he was attaching himself to an urban and decidedly 'lower-class' vocabulary of religious millenarianism; even if he was sane, he was certainly not well-bred.

Yet he was not altogether being ignored, and his work was well enough known to be the subject of comment and debate. There was no reason why he should restrict himself to his own artistic experiments and indeed there was, now, a good commercial reason for his discontinuing work upon them: he had received the largest commission of his life from a sympathetic publisher. He was asked to illustrate Young's *Night Thoughts* (he had been reading it over, in his Lambeth study, when Gabriel appeared to him), but on a scale large enough to bear comparison with Boydell's 'Shakespeare Gallery' or Thornton's *Temple of Flora*. The commission had come from a young bookseller, Richard Edwards, who knew Blake's work very well – his brother, James, was also a bookseller and with Joseph Johnson had been responsible for the publication of Stedman's *Narrative*. James Edwards had previously asked Blake to engrave after Fuseli for the 'Milton Gallery' and had arranged for him to do some work on an edition of Hume's *History of England*; the fact that one project failed, and that the other did not in the end include work by Blake, is less important than the evidence of sympathy and collaboration. It was James Edwards, after all, who allowed artists to inspect the collection of medieval manuscripts that was preserved at his bookshop in Pall Mall; the association of Blake's own prophetic books with medieval illuminations has often been made, and it is certainly possible that his examination of the Bedford Book of Hours, on display in Pall Mall, affected his conception of his own art.

Richard Edwards had his book and print shop in New Bond Street, where he kept his own rarities. He had Edward Young's personal copy of *Night Thoughts*, with corrections in the author's hand, and his original plan may simply have involved Blake in furnishing extra illustrations for what was already an interesting volume. But the project rapidly grew in importance, and it was agreed that Blake should provide watercolours for each of the 537 pages of the poem. This was itself a large undertaking, but Farington's diary reveals another aspect of this venture: 'Fuseli understands that Edwards proposes to select abt. 200 from the whole and to have that number engraved as decorations for a new edition.'[5] Blake wanted one hundred guineas for the watercolours but Edwards said 'He could not afford to give more than 20 guineas for which Blake agreed.'[6] This is not a large sum, amounting to a little over ninepence a drawing, but no doubt Blake assumed that much more would be earned from the engravings themselves; an approximate price would have been something like forty guineas an engraving (no records of his agreement with Edwards survive), and a commission for two hundred would have provided him with a 'comfortable' income. It was not excessive – William Sharp earned twelve hundred guineas for engraving Copley's 'Death of Lord Chatham', while Charles Heath spent some nine years on that same painter's memorial to Major Pierson. The scale even of Blake's enterprise was soon reduced, however; the two hundred engravings became one hundred and fifty, and eventually the edition was advertised with only forty; there may have been a lack of capital for copper plate and paper, or it may be that Blake found himself quite unable to complete so much work in so short a time. Yet it was still, for him, an ambitious and unusually lengthy project; for two years he laboured over the watercolours and the engravings, choosing the line from each page that he wished to illustrate and then fashioning his design around the window of text. In fact the actual appearance of each page, with the words surrounded by painted images, bears some resemblance to his own illuminated books; there is no doubt that he conceived *Night Thoughts* as a variant upon his own novel methods. He left a blank square on each page, where the text could be pasted down, and then drew a red border around it; with that as his guide he could experiment with the figures and images with which he wished to decorate Young's words. There are a few preliminary sketches but most of the preparatory work was done on the page itself, with Blake erasing unwanted pencil lines with bread. Watercolours and firmer outlines were then added when the figures were completed to his satisfaction, and it seems that he also worked on the final copperplate engravings even as he finished the watercolours. It was a continuous, technically difficult, process; but there is no doubt, also, that it was a labour of love.

Blake had always admired *Night Thoughts*, and the obscurity into which Young has now fallen should not blind us to the merits of his verse. With its Miltonic cadence, its Shakespearian diction and its exultant sepulchralism, the poem is closer to Blake than might be expected; certainly it elicited some of his most extraordinary illustrated work, and there are occasions when Blake needed the stimulus or goad of another's imagination before he could fully release his own. But Young also possessed a very fine sense of the sacred:

> Angels are Men of a superior Kind . . .
> And Men are Angels, loaded for an Hour.[7]

It is a much more splendid vision of human destiny than that offered by latitudinarians or deists, and it is one with which Blake found himself in complete agreement. He even went so far as to imitate Young when the proper occasion arose, and Young's forgotten line, 'Thy Master, *Satan*, I dare call a Dunce',[8] lies behind a poem by Blake that is very much shorter, and now much more famous, than the entire *Night Thoughts*:

> Truly My Satan thou art but a Dunce
> And dost not know the Garment from the Man
> Every Harlot was a Virgin once
> Nor canst thou ever change Kate into Nan
>
> Tho thou art Worshipd by the Names Divine
> Of Jesus & Jehovah: thou art still
> The Son of Morn in weary Nights decline
> The lost Travellers Dream under the Hill[9]

Blake's interest in the poem, as well as the speed with which he was compelled to make his illustrations (at the rate of about five a week), meant that he often translated Young's images and arguments in a highly literal manner. He marked the line from each page that he wished to employ with an 'X'; and the means by which he chose to interpret Young throws some light upon the characteristics of his imagination. The phrase 'drove me to the brink' is illustrated with a human figure being literally hounded to the edge of a precipice, and for the line 'Open thy Bosom, set thy Wishes wide' he shows a young man opening up his chest to allow three small winged creatures to emerge; he sees concepts such as Time and Death as monstrous human figures, and tends to convert abstractions into dramatic activity and confrontation. (Even the 'Atoms' of Newton are depicted as human figures, in a further attack upon his impersonal physics.) What this suggests, in turn, is that Blake already possessed a coherent system of artistic signs that he could redeploy as the occasion demanded; it comes from the narrative of his prophetic books but it also derives from that art of gesture which he had perfected in the twelve colour prints of the year before. He does not so much reinterpret Young's poem as find equivalents for its meaning within his own imaginative repertoire. It is also worth remarking that, once again, he tends to create symmetrical pairs of illustrations so that on a double-page spread they will be seen in active combination or confrontation with one another; it is one aspect of his training as a copy-engraver that he could never relinquish since, as one twentieth-century printmaker has put it, 'The Printmaker is a most peculiar being . . . he takes pleasure in working backwards or in opposites . . . left is right, right is left. Backwards is forwards.'[10]

Blake's work on *Night Thoughts* has sometimes been described as laboured, mechanical, or unfinished; it is certainly repetitive, but the necessity of completing more than five hundred watercolours in two years may help to explain the deployment of certain stock figures. The poem itself is full of them. In fact much of his work here is powerful and suggestive, with a striking alignment of text and design that is derived from his prophetic books; but if his figures have the same formal and gestural attitudes as in his previous work, they are also conceived with a fluency and freedom that suggest relief at the end of his own creative labours on illuminated printing. The human or allegorical figures of Young's poem are extravagantly, even carelessly, conceived by Blake; they rise and descend, or recline upon the rectangular boxes that hold the text, or soar around it. A young man looks aghast at a sundial, Death pulls down the sun, and a bearded figure points towards a raging ocean. The human figures here are not realistically conveyed but, in the world of Blake's vision, they are vessels or allegories of a spiritual state; these figures are pressed out of shape, or distorted, by forces both above and below. Yet, despite the poem's emphasis upon Death and Time, he continually stresses the possibility of rebirth.

It has been remarked that, for the printmaker, there is a pleasure to be derived in working 'backwards or in opposites'; but this need not be confined to Blake's use of symmetrical oppositions within the illustrations of *Night Thoughts*. While engaged upon Young's verses, for example, he began to write a poem of his own in direct contrast to them. Its original title was probably 'The Book of Vala', in which Vala herself is to be seen as Nature, the veil of the fallen world and the emblem of veiled sexuality. An early fragment of the poem describes eternal creatures who are also hermaphrodites: 'Female her form bright as the summer but the parts of love / Male . . .'[11] At a later date he would draw explicit illustrations of these sexual fantasies, but in the verse he confined himself to the depiction of 'struggling copulation'.[12] Then he discarded this fragment when, in a beautiful copperplate hand, he wrote out thirty-five pages of new text. He even drew in faintly ruled lines to keep the verses straight, and tended to treat each page as if it were a plate that he was engraving; he erased lines and then wrote neatly over them, he placed his additions in carefully boxed spaces and generally kept within the formal bounds that his early training had laid out for him. The verse itself is a continuation of his earlier Lambeth poems, in which sexual jealousy and repression are seen as aspects of mechanical vision and the material world, and it contains such figures as Los and Urizen who had dominated the earlier poetry; the consonance of this work with its predecessors is to be seen in the title itself, which Blake penned with a few flourishes on the first page – 'VALA, OR The Death and Judgement of the Ancient Man'. But then, in an extraordinary act of imitation, he subtitled the work 'A DREAM of Nine Nights',[13] just as Young's poem finished with 'NIGHT the NINTH and LAST';[14] it is as if he ccould not work long upon one man's verse without wishing to oppose it, to set up a contrary, to draw an alternative image. He seems to have realised how debilitating Young's measured verses might become, and it is likely that he turned to his own poem for relief and release from his enforced subservience to another man's vision. If there is a problem with Night Thoughts it is that Young's maintenance of the same cadence encourages a sense of calm and resignation that also pervades the poem at a thematic level. Blake knew that by breaking the cadence he could also break down that placid serenity which had never been part of his own nature. But it is an extraordinary indication of the oppositions within his work – striking originality combined with equally striking imitation – that he should conceive and describe his poem in terms taken from Young. At a later date he would even write his verses upon the discarded proofs of his edition of Night Thoughts, using the same boxed areas in which Young's letter-print had been pasted. But no doubt he had also begun work on his poem at the time of Night Thoughts because he simply could not help himself. He had for so long been combining art and poetry in his own work that he must have found himself constitution-ally incapable of concentrating upon one single aspect of his skills. The habitual daily labour upon the illustrations to Young may have actively encouraged his composition of Vala, and in this long poem he was writing some of his finest verse:

> What is the price of Experience do men buy it for a song
> Or wisdom for a dance in the street? No it is bought with the price
> Of all that a man hath his house his wife his children
> Wisdom is sold in the desolate market where none come to buy
> And in the witherd field where the farmer plows for bread in vain[15]

In these carefully measured, and carefully handwritten, cadences we come closer to the centre of Blake himself – measured, aphoristic, didactic, tightly controlled. Yet they will eventually be seen as part of a vast, rambling and unfinished epic that was continually being altered and revised, deleted and rewritten, until it became confused and on occasions incomprehensible. And here too, in this movement between discipline and disorder, control and chaos, we come closer to the paradoxes within Blake.

The edition of *Night Thoughts* was first intended for publication in the summer of 1796, but by then he had completed only twenty-two plates; it was advertised again at the end of the year by Richard Edwards, noting 'the bold and masterly execution' of Blake's work, and a prospectus was issued in the following spring. The print run would have been small, and approximately two hundred copies were issued; some of these were coloured, and it is possible that Blake made a 'master copy' that was then used as a model by professional colourists. *Night Thoughts* finally appeared in the winter of 1797, but in a much less ambitious form than had originally been proposed. Only four nights were illustrated, the number of volumes had been reduced from four to this single book, and there were forty-three rather than two hundred engravings. A copy printed on vellum was placed on view in James Edwards's shop in Pall Mall, while Blake's water-colours were no doubt displayed in Richard Edwards's own establishment. It was not a wholly propitious time to publish such an expensive edition, but the main reason for its truncated appearance seems to have been a loss of interest on the part of Richard Edwards himself. He came into an inheritance, and abandoned publishing in the following year in order to become a senior civil servant in Minorca. Blake wished to complete the project to his own satisfaction, however, and arranged the finished watercolours in two volumes before handing them to Edwards. It is not clear if he was paid in full for his work over these two years but it seems likely that, for part of his remuneration, he was given the copper plate he had used for the engravings as well as any surplus paper. There is a possibility that he tried to publish another edition of the engravings for his own financial purposes, but no record of any such enterprise survives.

Once more his hopes for public success and financial independence had not been fulfilled; he earned far less than he had expected, and there were no reviews of the edition itself. He does not seem to have been particularly dejected, however, and the following year he offers one clue to his state of mind in this period of neglect and frustration: 'He who has few Things to desire cannot have many to fear'.[16] Almost immediately he started work upon another project. He took the unused paper that had come from Edwards and began to make a fair copy of the poem which he had been composing while working on *Night Thoughts*. Its actual nature will be discussed at the time when he came close to completing it, but it is enough to note now that he designed it to be printed in a much more orthodox form than any of his illuminated books. The experience of working on so 'public' a poem as Young's, with its projected sale of two hundred, may have encouraged him to believe that he might be able to create something of a similar kind; his would be a poem, also in nine nights, which might find subscribers of a fashionable or conventional sort. The illuminated prophecies had not been the culmination of Blake's artistic ambitions but, rather, one stage in a continuing process.

Certainly he now became more accommodating with individual commissions, and more compliant with specific patrons. John Flaxman's wife, Ann, had admired his work on *Night Thoughts*, and described Blake as 'a Native poet [& an Artist] & sings his wood notes [unfettered by any rule] whose genius soars above all rule'. She anticipated the production of the illustrated volume in an equally fulsome manner: 'twill be a [very] lily of the Valley or [Mountain daisy] the Meadows queen, twill be in short the choicest wild flower in Linneas System'.[17] It is interesting that she should characterise Blake in such conventionally sentimental terms, since it suggests that his real genius was quite overlooked even by those who were close to him. In the following year she repeated her praise in a similar way: 'Native Poet he & one who has sung his wood notes wild – of a Strong and Singular Imagination – he has treated his Poet most Poetically – Flaxman has employ'd him to Illuminate the works of Gray for my library.'[18] Flaxman's commission was no doubt designed to amuse and please his wife, but it was also a gentle and informal way of supporting his friend. There is no doubt that Blake relished the commission, however; he fully agreed with Gray's belief in the Celtic or bardic origins of poetry, and Gray's ode 'The Bard' was to inspire two separate paintings by him.

He purchased or was given an early edition of the poetry, from which he removed the introductory matter and concluding notes; then he pasted each page of the text upon the surplus paper that Richard Edwards had given to him, and very rapidly drew watercolour images around it. No preliminary drawings of these watercolours survive, and it is likely that Blake improvised as he went along. On the title page he wrote 'Drawings By William Blake', and added a small image of a young man with a lyre riding upon a swan's back. He seems deliberately to be projecting here the sentimental image that Ann Flaxman had conceived of him, and on the last page of the text he wrote a poem to her in which he used her own 'wild flower' imagery: 'A little Flower grew in a lonely Vale . . .'[19] There are times when he seems ready to subdue his own identity, and to adopt whatever persona or role is most agreeable to others. His illustrations to Gray are in fact more powerful than the botanical imagery might suggest. The fourteen illustrations to 'The Bard' alone are magnificent recreations of the epic spirit, his monumental image of the poet with white beard and star-spangled gown like some evocation of primeval magic. But Blake's particular ability to conjure such monumental images within so small a space has the consequence, intended or unintended, of lending an air of strangeness, and even on occasions monstrousness, to his creations. It is indeed as if they were derived from some ancient source of power. But other watercolours in the collection are more fanciful and decorative; they shimmer in pale blues, and yellows, and pinks and, like the best of Georgian pastels, look as if some portion of the sky had come down upon the earth and left its brightness there. They evince what Gray himself, in his 'Ode for Music', describes as 'The liquid language of the skies'.[20]

There were other commissions in this period, but he had resumed his work as a self-employed engraver at an unpropitious time. One of his profession declared that the privations and difficulties of war had consigned all artistic activity to 'an abject and almost expiring state',[21] while another contemporary wrote, 'The engraving of Pictures is at present but a dull business. The war occasions a scarcity of cash, people in general find it difficult to obtain the necessary comforts of life, and have not a surplus of money for elegancies.'[22] He placed his name in Holden's Triennial Dictionary as 'William Blake, Engraver, Lambeth Green', but in fact he was still largely dependent for friends upon the few commissions that he received in the years immediately following Night Thoughts.[23] Flaxman maintained the assistance he had given by employing Blake to engrave three designs for a 'Naval Pillar or Monument' that he proposed to set up in Greenwich as a memorial to various maritime heroes. George Cumberland, who had already helped him to obtain work on Stuart and Revett's *The Antiquities of Athens*, also commissioned him to design and engrave a map for his *An Attempt to Describe Hafod* – Hafod being a district in North Wales where Thomas Johnes had built a Gothic house that included, among other extravagant fancies, a 'Druid' temple. In fact Cumberland may also have hoped to introduce Blake to Johnes as a possible patron; Johnes was MP for Radnor but a civilised man who claimed to be able to trace his lineage back to the rulers of the ancient Britons and who had inherited a library of early Welsh manuscripts. He was also a patron of the contemporary arts, and at various times commissioned both Stothard and Fuseli to decorate his house with various medieval scenes. He was precisely the sort of person likely to have been interested in Blake's work and, indeed, Johnes purchased one copy of *Songs of Innocence*.

It cannot be said that Blake's journeyman work as an engraver, even for his friends, was in any degree remarkable – there is nothing so interesting as his illustrations for Stedman's *Narrative* – and the conventionality that he willingly adopted is perhaps seen to best effect in his engraving of a carpet advertisement which he executed at this time. It is a rather charming piece, showing various carpet-makers busied about their looms, and may, by a stretch of the biographical imagination, be related to a line he was later to write about those 'who labour in Tirzahs Looms for bread';[24] but it is hardly the kind of art upon which he wished to be engaged, at a time when his contemporaries were being celebrated for their more formal achievements. Nevertheless he needed to obtain work wherever he could find it since, as he explained in a letter to Cumberland, 'I live by Miracle . . . as to Engraving, in which art I cannot reproach myself with any neglect, yet I am laid by in a corner as if I did not Exist, & Since my Young's Night Thoughts have been publish'd, Even Johnson & Fuseli have discarded my Graver'.[25] In fact the last commission from those two gentlemen had concerned some engravings for Allen's *A New and Improved History of England* and *A New and Improved Roman History*; the reason for their neglect is not clear, although Blake claimed that both men had tried to dissuade him from continuing his own creative work, and that Johnson in particular had 'written such letters to me as would have called for the sceptre of Agamemnon rather than the tongue of Ulysses'.[26] So it is safe to assume that there were, at the very least, misunderstandings and perhaps arguments between Blake and his erstwhile employers. He was always sensitive, and rightly so, to the charge that his own creative work was of no real consequence.

Yet in the same letter where he lamented his being 'laid by in a corner', he mentioned a more promising venture. 'I am Painting small Pictures from the Bible . . . My Work pleases my employer, & I have an order for Fifty small Pictures at One Guinea each, which is Something better than mere copying after another artist.'[27] The 'employer' was Thomas Butts, and this first reference to him by Blake brings into his life a man who for the next twenty years was to become his most important friend and patron. Butts was a Swedenborgian, and was probably introduced to Blake by his co-religionist Flaxman; he was working as chief clerk in the office of the Muster-master General (which would soon be known as the War Office) and, like most government servants of the period, the system of fees and patronage allowed him to acquire a modest fortune. He owned a large house in Great Marlborough Street (where, according to the 1801 census, there were some nineteen females), and he speculated in various forms of shares and property ventures. Blake painted a miniature portrait of him that shows a slight and rather dandified man; he looks like a typically eighteenth-century 'man of feeling', so fully documented by Henry Mackenzie in his novel of that name, but he also possessed considerable commercial acumen and was blessed by a strong religious sensibility. The two men seem to have found enough in common, at least, to have become acquainted almost immediately; they were soon meeting regularly on Tuesday evenings, and Blake was even assisting Mrs Butts with the designs for her needlework. Butts treated Blake with respect touched by good-humoured condescension, while Blake seems to have considered Butts as a friend sent by providence to assist him. For the next ten years, in fact, he provided the artist with a modest but steady income and there is some truth to Samuel Palmer's claim that he was the one man who 'stood between the greatest designer in England and the workhouse'.[28]

The first of his commissions was the series of fifty biblical paintings Blake had mentioned to Cumberland, which he completed at an approximate rate of one each week. The subjects must have been chosen in consultation with Butts, but the technique and vision were all Blake's own. He actually followed much the same method of painting that he had used on the colour prints, with the difference that he was now generally working upon canvas rather than copper plate. Once more he was intent upon providing depth and mass to the surfaces of his pictures; his first step was to cover the canvas ground with a mixture of whiting and carpenter's glue, and then he began building up his image with thin layers of watercolour, which were themselves washed over with glue. In this way he achieved the effects of firmness and density, to such an extent that these paintings sometimes seem like exercises in bas-relief. He had spent his life working with materials of various kinds – inks, papers, coppers – and, in this period, he seems similarly preoccupied with the tactile nature of his medium. He did occasionally paint upon copper, perhaps when he found a piece of the appropriate size in his studio, and at least once he used what looks suspiciously like a piece of scrap metal – one of his most powerful works, 'The Agony in the Garden', is painted upon a fragment of iron covered with red lead. Perhaps he found it in his own garden, and decided that it was the appropriate object to depict the sacred scene. His painting medium itself is characteristically known as tempera but Blake sometimes referred to his works in this style as 'frescoes', with specific reference to what he considered to be the unjustly neglected art of the fifteenth century. But the term also suggests the kind of urban and public art to which he still aspired.

The paintings have the figural restraint and grace that are associated with the works of the Italian masters, and it is perhaps worth remarking in this context that Blake's religious imagery has very little to do with standard Protestant iconography. With subjects such as 'The Christ Child Asleep on a Cross' and 'The Child Christ Taught by the Virgin to Read' we are entering a world of Catholic art in which he 'dwelt with particular affection on the memory of Fra Angelico, often speaking of him as an inspired inventor and as a saint'.[29] For this series of temperas he took fifteen subjects from the Old Testament, and thirty-five from the New; he dwelt particularly upon the life of Christ, therefore, and portrayed him through the stages of his infancy, ministry and passion. He called his works 'Visions of Eternity' and in 1798, the year before he began the series, he was already trying to elucidate the eternal significance of Christ's pilgrimage upon the earth.[30] He was furiously annotating Bishop Watson's An Apology for the Bible, which he considered to be no more than a piece of vicious priestcraft designed to maintain 'The Beast & the Whore' against certain political subversives.[31] Yet he is less concerned with Watson's attack on Paine and on republicanism than on the true revelation of the Bible: 'the consideration of these things is the [entire] whole duty of man & the affairs of life & death trifles sports of time But these considerations business of Eternity'.[32] That is why he was so happy to undertake Butts's commission, where he could dwell within Eternity for the sake of his art. In one of these paintings, 'Christ the Mediator', the figure of Jesus is seen with his arms upraised in much the same posture as Blake depicted in 'Albion Rose'; it is the attitude that has become known as the 'Divine Human' or, as Blake had read in Boehme, 'God is not a person except in Christ'.[33]

There is another aspect of these temperas that is anticipated in his annotations. 'Christ came not to call the Virtuous,' he wrote. Indeed, 'The Gospel is Forgiveness of Sins & has No Moral Precepts'.[34] This is the spirit or animating breath within these extraordinary paintings, where Blake has composed each canvas as part of some intense and continuing drama of redemption; the characteristic movement is one of reverent and arrested gesture, as if the eternal significance of the scene has been caught for ever. In a certain sense they resemble the images of his earlier art, but these are quieter works precisely because they possess an independent and coherent significance of their own; the depiction of his private visionary world, in the colour prints and in the illuminated prophecies, tends towards stridency in its ambition to be immediately effective. But the figures of Jesus, of Mary and of the Old Testament patriarchs are already infolded within a known biblical narrative; as a result they seem fuller here, and less vehement. Critics and art historians have also suggested that, despite Blake's later tirades against the 'demons' of Venetian and post-Renaissance art, these temperas have in part been influenced by the respective works of Titian and of Rembrandt; in particular, Blake's use of light, characteristically radiating from one source, has affinities with what he would eventually call their 'Blots & Blurs'.[35]

In fact a proximate cause can be found for the alteration in his practice. At the end of 1798, just before he began work on the temperas for Butts, the most important exhibition of Old Masters hitherto held in London was opened to the public. At Mr Bryan's Gallery at No. 88 Pall Mall, and at the Lyceum in the Strand, a shilling admitted visitors to what was, for most of them, the first sight of Caravaggio, Veronese, Correggio, Raphael, Poussin, Michelangelo, Raphael, Titian and Tintoretto. The effect of this joint exhibition can perhaps best be described in the words of William Hazlitt: 'I was staggered when I saw the works there collected, and looked at them with wondering and with longing eyes. A mist passed away from my sight; the scales fell off . . . to see them face to face, to be in the same room with their deathless productions, was like

breaking some mighty spell – was almost an effect of necromancy!'[36] It
is not at all fanciful to imagine a similar response from Blake; when he
saw a somewhat inferior exhibition six years later he felt himself
'enlightened' and 'drunk with intellectual vision', and the impact
upon him of seeing Rembrandt or Veronese for the first time cannot
be over-emphasised.[37] Certainly it seems to have had a direct effect
upon his artistic method, since the series of tempera paintings are
imbued with a classical spirit quite different from the work he had
previously completed at Lambeth. There are reports that Fuseli urged
him to move in such a direction and abjure his more innovative and
apparently unruly productions, and there are signs that he took advice
of this or a similar kind. He even exhibited two of the temperas at the
Royal Academy after an absence of fourteen years – he showed 'The
Last Supper' in 1799 and 'The Miracle of the Loaves and Fishes' in
1800 – and this in turn suggests that he was intent upon rejoining the
main current of English art. He still maintained his emphasis upon a
central axis within each painting, with strong vertical symmetries
controlling the composition, but he enlarged his vision in order to
include more familiar 'classical' elements. In particular he introduced
effects of perspective, which he had previously eschewed, and
composed swelling landscapes of hills and buildings behind his central
figures that suggest he had intently studied Poussin or Claude Lorrain
in the Pall Mall gallery. The alteration may even be related to his
decision to publish his new poem in more conventional format; it
seems that his period of experiment was over and that, in want of
income or renown, he had decided to return to more orthodox styles.

Such attempts were not always successful, however. When he
executed the frontispiece to an edition of Bürger's *Leonora*, he was
accused by two periodical writers of creating 'an effect perfectly
ludicrous' and of possessing a 'depraved fancy'.[38] He could also be
unfortunate with his patrons. George Cumberland, perpetually eager
to help a friend whom he considered a man of genius, had introduced
him to the Reverend John Trusler; Trusler was a clergyman and
author who specialised in the 'how to' books that were so popular in
this period – *The Way to be Rich and Respectable* and *A Sure Way to
Lengthen Life* were two of his many titles. He commissioned Blake to
complete four watercolours, 'Malevolence' and 'Benevolence' to be
followed by 'Pride' and 'Humility'. As soon as he saw Blake's version
of 'Malevolence', however, the commission was cancelled.
Apparently Trusler considered it unreal and incomprehensible, and

in a letter Blake met his objections with something like fury. It is worth quoting his response in some detail because it represents the first surviving evidence of his private temper and attitudes. It begins with a rebuke to the 'Revd Sir' for questioning his judgment – 'I really am sorry that you are fall'n out with the Spiritual World' – and then goes on with an even more haughty reprimand. 'You say that I want somebody to Elucidate my Ideas. But you ought to know that What is Grand is necessarily obscure to Weak men. That which can be made Explicit to the Idiot is not worth my care.' Here are Blake's pride and anger in full force, and he asserts the worth of his own art by claiming that 'my figures . . . are those of Michael Angelo, Rafael & the Antique, & of the best living Models'. This was not the first or last time that he would compare himself to the great masters of the past, although he tended to do so when he was crossed or criticised in some manner. But then, after delivering these opinions, he launches into an exposition of his own beliefs. 'And I know that This World Is a World of IMAGINATION & Vision. I see Every thing I paint In This World, but Every body does not see alike. To the Eyes of a Miser a Guinea is more beautiful than the Sun, & a bag worn with the use of Money has more beautiful proportions than a Vine filled with Grapes. The tree which moves some to tears of joy is in the Eyes of others only a Green thing that stands in the way.' This is a remarkable passage, which demonstrates Blake's characteristically urgent and vigorous prose, and it is followed by an important statement of principle. 'But to the Eyes of the Man of Imagination, Nature is Imagination itself . . . To Me This World is all One continued Vision of Fancy or Imagination.'[39] He may have been speaking literally here – his own visions were persistent, and when we hear reports of Blake being 'abstracted' in company he was seeing that which others could not see. But there is also a more dogmatic or doctrinal air to his remark that 'Nature is Imagination'; he might almost have been quoting Paracelsus. Trusler sent Blake's fierce letter on to Cumberland, no doubt to explain why he could not continue to support such a man. Cumberland put it away with a scribbled note – 'Blake, dim'd with superstition'.[40]

It is not immediately clear what he meant by that, although a comment by Thomas Butts to Blake sets a partial context for it. In these late Lambeth years, according to Butts, Blake had relied upon 'certain opinions imbib'd from reading, nourish'd by indulgence, and rivetted by a confin'd Conversation . . . equally prejudicial to your

Interest & Happiness'.[41] This comes from a rough draft of a letter that
Butts sent to Blake in the autumn of 1800 – typically, Blake did not
bother to keep the original – and it is hard accurately to judge the tone
of Butts's comments, which seem to veer from irony to sense and back
again. But he does add, in the next sentence, an almost jocose
reference to Blake's interest in 'dim incredulity, haggard suspicion, &
bloated philosophy'.[42] If it is a serious comment, what does it mean or
imply? Any answer must be conjectural at best, but the supposition
can be only that Blake was involved with the more exotic aspects of
religious enthusiasm; 'dim incredulity', 'indulgence' and 'confin'd
Conversation' suggest the presence of a small group of people who
held what even Butts, a Swedenborgian, considered highly un-
conventional views. Perhaps a clue is to be found in Blake's friend and
colleague, the painter Richard Cosway, who had already praised him
to Farington as a man 'of extraordinary genius and imagination'.[43]
Cosway was not only a famous and fashionable painter; he was also a
mesmerist and magician who practised *arcana* related to alchemical
and cabbalistic teaching. There are reports of erotic ceremonies, the
imbibing of drugs or 'elixirs', and ritual nudity.[44] Blake was no
stranger to the symbols or beliefs of a man such as Cosway – the
manuscript of the poem he was now writing contains many drawings
of bizarre sexual imagery, including women sporting giant phalli and
children engaged in erotic practices with adults. In a shorter poem
which he wrote at this time he depicts, albeit in half-jocular fashion,
his own casting of a spell: 'And turnd himself round three times
three'.[45] But his actual belief in the potency of magic never left him,
and some years later he believed that one of his drawings had been
effaced as the result of what he called 'some malignant spell' by
Thomas Stothard.[46] There are other currents of strange belief that
swirl around him in this period. Many of his friends and acquaintances were, as has been noted, Freemasons; in this period that group
was connected with political radicalism and revolutionary politics
but, in the words of one contemporary pamphlet, entitled *Proofs of a
Conspiracy Against all the Religions and Governments of Europe carried
on in the Secret Meetings of Free Masons, Illuminati and Reading Societies*,
it was also associated with 'the mystical whims of J. Behmen and
Swedenborg – by the fanatical and knavish doctrines of the modern
Rosycrucians – by Magicians – Magnetisers –Exorcists'.[47] So an
interest in Boehme and Swedenborg was considered close to belief in
magic and faith healing.

There were other groups, who met at the Green Dragon in Cripplegate, or the Angel in Cecil Court, or in the debating room near Bunhill Row. There were the 'Ancient Deists' of Hoxton, for example, who included 'Alchymists, Astrologers, Calculators, Mystics, Magnetisers, Prophets and Projectors of every kind'; in their assemblies there was talk of spirits and prophecy, while 'any visitor not in the habit of hearing supernatural voices, or not informed of the common occurrences of the day, by the ministration of Angels, would have been treated as a novice'.[48] There is a strain of thought here that is connected to Blake's own speculations. Magical belief is generally considered to be the resort of the thwarted or powerless, who feel that they can exercise control in no other way; this is why it is also appealing to the paranoid and the fantasist. That is one way of looking at it and, indeed, Blake succumbed to many such sensations and fears in the course of his life. But it is perhaps an anachronistic way of considering magical practice, which in the late eighteenth century had more serious purposes. It was of course related to the old popular and urban traditions of which Blake was the instinctive heir (hence his attacks upon Newton and upon Locke) but it was also seen, through the agency of mesmerism, as a powerful and innovative way of understanding or controlling the world. Mesmerism, in particular, was considered to exercise a profound influence over the vital fluids and spirits of the universe. If he ever sensed an incompatibility between his extraordinary images of Christ or of Mary and these magical beliefs, then he needed only to consider the example of Paracelsus as one who was both a devout Christian and a practising magician in a world where 'everything that lives is holy!' If the heavens are within man, then man can control the heavens. Christ himself is the paradigm of the 'Divine Human', and the great exemplar of Paracelsus's magical belief that 'Each man has the essence of God, and all the wisdom and the power of the world within himself'.[49] This is the area in which all of Blake's beliefs also come together.

It is, at least, a possible reconstruction, and one that would have been very disturbing to those who took a more orthodox attitude to matters of faith and worship. Certainly both George Cumberland and Thomas Butts believed that he had lost his way among superstition and dim credulity. But in fact his own remarks betray a certain ambivalence about the course of his life at the very end of the eighteenth century. There are times when it seems that he never made any decisions about his worldly career, and was happy to move along in his own abstracted and distracted manner. He is somehow lost in the world, unable to deal with its claims or cope with its responsibilities, trusting entirely to the sacredness of his visions and the truth of his visionary art. His ferocious reply to Trusler suggests how sensitive he was to criticism, and yet at the same time he appears entirely sanguine about his prospects. He explains to Trusler that he is always guided by 'my Genius or Angel',[50] and then goes on to assert that 'I am happy to find a Great Majority of Fellow Mortals who can Elucidate My Visions',[51] while to Cumberland he explained, 'I laugh at Fortune & Go on & on. I think I foresee better Things than I have ever seen.'[52] This becomes one of his constant refrains, and there was an element of exuberant hopefulness in him that had always to contend with feelings of doubt and despair. In the same letter to Cumberland he remarks that 'Tho' I laugh at Fortune, I am perswaded that She Alone is the Governor of Worldly Riches, & when it is Fit She will call on me; till then I wait with Patience'.[53] It is the same attitude, subtly modified, that he expressed in his annotations to the essays of Francis Bacon (which he detested for their worldly and 'civilised' air); he asks, 'What is Fortune but an outward Accident for a few years sixty at most & then gone'.[54] There may be a plaintive or dismissive note here, according to reading, and the ambiguity is strengthened by a small detail he added in his illustrations to Gray's poems. In his designs for 'Elegy Written in a Country Church-Yard', as an example of 'th'unhonoured Dead', he puts his own name upon a tombstone. But then in a succeeding drawing his soul is seen soaring towards the sky. His enthusiasm and optimism struggled with a sense of defeat or neglect, while his religious quietism was opposed by the anxieties of thwarted ambition. At the turn of the century he was forty-three years old, and with only a confused sense of his direction. His next move was to be away from Lambeth, and out of London.

NINETEEN

Felphams Vale

I t began with a death. The natural son of William Hayley, Thomas Alphonso, was crippled by a disease related to the curvature of his spine; he was only nineteen, but he was already a proficient linguist and artist. His father had taught him well: he could 'spout Shakespeare' at three, and was learning Latin at four.[1] But his central interest was in art, and when John Flaxman returned from Italy he agreed to take on the boy as an apprentice sculptor. Even at this time Thomas Alphonso knew, or knew of, Blake; in the summer of 1796 he wrote to his father, 'I have not yet seen anything of Blake or his drawings . . . I may if possible take a walk to his house tomorrow morning';[2] it was, as he said, a 'great distance' from Flaxman's house in Fitzroy Square to the Blake household in Lambeth, but he did meet them at a later date. There is, at least, a reference, to the fact that 'he drank tea on the other side of the river'.[3]

Three years later Thomas Alphonso was dying. His father, in great anxiety and perturbation of spirits, wanted his son's work to be memorialised in some way. Hayley had been writing a series of verse epistles to John Flaxman, under the title of *An Essay on Sculpture*, and he wished to include in that intended volume an engraving of his son's drawings of Pericles and Demosthenes as well as a portrait of the boy himself. Flaxman suggested Blake as an appropriate choice as engraver, and in the early months of 1800 Blake set to work on the commission. But, even though Thomas Alphonso lay dying, he was once again late in finishing and delivering his work; he seems to have managed the image of Demosthenes but he was very slow in finishing the portrait head of the young artist, who was called by his father the 'interesting Invalid' or 'beloved Cripple'.[4] In March Flaxman wrote to

Hayley to tell him that Blake had been sent the portrait medallion of Thomas Alphonso, which he was to copy, some four weeks before: 'but perhaps You are not acquainted with Mr Blake's direction? it is No 13 Hercules Buildings near the Asylum, Surry Side of Westminster Bridge'.[5] Blake soon became aware that his work was impatiently expected, and 'With all possible expedition I send you a proof of my attempt to Express your & our Much Beloved's Countenance'; he went on to pray that 'Jesus and his Angels' might alleviate the young man's suffering.[6] He may have worked on it too hastily, however, since it did not please Hayley at all – to a friend he described the engraving as 'a most mortifying disappointment' and the 'dear cripple' himself had agreed. Hayley was extremely delicate with Blake, however: 'Truth, precision, & Force of character,' he wrote, '. . . is so apt to escape from the firmest & ablest Hand.'[7] In any case it was hardly a situation in which Blake could become aggrieved or resentful; so, at Hayley's request, he altered the plate on two separate occasions. But he did not manage to finish the final version in time; at the beginning of May, Thomas Alphonso died. A few days later Blake sent a letter of condolence: 'I know that our deceased friends are more really with us than when they were apparent to our mortal part. Thirteen years ago I lost a brother & with his spirit I converse daily & hourly in the Spirit and See him in my remembrance in the regions of my Imagination. I hear his advice & even now write from his Dictate. Forgive me for Expressing to you my Enthusiasm which I wish all to partake of Since it is to me a Source of Immortal Joy: even in this world by it I am the companion of Angels.'[8] Here he is not necessarily describing those visions that surrounded him continually; he is depicting those 'Angels' or 'Spirits' which, like that of his dead brother, he sees in 'remembrance' and 'in the regions of my Imagination'. These are the 'Eternals' who 'Dictate swift winged words' of his verse, just as his brother dictates this letter to Hayley;[9] they are the powers of memory and the imagination that create art and that, in Blake's non-Newtonian universe, are not abstract forces but spiritual beings. His letter then goes on to combine, in characteristically Blakean style, the visionary with the practical: 'The Ruins of Time builds Mansions in Eternity. – I have also sent A Proof of Pericles for your Remarks.'[10] Thus began the strange friendship between William Blake and William Hayley.

They may first have encountered one another almost thirty years before, when Blake was an apprentice with James Basire: William

Hayley then lived with his mother at No. 5 Great Queen Street, just a few yards from the engraver's shop. Then, in 1784, Flaxman had sent Hayley a copy of *Poetical Sketches* with the letter apologising for Blake's lack of education. So there was already a connection between the two men. Blake, in turn, could hardly fail to be aware of Hayley; he was one of the most famous and popular poets of the age, considered by some to be the 'greatest living poet' (at least according to Algernon Swinburne), [11] although others took a rather different view. Byron's comment is succinct: 'His style in youth or age is still the same, / Forever feeble and forever tame.' [12] Southey was a little more charitable: 'Everything about that man is good except his poetry.' [13] Hayley, whatever his merits, was certainly prolific. He was a dramatist as well as a composer of funereal odes and epitaphs; he was the biographer of Milton, the first English translator of Dante, and the composer of such aesthetic treatises as *An Essay on Epic Poetry* and *An Epistle on Painting*. By the time that Blake met him his most famous poem, *The Triumphs of Temper*, had just been published in its twelfth edition and he had even turned down the post of Poet Laureate. He was twelve years older than Blake and came from a quite different background: he had been educated at Eton and Cambridge, and tried his luck at drama before finding his métier with epic poetry of a fashionable sort. His marriage was not a success, and the crippled Thomas Alphonso Hayley sprang from his liaison with a housekeeper.

He was a tall man, of what used to be called a military bearing, but with a pronounced limp, which he had contracted after his hip joint had been affected by a childish fever. He was in certain respects what would now be considered eccentric; but in the latter part of the eighteenth century he was deemed only a little out of the ordinary. In particular, he carried a parasol or umbrella with him, which he unfurled whenever he rode upon a horse. As a consequence, and as a result of the injury, he was always falling out of the saddle and ending with upturned umbrella upon the ground. His autobiography is one of the most inadvertently comic narratives of the early nineteenth century; it is written in an ornate and convoluted prose in which he refers to himself throughout as 'Hayley' or 'the Poet' – 'The projects of Hayley,' he wrote of himself, for example, 'were generally formed in all the ardour of benevolence; and often with more zeal than discretion.' [14] Of his propensity to write funereal epitaphs and lamentations on death, he explains that it is 'a species of composition to which Hayley was so much inclined, by his native tenderness of heart'.[15] He had a commanding and impetuous disposition, but this was mitigated by an amiable and enthusiastic temper. He was active and sanguine, always rushing to do good, often prone to tears, and generally *con spirito* in the affairs of life. He patronised Flaxman and other artists of the day; he was a friend of the great historian Gibbon; he was closely acquainted with Romney and together they elaborated schemes for the combination of poetry and design; he supported Cowper at a time when his mania was beyond the comprehension of even the most enlightened contemporaries. Hayley must have seemed, then, an ideal employer for William Blake.

After he had written his letter of consolation on the death of Hayley's son, Blake himself succumbed to a profound depression. He explained to Cumberland that he had fallen into a 'Deep pit of Melancholy, Melancholy without any real reason for it';[16] in such a state he tended to avoid company, and visited only a very few people. But Hayley had come up to stay with friends in Kew after his son's funeral, and it seems likely that they met during the course of this visit – it was at any rate agreed that Blake should travel down to Hayley's house in Felpham, Sussex, in order to work on another portrait of the dead boy. He went in July, carrying with him in the chaise a bas-relief by Flaxman that Hayley had commissioned, and then decided to stay longer than he had originally planned. A few days later, towards the end of July, he and Hayley came to an important decision: Blake would rent a cottage in the small Sussex village and work, as Hayley put it to a friend, 'under my auspices'. Hayley was always full of plans and schemes, and there is no doubt that Blake saw his own prospects in a very favourable light. It was an extreme measure, to leave London and live immured in the countryside, but it must have seemed a necessary one – better to work in the country than starve in the city. Flaxman gave his blessing to the idea, in terms that suggest the neglect and insensitivity with which Blake had constantly to deal. 'I hope,' he wrote to Hayley, 'that Blake's residence at Felpham will be a Mutual Comfort to you & him, & I see no reason why he should not make as good a livelihood there as in London, if he engraves & teaches drawing . . . as also by making neat drawings of different kinds but if he places any dependence on painting large pictures, for which he is not qualified, either by habit or study, he will be miserably deceived.'[17] Blake's poetry is not even mentioned, displaying an indifference all the more serious since it was Flaxman who had originally sent *Poetical Sketches* to Hayley. Blake's later work in that medium was clearly considered to be of no consequence. It was not, perhaps, a happy omen for his new life.

But it began cheerfully enough. At the beginning of September 1800 there was a round of farewell tea parties, with the Buttses and with the Flaxmans; Catherine Blake wrote to Nancy Flaxman, in a letter composed entirely in her husband's hand, while Blake thanked Flaxman himself for his assistance. 'It is you,' he wrote, 'that I owe All my present Happiness.'[18] He even added a poem of appreciation, which ended with a flourish:

> And My Angels have told me that seeing such visions I could not
> subsist on the Earth
> But by my conjunction with Flaxman, who knows how to forgive
> Nervous Fear.[19]

An inspection of this 'penny-post' letter, sealed with red wax, reveals that he originally wrote 'Nervous' with a small 'n' before changing it into a capital – which suggests, perhaps, a sense of drama or of occasion. He also hoped that 'you will forgive the Poetry', as if it were an indiscretion or extravagance on his part which his friend might not appreciate.[20] In the letter supposedly written by Catherine Blake, he also appended a poem to Nancy Flaxman, of which the following couplet is typical:

> The Bread of sweet Thought & the Wine of Delight
> Feeds the Village of Felpham by day & by night[21]

The reference to bread is more than symbolic in this context, however, since, during the weeks and days when the Blakes were preparing to leave Lambeth, London itself was the scene of intermittent but ferocious riots over the price of that staple commodity. In this same letter Blake, or his wife, referred to 'the terrible desart of London';[22] for them it truly had been a desert, with little relief in sight, and no doubt they considered themselves justified in fleeing from it. But there is also an indication of more general devastation here, in a capital where a bad harvest, Napoleon's European blockade and diversion of grain to the troops, meant that there was often no bread to eat at all. Three days before the Blakes left for Felpham, the Corn-market was stormed after some handbills were pasted on the Monument declaring 'Bread will be Sixpence the Quartern If the People will Assemble at the Corn Market on Monday'.[23] On Tuesday, after the riots in the market, some bakers' shops in Whitechapel were attacked by a mob, and on the next day a handbill was addressed to 'Starved fellow Creatures' asking them to come the following night 'with proper weapons in St Georges fields, where You will meet friends to defend Your Rights Never mind the blood thirsty Soldiers We shall put them to flight . . . The Cause is honourable & ought to be prosecuted as such Rouse to glory Ye slumbering Britons'.[24] That was the day on which the Blakes travelled to Felpham.

There had been a slight delay in their departure; Catherine had become exhausted although, as Blake explained to Hayley, she 'is like a flame of many colours of precious jewels whenever she hears it [Felpham] named'.[25] He maintained the alchemical note in a postscript – 'My fingers Emit sparks of fire with Expectation of my future labours'.[26] Finally, on Thursday morning, they left Lambeth for ever. They had packed everything in sixteen heavy boxes; among other things they had to store his copper plates, containing all of his engraved work, as well as the stock of illuminated books that had already been printed. Then there was all the unused paper, the inks and graving tools as well as the wooden press itself. There was a small quantity of furniture, clothes (which Catherine made), and domestic necessities. In fact Blake's sister, whose presence is rarely felt in this biography, had to be enlisted for the journey as an extra 'hand'. They set off from one of the coaching inns between six and seven in the morning, and arrived at their new cottage just before midnight; the journey of some seventy miles had taken seventeen hours. They had to change seven times, but it was a fine day for travelling and 'Our Journey was very pleasant . . . No Grumbling, All was Chearfulness & Good Humour'.[27] The next morning Blake came out of his cottage and found a ploughman at work in a neighbouring field. At this moment the ploughboy working with him called out 'Father, the gate is open'.[28] For Blake this was an emblem of his new life, and of the work that he was about to begin.

The same sunny mood continued, and two days later he wrote a letter to Flaxman – addressing him as 'Sculptor of Eternity' – in which he extolled the virtues of the cottage, of Hayley, and of Felpham.[29] His was one continual hyperbole of enthusiasm, in which what Hayley called the 'marine cottage' was described as 'the Spontaneous Effusion of Humanity, congenial to the wants of Man';[30] at a later date he was to take a less sanguine attitude towards it, when he realised that the effusions were also those of damp and cold. It is worth remarking that at once he begins to talk about his visions – in Felpham 'voices of Celestial inhabitants are more distinctly heard, & their forms more distinctly seen, & my Cottage is also a Shadow of their houses'.[31] In fact this becomes a distinctive pattern in his expression during this period, with the material world characteristic-ally being conceived as a 'shadow' of some eternal drama elsewhere, and where his 'mortal life' or 'mortal part' is considered to be distinctly unimportant. This sounds different from his earlier celebrations of sexual energy and radical optimism, and suggests not only that he was growing older but that his 'mortal' hopes and aspirations were now being devalued or discounted. Perhaps he had decided to make a virtue out of his withdrawal from the city. His self-confidence and ambition were directed elsewhere and, as he explained in this same letter to Flaxman, 'I am more famed in Heaven for my works than I could well concieve. In my Brain are studies & Chambers fill'd with books & pictures of old, which I wrote and painted in ages of Eternity before my mortal life; & those works are the delight & Study of Archangels. Why, then, should I be anxious about the riches or fame of mortality.'[32] He had abandoned any expectation of earthly success, in other words, and resigned himself to neglect; now, having left London, his visions were a true comfort. They suggested the reassurance of a world beyond this one, and may even have assuaged his 'Nervous Fear'. Thus, as he closed his letter to Flaxman, he repeated, 'I look back into the regions of Reminiscence & behold our ancient days before this Earth appear'd in its vegetated mortality to my mortal vegetated Eyes'.[33] Two days later he wrote a letter to Thomas Butts in which he was much more circumspect about his visions: 'Meat is cheaper than in London, but the sweet air & the voices of winds, trees & birds, & the odours of the happy ground, makes it a dwelling for immortals'.[34]

Felpham was a country village near the Sussex coast, a little over a mile northeast of Bognor, with a population of five hundred. Blake rented his cottage, for twenty pounds a year, from the landlord of the Fox Inn; it was a modest thatched dwelling of a standard Sussex kind. It might have been cheaper, but sea-bathing was becoming a fashionable health cure (it was considered particularly useful in treating diseases of the glands) and Bognor was beginning its development into a proper seaside town. As Blake's landlord, Mr Grinder, put it, 'Why here are several cottages that might have been let heretofore for four or five pounds a year that [are] being now furbished up and whitewashed, with a little furniture and staircase carpets put into them.'[35] Blake's was a narrow two-storeyed cottage at right angles to the country lane that winds from the village to the shore. There were three rooms downstairs, one of them a small and cheerful kitchen with a stove. There were staircases at either end of the dwelling – one wide and very steep, the other narrow and circuitous – leading to three bedrooms. Two of these were of a rounded shape, looking like the interior of an eggshell or what Blake might have called the 'Mundane Egg', while the third and largest room, used by the Blakes, had a fireplace, a tiny wooden cupboard above the bed and a small alcove on either side of it. It was, and is, a very tranquil house, which emanates great peacefulness. From the windows at the front the Blakes gazed out upon a narrow strip of garden, cornfields, and then the sea. There was clematis over the gate, and at the back of the house, which looked towards the Sussex Downs, there stood an elm tree. He drew his new home in the pages of his long epic poem *Milton*, with a representation of himself standing on the path; in some copies he added flowers and shrubbery along the door. The cottage survives, but there was one other element in his composition which is now rarely to be seen – an angelic visitant hovers over the small garden.

> For when Los joind with me he took me in his firy whirlwind
> My Vegetated portion was hurried from Lambeths shades
> He set me down in Felphams Vale & prepard a beautiful
> Cottage for me that in three years I might write all these Visions
> To display Natures cruel holiness . . .[36]

It was a retired place, then, surrounded by fields and meadows, noticeable for the scent of wild purple thyme and for the sound of larks. Blake had never before seen the sea; he could now reach it after a walk of two minutes, and he could watch it at all times and in all seasons. The shingle was filled with tiny pebbles that reflected the extraordinary light coming off the surface of the water, and it was while sitting upon the yellow sands of the beach that he was granted his first Felpham vision: he saw 'particles bright' forming the shape of a man.[37] Once more Newton's theory of particles had been given a mystical dimension. Then that vision expanded 'Like a Sea without shore', and he saw the entire natural world as 'One Man'.[38] He was later to believe that he could only maintain his 'visionary studies' in London,[39] but in this period he was entranced by 'the shifting lights of the sea',[40] while along its shore he saw the spirits of ancient poets and prophets all, as he said, 'majestic shadows, grey but luminous, and superior to the common height of men'.[41] With this description, too, he comes close to the common depiction of what have been termed by those who see them as 'spectral bodies' or 'astral bodies', as if the light of the sea itself had acquired human form.

On his return to the cottage he might have gone past his own gate and walked sixty yards to the Fox Inn, on the left-hand side of the lane, where Mr Grinder lived with his wife and daughter; two hundred yards further along this winding lane was Hayley's own residence, Turret House, which took its name from the tower that he had built to contain his library and study. This house and its garden were shielded by high pebbled walls, and it seems that Hayley's presence in the small village aroused curious rumours. Yeats, writing in 1905, claimed that 'The people of Felpham remember Hayley to this day . . . He had two wives, they say, and kept one in a wood with her leg chained to a tree-trunk.'[42] This is probably a rustic conflation of the facts that he had an illegitimate son and was lame in one leg. A few hundred yards to the west stood the church, which was of course the focal point of this small community. Neither Hayley nor Blake is known to have attended it.

For Blake, there now opened a period of happy industry. Four days after his arrival he began work on etching and illustrating a ballad that Hayley had written on 'Little Tom the Sailor', a child who had died at sea; his mother, a Folkestone widow of straitened means, was intended to benefit by the sales of this broadsheet. Blake etched two illustrations, and Catherine Blake printed the copies on their wooden press, which they had already set up in the cottage. It is not an uninteresting production, and can be noted as one of the first examples of what he called, confusingly, 'Woodcut on Pewter', where the ground of the metal was smoked and the outlines then traced or scraped upon the dark surface.[43] It was also his first commission at Felpham, and no doubt he took care to make it a successful one. The fact that he was now illustrating the work of a poet far inferior to himself cannot have escaped his attention, although, in a depressingly humble letter to Hayley, he declares that he and his wife 'determine . . . to be happy'.[44] He might have been less happy if he had known that Hayley was now referring to him as 'my secretary'.[45]

But the decision to leave London must have then seemed a correct one, since Hayley immediately began showering him with commissions. As soon as he had finished 'Little Tom the Sailor', for example, he was set to work upon a series of 'Poetic Heads', which were to adorn the new library in Turret House. These were pen and tempera paintings on canvas, designed to look like the bas-reliefs on classical medallions, which depicted the great heroes of Hayley's literary world – eighteen of them, including Homer, Dante, Chaucer, Tasso, Milton, Spenser, Shakespeare, Otway, Dryden and Cowper. His dead son, Thomas Alphonso, was also included. Blake took great care with them, adopting very pale effects of tempera, which he had not employed before, and making sure that he included motifs that Thomas Alphonso had designed before his death. He could have got all of the 'heads' themselves from the frontispieces or illustrations in the books in Hayley's voluminous library; in particular he copied from engravings by George Vertue, which may have reminded him of the time when he studied such work as an apprentice. He painted in the cottage but made some late alterations in the library itself, which had only recently been completed. It was a long and narrow room, while leading off from it were two bedrooms and what was then known as the 'closet'. Presumably it was this propinquity of the library and lavatory that sparked off one of Blake's less flattering couplets about Hayley:

> Thus Hayley on his Toilette seeing the Sope
> Cries Homer is very much improvd by Pope.[46]

For his actual painting of Homer he added a frog and a mouse; it is an obvious reference to Batrachomyomachia, 'The Battle of the Frogs and the Mice', then attributed to the poet, but it is hard not to discern some ironic reference intended by Blake. He gave Milton a serpent and a wreath of oak, which may suggest the perils of the material world, while Shakespeare's image is surrounded by ghosts. They are striking representations and form an apt prelude to his later 'visionary heads'; it is always worth looking at the eyes of his portraits and, in this series, they are wonderfully alert and revealing. It is as if he had seen them in life, so perhaps these are the great figures he observed walking upon the sea-shore. He was also something of an amateur expert in physiognomy, having read Lavater's treatise on the subject, and he may have paused to reflect on his own visage as he traced those of his literary ancestors. George Richmond certainly saw in him a 'quivering intensity' aligned with a 'stubborn English chin',[47] while Algernon Swinburne has noted 'a preponderance of brow and head;

clear bird-like eyes, eloquent excitable mouth, with a look of nervous and fluent power . . . It is not the face of a man who could ever be cured of illusions.'[48] He also noticed that his forehead was largest above his eyes, which gave him 'an eager steadiness of passionate expression . . . the look of one who can do all things but hesitate',[49] while others have noted that the bump of ideality, at least according to the system propounded by Gall, is very pronounced upon the cerebellum.

'Mr Hayley acts like a Prince,' he told Butts, and indeed he was princely in his patronage.[50] He was seized by the idea of publishing a series of ballads, to be illustrated by Blake, which could be sold by his friends in Bath, Chichester, London and elsewhere. He proposed Blake as a drawing tutor to some of the eminent families in his neighbourhood, and he began to 'teach' Blake the art of miniature painting as a way of earning additional income. Hayley had once set out to be a miniature-painter, while he was at Cambridge, but had to retire from that employment when he found, according to his own grandiloquent testimony, that his eyes became 'drowned in blood'. He was pleased by the progress of his pupil, however, and wrote to a friend, 'I have an excellent enthusiastic Creature, a Friend of Flaxman, under my own Eye residing in this village; he is by profession an Engraver, but he says I have taught Him to paint in miniature, & in Truth He has improved his excellent versatile Talents very much in this retired scene.'[51] Hayley had originally written 'taught Him to paint' and then inserted 'in miniature' afterwards, which suggest how little he knew – or had been told – about Blake's real abilities. Blake was actually an excellent miniaturist, as might be expected from a man who had spent his life with a graver's burin, and he completed several commissions. Some of them were undertaken for Hayley himself, or for Hayley's friends, but he also presented one to Thomas Butts and continued to produce them intermittently over the next few years – 'Miniature,' he explained to Butts, in one of those phrases by which he gave life and form to all activities, 'is become a Goddess in my Eyes, & my Friends in Sussex say that I Excel in the pursuit.'[52] In fact he redeployed the economical use of stipple, so essential to miniature, in many of his later and larger works: he was an expert technician who never forgot an appropriate lesson. Even while experimenting with this new medium, however, other commissions crowded upon him – Flaxman sent on a request from a collector while, at the same time, Blake was beginning work upon illustrating the ballads that Hayley was writing. Then there was the prospect of additional work when Hayley agreed to write the life of his old friend William Cowper.

Cowper had died in the spring of 1800, just a week before the death of Hayley's son, but this double burden of grief did not mitigate Hayley's usual industry. And as soon as he had decided to write the biography he asked Blake to undertake much of the engraving work for it with portraits of Cowper and of Cowper's mother. There were certain problems that complicated the project, however, the largest of them being Lady Hesketh. She was Cowper's cousin, a woman of decided and sometimes hysterical views about her famous relative. When Hayley sent her a miniature of Cowper that Blake had executed from a painting by Romney, she replied, 'the Sight of it has in *real truth* inspired me with a degree of *horror*, which I shall not recover from in haste! . . . I cannot restrain my Pen from declaring that I think it *dreadful*! *Shocking*!'[53] There would be further outbursts from her over the next few months, but Hayley generally managed to surmount her objections with tact, benevolent compliments and charming vignettes of what he described as 'the Engraver & the Hermit' – meaning Blake and himself.[54] Blake is 'the friendly artist by my side . . . the friendly Zealous Engraver who daily works by my side . . . my worthy artist who works constantly in my study'.[55] He was to be seen, therefore, as very much Hayley's creature.

Lady Hesketh was most troubled, and incensed, by any suggestion of Cowper's insanity; she vigorously objected to any traces of 'enthusiasm' in Blake's engravings of his features, and indeed any hint of wildness was removed from the finished portraits. Cowper had suffered from religious mania of an extreme kind, and believed that he was irrevocably damned; he had spent some time in an asylum, but in the latter years of his life had been looked after by friends and relatives. He remained 'a stricken deer, that left the herd / Long since'.[56] As such he must have been of interest to Blake, who had himself suffered from the imputation of insanity and even religious mania – 'dim'd with superstition' had been Cumberland's phrase. He must have discussed Cowper with Hayley, even as he worked upon his visage, and he became acquainted with some of those who had known Cowper well. In fact the story of his depression and madness stayed with Blake for a long time, and almost twenty years later he added a handwritten note to Spurzheim's *Observations on Insanity*, which he had been reading with great attention: 'Cowper came to me & said. O that I were insane always I will never rest. Can you not make me truly insane. I will never rest till I am so. O that in the bosom of God I was hid. You retain health & yet are as mad as any of us all – over us all – mad as a refuge from unbelief – from Bacon Newton & Locke.'[57] This represents a very subtle appreciation by Blake of what would now no doubt be described as the cultural origins of insanity; he understood that the charge of madness would be laid against those who refused to accept the mechanical world of late eighteenth-century science and philosophy. He is also implying that 'madness' is simply an analogue for religious belief in an increasingly secular and deistical world. That is why Blake was considered to be insane. But the despairing poet had not seen as far as Blake – 'Can you not make me truly insane,' he asks him. Cowper had succumbed to fears and delusions because he had accepted the conventional view of insanity, and had not trusted his own capacity for religious reawakening. It is a crucial point in Blake's understanding of himself because the more orthodox philosophers in this period tended to equate any form of religious enthusiasm with mental derangement; to claim divine inspiration, as Blake often did, was to be almost automatically labelled insane. If he had lived in the early decades of the seventeenth century his descriptions of 'Spirits' and 'Angels' would have been considered exceptional but not necessarily inaccurate or fantastic; by the latter half of the eighteenth century they were considered the delusions of madmen. Blake knew instinctively how to withstand the orthodoxies and fashions of his time, however, but Cowper had doubted himself – and that, in Blake's eyes, was perhaps the single greatest mistake of an artist's life. It seems likely that the shade of Cowper is incorporated into the 'Spectre' who torments Los in *Jerusalem* and who delivers one of the most extraordinary and accurate versions of depressive madness in the eighteenth century:

>   the joys of God advance
> For he is Righteous: he is not a Being of Pity & Compassion
> He cannot feel Distress: he feeds on Sacrifice & Offering:
> Delighting in cries & tears & clothed in holiness & solitude
> But my griefs advance also, for ever & ever without end
> O that I could cease to be! Despair! I am Despair
> Created to be the great example of horror & agony . . .
> To be all evil, all reversed & for ever dead: knowing
> And seeing life, yet living not; how can I then behold
> And not tremble; how can I be beheld & not abhorrd[58]

So the story of Cowper's life acted as both a lesson and a warning to Blake – a lesson on the need for courage and self-confidence, and a warning against self-doubt and melancholy. He had known both confidence and despair – indeed it might be said that his life in these years was poised between the two – but at least he had never for long lost faith in his visions.

About a year after he had moved to Felpham he was walking through the fields to the nearby village of Lavant, in order to meet his sister who was arriving on the London coach, and once more he had one of those spiritual epiphanies in which the meaning of his life was vouchsafed to him. It is difficult to understand the precise nature of this particular vision, since his description is couched in a set of cryptic verses, but it seems to concern the question of whether he should return to London or stay at Felpham. The dead members of his family surround him, as do various angels and demons in concert together; a thistle is transformed into an old man who warns Blake not to return to the capital, while the sun becomes an image of Los descending to the ground 'in fierce flames'.[59] In some way Blake defies him, and then he goes on to celebrate the very faculty of vision itself, which allows him to rise above human claims and preoccupations:

> Now I a fourfold vision see,
> And a fourfold vision is given to me.[60]

But the visions did not necessarily interfere with his work, as they had done in London, and these first months were a time of great industry and application – 'Engraving, of all human Works, appears to require the largest Portion of patience,' Hayley wrote to a friend, 'and he [Blake] happily possesses more of that inestimable Virtue, than I ever saw united before to an Imagination so lively & so prolific!'[61] Indeed Hayley seems to have thought more highly of his colleague's powers than Flaxman, who declined an invitation to visit Blake on account of his busy employment in London. And whatever Blake may have thought or said at a later date, he did feel a genuine affection for Felpham and for Hayley during this period. As Hayley wrote to Flaxman, 'our good Blake grows more & more attach'd to this pleasant marine village, & seems to gain in it a perpetual increase of improving Talents & settled Comfort'.[62]

It was in certain respects a life of routine, even if the routine was primarily one of work – all the more arduous because the thatching over the ground-floor windows blocked out much of the light. Hayley was astonished once to enter the cottage, in the heat of an August afternoon, and find him 'grinding away, graver in hand'.[63] There were still moments when his visions gained mastery over him and he would be abstracted, brooding, until he again displayed 'the quiet pluck with which he always buckled to etching when Mrs Blake placed the "empty plate" upon the little round oak table'.[64] On other occasions he worked with his patron in the new library, and in Hayley's correspondence there are constant references to 'we' – 'I say we, for the warm-hearted indefatigable Blake was daily by my side'.[65] They remained together in their leisure hours, too, and it was Blake's habit to join Hayley on his Tuesday and Friday visits to Miss Harriet Poole in nearby Lavant; they rode out there for breakfast, Blake mounted on a horse called Bruno, and in the company of 'Paulina', as the lady was known, Hayley would write letters and correct proofs, which had been sent ahead, read aloud from his latest works, and engage in what was then described as 'general conversation'. It seems, however, that the good Paulina 'was perpetually uneasy on account of Hayley's open umbrella; and when they left her to return to Felpham, she would watch them with her telescope, and once she had the fright of seeing Hayley thrown – "tost into the air" '.[66] No doubt the umbrella broke his fall.

There were other friends and visitors who, according to their extant correspondence, seem to have warmed to the Blakes as much as Hayley himself. One acquaintance even wanted to present them with a white kitten (Blake always preferred cats to dogs). An undergraduate from Oxford, Edward Garrard Marsh, made frequent visits to Felpham; he was also a poet and read, or sung, his verses to the two older men. Blake, fitting in with the general tenor of Hayley's magniloquence, described him as 'the Bard of Oxford' whose verses 'still sound upon my Ear like the distant approach of things mighty & magnificent' – given the feeble nature of Marsh's poetry, this demonstrates that Blake was also given to hyperbole and exaggeration on appropriate occasions.[67] Marsh returned the compliment when, in a letter to Hayley mentioning 'the poetical sculptor' (or engraver), he adds, 'I long to hear Mr Blake's devotional air, though (I fear) I should have been very awkward in the attempt to give notes to his music. His ingenuity will however (I doubt not) discover some method of preserving his compositions upon paper, though he is not well versed in bars and crotchets.'[68] Here again is an account of Blake singing his own lyrics, and even composing or improvising music for them; it corroborates the earlier record of his 'songs' in the drawing-room of Mrs Mathew, and we will discover that in old age he also sang his own work. It suggests, of course, how intimately some of his poetry is tied to music while at the same time it confirms how close he came to the popular urban tradition of ballads and street songs. The identity of the 'devotional air' he performed at Felpham is not at all clear; the only real example that survives is the famous poem that he placed at the beginning of one of his epics. It is interesting to consider Blake singing, then, in the study of Hayley's home in Felpham,

> And did those feet in ancient time,
> Walk upon Englands mountains green.[69]

It is not necessarily a fanciful notion, either, since in a verse letter from Felpham of this date he uses much the same imagery which he would employ in the poem itself:

> With the bows of my Mind & the Arrows of Thought –
> My bowstring fierce with Ardour breathes,
> My arrows glow in their golden sheaves.[70]

This is not far from

> Bring me my Bow of burning gold:
> Bring me my Arrows of desire.[71]

So the famous lyric now known as 'Jerusalem' might have been written at a little cottage by the Sussex shore, as Blake considered the work he had to do for William Hayley.

There was work for others, also. Hayley had made a point of introducing him to the grandees of the district, such as Lady Bathurst and Lord Egremont, who either gave him employment as a drawing-master or commissioned him to paint miniatures. He used to say that he had only refused one such offer of work – 'to paint a set of handscreens for a lady of quality', according to one of his earliest biographers.[72] The lady was probably Lady Bathurst herself, but he did remain on good enough terms to act as a part-time tutor to her family.

There were of course occasions when he rested from his labours. Most surprising, perhaps, is the fact that he seems to have taken up landscape drawing for a time. There are certain extant pencil and watercolour sketches that depict the church at Felpham, a wood, and a garden path; on one occasion he and Hayley made a journey to

Hayley's previous house in Eartham, where Thomas Alphonso had died, and Blake quickly sketched the exterior of it. This was also the occasion when they witnessed the death of Hayley's old servant – 'my good William who closed his height of cheerful and affectionate existence (near eighty) . . . in the great house at Eartham where Blake and I had the mournful gratification of attending him (by accident) in the few last hours of his life'.[73] Death was for Blake a joyful moment, symbolising release, and his attendance upon the servant might have helped to inspire his later etching of 'The Death of the Good Old Man'. The landscapes themselves are competent enough, with a dash of bright green for the trees and lawns in the Eartham drawing, but they display nothing of his genius; the external and material world meant very little to him for, as he said himself, 'Nature & Fancy are Two Things & can Never be joined; neither ought any one to attempt it, for it is Idolatry & destroys the Soul'.[74]

There were also expeditions with Catherine Blake as well as with Hayley: they sometimes walked into Chichester together, some seven miles away, to purchase what he called 'most Conveniences';[75] he thought it a 'very handsome City' and there are resemblances that suggest he used it as one of his models for the visionary city of Golgonooza that emerges in his later epic poetry.[76] He made certain acquaintances here, too, and was sometimes in the company of a printer named Seagrave and a woodcarver named Weller. No doubt he was more at ease with them than with Lady Bathurst or Lord Egremont. He and Catherine had their own pastimes in the evening, and there is extant a list of riddles – 'Love errs' equals 'Lovers', while 'an Ell [L] taken from London is Undone'.

But there was never really any chance of removing himself from the sphere of Hayley's busy benevolence. As the 'Hermit of Felpham' put it in his autobiography, he possessed a 'restless desire to subserve the interest of his friends, even when these friends were as unpardonably indolent in prosecuting their own concerns'.[77] He also explained, in one of his usual third-person references to himself, that 'The chief occupation and delight of Hayley seems to have consisted in zealous and constant endeavours to serve his friends, while they lived, and to celebrate their talents and virtues after their decease.'[78] Blake certainly still lived and, being so close to hand, became immediately subject to Hayley's high-minded attention. In the library of Turret House, he began to teach Blake the Greek and Latin languages. They pored over the Bible in Greek, and closely followed a translation of the *Iliad* with the original – biblical Greek is easier to follow than that of Homer but, in any case, Blake made enough progress to be described by his self-appointed tutor as a 'Grecian'.[79] He had a good ear and eye for languages, and his knowledge of that ancient tongue progressed further than is generally supposed – a notebook has recently been discovered in which Blake has translated parts of *Ajax* by Sophocles and then, on some subsequent pages, has made notes of the same dramatist's *Philoctetes*.[80] It shows great skill and determination for a middle-aged man to learn Greek well enough to be able to read Sophocles, but he did not stop at that point. As he explained to his brother in a letter from Felpham, 'I go on Merrily with my Greek & Latin; am very sorry that I did not begin to learn languages early in life as I find it very Easy; am now learning my Hebrew . . . I read Greek as fluently as an Oxford scholar & the Testament is my chief master'.[81] Perhaps he learned Hebrew for the same reason as Carlos Blacker, so he could speak to God in the Almighty's own language. Hayley, who much enjoyed the sound of his own voice, noted in his auto-biography, 'It was a favourite custom with Hayley to animate himself (or any fellow-sufferer from tender health) to new literary exertions by the citation of favourite passages from the great authors of Rome and Greece.'[82] But his ambitions for his pupil ranged even wider; he began to read aloud some French authors to Blake, who declared later 'that he learnt French, sufficient to read it, in a few weeks'.[83] He also began to study Italian and, in particular, the work of Dante. He corrected mistakes in Boyd's English translation of the *Inferno* and annotated his *Historical Notes* on the poet with his customary polemic: 'the grandest Poetry is Immoral the Grandest characters Wicked . . . Poetry is to excuse Vice & shew its reasons & necessary purgation'.[84] He had very decided and specific views about poetry, therefore, but it is unlikely that he chose to communicate them to Hayley; it was his habit to keep his most important and idiosyncratic opinions to himself, and to his employer he remained 'mild' and 'amiable'. There were difficult moments, of course, and Blake was once

> Rememb'ring the Verses that Hayley sung
> When my heart knock'd against the roots of my tongue.[85]

This may have been the time when Hayley read out, translating as he went along, the first two hundred lines of Tasso's *Le Sette Giornale del Mondo Creato*; Blake dutifully transcribed the verse as Hayley dictated it, and thus literally earned the name of 'secretary' that Hayley had once given him. There was also the occasion when Hayley recited some verse of the German poet Klopstock, to whom Blake had a decided aversion. In the months before he left London he had even written a satirical poem deriding that poet and proclaiming himself as 'English Blake' against the claims or criticisms of any foreigner.[86] He ended with a characteristic flourish, which marks him as much a Cockney as an Englishman:

> If Blake could do this when he rose up from shite
> What might he not do if he sat down to write.[87]

He had written this among the limekilns and dilapidated pleasure gardens of Lambeth. If he had read the public prints, now that he was at Felpham, he would have known that the revolutionary Colonel Despard had been seized at the Oakley Arms public house, close by Blake's old home in Hercules Buildings, tried for high treason and hanged a few months later. He could not have known that the young Thomas De Quincey was even then wandering through the streets of London which seemed to him a 'mighty labyrinth';[88] he sat in Golden Square, the site of Blake's own childhood, and contemplated the extent of his sufferings among the 'dreamy lamp-light' and the melancholy airs of the barrel-organ.[89] But Blake was now far removed from that city he had known so well, 'sitting at tea by a wood fire in our Cottage, the wind sighing above our roof & the sea roaring at a distance'.[90] Yet there were visionary intimations even among the homeliness; when 'the wind sweeps over a Corn field' it seemed to him 'the noise of souls / Thro all the immense borne down by Clouds';[91] and before the rising of the sun he could sometimes hear 'the sound of harps'.[92] He also confesses his continual 'remembrance of Felpham's waves',[93] and he is supposed to have declared that one of his later drawings was inspired by just such a memory; it is entitled 'The Spirit of God Moved Upon the Face of the Waters'. In his garden he saw other visions of beneficence: 'there was great stillness among the branches and flowers, and more than common sweetness in the air; I heard a low and pleasant sound and I knew not whence it came. At last I saw the broad leaf of a flower move, and underneath I saw a procession of creatures, of the colour and size of green and grey grass-hoppers, bearing a body laid out on a rose-leaf, which they buried with songs, and then disappeared. It was a fairy funeral!'[94]

There were sprites and fairies, too, in one of his few works at Felpham that was not commissioned by William Hayley. Flaxman had written to Blake a few months after his arrival with the news that a connoisseur, the Reverend Joseph Thomas, wished him to sketch scenes from Milton's *Comus* and from some of Shakespeare's plays, 'for which he will give a Guinea each, the dimensions as follow the paper, an upright square of 12 Inches & half by 8 Inches, within this Space leaving a moderate margin, the principal figure not exceeding 6 Inches high'.[95] It was not a handsome remuneration, but money was always necessary and the Reverend Thomas himself called upon Blake at Felpham to discuss the designs. He was a man of some taste, who was known also to be one of '*liberality* – not merely amateur in art, but as a patron and friend to *living Artists*'.[96] So Blake began work upon *Comus*, and finished some eight designs in pen and watercolour. They are in a quite different style and mood from the temperas he had been painting for Butts (he had three of these to finish, and had brought down three bare canvases from Lambeth for them), although the change in medium from tempera to watercolour might in part have been dictated by the change in residence: the cottage had much less room than the Lambeth house, and to work in tempera was a messy and complicated business. In these cramped conditions Blake follows the scenic structure of Milton's masque very accurately, just as he carefully follows Thomas's instructions for the dimensions of the watercolours and size of the central figures. They are pretty sketches, bathed in a mild ethereal light, but they are essentially decorative rather than inventive; they are the work of an artist on commission, and lack any sense of real contact with the material of Milton's poem. In fact much of his work in this period seems tamed and constricted, as if his ancillary role to the 'Hermit of Felpham' materially affected his art. The country was not, in any case, conducive to his urban genius.

Yet the lack of inspiration can hardly be blamed on him alone, when the work he was asked to illustrate was often banal. He had agreed, for example, to interpret Hayley's *Ballads* on a variety of animals – the idea had been Hayley's, and his motives were as benevolent as ever. He wished to earn some money for Blake as well as 'to amuse the Artist in his patient labour, and to furnish his fancy with a few slight subjects for an inventive pencil, that might afford some variety to his incessant application, without too far interrupting his more serious business'.[97] (The 'serious business' was not any original work of Blake's but his engravings for Hayley's *Life of Cowper*.) Hayley went on to say that 'Since friendship induced this meritorious Artist

BLAKE

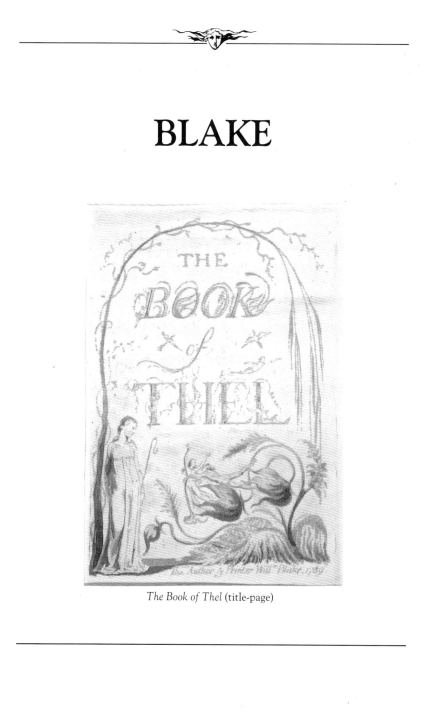

The Book of Thel (title-page)

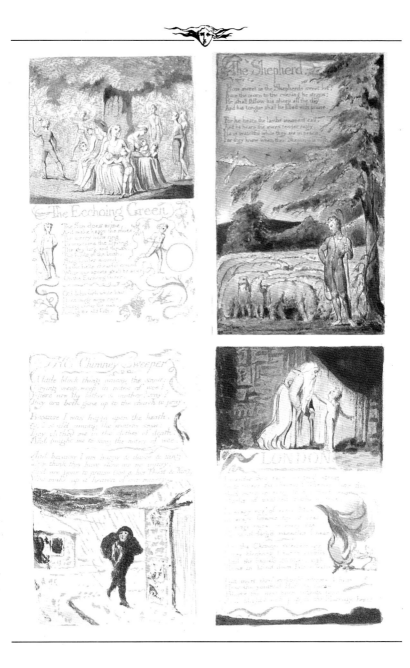

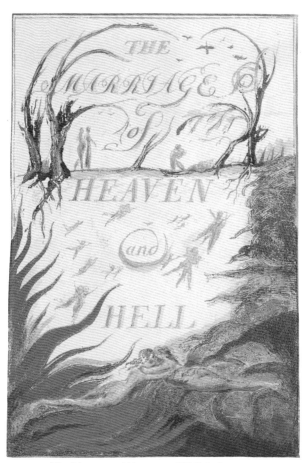

The Marriage of Heaven and Hell (title-page)

Opposite top left: *Songs of Innocence*: 'The Ecchoing Green' (an early print)
Opposite top right: *Songs of Innocence*: 'The Shepherd' (a late print)
Opposite bottom left: *Songs of Experience*: 'The Chimney Sweeper' (an early print)
Opposite bottom right: *Songs of Experience*: 'London' (a late print)

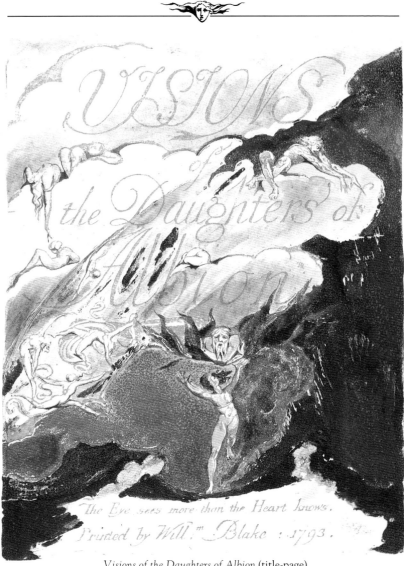

The Eye sees more than the Heart knows.
Printed by Will.ᵐ Blake : 1793.

Visions of the Daughters of Albion (title-page)

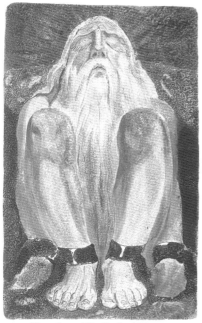

Plate from *The Book of Urizen*

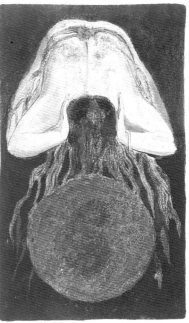

Plate from *The Book of Urizen*

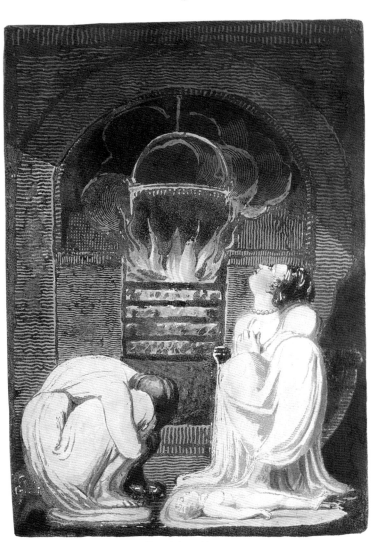

Plate 6 from *Europe*

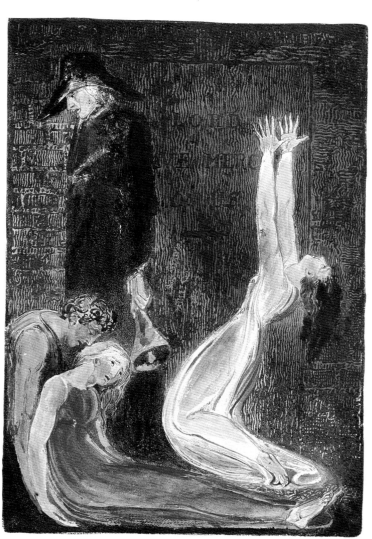

Plate 11 from *Europe*

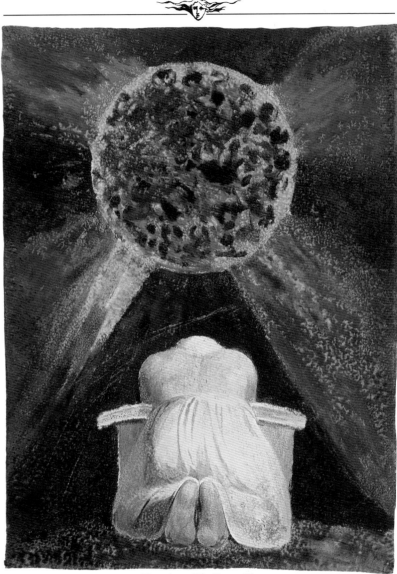

Plate from *The Song of Los*

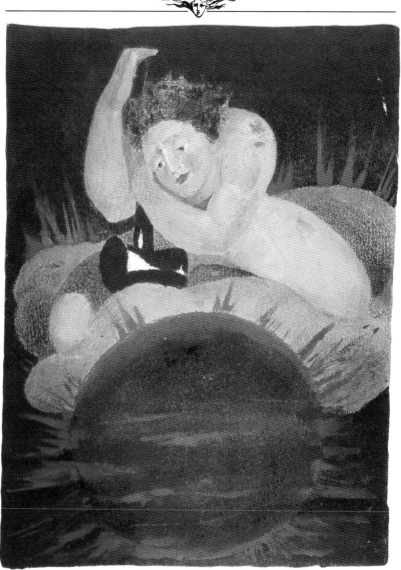

Plate from *The Song of Los*

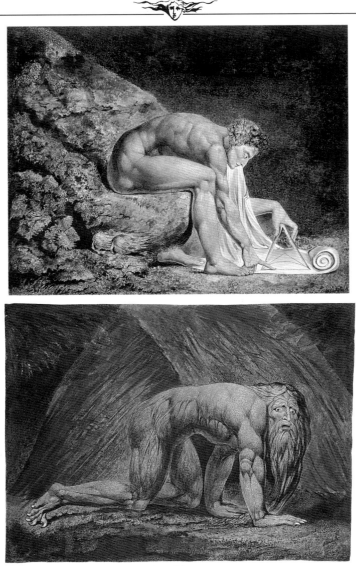

Top: *Newton*
Above: *Nebuchadnezzar*

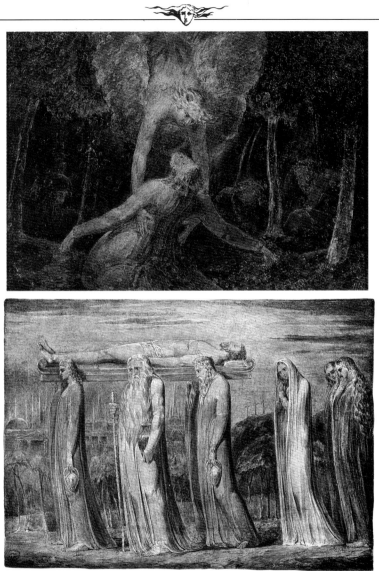

Top: *The Agony in the Garden*
Above: *The Body of Christ Borne to the Tomb*

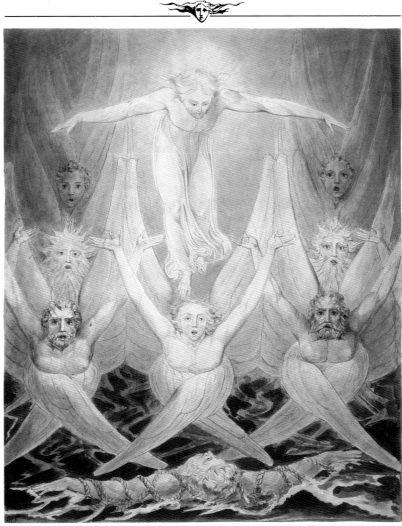

David Delivered out of Many Waters: 'He Rode upon the Cherubim'

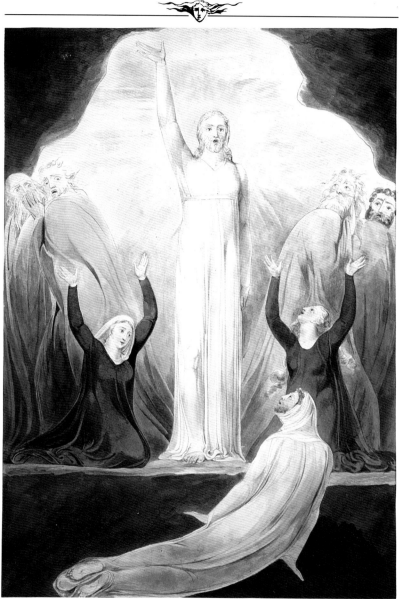

The Raising of Lazarus

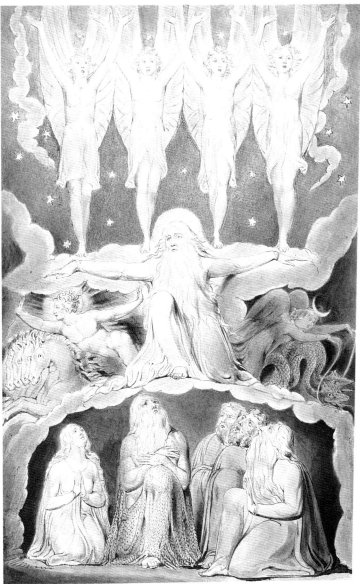

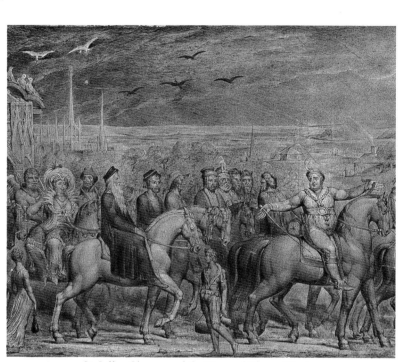

*Sir Jeffery Chaucer and the Nine and Twenty Pilgrims
on their Journey to Canterbury* (detail)

Opposite: *Illustrations to the Book of Job*:
'When the Morning Stars Sang together'

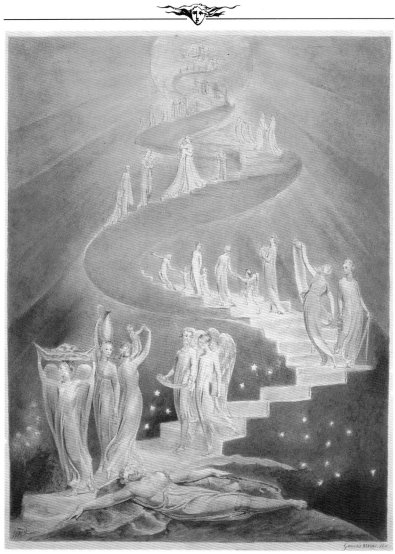

Jacob's Dream
Opposite top: *Six Illustrations to Milton's 'On the Morning of Christ's Nativity'*:
'The Descent of Peace'
Opposite bottom: *Twelve Illustrations to Milton's 'L'Allegro' and 'Il Penseroso'*:
'The Youthful Poet's Dream' ('L'Allegro')

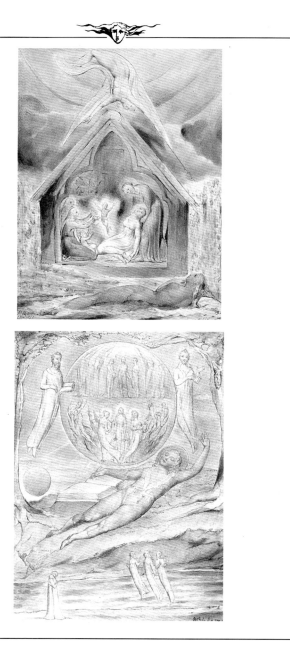

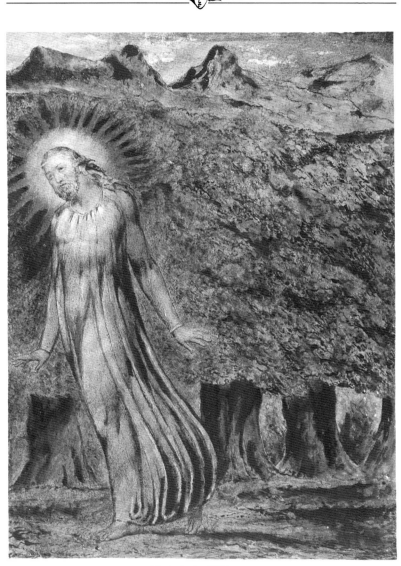

Christ in the Wilderness

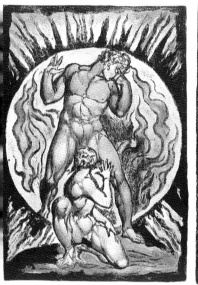

Plate from *Milton*

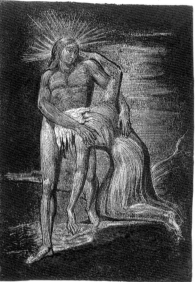

Plate from *Milton*

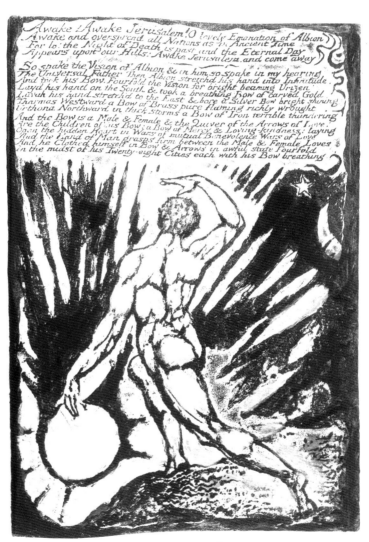

Plate from *Jerusalem*

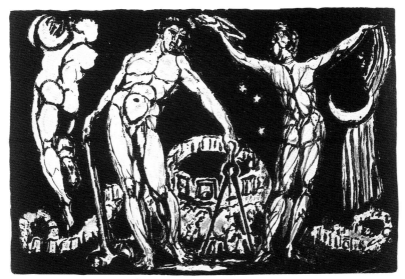

Plate from *Jerusalem*

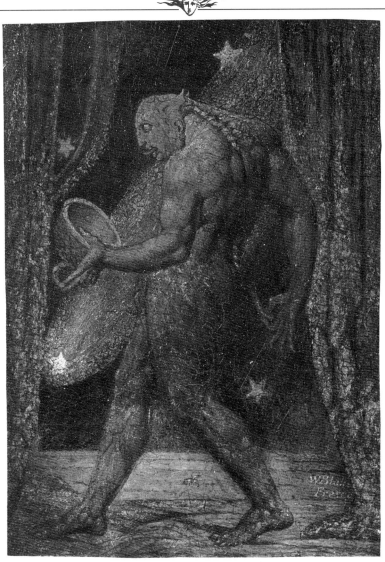

The Ghost of a Flea

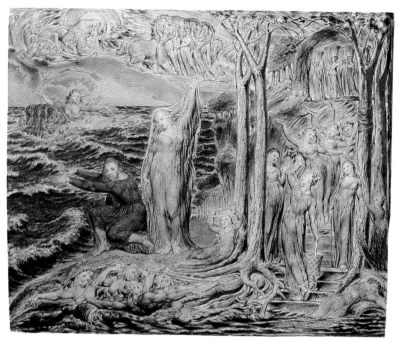

The Sea of Time and Space

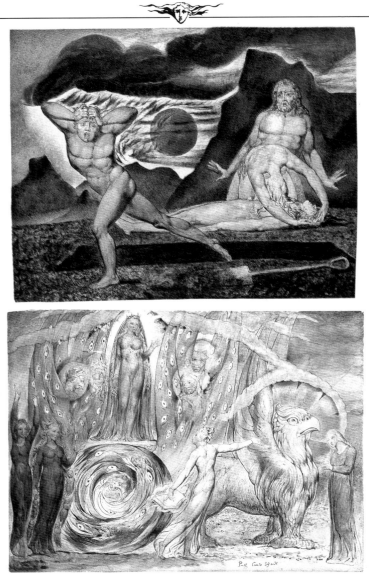

Top: *The Body of Abel Found by Adam and Eve*
Above: *Illustrations to Dante's Divine Comedy:*
'Beatrice Addressing Dante from the Car'

to leave London (the great lucrative theatre of talents!) for the sake of settling near me, it seems to be a duty incumbent of me to use every liberal method, in my power, to obtain for his industrious ingenuity, the notice and favour of my Countrymen.'[98] Blake had begun engraving a lion in the spring of 1801 but *Cowper* intervened, and he did not really start to work properly on the ballads until the following year. The plan was to issue one each month, together with three engravings, over a period of fifteen months and then to collect them within the covers of a quarto volume. They had also decided to dispense with the services of a bookseller and, with the help of the printer Seagrave in Chichester, to publish them privately and sell them – at half a crown each – through the agency of such friends as John Flaxman and Lady Hesketh. Blake himself purchased the paper, for thirty pounds, and the initial response of Hayley's correspondents suggested that it was likely to be a very profitable venture. It was in fact a perfectly orthodox enterprise, but there is no reason to believe that Blake thought any the worse of it for that; it would be quite wrong to cast him in the Romantic role of the poet who rejects the lure of gold. He was always trying to make money out of conventional publishing, whenever the opportunity arose to do so, and was quite happy to follow Hayley's lead. 'I should never have known the nature of Publication,' he told his brother, 'unless I had known H. & his connexions & his method of managing.'[99] This in turn suggests that his experiments with relief etching and with illuminated books, both in Poland Street and in Lambeth, were not considered by him to be proper 'Publication' at all.

In the summer of 1802 he produced three engravings illustrating 'The Elephant', which was followed over the next three months by 'The Eagle', 'The Lion' and 'The Dog'. No doubt he knew Oudry's engravings for the fables of La Fontaine, and the subjects of the various ballads gave Hayley the opportunity for facetious remarks about Blake giving birth to a lion cub, launching an eagle and so forth. But their initial hopes of profit were not realised; there were a few sales but the subscription was not large enough to guarantee the success of the venture, and no more ballads were printed or issued. It cannot be said that Blake's own artistic endeavours were anything more than proficient on this occasion, however; Hayley's verse was not likely to inspire him and the illustration of 'The Tyger' has already suggested that he had difficulty with the drawing of animals. His serpents and his dragons often look ridiculous, while his efforts to depict elephants and dogs remain in the sphere of what might be called pious verisimilitude. Ruskin liked his horse, although Dante Gabriel Rossetti thought it to be 'snuffling with propriety'.[100] The truth is that he could only really depict the 'human form divine', which, in its various aspects, was at the centre of his own cosmogony. He saw the universe in the form of 'One Man' or the 'Divine Human'; that was the shape which inspired him, therefore, and so the animals were not a success. He eventually used the unsold copies, and the stock of discarded paper, as scrap material for his own work; but the failure of the enterprise was yet another example of his general failure in business. 'He is an excellent creature,' Hayley wrote, 'but not very fit to manage pecuniary Concerns to his own advantage.'[101]

This episode may also have affected his relationship with Hayley, which, in the latter months of 1802, was undergoing a profound change. There had been the ordinary problems and inconveniences of living in an unfamiliar place. The cottage was damp, since it had no cellar and was placed low on the earth between the Downs and the sea; Catherine was particularly affected by it, and suffered inter-mittently from 'ague' and rheumatism. The purple thyme of the region was supposed to act as a curative for such problems, but it can have had very little effect upon her since she continued to be disturbed by the same symptoms even after their return to London. Blake suffered from colds and fevers, too, in a pattern that suggests his mortal part was expressing his spiritual anxieties. There were also tensions within the household itself. His sister lived with them for long periods and, according to his own testimony, she and his wife were not wholly at ease in each other's company:

> Must my Wife live in my Sister's bane,
> Or my Sister survive on my Love's pain?[102]

In the same verse, transcribed in a letter to Butts, he also expresses his fears that he might be losing the affection of Butts himself as well as his other London friends. The poem was written after only one year at Felpham but he already depicts his life in despondent terms:

> My hands are labour'd day & night,
> And Ease comes never in my sight.
> My Wife has no indulgence given
> Except what comes to her from heaven.
> We eat little, we drink less;
> This Earth breeds not our happiness.[103]

There is more than an element of exaggeration here, since there is no evidence that they suffered from malnutrition in Felpham, and the catalogue of woes may simply be a prelude to the last line quoted, which established his general philosophy. In the following spring, however, Hayley announced that both Blakes were suffering from a 'severe Fever',[104] but then, in the following month, he reported that Blake was now in 'triumphant spirits'.[105] These spirits did not last long, since he was ill again for much of July. 'But I trust,' Hayley added, 'he will speedily revive under the care of perhaps the very best Wife that ever mortal possessed, at least one that most admirably illustrates that expressive appellation *a Helpmate*.'[106] It is worth noting here that there are no remarks about her 'low' origin of the kind that Fuseli and others made. It was always said, in the patois of the day, that Hayley was a 'gentleman'.

In this month, too, Lady Hesketh was openly doubting Blake's abilities, and reporting to Hayley that those with 'pretensions to Taste, find many defects in your friends engravings'.[107] When she reiterated her complaint in another letter, he replied with a description of Blake that displays genuine sympathy and affection. In the first place, rather tactlessly, he compares him to Lady Hesketh's cousin, the insane William Cowper: 'He resembles our beloved Bard in the Tenderness of his Heart, & in the perilous powers of an Imagination utterly unfit to take due Care of Himself. – with admirable faculties, his sensibility is so dangerously acute, that the common rough treatment which true genius often receives from *ordinary Minds* in the commerce of the World might not only wound him *more than it should do*, but really reduce Him to the Incapacity of an Ideot.'[108] It is significant that he uses the phrase 'true genius', and in fact repeats it a little later; it is interesting, too, that he is referring here to Blake's artistic, not poetic, gifts. His description of his mental state is astute (that dangerous sensitivity would eventually be turned against Hayley himself), and he then goes on to give the fullest surviving description of the Blakes' marriage: Catherine was 'the only female on Earth, who could have suited Him *exactly*. They have been married more than 17 years & are as fond of each other as if their Honey Moon were still shining – They live in a neat little cottage, which they both regard as the most delightful residence ever inhabited by a mortal; they have no servant: – the good woman not only does all the work of the House, but she even makes the greatest part of her Husbands dress, & assists him in *his art* – she draws, she

engraves, & sings delightfully & is so truly the Half of her good man,
that they seem animated by one Soul, & that a soul of indefatigable
Industry & benevolence – it sometimes hurries them both to labour
rather too much . . .'[109] It is a little patronising in tone, perhaps, but it
is hardly the expression of a man of whom Blake was later to write:

> And when he could not act upon my wife
> Hired a Villain to bereave my Life.[110]

Hayley's sympathy and friendship were also evident in his continual
efforts to secure new patrons and new commissions for Blake's art;
these were often successful and, after he had written a letter to the
Countess of Portarlington, that lady's brother bought an edition of
Songs of Innocence from Blake's stock. In fact copies of that particular
book were growing low – it was his most accessible, after all – and at
some time in 1802 he and his wife printed another three on their press
at Felpham.[111]

Yet by the end of that year it was clear that Blake was depressed and
unwell. He had been working on some engravings for the next edition
of Hayley's *The Triumphs of Temper* (a copy of which Hayley with due
ceremony presented to Catherine Blake), but he knew clearly enough
that such work was unworthy of him – 'if it was fit for me, I doubt not
that I should be Employ'd in Greater things'.[112] He was being asked to
illustrate the verse of an inferior poet, and even had the indignity of
engraving after original designs by Maria Flaxman; he was truly acting
as a factotum, and the somewhat gloomy and dispiriting tone of these
illustrations may plausibly be related to his own state of mind. He told
Butts, in November, that he had been 'very Unhappy' – precisely
because he was compelled to work for others and was thus unable to
continue with his true art.[113] His great fear was always that he was
being forced to betray his own gifts. But, as so often when he was faced
with misfortune or lack of recognition, he became more assertive and
determined than ever; in the same letter he explained to Butts, 'I have
travel'd thro' Perils & Darkness not unlike a Champion. I have
Conquer'd, and shall still Go on Conquering. Nothing can withstand
the fury of my Course among the Stars of God & in the Abysses of the
Accuser.'[114] A few weeks later he was complaining that he had
'Spiritual Enemies of . . . formidable magnitude',[115] and it is clear
that he believed the drama of his life was also being played out in
another and much larger sphere than that of Felpham; even now he
was talking about Jesus, and about his own 'Station as a Soldier of

Christ', since his Christianity was intimately bound up with a sense of his own divine destiny.[116] Then he returned, as he always did in this context, to the experience of his visions – he explained to Butts, 'I am under the direction of Messengers from Heaven, daily & nightly.'[117] Who is to say that this is madness? It was, for him, the most plausible explanation for the phenomena that surrounded him continually. So he tried to remain patient on his journey through 'the sea of time & space', and hope for better things.[118] But, in the first months of 1803, he had determined to return to London.

He explained the decision to his brother James, the hosier; he told him that Hayley 'is jealous as Stothard was & will be no further My friend than he is compell'd by circumstances. The truth is, as a Poet he is frighten'd at me & as a Painter his views & mine are opposite.'[119] It is an obvious example of his extreme sensitivity, but it may be that he divined an element of his patron's character that was not even known to Hayley himself. What does the available evidence suggest? There is no doubt that Blake felt, as he put it, 'imposed upon'.[120] The general feeling among Hayley's acquaintance was that the good poet of Felpham had brought down from London a worthy engraver to act as general assistant; that was the impression that Hayley himself gave, and Blake could not have been unaware of it. It ought to be remembered that he had never before been in close proximity to another poet – certainly not one of Hayley's public eminence – and that in itself might have made him apprehensive and unsure. His feelings would have been compounded by the fact that he had left London precisely because he had failed there. He felt that he was being asked to do work of a trivial nature simply for the sake of the money, and that his real genius was being neglected or ignored. This was his constant complaint against his friends, and it was one that he now began to level at Hayley. He believed that Hayley was envious of his gifts, both as a painter and as a poet, but it is more likely that he did not understand them. Hayley had already stated his belief that Blake had 'true genius' but, in his somewhat bland and grandiloquent vocabulary, it is hard to know precisely what he meant by that; it is probable that, in Blake's lyrics, he saw evidence of a 'genius' that had gone sadly awry in the productions of later years. He thought more of the paintings, and there is no reason to doubt his genuine enthusiasm for some of Blake's work. But, as far as he was concerned, they were still the productions of an 'Engraver' – no doubt in a typically late eighteenth-century manner he admired the effusions of such an 'original' and 'simple' mind – and not at all in the same class as, for example, the sculptures of Flaxman or the paintings of Romney. So, with the best intentions in the world, he continued to recommend Blake as an engraver and journeyman artist to his friends. Blake was the 'dear', 'amiable', 'good-hearted' and 'indefatigable' worker whose original poetry and painting were delightful adornments to what should remain a workmanlike career.

Blake understood this perfectly, of course, and accurately summed up Hayley's attitude as one of 'Genteel Ignorance & Polite Disapprobation'.[121] He accepted the situation at first but gradually over the three years he and his wife remained at Felpham it became a source of frustration, resentment and anger. His friends sometimes accused him of 'irritability' or of being, in Hayley's phrase, 'quick-spirited' – 'irritation' being a stronger word then than it is now, with connotations of extreme sensitivity. It was linked to paranoia and, interestingly enough, to the seeing of visions – 'Such spectra,' one doctor wrote, 'are by no means rare among studious men, if of an irritable temperament, and an imaginative turn.'[122] But Blake was not to be patronised in this fashion; he knew himself to be a great artist and visionary who was systematically being ignored or marginalised. It is no wonder that he sometimes became angry, or behaved irrationally; the real wonder is that he remained patient and 'mild' for such long periods. Lesser writers such as Richard Savage and Thomas De Quincey found refuge from the world in alcohol, or opium, or the madhouse; Blake, the greatest and least respected of eighteenth-century artists, continued his profession as an engraver until the end of his life. There is an heroic achievement even in that.

But this is to move too far from Felpham, where in the summer of 1803 Blake made an effort at self-assertion. Hayley described the incident to Flaxman: 'Blake surprized me a little in saying (after we had settled the price of 30 Guineas for the first, the price which He had for the Cowper) that Romney's head would require much Labor & he must have 40 for it – startled as I was I replied I will not stint you in behalf of Romney – you shall have 40 – but soon after while we were looking at the smaller & slighter drawing of the Medallion He astonished me by saying I must have 30 G for this – I then replied – of this point I must consider . . .'[123] This is not a question of avarice on Blake's part – the pity of the situation lies in the fact that he could only assert his true worth by suddenly asking for more money. It was the only price ascribed to him by those such as Hayley, who advised him to continue with the 'drudgery of business';[124] since his real value was hidden to them all, he was compelled to fight back on their terms and simply demand larger payments for his productions. He was caught in the trap of their expectations, and this served only to frustrate and infuriate him further. So in his letters he became ever more grandiloquent, as lack of recognition compelled him to new and further heights of self-definition –'I know that the Public are my friends & love my works,' he told his brother, '& will embrace them whenever they see them.'[125] In a slightly later correspondence with Butts, he expanded upon that newly awakened sense of self-worth, which he felt it necessary to demonstrate after three years in Felpham: 'Now I may say to you, what perhaps I should not dare to say to any one else: That I can alone carry on my visionary studies in London unannoy'd, & that I may converse with my friends in Eternity, See Visions, Dream Dreams & prophecy & speak Parables . . .'[126] He seems almost to be comparing his life with that of Christ here, but there is a significant addition when he makes it clear that, at least in London, he will be 'unobserv'd & at liberty from the Doubts of other Mortals; perhaps Doubts proceeding from kindness, but Doubts are always pernicious, Especially when we Doubt our Friends. Christ is very decided on this Point.'[127] It is what Blake feared and hated, the 'doubt' that he ridiculed in 'Auguries of Innocence':

> If the Sun & Moon should Doubt
> Theyd immediately Go out.[128]

But what if Blake should suffer self-doubt, what then? Then the visions would seem madness, and his work a wasteland, and his life a failure. So he fought against 'words of Doubt' all his life.[129] The friendly, but nevertheless pernicious, doubter in Blake's letter is Hayley, whom he described as a 'corporeal' friend but a 'Spiritual' enemy;[130] this in turn raises the question whether he ever intimated to his patron any of his own visions and beliefs? Did he tell him, as he told Butts and Flaxman, that he was surrounded by 'Eternals' and by 'Spiritual Messengers'? There is some evidence that he did introduce him to his spiritual world, since Hayley told both Edward Marsh and Lady Hesketh that Blake believed 'all the Demons, who tormented our dear Cowper when living, are now labouring to impede the publication of his Life'.[131] The tone is jocular rather than serious, and this may suggest his general attitude towards Blake's visionary conceptions – to treat them lightly, and to rely upon Blake's general mildness, was to dismiss the subject. Blake had also shown him part of an epic poem he was writing in the cottage but, according to Blake himself, his attitude had been one of 'contempt' – 'he is as much averse to my poetry as he is to a Chapter in the Bible', by which he meant that Hayley did not have the spiritual capacity to understand him at all.[132] There has been much speculation about the more oblique aspects of their relationship – a plausible case can be made for considering Hayley in the line of 'father figures', for example, against whom Blake turned in fury.

The role of Catherine over the three years also deserves some consideration. Hayley thought highly of her, to judge from his correspondence, and she may have been able to maintain some sort of uneasy peace between the two men at the height of her husband's frustrations. It may also be that, in the presence of the busy and successful Hayley, Blake felt he had over the years in some way failed his wife by consigning her to a life of labour and poverty. Certainly in that later hysterical couplet when he claimed Hayley tried to 'act upon my wife', he is clearly asserting some kind of connection between them that enraged or perturbed him – but this was written at a much later date, at a time of great mental disturbance, and all the evidence suggests that Catherine remained what she had always been, the loving and compliant wife.

Of course there had been some advantages to the time at Felpham. He had remained steadily in work; he had made several 'connections' with future employers such as the Egremonts at Petworth; and he had discovered (or so he thought) a manner of publication that would prove useful to him. As he told his brother, he had learnt so much from Hayley's informal system of publishing and distributing the Ballads that 'It now would be folly not to venture publishing' on his return to London.[133] He also explained that 'The Profits arising from Publications are immense, & I now have it in my power to commence publication with many very formidable works, which I have finish'd & ready'.[134] One of those works was the poem that he had been writing since his last years in Lambeth, and it could fairly be said that Hayley's most profound effect upon Blake can be seen within the very texture of this verse.

Hayley's role as a biographer and theorist is more important here than his reputation as a poet. In particular he had written a life of Milton, in which he had reasserted the English epic tradition and placed it within the context of Milton's political radicalism. Of course

Blake had been acquainted with Milton's work from his apprentice days, but the poet now seems to acquire a distinctive presence in his life – he and Hayley were planning an engraved edition of Cowper's translations of Milton's Latin and Italian poetry (like many such ventures, it came to nothing); he had painted the poet's portrait for Hayley's library; he had illustrated *Comus* with a sequence of watercolours; and now he began to mention Milton in his correspondence. Hayley had also recently completed *An Essay on Epic Poetry*, which again affirmed the importance and centrality of the epic tradition in England – in his usual grand fashion, he urged younger writers to adopt it as the true standard of poetic excellence. He would have found a willing listener in Blake, and it cannot be a coincidence that it was during these Felpham years that Blake for the first time produced his own version of epic.

He had been working on the poem for some years, writing verses quickly while inspired, 'twelve or sometimes twenty or thirty lines at a time';[135] he had entitled it *Vala* and, while still at Lambeth, he had written out the first thirty-six pages in an elaborate copperplate hand. It was to be the story of the Ancient Man, or Eternal Man, whose faculties are dimmed and divided when he falls into the material world; but, like much of the work he completed at Lambeth, it is also a celebration of sexual energy and a hymn to human fulfilments and aspirations when the scattered portions of that eternal body are eventually reconciled. He had taken these pages of the poem with him to Felpham, where he continued working upon it in an informal and sporadic way. He had many mundane tasks to perform and in any case, as he said of his painting at this time, his work was best 'done in the heat of My Spirits' – an ambiguous reference, which hints at the inspiration he may also have derived from his glowing visions.[136] So he wrote lines and passages of the poem on scraps of paper; but then, in the summer of 1802, he decided to transcribe a fair copy and turn these verses into a coherent work of art. There were many reasons why he should wish to return to his poetry, one of them being his optimism that the 'Public are my friends & love my works'. His experience with the *Ballads* had demonstrated to him that material could be printed and distributed relatively cheaply as long as it remained out of the hands of booksellers; he had followed that precept with his illuminated prophecies but only a few copies could be printed in any one session. Seagrave, Hayley and Blake had between them been able to print out far more copies of the *Ballads* at a quicker and cheaper rate. It seemed an appropriate form, then, for the new poem, which, as he explained to Butts, 'shall, by Divine Assistance be progressively Printed & ornamented with Prints & given to the Public'.[137] The verses would be printed in conventional letterpress and, as with the *Ballads*, an engraving would be placed at the end of each 'book' or 'chapter'. He had calculated the costs involved and was happy to explain them to his brother, the small businessman and shopkeeper: 'A Book price half a guinea may be got out at the Expense of Ten pounds & its almost certain profits are 500 G[uineas]. I am only sorry that I did not know the methods of publishing years ago.'[138]

The new method of publication may have crystallised his plans for the poem, but of course there were other forces involved in its preparation and composition. It was in this period, as we have seen, that he became closely acquainted with Hayley's conception of an English epic tradition in general and of Milton in particular. In many respects Blake was highly impressionable – his occasional docility is the complementary side of his fierce inventiveness – and it seems that almost at once he had taken up Hayley's aspirations and decided that he would compose his own English epic. The original thirty-six pages of *Vala*, written in Lambeth, had been composed in that tone of biblical and lyrical lament which was all his own. Now, as he continued work upon the poem in Felpham, he introduces a Miltonic resonance; in one of the chapters or 'Nights', as he called them after Young, he even copies the motif of Satan's journey from the second book of *Paradise Lost*. By combining a Miltonic cadence with the biblical sonority that came so naturally to him, he also managed to rediscover an aspect of English poetry that had been neglected since the seventeenth century; he had recreated the language of declamation and prophecy. He had also determined that this was to be a long poem – the longest poem he had ever written – in compliance with the high demands of the epic form. He still had the discarded proof sheets of the *Night Thoughts* engravings, and he used these to transcribe his fair copy; he wrote it out quickly, with very few revisions or deletions, and filled some forty pages with closely packed handwriting.

He explained to Butts, some months after he had begun this transcription, that the poem was in part imbued with the events of Felpham – he had even employed his new knowledge of classical Greek to write an epigraph in that language. 'But none can know the Spiritual Acts of my three years' Slumber on the banks of the Ocean, unless he has seen them in the Spirit, or he should read My long Poem descriptive of those Acts; for I have in these three years composed an immense number of verses on One Grand Theme, Similar to Homer's Iliad or Milton's Paradise Lost, the Persons & Machinery intirely new to the Inhabitants of Earth (some of the Persons Excepted)'.[139] The references to Homer and to Milton, as well as to what was then known as 'epic machinery', suggest once more the debt to Hayley. 'I have written this Poem from immediate Dictation . . . without Pre-meditation & even against my Will; the Time it has taken in writing was thus render'd Non Existent, & an immense Poem exists which seems to be the Labour of a long Life, all produc'd without Labour or Study. I mention this to shew you what I think the Grand Reason of my being brought down here.'[140] A few weeks later he returned to the subject with Butts, when he described 'a Sublime Allegory, which is now perfectly completed into a Grand Poem. I may praise it, since I dare not pretend to be any other than the Secretary; the Authors are in Eternity. I consider it as the Grandest Poem that this World Contains.'[141] Once more he refers specifically to his time in the country since this great poem is in part the 'Sublime Allegory' of 'our three years' trouble'.[142] In the margin of one of its sheets he has also scrawled in crayon an epigram about 'injury' and 'the distrest', which has some bearing upon his complaints of that time.[143]

In fact there are specific references to Felpham and its vicinity within the poem. There are allusions to Chichester, and to the 'polypus' that he would have observed along the sea-coast and which became in his vision 'a Human polypus of Death';[144] there are also observations of country life, 'Where the herds low after the shadow & after the water spring', and where 'the grasshopper the Emmet & the Fly', 'the golden Moth' and 'the strong Bull' can all be found.[145] But this is no longer the lyrical and meditative poem that he had begun at Lambeth; he has taken his epic ambitions very seriously indeed, and this is a dramatic and rhetorical performance that uses his 'three years' trouble' as the inspiration of a grand vision. It is an epic poem indeed, but it is an epic of the individual human psyche in which conflict, repression and the urge for power make up the 'Machinery'. Nothing quite like it had ever been attempted before in English poetry, and it was Blake's isolation and frustration – the frustration of a man of genius – that made it possible. In his correspondence he had talked about Hayley's envy, and about his own sense of being 'imposed upon'; here, in the verses that he was rapidly copying out onto discarded proofs, he creates a visionary world in which a 'fiery boy' is held down by 'the Chain of Jealousy', in which epic figures struggle for mastery and dominion over each other, and in which divided faculties are the constituent parts of some eternally fallen world.[146] It was a time when Blake was forced to labour over the work of other men, and within the texture of the poem there is an uneasy violence directed against those who 'Reduce all to our will as spaniels are taught with art'.[147] He was known as 'poor Blake' and yet the character of Orc declares:

Thy Pity I contemn scatter thy snows elsewhere
I rage in the deep for Lo my feet & hands are naild to the burning rock
Yet my fierce fires are better than thy snows.[148]

It is hard, knowing the circumstances of the composition, not to see Hayley himself turned into an aspect of the terrible Urizen whom Orc denounces:

yet thou dost fixd obdurate brooding sit
Writing thy books. Anon a cloud filld with a waste of snows
Covers thee still obdurate still resolvd & writing still.[149]

It was a period when Blake was troubled by much 'uneasiness' and 'unhappiness', as we have had reason to observe, and now as he wrote out the poem in his cottage he introduced for the first time the 'Spectre'; it is the shadow side of a man filled with doubts and fears of futurity, an aspect of the mind that is cruelly obsessed with laws and the conventional dictates of reason:

The Spectre rose in pain
A Shadow blue obscure & dismal. like a statue of lead
Bent by its fall from a high tower the dolorous shadow rose.[150]

It is the image of weak hope and despair hovering above the fallen body of the eternal man, a shadow that will in the end become an insane devouring creature. Blake said that the poem was dictated to him, sometimes against his will, and in the process all his private agonies and resentment against Hayley have been transformed into a vast epic of human fear and repression:

Compell the poor to live upon a Crust of bread by soft mild arts
Smile when they frown frown when they smile & when a man looks pale
With labour & abstinence say he looks healthy & happy
And when his children sicken let them die there are enough
Born even too many & our Earth will be overrun.[151]

This is a world driven by material power and by the forced enslavement of the finest faculties of mankind, yet sometimes the verse lament is overwhelmed by the extraordinary peace of the visionary moment, breaking through like the birdsong around Blake's cottage. He could sense the truth of his visions as he walked through the cornfields of Felpham, or along the shore, seeing in the flight of the birds or the breaking of the sea some lost happiness or completeness, some possibility of infinite life that had been fore-closed. He was one who was continually 'Seeking the Eternal which is always present to the wise'.[152] He believed that the authors of *Vala* itself were in eternity – and indeed who could have expected that some of the most significant and percipient poetry of the century, employing lyrical meditation to reveal the nature of the social and public world, should have come from the pen of a journeyman engraver living in a Sussex cottage? Passages of pastoral description and private lamentation are succeeded by very subtle analyses of what Blake called 'mental states' and by paragraphs of magnificent denunciation: in the form of the poem, then, we may be able to perceive something of Blake's bearing in the world, where amiability was succeeded by anger, and where the steady discipline of his engraving was followed by the 'heat of My Spirits' as he wrote by divine dictate.

By the spring of 1803, as we have seen, Blake and his wife had decided not to renew the lease on their cottage, and to return to London; Hayley was told of their determination, and seemed to make no effort to change their course. They were to leave in the autumn, but already Blake's imagination was filled with bright visions of his own city; he was ready to see 'fine Pictures, and the various improvements in Works of Art going on in London'.[153] He considered the peace with France established by the Treaty of Amiens as an occasion for exhibitions and public works and, no doubt, an opportunity of earning money for himself through engraving or through his new trade as 'publisher' of his own engraved books. But he was also in need of a reliable patron and, with his separation from Hayley only a few months away, he began writing once more to Thomas Butts. He had been somewhat neglectful of his old friend and employer while he had been at Felpham; Butts had commissioned him to complete some watercolours of biblical scenes, in addition to the temperas, but the dilatory or distracted artist had managed only to send preliminary sketches from which Butts was meant to choose the designs. He had finished the three remaining temperas some two years after the removal to Sussex, on canvas which he had brought down especially for that commission, and had written in advance with the hope that Butts would 'excuse my want of steady perseverance'.[154] But he began work on the watercolours themselves only a few months before the return to London, and once more he was writing to apologise for, and explain, his inactivity. An explanation might well have been necessary, since Butts tended to pay him in advance, but, when it came, it was of a most unusual kind. 'I would not send you a Drawing or a Picture,' he wrote, 'till I had again reconsider'd my notions of Art, & had put myself back as if I was a learner.'[155] What he had learned, however, was that 'I am Right'.[156] He had said at the beginning of this letter that 'I have now given two years to the intense study of those parts of the art which relate to light & shade & colour, & am Convinc'd that either my understanding is incapable of comprehending the beauties of Colouring, or the Pictures which I painted for you Are Equal in Every part of Art, & superior in One, to any thing that has been done since the age of Rafael.'[157] He then went on to compare himself with 'Carrache or Rafael'.

It is in fact the key to the work he was now belatedly resuming. He had executed a few earlier watercolours for Butts, before he left London; they are intensely dramatic and expressive works, after the calm grandeur of the temperas, showing the soldiers gambling for Christ's garment, a blasphemer being stoned, the ghost of Samuel rising out of the ground. The vivid colouring, the powerful chiaroscuro and the general violence of the compositions mark a strong development in his art, and prompted him to reflect upon his general direction. That had been the one advantage of Felpham. 'One thing of real consequence I have accomplish'd by coming into the country, which is to me consolation enough: namely, I have recollected all my scatter'd thoughts on Art and resumed my primitive & original ways of Execution in both painting & engraving, which in the confusion of London I had very much lost & obliterated from my mind.'[158] He was, in other words, returning to the example of Raphael and the art of fifteenth-century Florence. He managed to complete only seven new watercolours in the summer of 1802, and realised that he would not be able to finish any more for Butts until he had settled in the city; but even in these Felpham works we observe the extent of his renewed interest in Raphael. Such paintings as 'The

Angel of the Divine Presence', 'The Death of the Virgin' and 'The Three Maries at the Sepulchre' have that balance of shape and gesture, that lucidity of formal arrangement, that miraculous use of shallow space, which he had studied in the engravings taken from the Italian masters. Perhaps we might not judge them to be as great as those works in the papal apartments of the Vatican but, then, Blake was not working within a grand or settled inheritance. He had reinvented the language of prophecy in *Vala*, and in his painting he was attempting to rediscover the tradition of sacred art that had been lost in England for many centuries. Baudelaire once said that the Germans find beauty in outline while the English find it in perspective; there is a truth to that, but Blake's style was always one that removed perspective for the sake of uncovering some more ancient truth of a spiritual art. One also sees in such works as 'The Death of the Virgin' the extraordinary devotion of his nature; it was his genius to create the effects of monumentality within a small space but that sense of scale, like the strange light with which these vibrant watercolours are imbued, is the expression of reverence and worship. To this day he is not much admired by secular critics, largely because they refuse to understand the mysteries that he wished to reveal as much in his art as in his poetry:

> Pitying the Lamb of God Descended thro Jerusalems gates
> To put off Mystery time after time & as a Man
> Is born on Earth so was he born of Fair Jerusalem. [159]

He completed some eighty watercolours over the next few years, working on them intermittently when no other commissions were available, and they form a series that might well be termed 'Blake's Bible Gallery' after the fashion of the time; he inscribed the appropriate biblical reference in the lower right-hand corner, under the painting itself, and in his characteristic way arranged them in pairs or in parallels. But even though they had been privately commissioned, they were not necessarily meant to be private works; one of the motives for his return to London, in fact, was precisely to reacquaint himself with the art market of the capital. Just as he intended his new poem, *Vala*, to be published in a conventional manner, so he was pleased to find that Butts was planning to exhibit two of his biblical temperas at a gallery in Berners Street known as 'The British School of Painting'. It is another example of his ill luck in the world that the gallery closed down before any such exhibition could take place, but there is no doubt that in this period he was again much exercised over the prospect of joining the movement towards public or national art. He had already congratulated his friend George Cumberland on his idea for a national gallery (there was to be no such institution for more than twenty years), and the prospect of European peace persuaded him to believe that 'The Reign of Literature & the Arts Commences'.[160] But his enthusiasm was wasted; even before he left Felpham for London, war with France and Napoleon recommenced. In that same period, too, he suffered the gravest crisis of his life.

TWENTY

Scofield the Accuser

The affair started outside Blake's cottage on the twelfth of August. A soldier, who was billeted at the Fox Inn just down the lane, came into the garden in order to speak to the ostler from the inn who was working there: Private John Scofield was leaning against the wall, 'lounging about' as was later related, when Blake came out. He did not realise that his gardener had asked the soldier for assistance, and wondered what he was doing on his premises. Some words were then exchanged, which the gardener, William, testified he had not heard. At this point Blake seems to have lost his temper and, taking the private soldier by the neck and back, he marched him up the lane to the Fox Inn. There were now some witnesses, among them the landlord of the tavern and his wife as well as another soldier billeted there. Blake and Scofield were then separated, after more angry words were spoken. It might have been a common enough incident, but these were not common times. Five months later Blake faced trial in Chichester for sedition.

The summer of 1803, after the resumption of war with France, was a period of alarm and speculation when it appeared very likely that Napoleon's fleet would invade England. It was a time of what was called 'volunteering', while the south coast was fortified with beacons and Martello towers. The countryside around Felpham was one of those areas where the soldiery were stationed in makeshift tents or in billets such as the Fox Inn. To be accused of sedition, in such circumstances, was to risk a great deal. Private John Scofield was part of the First Regiment of Dragoons, then stationed at Chichester; he had once risen to the post of sergeant but had been reduced through the ranks for some unspecified offence until he was now once again a 'common soldier'. He had been a fustian cutter in Manchester, was no doubt in want of money, and he may have believed that the deposition he swore against Blake – especially at a time of war – would be rewarded. Here is the substance of what he claimed Blake had said to him in the cottage garden: 'The People of England were like a Parcel of Children, that they would play with themselves till they got scalded and burnt, that the French knew our Strength very well, and if Bonaparte should come he would be master of Europe in an Hour's Time, that England might depend on it, that when he set his Foot on English Ground that every Englishman would have his choice, whether to have his Throat cut, or to join the French, & that he was a strong Man, and would certainly begin to cut Throats, and the strongest Man must conquer – that he damned the King of England – his Country, & his Subjects, that his Soldiers were all bound for Slaves, and all the Poor People in general.'[1] Scofield testified that at this point Catherine Blake came running out of the cottage and declared that 'the King of England would run himself so far into the Fire, that he might [not?] get himself out again. & altho' she was but a Woman, she would fight for as long as she had a drop of Blood in her'.

BLAKE: My dear, you would not fight against France.

CATHERINE: No, I would for Bonaparte as long as I am able.

BLAKE (to Scofield): I have told what I have said before greater People than you. You have been sent by your Captain to Esquire Hayley to hear what I had to say. Go and tell them.

CATHERINE: Turn him out of the garden.

At which point Blake pushed him out into the road, and took Scofield by the collar while repeating 'Damn the King. The soldiers are all slaves.'[2]

Blake himself gave an altogether different account of the incident. He said that he simply asked Scofield to leave his garden, not knowing the reason for his presence there, and that he 'made me an impertinent answer. I insisted on his leaving the Garden; he refused. I still persisted in desiring his departure; he then threaten'd to knock out my Eyes, with many abominable imprecations & with some contempt for my Person; it affronted my foolish Pride. I therefore took him by the Elbows & pushed him before me till I had got him out; there I intended to have left him, but he, turning about, put himself into a Posture of Defiance, threatening & swearing at me. I, perhaps foolishly & perhaps not, stepped out at the Gate, &, putting aside his blows, took him again by the Elbows, &, keeping his back to me, pushed him forwards down the road about fifty yards – he all the while endeavouring to turn round & strike me, & raging & cursing, which drew out several neighbours.'[3]

Blake managed to get him to the door of the Fox Inn, where the neighbours had already gathered. The landlord persuaded Scofield to return inside with the other soldier, Private Cox, but Blake believed that both men were soon plotting to have their revenge by accusing him of the seditious words that Scofield reported. But they had no witnesses. None of the neighbours had heard Blake utter anything of that kind while he was outside the Fox Inn, while the only independent witness to the conversation in the garden was the gardener himself. William could recall nothing, however, except the moment when Blake turned out Scofield. The two accounts clearly differ so widely that any interpretation of the evidence must be marshalled very carefully. There is no doubt Blake could utter remarks that to an ordinary soldier would sound 'seditious'; although he would never have been as commonplace as those radical agitators who used as their toast 'May the last of Kings be strangled with the guts of the last priest', he had attacked George III in various mythic incarnations and had once written a charming little verse:

> The Angel that presided oer my birth
> Said Little creature formd of Joy & Mirth
> Go love without the help of any King on Earth.[4]

It is at least possible then that, in the course of a violent argument, Blake's sometimes ferocious temper provoked him to expressions that would have been better left unsaid. And what of Catherine's role in the affair? She does not seem likely to have pledged herself to fight for Bonaparte, but a friendly acquaintance did report her as saying, some years later, 'if this Country does go to War our King ought to lose his head'.[5] So it is not inconceivable that she also uttered what, in the context of the times, were seditious words.

Scofield and Cox were now going around Felpham claiming that they would have Blake hanged (Scofield apparently also accusing him of being a 'military painter', since he had misheard or mistaken the term miniature-painter), as well as abusing witnesses who refused to testify on their behalf. Three days later Scofield made a formal complaint against Blake in front of the justices at Chichester, and on the following morning the poet appeared before them and pleaded not guilty. He was 'bound over' for the next quarter sessions, while Hayley and Seagrave put up the bond money of £100. Blake was now in a very serious predicament. He was being tried under common law, not the new legislation intended to stifle internal political debate, and he would not have been hanged; but he would have been fined, and might have had to serve some term of imprisonment. It is hard to imagine the fear and anxiety into which he was now plunged; it was as if the event he had dreaded most in his life (one should recall his own nervous attempts at self-censorship in earlier years) was now about to take place. He had always been susceptible to anxious terrors, and at the very end of his life he once again described the 'doubt & Fear' that seemed always to attend him.[6] His memory of the incident up the Medway, when he was briefly detained as a possible 'spy', would no doubt have redoubled that 'Fear'. His friends knew very well what he was suffering now, and in a letter to Hayley Flaxman commented upon Blake's 'afflictions' and noted that his 'irritability as well as the Association and arrangement of his ideas do not seem likely to be soothed or more advantageously disposed by any power inferior to That by which man is originally endowed with his faculties'.[7] But what was this 'Association and arrangement of his ideas' that so troubled Flaxman? It seems for a while Blake believed he had been the victim of a paid spy or informant set to entrap him; there is even a vague suggestion that he believed Hayley to be partly responsible for the plot. There may have been elements of paranoid fantasy here, but it was not unusual for spies and informants to act against specific targets. He felt himself in great danger, therefore, and prepared an elaborate memorandum on the facts of the matter. He wrote to Thomas Butts, who still worked in the office of the Muster-master General, and asked him to discover anything he could about Scofield. In the same letter he lamented his fate:

> O why was I born with a different face?
> Why was I not born like the rest of my race?
> When I look each one starts! when I speak, I offend;
> Then I'm silent & passive & lose every Friend.[8]

It is the agony of a man who feels himself set apart, and who believes that he can never behave appropriately. It must have seemed that his time at Felpham had proved beyond any doubt that he was trapped; if he adopted what he called a 'too passive manner' then his real work was overlooked and despised, but if he gave expression to his 'active physiognomy' he found himself being taken before a bench of judges.[9] To be tried and condemned – that would be the primal scene of disaster for a visionary who had rebelled against his father and his father's world, who had consistently defied authority, who had been acquainted with political radicalism, and who in his poetry attacked the very foundations of late eighteenth-century culture as wicked or corrupt. To stand so far outside the forces of convention, however, led also to the fear that he might one day be crushed by them. This was the dread that lay within what he called his 'perilous adventure'.[10]

There is a glass goblet known as a 'rummer', which was used for drink in this period. One has recently been found that has the vaguest outline of an angel engraved upon it, while on the other side two lines of verse have been more crudely cut with what looks like a diamond-pointed tool:

> Thou Holder Of Immoral Drink
> I Give Thee Purpose Now I Think[11]

It transpired at the trial that Scofield may have been drunk on the occasion of his quarrel with Blake. And there, on the stem, is another inscription: 'Blake In Anguish Felpham August 1803'. In this same period he took out his old engraving of fear and misery, once entitled 'Our End is Come', and retitled it 'A Scene in the Last Judgement. Satan's Holy Trinity. The Accuser, the Judge, and the Executioner'.

The Blakes left Felpham in mid-September, at the time when the lease on their cottage had expired, and with all the paraphernalia of their life and work made the slow trek by post-chaise to London. It was a very different journey from the one they had begun three years before, however, when they had come to the Sussex village in search of what Blake had then called a 'New life' in 'Spiritual' Felpham.[12] For the first three weeks they stayed at his brother's house in Broad Street, while they looked for suitable lodgings; there was no question now of finding a house as large as the one they had left in Lambeth, so much poorer they had become in that interval of three years, and instead they searched for smaller apartments in the vicinity of Broad Street itself.

At the beginning of October Blake had to return to Sussex, in order to appear at the quarter sessions in Petworth; at this stage he had no formal defence or legal representation and, since he once more pleaded not guilty to charges of sedition and assault upon Scofield, a true bill of indictment was found against him. He was pledged to appear at the next quarter sessions, and so was compelled to endure another three months of nervous agony. But Hayley was stirred up and asked an old friend, Samuel Rose, to act as Blake's barrister while a solicitor was found in Chichester. It seems more than probable that Hayley also offered to pay all the costs of the matter and, naturally enough, Blake's previously low opinion of his patron began to change. He told Butts, to whom he had complained about Hayley, that he should 'burn what I have peevishly written about any friend. I have been very much degraded & injuriously treated; but if it all arise from my own fault, I ought to blame myself.' He also now maintained, 'If a Man offends me ignorantly & not designedly, surely I ought to consider him with favour & affection. Perhaps the simplicity of myself is the origin of all offences committed against me.'[13] Certainly he had no wish to alienate or offend Hayley now, especially when there were others who were already inclined to doubt his innocence. Lady Hesketh told Hayley that Blake had 'appeard to me much to blame, even upon his own representation of the matter, but if I may give credit to some reports which reachd me at that time, Mr B: was more *Seriously* to blame than you were at all aware of I believe – but I will only add on this Subject – that – *if he was*, I sincerely hope that you are no Stranger to it!'[14] This is all very mysterious but it seems their mutual friend Samuel Rose may have imparted information to her that he discovered during the course of preparing the defence. It might have concerned Blake's past association with such radicals as Joseph Johnson or William Sharp – one other correspondent, for example, told Hayley, 'I know our friend's eccentricity, and understood that, during the crisis of the French Revolution, he had been one of its earnest partisans.'[15] But Lady Hesketh's misgivings may also have been related to the unwillingness of the Felpham villagers to speak against Blake. Soldiers were not necessarily popular with the natives of Sussex among whom they had been consigned; they were thought to force up the price of commodities, and the military commanders were resented for their use of fields and farms in the neighbourhood. Neither were the locally enlisted men always happy to serve, and there were occasions when the Chichester Volunteers came close to mutiny. So there may be reason to believe, then, that a conspiracy of silence had been formed by the Felpham villagers in order to protect Blake from his military persecutors. But this is surmise only.

After the quarter sessions were over, Blake returned to London, where his wife remained anxious and ill. In this condition of nervous perturbation they still had to make their way in the great city, however, and their first step was to leave James Blake's house and move to lodgings at No. 17 South Molton Street. They rented two rooms on the first floor, no doubt above some kind of commercial establishment, in a narrow street just south of the point where Oxford Street became the Tyburn Road. Their landlord was a certain Mark Martin, and they were poor enough to remain here for the next seventeen years. The rooms were not large, but they were light and airy enough; from the back he could see the outline of Hyde Park, and from the front he looked out upon a row of shops and houses. But there were no trees here, no garden, no view of the Thames – as there had been in Lambeth – only the dark and muddy passages of central London that he had known since childhood. Behind the house was a malodorous street known as Poverty Lane. Blake had returned home. Here was 'Calvarys foot', since the old hanging garden of Tyburn was only a short distance away;[16] that is why there was an eternal gate hovering 'from Hyde Park / To Tyburns deathful shades'.[17]

> I behold London; a Human awful wonder of God!
> He says: Return, Albion, return! I give myself for thee:
> My Streets are my, Ideas of Imagination . . .
> I write in South Molton Street, what I both see and hear
> In regions of Humanity, in Londons opening streets.
> I see thee awful Parent Land in light, behold I see![18]

But what a homecoming it was. He found at once he was forgotten or out of favour. Hayley employed him to act as a kind of paid messenger for his research on a life of Romney, and Blake busied himself by listing the various locations of the painter's work. Flaxman also managed to place some small commissions for Blake's graver, including designs from the *Iliad*, and Fuseli provided him with two small Shakespearian scenes. But there was little else for him, and after 1804 there were to be no other commercial designs for eleven years – from which obscurity he would eventually emerge in the glorious role as an illustrator to one of Wedgwood's porcelain catalogues. 'How is it possible that a Man almost 50 Years of Age,' he complained to Hayley, be considered to be 'inferior to a boy of twenty, who scarcely has taken or deigns to take a pencil in hand . . . how is it possible that such a fop can be superior to the studious lover of Art can scarcely be imagin'd'. But then, as in all such situations of neglect, his vision breaks through with its own consolations. 'Yet I laugh and sing, for if on Earth neglected I am in heaven a Prince among Princes . . . I shall live altho' I should want bread – nothing is necessary to me but to do my Duty & to rejoice in the exceeding joy that is always poured out on my Spirit.'[19]

It was a strange time to be under the charge of sedition and threat of punishment, for all around him he could see that London was preparing for war with Napoleon. Nevertheless, in his letters to Hayley, he remarks upon the beneficent changes since his departure three years before: 'The shops in London improve; everything is elegant, clean and neat; the streets are widened where they were narrow . . .'[20] The transformation can be explained by the effect of the Paving Acts, passed during the period, which both legislated for more regular cleansing of the streets and provided for the building of gutters and pavements of Purbeck stone rather than the familiar and uncomfortable cobbles. Within a few years, also, gas would take over from the oil-lamps shining in their crystal globes. The war had encouraged various forms of economic expansion (most notably the building of the Thames docks) and, as Blake knew well enough, the arts of manufacture and the art of war could not be easily distinguished. Whatever he thought of the 'improvements', as they were known, he always understood the secret life of what was now the largest city in the world. In the long poem that he had brought with him from Felpham and which he was soon to complete, the Eternal Man cries out 'war is energy Enslavd', and Urizen laments his creation of the religion of war:

Saying O that I had never drank the wine nor eat the bread
Of dark mortality nor cast my view into futurity nor turnd
My back darkning the present clouding with a cloud
And building arches high & cities turrets & towers & domes
Whose smoke destroyd the pleasant gardens & whose running Kennels
Chokd the bright rivers burdning with my Ships the angry deep
Thro Chaos . . .[21]

This, too, is his vision of London as he sat brooding in South Molton Street.

·

In the second week of January 1805, he returned to Sussex for his trial on charges of sedition and assault. It is not clear whether he stayed with Hayley, but the evidence suggests he visited him at Felpham, carrying with him some work that Fuseli had asked him to deliver, but then found temporary lodgings in Chichester for a day or two before the trial itself. Hayley had, in the meantime, suffered a small accident: he had once again fallen from his horse while trying to unfurl his umbrella, and had been pitched headlong onto a piece of flint on the ground. He was wearing a newly strengthened hat, fortunately enough, and sustained only a minor cut; but it did not prevent him from magniloquently asserting, 'living or dying, I must make a public appearance at the trial of my friend Blake'.[22]

It was to be held at the Guildhall in Chichester; that edifice had once been the chancery of an ancient Grey Friars monastery, and was only a little larger than the average church hall, but it is an odd coincidence that Blake should find himself brought to justice in the Gothic surroundings which otherwise he so much admired. The trial was supposed to take place on 10 January, but it was postponed and did not begin until four o'clock the following day. The presiding judge or chairman of the sessions was, ominously enough, the Duke of Richmond; he was a quondam parliamentary reformer but, in the emergency of war preparations, he had assumed the role of field marshal and had responsibility for the troops around Chichester. No doubt he wanted to make an example of this seditionist. Hayley certainly believed that he was 'bitterly prejudiced' against Blake and in the course of the trial made some 'unwarrantable observations'.[23] Another of the judges, John Quantock, had been appointed field officer of the 'volunteers' on the same day Scofield had complained about Blake's language and behaviour. Very frequently in this period the jury was inclined to override the prejudices of the judiciary, however, and so the omens were finely balanced. Much depended upon the testimony of the Felpham witnesses, as opposed to that of the soldiers, and upon the skill of Blake's defending counsel. Blake himself, according to the procedures of the time, would not be called to give evidence.

The transcript of the trial has not survived, but there are reports from Hayley, Blake and others. It seems that the witnesses in his defence were of the type that would have recommended itself to a jury – an ostler, the wife of a miller's servant – and they all declared he had said nothing at all approaching sedition, had not uttered 'Damn the

King' or any such words. His accusers were soldiers of the lowest rank, however, and somewhat dubious reputation. Scofield, as already noted, had been reduced in office some years before. Samuel Rose, in defence, made a powerful if somewhat disingenuous speech in which he claimed, 'Mr Blake is as loyal a subject as any man in this court' and that the crime of which he was accused was of such 'extraordinary malignity' that it would brand him for ever with 'indelible disgrace' – 'he feels as much indignation at the idea of exposing to contempt or injury the sacred person of his sovereign as any man'.[24] Then Rose proceeded to depict his client in the most equable light, before denouncing Scofield as a 'degraded' man who was not to be trusted. He continued to describe the testimony of the various witnesses but then, only half-way through his prepared defence, he was seized with some illness and could only conclude his remarks, according to Hayley, 'with apparent infirmity'.[25] He could not even reply to the prosecuting counsel's closing speech, but there was no need to do so. The conflicting testimony of the soldiers themselves seems to have decided the matter – at one point, during their examination, Blake shouted out 'False!' in a voice 'which electrified the whole court . . . and carried conviction with it'.[26] One citizen of Chichester who was present at the trial said that 'the only thing he remembered of it was Blake's flashing eye'.[27] The jury's verdict was swift, and the trial lasted only one hour. Blake was acquitted and, as the *Sussex Advertiser* reported a few days later, the verdict 'so gratified the auditory that the court was, in defiance of all decency, thrown into an uproar by their noisy exultations'.[28] Hayley also reported that those in court were 'loud in the honest exultation of their joy in his acquittal';[29] Hayley immediately went up to the Duke of Richmond and congratulated him for having 'the gratification of seeing an honest man honorably delivered from an infamous persecution'. The Duke replied, somewhat testily, 'I know nothing of him.'[30] The brief remark does reveal one interesting point, however; it is clear that the prosecution and the judges were not aware of Blake's earlier radicalism, and in particular had known nothing of his acquaintance with Joseph Johnson or Mary Wollstonecraft. Any such association, brought out in open court, would have been sure to harm him. It also tends to refute Blake's later belief that 'the Government, or some high person, knowing him to have been of the Paine set, "sent the soldier to entrap him" '.[31] It is not inconceivable in the atmosphere of those times, but it is unlikely. After the trial was over Hayley and Blake rode on horseback to see

Harriet Poole, or the 'Lady of Lavant', and 'this anxious day concluded with much joy'.[32] The conclusion was not so joyful for Samuel Rose, however, whose infirmity at the trial was an indication of incipient consumption; he died a year later. 'Farewell, Sweet Rose!' Blake wrote, 'thou hast got before me into the Celestial City. I have also but a few more Mountains to pass.'[33]

He knew well enough that the mind has mountains, too, and it can fairly be said that the effect of the trial stayed with him for the rest of his life. It was not simply a question of being given a suspect character, although in such an uncertain period even the taint of sedition might have lost him patrons. It was that he had, for the first time, become entangled with the Law, that terrible place where convention and oppression meet and of which he seems to have been truly fearful. Law itself then becomes a dark region for Blake, to be placed within his complex mythology – 'Bowlahoola is namd Law. by mortals'.[34] But then less than twenty lines later we read, 'Bowlahoola is the Stomach in every individual man.'[35] Is there not something in this strange association that suggests Blake's own sick, physical horror at the prospect of trial and imprisonment? The name of Scofield, as well as those of his other accusers and judges, recur throughout the rest of his poetry:

Scofield! Kox, Kotope and Bowen, revolve most mightily upon
The Furnace of Los: before the eastern gate bending their fury.
They war, to destroy the Furnaces, to desolate Golgonooza:
And to devour the Sleeping Humanity of Albion in rage & hunger . . .

Go thou to Skofield: ask him if he is Bath or if he is Canterbury
Tell him to be no more dubious: demand explicit words
Tell him: I will dash him into shivers, where & at what time
I please: tell Hand & Skofield they are my ministers of evil
To those I hate: for I can hate also as well as they![36]

And so it goes on, with other references to this private soldier as 'Adam who was New-Created in Edom' and one of the 'Giants' who created the fallen material illusion of our world.[37] Scofield is enlarged in Blake's mythology because he was the porter who opened the gate into Blake's private hell. He was the emblem of all that he feared – the accuser, the summoner up of childhood woes. He was the destroyer, and yet he may also have been a creator; the experience of anxiety and relief, of despair and exaltation at his acquittal, helped to change Blake's sense of his self and of his art. In the months after his trial he was to experience a new revelation.

TWENTY-ONE

Despair

He had escaped from 'the arrows of darkness', he said.[1]
Catherine had been 'near the Gate of Death' as a result of his
ordeal, and had been nursed by a fellow-lodger in South
Molton Street while he remained in Chichester.[2] But his safe
homecoming prompted her own return to health, and for all this
Blake could hardly express his thanks to Hayley: 'Gratitude is Heaven
itself; there could be no heaven without Gratitude. I feel it & I know
it. I thank God & Man for it & above all You, My dear friend &
benefactor in the Lord.'[3] His own reaction to these events was to
contract some kind of violent cold or fever, which consigned him to
bed for three days, but as soon as he recovered he began to act for
Hayley. One of his most urgent commissions was of course to discover
the location of Romney's paintings and drawings, but he was also
involved in some engraving work for his old patron. He was working
on the design for a memorial to Cowper, and he was expecting to
complete many of the plates for Romney's biography as well as those
for the new edition of Hayley's *Triumphs of Temper*; both men had also
been discussing the prospects for an edition of Cowper's translations
from Milton, and a new edition of Cowper's own work. Blake always
addresses Hayley as 'sir' in his correspondence, and shows perhaps
excessive subservience both to him and to Flaxman. It would seem
that the experience with the soldier had thoroughly unnerved or
demoralised him, and the letters from the months after the trial show
little sense of his own worth as an artist or as a man. 'I will not advise
any thing till Flaxman sees them . . . Your anxiously devoted Will
Blake . . . I beg your remarks also on both my performances, as in
their present state they will be capable of very much improve-

ment . . . Your beautiful and elegant Venusea grows in our estimation on a second and third perusal . . . I will neither Do nor say but as you Direct.'⁴ And so it goes on. There may have been some excuse for him to defer to Flaxman's judgment, since he was considered to be one of the greatest artists in Europe, but he was perhaps over-gilding the lily of gratitude when he professes admiration for all the books that Hayley sent him: 'I will again read Clarissa &c., they must be admirable . . . I have read the book thro' attentively and was much entertain'd and instructed . . . I thank you sincerely for Falconer, an admirable poet, and the admirable prints to it by Fittler. Whether you intended it or not, they have given me some excellent hints in engraving; his manner of working is what I shall endeavour to adopt in many points.'⁵ The engraving to which he refers is 'The Shipwreck' and the title might aptly refer to Blake's own hopes of future patronage – it was the only engraving of his that was eventually published in Hayley's *Life of Romney*.

It is a mark of Blake's essentially solitary character that his attempts to work with, or for, others seem always to have been frustrated: it was in these months, too, that he tried unsuccessfully to interest Hayley in the editing of a periodical to be entitled *The Defence of Literature*. The idea had emerged from Blake's conversations with Prince Hoare, the foreign secretary of the Royal Academy whose pamphlet on art had been illustrated with a rather sketchy engraving by him a few months before; Hoare in turn introduced him to Richard Phillips, a radical bookseller and publisher who had once been imprisoned for distributing Tom Paine's *Rights of Man*. 'So you see,' Blake wrote to Hayley, 'he is spiritually adjoin'd with us.'⁶ Hoare and Phillips intended to establish a periodical to act as an antidote to what they considered the corrupt 'pests' of the literary press and perhaps as a radical alternative to the Whiggish mores of the recently established *Edinburgh Review*.⁷ Hayley was to be its editor, and Phillips would contribute two thousands pounds a year to ensure the journal's quality and circulation. But Hayley prevaricated, nominated a deputy, who duly went to Russia, and the project failed altogether. Blake had hoped for some 'bulwark for Genius', no doubt including his own.⁸ Not for the first time in his life, he was disappointed.

In fact there was nothing but disappointment and defeat ahead of him now. Of all the projects that he and Hayley had discussed, for example, only two were ever completed. Even while Blake was busy with pictorial research for the *Life of Romney*, Hayley was actively looking for other engravers; even Flaxman was recommending another man, Cromek, for work on that volume. But the fault was not necessarily theirs; Blake was at this stage excessively undependable. Hayley had continually to press him to complete two plates depicting Cowper's monument; although he promised 'Proofs in another week', they were not finally despatched until six weeks later.[9] 'The fresh Engravings we expected from Blake by the Coach of Tuesday,' Hayley wrote, 'were not arriv'd when Seagrave met me at the Cottage on Friday – our mutual Consternation was extreme . . .'[10] It was the same pattern of tardiness that disrupted work on the one plate he completed for Hayley's Life of Romney: 'I am going on briskly with the Plates,' he had written to him in the first weeks of 1804, '& if God blesses me with health doubt not yet to make a Figure in the Great Dance of Life that shall amuse the Spectators in the Sky.'[11] A year later he had still not finished them. His own explanation for this slowness in the production of his engravings was 'my solicitude to bring them to perfection', which included 'giving the last touches, which are always the best'.[12] Of course there was truth to this, although his tendency to overelaborate and overwork a plate or painting was one for which he often castigated himself; but the patience of his employer could not have been improved by Blake's subtle, and sometimes not so subtle, requests for money. He was at pains to inform Hayley how busily employed other engravers were, thus preventing them from doing other work, and how much they customarily charged for their services. On some occasions he also asked directly for more cash on account: 'I must now tell my wants, & beg the favour of some more of the needful: the favor of ten Pounds will carry me thru this Plate & the Head of Romney, for which I am already paid.'[13] At the same time he was unnerved by the competitive life around him – 'I must say that in London every calumny and falsehood utter'd against another of the same trade is thought fair play . . . we are not in a field of battle, but in a City of Assassinations.'[14]

It was in every respect a troubling time for him, and there is reason to believe that he felt some shame for his financial demands and his own commercial ineptitude. He was not really fit to ply his wares in the market place, despite his grandiose ambitions, and he knew it. Indeed there were periods, such as this one, when he became so vulnerable to the world that the various elements of his character unravel and display themselves without the chastening effect of his genius. So we have, in the space of one letter to Hayley, an encomium on 'Eternity' and 'Spirits' as well as a direct request for money couched in ingenuously visionary terms – 'Now, My Dear Sir, I will thank you for the transmission of ten Pounds to the Dreamer'.[15] There are occasions when it seems he has almost lost control over his personality or, rather, that its various aspects jostle for attention – the visionary and the tradesman, the poet and the fantasist, the prophet and the hypocrite, the passive servant and the self-righteous autodidact. All these various selves seem then to strive for mastery, and it is possible to see even here in the chaos of Blake's despair one of the sources for the drama of his Prophetic Books, where various faculties and aptitudes are engaged in a constant battle for supremacy. In moments of vision, however, all is reconciled – just as in his life the bewildering complexities of his behaviour can be transformed in an epiphany and, for a moment, all is healed.

It happened in the autumn of 1804, when he entered the Truchsessian Gallery in the New Road opposite Portland Place. Count Truchsess had lost his fortune in the French Revolution, according to his own account, and was obliged to bring his collection of paintings to England, where by means of subscription he intended to form a permanent gallery. The required amount for this venture was sixty thousand guineas, and whether or not he acquired that very large sum he did indeed transport nine hundred works of art. These were the paintings Blake now saw. 'Suddenly, on the day after visiting the Truchsessian Gallery of Pictures,' he wrote to Hayley, 'I was again enlightened with the light I enjoyed in my youth, and which has for exactly twenty years been closed from me as by a door and by window-shutters.' It is an extraordinary letter, which goes on with another revealing passage: '. . . excuse my enthusiasm or rather madness, for I am really drunk with intellectual vision whenever I take a pencil or graver into my hand, even as I used to be in my youth, and as I have not been for twenty dark, but very profitable years. I thank God that I courageously pursued my course through darkness.'

He is very specific about the period of darkness he has had to undergo, with a duration of twenty years up to this year of 1804. 1784 was the year in which his father died and in which he set up the print-selling business with James Parker in Broad Street. It was the beginning, then, of his life as a tradesman, conducted perhaps in emulation of his dead father. But Blake's letter offers other direct evidence about his state of mind. The description of his revelation in

the gallery on New Street is prefaced by one significant reference –
'Our good and kind friend Hawkins is not yet in town – hope soon to
have the pleasure of seeing him, with the courage of conscious
industry, worthy of his former kindness to me.' John Hawkins was the
man who, exactly twenty years before, had tried to raise a subscription
to allow Blake to continue his artistic studies in Italy; the effort had
not proved successful, but clearly Blake had not forgotten it or
misunderstood its possible significance in his life. If he had been able
to travel to Italy, to study the great masters he revered, he would not
have been forced into commercial life. He might never have been
compelled to earn his living as a copy-engraver. He would have been
an artist, not an artisan. So now, after twenty years 'as a slave bound
in a mill among beasts and devils', what is the nature and force of his
'intellectual vision'?[16] He declares that his life and art have been
renewed by it, so perhaps we can look for the source of renewal in the
works which he saw on that autumn day.

He was once more in the presence of those masters whom he had
loved since childhood – Dürer, Giulio Romano, Michelangelo – and
in this revelation there is almost a nostalgic longing for the sense of
the sacred that he had possessed as a child. He had been through so
much in his life, but now he was back at the pure well of his original
inspiration. On display in the Truchsessian Gallery among these great
works he had revered in youth were certain artists of the early German
and Netherlandish Schools – Schongauer, Gossaert, Matsys – whose
spiritual intensity and formal refinement were so much a part of the
'Gothic' sensibility that he had imbibed while young. As he said, 'I
was again enlightened with the light I enjoyed in my youth', and out
of that reawakening came a new sense of life and of his duty to his art.
It is significant that after this time he speaks only with loathing for the
work of Rubens, of Rembrandt and of Correggio. These artists (or
works from their studio) were also on display in the gallery, and it is
clear that, in their proximity to the great works of his youth, they
seemed to him only blurred and indistinct visions of the material
world that he despised. But there was also another aspect to his
distaste, which in part explains the fury that he would direct against
them – there is no doubt that in the work he had completed over those
last twenty 'dark' years he had been influenced both by Rembrandt
and by Correggio. There are certain of his temperas, for example, that
employ soft tints and reflected lights in a manner which he came to
abhor. So he was expelling his own demons when he attacks those

artists who 'cause that the execution shall be all blocked up with brown shadows. They put the original Artist in fear and doubt of his own original conception.'[17] That 'original conception' was what he had rediscovered in the gallery, and it was to take him forward into the next stage of his art. 'I have lost my Confusion of Thought while at work,' he told Hayley a few weeks later, '& am as much myself when I take the Pencil or Graver into my hand as I used to be in my Youth.'[18]

So he realised now that journeyman commerce and mechanical engraving had come close to ruining his life and his work. This was the 'spectrous Fiend' who had also been 'the enemy of conjugal love', a reference that suggests his sexual nature had also been thwarted by the pursuit of money and of work.[19] It is significant that he did no more commercial engraving for eleven years; he had found 'the courage to suffer poverty and disgrace, till he ultimately conquers'.[20] But the consequences of his revelation were also of a more positive kind. He knew instinctively he should return to that 'true Art Calld Gothic in All Ages', an art of form and outline, which are themselves the lineaments of the spirit;[21] he believed he had rediscovered the art that expressed 'the eternal Principles that exist in all ages'.[22] He had recollected his childhood experiences in Westminster Abbey and now once more asserted the necessity of 'Conversing with Eternal Realities as they Exist in the Human Imagination We are in a World of Generation & death & this world we must cast off if we would be Painters'.[23] From this period, too, he throws off the influence of classical art as inimical to true vision and, as a result, believes himself to be returning to his native English style.

There is a watercolour that he painted in the months after visiting the Truchsessian Exhibition; it is entitled 'Christ in the Sepulchre, Guarded by Angels' and displays two angels hovering in prayer above the body of the Lord, their wings almost in the form of a canopy. Blake said in a later description that he wished to see this painting in fresco, and enlarged to such a size that it would be an 'ornament' within a church.[24] Yet that is precisely where he had once seen something very much like it; the composition of this painting closely resembles the tomb of Countess Aveline in Westminster Abbey. He had drawn it for Basire, thirty years before, and the reawakening of his artistic vision is in that respect a continuation of the spiritual revelation he had experienced as a boy. The first sight of that tomb seems to have become for Blake a primal form, an image of art and

holiness itself, and in the verses he now wrote in South Molton Street
he returns to it yet again:

> Two winged immortal shapes one standing at his feet
> Toward the East one standing at his head toward the west
> Their wings joind in the Zenith over head
> Such is a Vision of All Beulah hovring over the Sleeper . . .
>
> Then Los said I behold the Divine Vision thro the broken Gates
> Of thy poor broken heart astonishd melted into Compassion & Love.[25]

He goes on to invoke the 'Lamb of God', and one of the consequences
of his artistic renewal is a return to the original biblical sources of his
inspiration; in the later sections of *Vala*, completed in London, he
introduces a large number of names ultimately derived from the Old
Testament, and it is as if the memory of his revelation in Westminster
Abbey had stirred all his childhood recollections of the Bible.

But it is no longer the Bible of angels and prophets, whose images
he had seen in visions around him, since now he emphasises more
than ever before the presence of Christ the Redeemer, the spiritual
outline of the Divine Man. But, in a period when Blake felt himself to
have been suddenly 'free from fetters' of the past,[26] he depicts 'The
Raising of Lazarus', 'The Angel Rolling the Stone away from the
Sepulchre', 'The Resurrection', 'The Transfiguration' and 'The
Ascension'. It was now that he took out his early engraving of 'Albion
Rose', showing a youth with arms outstretched in liberation, and
began infinitely to lighten it with burnishing. He had completed that
work in 1780, at the end of his apprenticeship, but now the joyful
figure had a further resonance for Blake, who added beneath the
image, 'Albion rose from where he labourd at the Mill with Slaves /
Giving himself for the Nations he danc'd the dance of Eternal Death'.
Through the nets of hatching and cross-hatching shines the bright
burnishing around the head and upper body of Albion, as if that
spiritual light might banish the codes and bonds of commercial
engraving. It is in this period, too, that Blake begins to adopt the
Swedenborgian word 'translucence', and in his art there is a fresh
sense of light as a form of spiritual revelation.

It was not his art alone that was affected by the pictures at the
exhibition; in the same year he visited the gallery in the New Road,
he also engraved the frontispieces for two new poems, *Milton* and
Jerusalem, which he was not to complete for some years. In this time of
freedom and exaltation he could see ahead of him the shadowy forms

of new and sublime works. Now, once again, he took up his brother's old notebook. He had begun to use it while at Felpham, to sketch out some designs for Hayley's *Ballads*, but at this moment he returned joyfully to the lyric stanzas of his early *Songs*. One of the poems is very short, scribbled in pencil as if it had emerged fully complete:

> Throughout all Eternity
> I forgive you you forgive me
> As our dear Redeemer said
> This the Wine & this the Bread.[27]

But there were other forms of vision that directly affected the life of the Blakes in South Molton Street. Catherine had become sick again of the rheumatism she had contracted in the dampness of the Felpham cottage, and she was being treated by 'Mr Birch's Electrical Magic'[28] – two years before, Joseph Johnson had published Birch's *Essay on the Medical Application of Electricity*, in which was described 'The application of the electric fluid to the diseases of the human body . . . under the form of a star'.[29] In a later etching Blake would show his own figure being touched by a star, entering through his left foot, and it is hard not to associate his belief in electricity with his older attachment to various forms of magical activity. Indeed the magician and magnetic healer Richard Cosway now lived around the corner from the Blakes in Stratford Place; they resumed their old acquaintance, and no doubt discussed the arcana of 'modern Magical Science' in which the ancient theories of Paracelsus and sexual occultism were compounded with the recent discoveries of Mesmer and Birch himself.[30] Various organs of the human body were supposed to harbour different spiritual fluids or emanations, which could be manipulated by the animal magnetiser, and there were some adepts who believed they could actually see the organs of those whom they treated. Such beliefs may explain some of the more puzzling areas of Blake's mythic poetry:

> The First State is in the Head, the Second is in the Heart:
> The Third in the Loins & Seminal Vessels & the Fourth
> In the Stomach & Intestines terrible, deadly, unutterable
> And he whose Gates are opend in those Regions of his Body
> Can from those Gates view all these wondrous Imaginations.[31]

Yet Blake's visionary dreams and revelations were no stay against the claims of the world and, even after his experience at the exhibition, he was not able to remove himself altogether from commercial considerations. He had decided to abandon journeyman engraving, but he still had to earn a living. He was particularly eager to have an edition of Hayley's *Ballads*, with his own engravings, published in small volume form; he entered negotiations with Richard Phillips, whose enthusiasm for Hayley, if not for Blake, had survived the disappointment over *The Defence of Literature*. There were problems with printers and contracts, however, which threw him into another furious bout of nervous anxiety – 'I am chiefly concerned for Poor Blake,' Phillips told Hayley, 'who has been sadly tortured by these untoward circumstances', with the use of 'Poor Blake' once more emphasising the pity which he inspired in those who knew him.[32] The book was eventually published – 'this beautiful little estate' Blake called it, since Hayley allowed him to retain all the income from its sales, but there is no evidence of its success.[33] In fact, in the early months of 1805, he was still acting as Hayley's agent while praising him somewhat effusively; but there were certain signs of tension. He professed himself unhurt when his patron began to look for new engravers for *The Life of Romney*, but he could not have been particularly happy with the decision. And Hayley himself, although still defending his erstwhile protégé, was becoming distinctly less enthusiastic about his artistic skills; he sent the new volume of *Ballads* to Lady Hesketh with the request that she 'smile on his gratitude tho you will frown on some productions of his pencil, particularly *the last*, in the little volume, which He thinks the best – so little can artists & authors judge of their own recent Composition'. He then described Blake's engravings for the Cowper volume as exhibiting '*more Zeal*, than *Success*'.[34] There was here, then, at least the possibility of disagreement.

But there was one patron who never seemed to doubt his genius and, as the interest of Hayley began to diminish, Thomas Butts once more took over the role of Blake's principal employer; for the next five years he gave him regular payments that allowed him to maintain a steady if modest income. At the beginning of this period he was still working upon the biblical watercolours which Butts had commissioned; he had begun them before he left for Felpham but now, after the revelation in the Truchsessian Gallery, there is a subtle but nevertheless noticeable difference of emphasis. They are executed upon thick drawing paper, with the watercolours perfectly boxed and outlined in Blake's familiar meticulous way. But they no longer possess the dramatic configurations and shadowy contrasts of the earlier watercolours; they are much more formal and hieratic compositions. They are no longer theatrical; they are emblematic. 'The Resurrection' depicts the risen Christ, bathed in a bright effulgent light, as he soars from the unsealed stone archway of the tomb; 'And the Angel which I Saw Lifted up his Hand to Heaven' shows the mighty figure of Revelation surrounded by brightness as the sea turns to fire where his feet have touched it. In all of these watercolours there is an exultant spirituality that is quite new in Blake's art. There is also more splendour and nobility in the conception of the human figures, who seem touched by some mystery, a mystery that Blake characteristically suggests through the powerful use of light and an intense concentration upon the central numinous figure. This formal intensity is highly reminiscent of the fifteenth-century art that he had rediscovered – one of his watercolours takes the shape of a medieval roof boss – and there is the sense that, for him, grace and revelation have become matters of immediate import. Everything takes place upon the surface of the painting; this is not because he has managed to unlearn the rules of perspective (although he was never very concerned with them) but because he is returning to an art in which there was no need for ambiguity or indeterminacy. The watercolours have faded over the last two centuries but, in some of them, the vivid blues linger upon the surface of the paper as a reminder of the brightness that had once existed there. It is an art, of course, which reflects his own temperament. He also went on to complete, for example, nineteen watercolours from the story of Job. The sufferings of that patriarch had already been depicted by him, but this was the first series of paintings devoted to the theme; they have great formal control and fluency but, in the narrative of Job's miseries and their eventual alleviation, it is hard not to see Blake creating an allegory of his own life. In fact the story of Job was to become of central importance to him, and he devoted more than seventy paintings and engravings to its exposition. And why should he not do so? It would be fair to say that few artists of genius had endured as much neglect and derision as he.

So Blake created new works for Butts but, no doubt on the well-founded if unspoken grounds that Butts was becoming a kind of artistic guardian, he also provided him with examples of his previous art. He completed new versions of the twelve 'colour prints' he had made ten years before, 'Newton' and 'Nebuchadnezzar' among them;

he may have kept the original millboards or coppers with him over that period, and applied fresh glue-based colours before printing them out. It is more likely, however, that he already possessed certain printed impressions upon which he now elaborated with pen and watercolour. He also gave Butts copies of *The Marriage of Heaven and Hell*, *The Book of Urizen* and *Songs of Innocence and of Experience*, which he still had in stock, the latter having to be in parts repainted and strengthened in the same fashion as the colour prints. Blake was also being paid to teach Butts's son the art of painting for the sum of twenty-five guineas a year. He was not in immediate want, therefore, and the best computation of his annual income over these years is between seventy and one hundred pounds; this is a little more than a competent journeyman engraver would have received, but of course very much less than such contemporaries as Sharp or Cosway or Parker. Blake was fully aware of this and, although he had reduced the 'spectrous Fiend' of commerce to its properly subordinate role, he believed 'works of Art can only be produced in Perfection where the Man is either in Affluence or is Above the Care of it'.[35] He particularly despised the 'Vile' arguments of those who professed to believe that poverty, and lack of proper patronage, were somehow good for him; he knew that penury and absence of recognition had only caused his art to suffer.

That was why he was so eager to take up a commission proposed to him in the autumn of 1805. He was approached by Robert Hartley Cromek, a thirty-five-year-old engraver who had decided to turn to the more lucrative trade of book publishing and selling. If we are to believe Blake's later accounts of him, he was a liar, a cheat and a hypocrite; in fact he was an enterprising and intelligent man who wished to serve Blake's best interests as well as his own. He had been a pupil of the great Italian engraver Bartolozzi, and had himself become an expert craftsman much admired by Flaxman and often employed by Stothard; ill health and a nervous constitution, however, made it impossible for him to sustain the patient drudgery and close confinement incumbent upon the engraver's task. So he set up as a bookseller, and his first venture was to produce an illustrated edition of *The Grave* by Robert Blair. It was one of the most popular works in the 'graveyard school' of mid-eighteenth-century English poetry and, as such, would already have been of some interest to Blake. It is probable Flaxman suggested to Cromek that Blake was the best possible illustrator for such a venture; but in any case Cromek, knowing George Cumberland, as well as Flaxman and Stothard, would have been well acquainted with his work. So he approached Blake, and proposed that the artist should prepare some forty designs in illustration of the poem. It was intended to be a handsome volume, purchased on subscription, and there is no doubt that Cromek was taking a calculated risk in choosing so unfashionable an artist as Blake had become. His proposal was not overgenerous since, at a guinea for each design, it was no more than Blake already received from Thomas Butts; but, as Flaxman said in a letter to Hayley, 'if he will only condescend to give that attention to his worldly concerns which every one does that prefers living to Starving, he is now in a way to do well'.[36]

Within two months he had completed twenty designs, of which Cromek seems to have approved; the bookseller showed them to the most senior Royal Academicians – among them Benjamin West and Thomas Lawrence – who were graciously pleased to honour the volume with 'Subscriptions and Patronage'.[37] Cromek also persuaded Blake's old friend Henry Fuseli to write an introduction. At the same time he issued a prospectus that promised 'FIFTEEN PRINTS FROM DESIGNS INVENTED AND TO BE ENGRAVED BY WILLIAM BLAKE; WITH A PREFACE CONTAINING AN EXPLANATION OF THE ARTIST'S VIEW IN THE DESIGNS AND A CRITIQUE ON THE POEM'.[38] He then exhibited the designs at his new shop at No. 23 Warren Street, by Fitzroy Square. It was proving a successful speculation, and so it was agreed that Blake should be allowed to engrave his own illustrations; twelve were chosen out of the twenty prepared, and at once he set to work on the first of them. It was entitled 'Death's Door', and within a week or two he presented it to Cromek for his sanction. But Cromek emphatically did not give it; he told Stothard that Blake 'had etched one of the subjects, but so indifferently and so carelessly . . . that he employed Schiavonetti to engrave them'.[39] Luigi Schiavonetti was a safe choice: he had been a fellow pupil with Cromek under Bartolozzi, and so both men knew each other well. But why was it that Cromek had found Blake's engraving work indifferent? 'Death's Door' does not seem careless at this late date, but Blake had made the mistake of attempting a bold and unfamiliar style; he had executed a relief etching entirely in 'white line', by which is meant that the normal processes of printing are reversed and the lines of the composition stand out white against a black background. It is similar in effect to the 'negative' print of a photograph, although Blake's methods are not simply confined to the techniques of the matter. It is a wonderful image, taken from various elements of his own earlier work – an old man seems to be blown towards the stone portal of death, while above that mournful edifice sits a naked and joyful young man who looks up towards the heavens. He is covered in radiance, and the essential effect of the 'white line' technique, as in the watercolours of the period, is to reinforce Blake's belief that there is a light to be found within all things. Cromek, however, thought otherwise: to him it seemed simply anomalous, incomplete, and primitive in execution. Certainly he did not believe it a suitable style for a fashionable volume – and no doubt everyone except Blake would have agreed with him. So he turned to his old colleague, and asked him to engrave something more suitable from Blake's designs. The salient fact was that, since both Cromek and Schiavonetti had once worked for the supreme stipple engraver of the day, they were both highly skilled in a style that was variously described as 'soft', 'sweet', 'graceful' and 'tender'. In all respects, then, their techniques were quite the opposite of those which Blake might be inclined to admire.

A new prospectus was issued by Cromek, indicating now that *The Grave* was 'TO BE ILLUSTRATED WITH TWELVE VERY SPIRITED ENGRAVINGS BY LOUIS SCHIAVONETTI, FROM DESIGNS INVENTED BY WILLIAM BLAKE'.[40] The finished engravings are in fact skilful and evocative works; Blake's extraordinary technique has obviously gone, but some of his power remains. Cromek is generally considered to have been at fault in this arrangement, largely because of Blake's later complaints, but it is easy to understand why he acted as he did. He was not out of sympathy with Blake's beliefs or with Blake's art, and indeed a surviving letter from him to another poet suggests that he had great sympathy with him; he talks of Blake's 'usual Characteristics – Sublimity, Simplicity, Elegance and Pathos, his wildness *of course*'. In the same letter he describes his 'Noble though extravagant Flights' and makes a half-joking reference to 'wild and wonderful genius'.[41] But here, also, lies the reason why he rejected Blake's engraving: it was too 'wild', too 'extravagant' for his proposed volume. Luigi Schiavonetti tamed his genius and subdued his art to the taste of the time; it is hard to believe that any other bookseller would have acted differently. Indeed Flaxman himself seems to have agreed with Cromek's decision – although he does not refer to it directly, in a letter about Blake during this period he remarks, 'I fear his abstracted habits are so much at variance with the usual modes of human life, that he will not derive all the advantage to be wished from the present favourable appearances.'[42] There is an obvious meaning here, from a successful artist such as Flaxman, but also a more ambiguous one; 'abstracted habits' is a vague phrase, but it may well summarise Blake's continual visionary capacity as well as his fervent belief in the 'Spirits' which surrounded him. That had never changed over the years.

And what of his own feelings in the matter? He was, naturally enough, disappointed; there is an indication of his hurt in a letter to Hayley at this time when he says, 'my Fate has been so uncommon that I expect Nothing. I was alive & in health & with the same Talents I now have all the time of Boydell's, Macklin's, Bowyer's, & other Great Works. I was known by them & was look'd upon by them as Incapable of Employment in those Works; it may turn out so again, notwithstanding appearances.'[43] He is referring here to his previous inability to find work upon the 'Galleries' or series of engravings that became popular in the 1780s and 1790s; but there is also a clear indication that he does not expect very much from Cromek. At this stage, however, even after the publisher had diverted the engravings to Schiavonetti, they remained on relatively friendly terms. In fact Blake had some cause to be grateful to Cromek, despite 'appearances', since, as his mid-Victorian biographer reported in the 1860s, it was 'that series of Drawings illustrative of Blair's Grave by which . . . Blake is most widely known – known at all, I may say – to the public at large'.[44] That was also true within Blake's own lifetime, as Cromek had something of a genius for promoting his wares. He had displayed Blake's designs in his shop and had solicited the approbation of the Royal Academy for them, as we have seen, but now he went to great lengths to advertise *The Grave* in the provincial newspapers. He also commissioned Thomas Phillips to paint Blake's portrait, which Schiavonetti then engraved as a frontispiece; it is a striking, if somewhat idealised, picture of Blake as the inspired artist. We see what another contemporary noticed with 'his head big and round, his eyes . . . large and lambent',[45] but it is also worth recalling that it was while sitting to Phillips that Blake told the story of the visiting angel who claimed to have been painted by Michelangelo. Perhaps that accounts for what one reviewer of the painting called 'a wildness in the eye'.[46] Mrs Blake never liked the portrait but, in gratitude, Blake presented Phillips with a copy of *Songs of Innocence and of Experience*.

Cromek may also have played some part in arranging the first extended description of Blake in published form; it came in a preface to a book by a friend of Cromek, Benjamin Heath Malkin, who privately published a memoir of his dead son entitled *A Father's Memoir of his Child*. Blake designed the frontispiece, picturing the dead child, and made an engraving from it; Cromek then erased Blake's engraving, and did one of his own. There may have been some small disagreement over this, but the most important element in the publication is the account that Malkin gives of Blake's life and genius. It represents the first accurate description of his youth and early career, undoubtedly derived from Blake himself, and includes a fine tribute to his 'warm and brilliant imagination'.[47] There is also more than a trace of Blake's own opinions in Malkin's attack upon those sceptics and rationalists who have disparaged the poet: 'By them have the higher powers of this artist been kept from public notice, and his genius tied down, as far as possible, to the mechanical department of his profession. By them, in short, has he been stigmatised as an engraver, who might do tolerably well, if he was not mad.'[48] This is the first direct reference to his 'madness', no doubt broached by the poet himself, and suggests the way he must have complained to his friends about his neglect. But it is clear that Malkin and Cromek did believe in his genius, and were making every effort to promote it. Henry Fuseli still had faith in his old acquaintance, also, and provided Cromek with an encomium on his designs, which 'claim approbation, sometimes excite our wonder, and not seldom our fears, when we see him play on the very verge of legitimate invention; but wildness so picturesque in itself, so often redeemed by taste, simplicity and elegance, what child of fancy, what artist would wish to discharge?'[49] Fuseli, like Cromek, mentions the 'wildness' but it cannot be said that, at this stage, Blake lacked admirers.

The Grave sold well, and Cromek described it as 'very lucrative' as well as a 'very honourable Speculation'.[50] Blake had not profited financially from it, at least not on the same scale as Cromek and Schiavonetti, but he thought highly enough of his designs to consider publishing them separately in a portfolio. He composed a title page, and although nothing further came of that project he was right to consider them worthy of separate notice. They represent some of his finest illustrated work; such designs as 'The Reunion of the Soul and the Body' and 'The Soul hovering over the Body reluctantly parting with Life' affirm once more that vibrant spirituality and formal intensity which were so much part of his biblical watercolours. The light of the Truchsessian Exhibition and Westminster Abbey is visible here in various images that haunted him – once again the formal shape of Countess Aveline's tomb is repeated, and in works such as 'The Counselor, King, Warrior, Mother & Child in the Tomb' he explicitly reverts to his earliest influences.

But the critical reaction to them was harsh. Robert Hunt, in *The Examiner*, described Blake's designs as 'absurd', while in the course of a long attack the *Anti-Jacobin* described them 'as the offspring of a morbid fancy'.[51] The critic then commented on a prefatory poem that Blake had composed. 'Should he again essay to climb the Parnassian heights, his friends would do well to restrain his wanderings by the strait waistcoat. Whatever licence we may allow him as a painter, to tolerate him as a poet would be insufferable.'[52] Once again the imputation of madness had been cast upon him, and we may judge his reaction from a letter he had written to Hayley at the time when he was being attacked by the newspaper reviewers for his illustrations to the *Ballads*. 'Receiving a Prophet As a Prophet is a Duty,' he wrote, 'which If omitted is more Severely Avenged than Every Sin & Wickedness beside. It is the Greatest of Crimes to Depress True Art & Science . . . I know that such Mockers are Most Severely Punish'd in Eternity. I know it, for I see it & dare not help. The Mocker of Art is the Mocker of Jesus.'[53] He still saw himself as a prophet, therefore, and it is possible to detect here some reason for the intensity he conveyed within his biblical watercolours. He knew well enough that, as haters of true art and of Blake's visionary conceptions, the worst punishment of such critics was simply to be themselves. But still he detested what he called 'Sneerers',[54] and a few months later he wrote an indignant letter in defence of Fuseli, who had been subject to 'widely diffused malice' by 'those wretches who, under pretence of criticism, use the dagger and the poison'.

There is no doubt that he also felt himself to be under threat, and by the end of 1805 all the resentments, rebuffs and misfortunes seemed to gather around him. Cromek's decision to employ Schiavonetti to engrave Blake's own designs was only the latest in a series of humiliations: Hayley was rapidly losing interest in his former protégé and was now actively looking for other engravers, Richard Phillips had somehow managed to enrage him over the publication of the *Ballads* and, at the same time, a definite coolness had entered his relationship with Flaxman. It occurred just at the time when he was removed from *The Grave* project, and it may well be that he believed Flaxman to have supported Cromek's refusal to accept his engravings.

In the middle of December Flaxman wrote to Hayley, 'When You have occasion to write to Mr Blake pray inquire if he has sufficient time to spare from his present undertaking to engrave, my drawings of Hero & Leander, & the orphan family, if he has not I shall look out for another engraver. I would rather this question should be proposed by you rather than me because I would not have either his good nature or his convenience strained to work after my designs.'[55] It is difficult to believe that Flaxman could not send a message to South Molton Street, and it seems likely that he was deliberately avoiding Blake even as he tried to assist him. No such commission was given, however, and he did not work with Flaxman for another ten years; three years after this letter was written, Flaxman confirmed that he and Blake never saw each other. Blake had prayed for Hayley's eyesight in the spring of 1805 – 'after reading in his Bible of the eyes of the Almighty', he 'instantly went down on his knees and prayed that God would strengthen the eyes of his friend' – but his last letter to his patron was written in the closing weeks of that year.[56] There is no evidence that they ever met or corresponded again. He begins this final communication in characteristic style, 'I cannot omit to Return you my sincere & Grateful Acknowledgments for the kind Reception . . .'[57] But he was also scribbling couplets in his dead brother's notebook in quite another vein:

On H—— the Pick thank

I write the Rascal Thanks till he & I
With Thanks & Compliments are quite drawn dry.[58]

Hayley is the target of ten separate epigrams, although sometimes he is joined by other of Blake's erstwhile friends:

My title as a Genius thus is provd
Not Praisd by Hayley nor by Flaxman lovd.[59]

For the most part these short verses are written in a neat hand above and below the emblems he had once drawn for 'Gates of Paradise'. It may seem particularly eccentric on his part to divulge his most intimate expression in this manner but epigrams, part of the currency of the age, were widely circulated in private form. These were clearly not meant to be circulated at all, however, and once more suggest his isolation. Here is one addressed to Flaxman:

I mock thee not tho I by thee am Mocked
Thou callst me Madman but I call thee Blockhead.[60]

Another is addressed equally to Flaxman and to Stothard:

> I found them blind I taught them how to see
> And now they know neither themselves nor me.[61]

Cromek, too, receives his fair due of bitterness:

> Cr—— loves artists as he loves his Meat
> He loves the Art but tis the Art to Cheat
>
> A Petty sneaking Knave I knew
> O M^r Cr—— how do ye do.[62]

None of it is necessarily very serious, of course, except Blake's obvious sensitivity to being called a 'Madman' – indeed there are signs of obsession about that matter in certain of his comments. He not only attacks his friends but he also manages to deride Samuel Rose, the lawyer who had defended him and had died a year later. In one long and rather garbled poem he calls himself 'Death' – no doubt because of his role as illustrator of *The Grave* – and launches into a comprehensive attack on almost everyone involved in his life over the last five years. He seems to have completed it at the time when he made his final break with Cromek, and with all those whom he believed to be in league against him.

The origin of this latest and last dispute with Cromek is to be found in the months after Blake had been removed from *The Grave*. Cromek had been promoting that volume in Halifax, and while there he came upon a copy of Chaucer's *Canterbury Tales*; it may have been the Ellesmere edition, which has illustrations of the pilgrims in the margin, since Cromek at once saw the painterly possibilities of such a work. So, in the summer or autumn of 1806, he approached Thomas Stothard and asked him to fashion a painting that would show all of Chaucer's pilgrims on their journey from London to Canterbury: it would then be exhibited, and subscriptions taken for the engraving that would follow. Stothard readily accepted, not least because he had first sketched out such a subject, 'The Canterbury Pilgrims Leaving the Tabard Inn' for Ritson's *English Anthology* more than ten years before. It was a shrewd and, as it turned out, very successful idea; Cromek congratulated himself upon it in a letter to a friend – 'You must know,' he wrote, 'that I give myself great Credit for thinking of such a glorious Subject – it is true that it was sufficiently obvious – but, it is equally true that what is obvious is often overlooked.'[63] Blake would hardly have agreed with him, however, since in later years he always insisted that Cromek had stolen the idea from him. One of his contemporaries, who had the story from Blake himself, has explained that, after *The Grave* fiasco, 'Cromek had asked Blake what work he had in mind to execute next. The unsuspecting artist not only told him, but without the least reserve showed him the designs sketched out for a fresco picture: the subject Chaucer's "Pilgrimage to Canterbury", with which Mr Cromek appeared highly delighted.'[64] A short while after, Blake discovered that Stothard had been commissioned to paint the same picture in much the same style as his own sketches. This would be a clear case of double-dealing on the part of Cromek, and Blake added even more damning details when he explained the affair to John Linnell some years later: it seems that Cromek actually commissioned Blake to complete the picture, for the price of twenty guineas, but then gave the engraving work to Schiavonetti. Blake promptly 'refused to let him have' the painting and Cromek immediately turned to Stothard.[65] Linnell's account – or Blake's memory of the argument – seems to have confused the imbroglio over *The Grave* engravings with the controversy over the Chaucer painting; but, in any case, Blake's stories are not at all convincing. There is no evidence that he sketched any designs for a Chaucerian fresco before 1808 – a year after Stothard's painting was finished – and in any case Stothard had conceived just such a design in 1793. Indeed Blake's whole account of the affair is inherently improbable. This is what seems to have happened.

Cromek did indeed commission Stothard to paint the pilgrims; the two men lived in Newman Street, knew each other well enough, and Stothard was so delighted with the idea that he did extensive preliminary work and research. He completed it quickly, and by March of the following year it was ready to be exhibited at Cromek's house. It is possible that Stothard had suggested Blake might engrave it but Cromek, once again, turned to Schiavonetti. It is also possible that Blake had heard of Stothard's fee of one hundred guineas because, in May of this year, he demanded from Cromek four guineas for a vignette which would dedicate *The Grave* to the Queen. She may seem a strange patron but the affair was arranged by his friend Ozias Humphry, who wrote Blake's 'Statement' to the Queen and obtained her consent. Blake then wrote a dedicatory poem and conceived a design to accompany it, for which he requested that relatively small sum. But it was an intemperate letter and, as a result, Cromek sent an angry reply – '*I can do without it*' being the central message.[66]

But it is in itself an interesting piece of correspondence, and throws a revealing light upon Blake's customary demeanour in the world. Cromek insists that 'I neither have, nor ever had, any encouragement from *you* to place you before the public in a more favourable point of view'.[67] Could this be an example of Blake's reticence or nervous withdrawal, at the time when he felt himself to have been humiliated by Cromek over the engravings for *The Grave*? Cromek went on to declare, 'I had to battle with a man who had pre-determined not to be served. What public reputation you have, the reputation of eccentricity excepted, I have acquired for you.'[68] There is a certain truth to this, in that it was indeed through his designs for *The Grave* that Blake acquired a measure of public reputation, but it is also significant to note that he was already known for his 'eccentricity'. One can imagine him as a familiar figure on the streets of London, and there are anecdotes in a later period of his being pointed out and described as the man who sees spirits and talks to angels. Cromek then makes a more specific point – 'I believed what you so often have told me, that your works were equal, nay superior, to a Raphael or to a Michael Angelo!'[69] So Blake was in the habit of expressing in conversation what he often confided in writing; it is impossible to think of him as doing it in a boastful way but, rather, in the quiet and undemonstrative manner that has been described by his contemporaries. More remarkable still, perhaps, is that Cromek thought so highly of his artistic abilities that he did indeed agree with this self-assessment. And he goes on to say, '*I have imposed on myself* yet more grossly in believing you to be one altogether abstracted from this world, holding converse with the world of spirits!'[70] Again it is clear that Blake was quite accustomed to talk about his visionary experiences and, sometimes, to be believed. But now, towards the close of his letter, Cromek remarks upon Stothard's painting of Chaucer's pilgrims: 'Why did you so *furiously rage* at the success of the little picture of "The Pilgrimage"? Three thousand people have now *seen it and have approved of it*. Believe me, yours is "*the voice of one crying in the wilderness!*" You say the subject is *low* and *contemptibly treated*.'[71] Note here that Blake has not accused Cromek of stealing or copying his idea – surely he would have done so, in this 'furious' letter, if there had been any substance to the claim? In fact the clue to his later behaviour lies at the very end of Cromek's reply when, in relation to Blake's dismissal of Stothard's work, he quotes from a popular poem of the period:

But if any *great critic* finds fauit with my letter,
He has nothing to do but to send you a be*t*ter.[72]

And that, precisely, is what Blake set out to do; he determined to paint his own version of the Chaucerian pilgrimage, and thus outface Stothard. His decision was fuelled by several other factors also; he seems at this stage to have believed that Cromek was in league with the newspaper critics against him, and he was enraged by the number of the then fashionable 'puffs' which were being published in praise of Stothard's painting. It was in any event an enormous success, and Cromek took it to all the major cities of England; it proved to be Stothard's most famous work, and the subsequent engraving at a cost of six guineas or three guineas had 'the most extensive sale of anything of the kind published within the last hundred years'.[73] One of the most irritating or wounding pieces of puffery was that which Cromek wrote, and which he added as a 'Prospectus' at the end of *The Grave*; Blake's humiliation was compounded by the fact that, in advertisements for that work, his own contribution as the original artist was not even mentioned. He had also been suffering from a nervous skin condition, then known as 'the Erisepilas', perhaps exacerbated or even caused by his dispute with Cromek. This was the mood in which he set out to execute his own alternative 'Pilgrims'.

Why was it, then, that in later life he should claim to have been the sole originator of the project? Even in his last years he was inclined to accuse Stothard of theft or plagiarism – to such an extent that Stothard, the most peaceable and just of men, eventually refused to have anything to do with him. Blake seems also to have believed that Stothard had exercised some supernatural force over his work since, when he came to look at his original drawing one day, 'he found it nearly effaced: the result of some malignant spell of Stothard's, he would, in telling the story, assure his friends'.[74] Stothard was of a rather more prosaic character and, as a result of Blake's claims, found his original drawing of the pilgrims and wrote beneath it in explanation and defiance, 'The first drawing of the Canterbury Pilgrims – made for Ritson'. Blake's conduct was in many respects, therefore, very peculiar indeed. But it has to be remembered that he was a fabulist who insisted upon the truth and substance of his visions; once something was imaginatively conceived by him, then it must be true. It is not an uncommon quality among writers, in particular, and there is no doubt that he genuinely believed what he wished to believe. It is even possible that Cromek had once spoken to him of *The Canterbury Tales* as an artistic subject, while discussing it with Stothard, or that Blake himself had had a visionary comprehension of Chaucer at the time he was completing that poet's head for Hayley's library; whatever the reason may have been, he again created his own imaginative reality in which he was the victim of the world. In his notebook poem on the subject, savagely exulting in the death of Schiavonetti and Cromek only a few years later, he continued his assault upon those who he believed had wronged him:

> Come Artists knock your heads against This stone
> For Sorrow that our friend Bob Screwmuchs gone.[75]

But, however much he seems to suffer from conventional paranoia, there is little or no evidence of serious mental instability on his part. The best proof of this lies in the fine lyric poems that he was even then writing or transcribing in the same notebook as the epigrams. It is perhaps wrong to call them lyrics, however, since they are closer to prophecies in a lyric mode, where moods of loss, helplessness and incapacity are lent a bardic voice that is variously sombre or angry. One of them seems accurately to resemble his own state, for the simple reason that it takes a line from one of his letters and transposes it to another key. After the Scofield incident he had written the plaintive letter to Butts in which he had asked 'O why was I born with a different face?'[76] The same question is asked in a poem entitled 'Mary', and it ends sadly enough:

> And thine is a Face of sweet Love in Despair
> And thine is a Face of mild sorrow & care
> And thine is a face of wild terror & fear
> That shall never be quiet till laid on its bier.[77]

All of these poems, scribbled into the notebook, were at some point in this period carefully transcribed onto the spare pages of Hayley's *Ballads* paper (with Hayley's text discarded) and turned into a neat little notebook. It has been called 'The Pickering Manuscript', after the Victorian gentleman who once owned it, but it seems to be a fair copy for Blake's own perusal or for that of a friend. There are ten poems on eleven sheets of paper, all carefully paginated, and Blake has gone to great pains to erase mistakes and write over them in a neat hand. One thing becomes immediately clear on even the most cursory inspection, however: the poems are couched in regular ballad metres and are formally very precise, so there is no reason to suppose that the irregular verse of the Prophetic Books was anything other than deliberate on his part. It has sometimes been suggested that as his interest in Prophecies grew his poetic genius was diminished; but this is far from the case, and there are poems in 'The Pickering Manuscript' that bear comparison with any of his lyrics of earlier years:

> Seek Love in the Pity of others Woe
> In the gentle relief of anothers care
> In the darkness of night & the winters snow
> In the naked and outcast Seek Love There.[78]

There is of course a didactic note, but it is merely an intensification of his earlier manner; as his sense of neglect grew more profound, so all the more forcibly he claimed a prophetic role. But there is no loss of subtlety or of power as a result:

> God Appears & God is Light
> To those poor Souls who dwell in Night
> But does a Human Form Display
> To those who Dwell in Realms of day.[79]

To consider this quatrain in itself would require much elucidation, beginning with Swedenborg's remark, 'the Lord appears in a Divine angelic form which is Human to those who acknowledge and believe in a visible Divine',[80] but what is most immediately evident is the form Blake has chosen to convey his theme. The loose couplet, or 'proverbial couplet', is one of the oldest measures of ballad and folk poetry. So in the mid-fourteenth century a poem of similar import begins

> Jesu, Lord, welcom thou be,
> In forme of bred as I thee see.[81]

It is hard not to be reminded of the songs that were printed on coarse paper and sold for a farthing or a half-penny on the streets of London; they were known as stall-ballads or broadsides, and the greatest poem in 'The Pickering Manuscript' is closely modelled upon this most popular form of urban poetry:

> A Robin Red breast in a Cage
> Puts all Heaven in a Rage
> A Dove house filld with Doves & Pigeons
> Shudders Hell thro all its regions
> A dog starvd at his Masters Gate

Predicts the ruin of the State . . .
Each outcry of the hunted Hare
A fibre from the Brain does tear
A Skylark wounded in the wing
A Cherubim does cease to sing.[82]

The poem is entitled 'Auguries of Innocence', and takes its place among Blake's other ventures both into emblem literature such as 'Gates of Paradise' and into aphoristic compilations such as The Marriage of Heaven and Hell; despite his evident inability to find a public, he still instinctively aligned himself with popular forms and popular beliefs. But he was also involved in a private search for meaning. 'Auguries of Innocence' and the other poems in 'The Pickering Manuscript' are associated with his attempts to create a primal mythology, as well as with his elucidation of the biblical narrative in his watercolours. In all cases he is attempting to rediscover and redeploy some form of ancient wisdom that had ceased to be available to his contemporaries. We might even find the sum of his philosophy in the famous opening to this poem:

To see a World in a Grain of Sand
And a Heaven in a Wild Flower
Hold Infinity in the palm of your hand
And Eternity in an hour.[83]

He had seen eternity, and now, as he laboured under the humiliations and misfortunes of a life that seems singularly ill-starred, he continued work upon the epic poem he had been writing at Felpham. 'It will not be long,' he told Hayley, 'before I shall be able to present the full history of my Spiritual Sufferings to the Dwellers upon Earth.'[84] But the poem began to change as he worked upon it in South Molton Street. He scratched out the original title, 'VALA', and wrote above it in scrawled handwriting 'The Four Zoas', and then he added 'The Torments of Love & Jealousy . . . of Albion'. He began to revise the entire poem, erasing sections and writing on top of them, adding long passages and introducing new themes, placing some extraordinary pencil drawings in the margins. For the first time he began to introduce a Christian terminology and invoked 'the lamb of God' and the 'saviour', at the same time as he refers to aspects of Druidic worship. He is returning once more to his early attitudes and beliefs; he is reinventing them, just as he had done in his most recent watercolours, as a way of reaffirming the light of youth that had again been vouchsafed to him. He had already written one 'Night the Seventh' at Felpham, but now he wrote another; he completed the final two nights, but only after extensive rewriting and alteration. The manuscript is an extraordinary confusion of words and images; dense blocks of his scribbled but compact handwriting are placed among old proofs of his *Night Thoughts* designs, while two other pages are written on the back of an engraving of 'Edward and Elinor' that he had cut in half. This is no longer the work he had begun in beautiful and spacious copper plate; it is now a working manuscript that seems to have a furious momentum about it.

The three last 'Nights', which he wrote in London, have the strongest narrative, concerned as they are with the apparent victory of evil and the fallen world before the triumph of Christ, the Eternal Man, and the revelatory Harvest. But they begin with battles and with riots, as if the whole pressure of the war and the city were around him as he wrote by Tyburn's brook. Some of the first lines he completed in South Molton Street are upon this theme:

Now comes the night of Carnage now the flesh of Kings & Princes
Pamperd in palaces for our food the blood of Captains nurturd
With lust & murder for our drink the drunken Raven shall wander
All night among the slain & mock the wounded that groan in the field.[85]

Thousands had died during the bombardment of Copenhagen, at the battles of Vimeiro and Corunna, and Chatham's expedition to Flushing had ended in death and disease. And as Blake sat in South Molton Street 'All futurity / Seems teeming with Endless Destruction never to be repelld'.[86] This is indeed, in his wonderful phrase, 'the night of Time', when London itself has become part of the technology of war;[87] in one of those visions of extraordinary percipience, he understands once again that war, repressed sexuality and the new industrialism are aspects of the same process which threatens to overwhelm the world. 'For war is energy Enslavd',[88] and out of this oppression, out of the science and religion of the fallen world, spring all our future woes:

And all the arts of life they changd into the arts of death
The hour glass contemnd because its simple workmanship
Was as the workmanship of the plowman & the water wheel
That raises water into Cisterns broken & burnd in fire
Because its workmanship was like the workmanship of the Shepherd
And in their stead intricate wheels invented Wheel without wheel

To perplex youth in their outgoings & to bind to labours
Of day & night the myriads of Eternity. that they might file
And polish brass & iron hour after hour laborious workmanship
Kept ignorant of the use that they might spend the days of wisdom
In sorrowful drudgery to obtain a scanty pittance of bread
In ignorance to view a small portion & think that All
And call it Demonstration blind to all the simple rules of life.[89]

It is worth quoting such a passage at length, if only to demonstrate that Blake's prophetic works need be neither incomprehensible nor (to use Cromek's word) 'wild' or mad. Here is some of the simplest, most direct and most powerful poetry of the early nineteenth century. Yet his visionary conception did not rest upon the conflict and enslavement which he saw everywhere around him; he had already experienced that sense of liberation that came from a fresh recognition of 'the light I enjoyed in my youth', and the poem follows the path of his enlightenment with concluding passages of apocalypse and revelation.[90] There comes that moment out of time when the 'Spectres' and 'Bodies of Vegetation', which are our mortal part upon the earth, may see

With joy the bright Light & in it a Human form
And knew he was the Saviour Even Jesus & they worshipped.[91]

The Eternal Man will wake from his sleep of six thousand years and reassume 'his ancient bliss'.[92] Tyranny and Mystery will then be consumed and

Start forth the trembling millions into flames of mental fire
Bathing their Limbs in the bright visions of Eternity.[92]

It is an extraordinary vision of renewal and restoration, when all the finite faculties of fallen man are enlarged so that he can 'behold the depths of wondrous worlds' and all the 'Animal forms of wisdom', converse with 'little Children' and with Jesus the Divine Humanity himself. And then humankind asks itself in wonder:

How is it we have walkd thro fires & yet are not consumd
How is it that all things are changd even as in ancient times.[94]

And as he laboured upon his vision in South Molton Street, Blake strengthened the mythic elements of his narrative; he introduced the name of 'Albion' as the Eternal Man, perhaps because he had just re-engraved the image of that exultant youth who had risen 'from where he had labourd at the Mill with Slaves'. He brings in the concept of the 'Mundane Shell', adding it as a pencilled addition to the earlier poetry, and depicts it as the hardened crust that protects the material universe and its fallen dimensions. In the course of the poem, written over a period of some ten years, we can observe the movement of his thought as he struggles to understand the implications of his own vision and, indeed, of his own life. Now, in London, he began to develop the notion of 'Limits', named as 'Opacity' and 'Contraction', which through the mercy of Jesus are formed to bind and therefore to define error. In certain respects they resemble the clear and pure outline that he considered to represent the form of true art; but he has also borrowed from the vocabulary of Newtonian science to suggest a wholly new way of looking at the material world. It has been given shape and substance so that it may eventually be redeemed because, in seeing error, we may at last be able to cast it off. When 'the limit of Contraction' is fixed, in the poem, the Eternal Man begins to rise from his 'Couch of Death' and 'lifts the blue lamps of his Eyes'.[95]

His visionary conceptions are not the elements of theory, however, but matters of pressing and urgent significance. He was trying to do no less than change the entire nature of human perception and, in an addition to the doctrine of 'Limits', he propounds the notion of 'States', which allows an alternative understanding of what we would now call human psychology. There was a phrase of the period to describe inebriates – they were said to be 'in drink' rather than 'drunken'. The distinction may seem a subtle one but the emphasis shifts from the moral state of the human being and concentrates instead upon the power of 'drink'. It is as if the poor creature were immersed for a time in some other element before being rescued. It is a contemporaneous way, at least, of approaching Blake's own beliefs. His first mention of 'State' comes in the penultimate 'Night' or chapter of the poem in which he declares that it is necessary to know 'The Difference between States & Individuals of those States'.[96] He elaborated upon this in a later work of prose: 'These States Exist now Man Passes on but States remain for Ever he passes thro them like a traveller who may as well suppose that the places he has passed thro exist no more as a Man may suppose that the States he has passed thro exist no more Every Thing is Eternal'.[97] These States may be of desire, or rage, or longing; they may also be of the material selfhood itself, and the Individual passes through them while retaining an essential spiritual identity. It is a way of externalising sin and error, so that it can be cast off like a garment, and it also allows for final redemption. You can be 'in drink' for a while, but that does not mean you are a 'drunkard'. The theory was not wholly original – the movement of the late eighteenth century was towards the depiction of abstract and invariable 'Passions', and Boehme as well as Swedenborg had adumbrated concepts of 'state' that are similar to those of Blake. But it may be that the prime source of his inspiration here was the humble 'state' of each printed engraving, which might be erased or revised at any time. It was, at least, a way of understanding the bewildering range of feelings that seem to sweep across him on certain occasions; but it was also a way of considering the passage of the soul through the world without dwelling upon sin and guilt but rather upon forgiveness and redemption. Much of his prophetic symbolism can actually be understood without undue difficulty, but it requires in the reader a reawakening of what is essentially a clear and simple vision. He is a 'difficult' poet only if we decide to make him so.

He began, as usual, to sketch images around his words. He was using the proof sheets of *Night Thoughts*, which already had his engravings upon them, and there are times in his new drawings when he deliberately adopts complementary motifs or postures; there are occasions, too, when the old image on the page seems to have affected the content of the new poem and it may be that he examined his earlier work in order to use it as one of the sources of his inspiration. But there is something remarkable about his drawings in *The Four Zoas*; many of them are explicitly and elaborately erotic. The forty-fifth page of the manuscript was an original *Night Thoughts* sheet, showing Jesus raising Lazarus to illustrate Edward Young's pious sentiment – 'That touch, which charm celestial heals the soul.' On the facing page, Blake has drawn one of his mythological personages who has 'reard up his hands' in a gesture deliberately similar to that of Lazarus. But in place of Jesus is a naked woman whose genitals have been transformed into an altar or chapel, with an erect penis forming a kind of holy statue at the centre. It is an extraordinary image, closely related to his belief that the religion of mystery and of secrecy is part of the fallen world, but it also asserts the connection between the war of the four faculties or 'zoas' with phallic rituals and the worship of the 'female pale'. By breaking through the literary and pictorial codes of his period, he seems to have come close to certain universal truths. It is no wonder that *The Four Zoas* sometimes becomes divagatory or even incoherent: Blake is confronting so many forces at once that it is a miracle the poem succeeds at all.

There are also more specifically erotic drawings – hermaphroditic figures with huge phalli, a woman reaching to caress the large penis of a man while masturbating with a dildo, a small boy with an erection as he watches a scene of love-making; there are also sketches of anal penetration, fellatio, defecation and group sexuality. But the central motif is the erect phallus. It was clear from his earliest writings that he trusted the energies of sexual freedom and, at least in theory, believed in the possibility of complete sexual licence. But it is something of a surprise to find him, at this late date, indulging in such libidinous imaginations – especially in a context where he is affirming the possibility of spiritual renovation and the everlasting return of 'the Lamb of God'. That, of course, is the point. This was the context in which he placed his eroticism, because for him it still represented an approach towards eternity and the reawakening of the Divine Man who is within us. The image of the hermaphrodite, with penis and vagina, is an ancient one – for Blake it represents in literal form that time before the sexes were divided and human faculties thereby distorted or degraded. The images of the erect penis are in turn related to the comparative mythology of the period, when phallus worship was believed to be at the centre of most primitive ritual. There is also another parallel that can be drawn: he called himself 'English Blake', and there are occasions when he seems intuitively or deliberately to have expressed some rare native characteristics. The drawings in the margins of his poem, for example, are curiously close in spirit to the 'babooneries' or grotesque drawings sometimes found in the margins of medieval illuminated manuscripts and which are known to have 'originated in England'.[98] There are elements of the national consciousness that can be continued over many centuries and, even in so small a matter as this, we glimpse the pattern of artistic identity and sensibility. But there are also less obvious preoccupations that animate these images of buggery and fellatio, and it is hard not to see them as in part related to the humiliations and disappointments that he was suffering during the composition of the last sections of the poem. There is also a suggestion of repressed sexuality, or repressed energy, finding its way out of him. In some respect, then, they are the pictorial equivalent of the aggressive epigrams he was composing in his old notebook; in both fashions was he able to externalise all his fears and fantasies in a furious and secluded manner.

The Four Zoas is one of the most extraordinary documents of the decades spanning the eighteenth and nineteenth centuries. It was never published in Blake's lifetime and was only properly rediscovered in 1889 when his first editors, Ellis and Yeats, transcribed it in a somewhat careless manner. There are still difficulties about its arrangement, but even in its present state it clearly represents a new kind of verse – a kind of Gothic Augustanism. The prevailing neoclassical vocabulary of the period has been used to create a myth in which various mental states are given names as if they were classical deities and where public polemic is married with lyrical lament and nostalgic pastoralism. There are occasions when Blake is so obsessed with his vision that he allows it undistorted expression, sometimes within lines and passages of powerful poetic beauty:

> I wakend Enion in the Morning & she turnd away
> Among the appie trees & all the gardens of delight
> Swam like a dream before my eyes . . . [99]

and sometimes in passages that have the directness (at times even the clumsiness) of prose:

> Deformd that I am thus a ravening devouring lust continually
> Craving & devouring but my Eyes are always upon thee O lovely
> Delusion . . . [100]

This was the shape his vision took – sometimes plangent, sometimes harsh, sometimes repetitive – and you cannot have one aspect without all of the others. In a sense his work may be said to resemble his behaviour in the world, with his beneficence and his rage, his labour and his dilatoriness, his arrogance and his anxiety. In fact his private breath may animate the whole poem because, if it can be said to imitate any other form, it is that of late eighteenth-century oratory – the oratory of Edmund Burke, and of the contemporary theatre. We have heard how he used to sing his own compositions, both in London and in Felpham, and it is possible to sense within these swaying lines the inflections of Blake's own voice. So he finished the poem in South Molton Street with a triumphant flourish:

> In all his ancient strength to form the golden armour of science
> For intellectual War The war of swords departed now
> The dark Religions are departed & sweet Science reigns. [101]

Underneath these words he drew in pencil the most wonderful image of a human figure rising in triumph from a globe; and then he scrawled in ink, 'End of The Dream'. The dream had ended, but the world was still with him. At the top of one page of his notebook he wrote, 'Tuesday Janry. 20, 1807 between Two & Seven in the Evening – Despair'.

TWENTY-TWO

organized and minutely articulated

There was only one refuge from despair for Blake – 'endless labour' was his lot and now, 'incessantly labouring', he set to work upon his own painting of the Canterbury Pilgrims.[1] He did so partly in response to Cromek's challenge, but he also had a much greater motive: he would demonstrate all that he had acquired through his visionary understanding of art. He decided to hold a one-man exhibition, as many of his contemporaries now did, and to publish a pamphlet or book in which he would explain, among other things, 'my various Inventions in Art'.[2] He took up Reynolds's *Works*, which included his Royal Academy 'Discourses', just to check the words of the enemy before embarking upon his own; he had already annotated the first volume in pencil, probably when he was staying at the cottage in Felpham, but now he inked over some of them and added further furious remarks with his pen. On the title page he inscribed in black ink, and in large letters, 'This Man was Hired to Depress Art', and then he wrote on the back, around the edges of the dedication to the King on the following page, and above the first page of text, in what seems to be a terrible fit of anger and frustration and sorrow: 'Having spent the Vigour of my Youth and Genius under the Oppression of Sr Joshua & his Gang of Cunning Hired Knaves Without Employment & as much as could possibly be Without Bread, The Reader must Expect to Read in all my Remarks on these Books Nothing but Indignation & Resentment While Sr Joshua was rolling in Riches Barry was Poor & Unemployd except by his own Energy Mortimer was called a Madman & only Portrait Painting applauded & rewarded by the Rich & Great. Reynolds & Gainsborough Blotted & Blurred one against the other & Divided all the English World between them.' At the close he added 'I was hid'; but then he crossed out 'was' and wrote 'I am hid'.[3]

There then follows, in a series of remarks and asides, what amounts to a wholesale attack upon the aesthetics and epistemology of his period. In a later poem the spirit of creative labour, Los, who 'kept the Divine Vision in time of trouble',[4] cries out 'I must Create a System, or be enslav'd by another Mans';[5] this is Blake's own cry, one that resounds through all his writing, and in these annotations he is actively fighting against the 'System' that held him back and threatened to destroy him. We can almost hear Reynolds's voice, as he discourses upon the 'Polite Arts' in the lecture theatre of the Royal Academy, where Blake had heard him nearly thirty years ago – 'The Venetian is indeed the most splendid of the schools of elegance . . . An History-painter paints man in general; a Portrait-painter, a particular man.' But Blake is murmuring to us: 'I consider Reynolds's Discourses . . . as the Simulation of the Hypocrite who Smiles particularly where he means to Betray. His Praise of Rafael is like the Hysteric Smile of Revenge.' And then, as Reynolds goes on to state that Raphael learned from the example of Michelangelo, Blake says a wonderful thing: 'I do not believe that Rafael taught Mich. Angelo or that Mich. Ang taught Rafael. any more than I believe that the Rose teaches the Lilly how to grow or the Apple tree teaches the Pear tree how to bear fruit.' As Reynolds talks, Blake continues to damn him. 'Abundance of Stupidity. Infernal Falsehood. Damnd Fool. A Polishd Villain. A Lie. Here is Nonsense.' But his annotations are not simply explosions of rage, because in the midst of them he states his own central beliefs more clearly than in any other place. 'Knowledge of Ideal Beauty,' he writes, 'is Not to be Acquired It is Born with us Innate Ideas are in Every Man Born with him . . . Man Brings All that he has or Can have Into the World with him. Man is Born Like a Garden ready Planted & Sown This World is too poor to produce one Seed . . . He who does not Know Truth at Sight is unworthy of Her Notice . . . The Man who never in his Mind & Thoughts traveld to Heaven Is No Artist.'[6] Few artists have thought so deeply about the nature of perception and, in his effort to remain free of the 'System', he was also able to launch a coordinated attack here upon Locke and Newton as the true progenitors of Reynolds's aesthetic and as gaolers of the prison in which Blake believed his epoch to be consigned.

No doubt these were matters he would have raised in his own projected book, but the idea came to nothing; throughout 1808 he

was preparing work for his exhibition, which would have at its centre
the painting of the Canterbury Pilgrims. He also managed to display
three other pictures at that year's Royal Academy show, where he had
the dubious pleasure of being part of an exhibition in which the
paintings were hung along the walls in no particular order, squeezed
into every available space, and sometimes stacked six in a vertical
row. But his largest hopes now rested upon what he called his
'Exhibition of *Paintings in Fresco*, Poetical and Historical Inventions,
By Wm. Blake'. He wrote out his prospectus in a very neat hand, and
gave it to a neighbouring printer in South Molton Street; the leaflet,
or advertisement, was then sent out with the following message: 'The
ignorant Insults of Individuals will not hinder me from doing my duty
to my Art . . . those who have been told that my Works are but an
unscientific and irregular Eccentricity, a Madman's Scrawls, I
demand of them to do me the justice to examine before they decide.'
He again compares himself to Michelangelo and Raphael, before
asserting the public and social nature of art itself: 'if Art is the glory of
a Nation, if Genius and Inspiration are the great Origin and Bond of
Society, the distinction my Works have obtained from those who best
understand such things, calls for my Exhibition as the greatest of
Duties to my country'.[7] Once more he had taken refuge in self-
assertion and angry grandiloquence, as a way of salvaging his identity
from the threats that had been levelled against it by Cromek and
others. He quoted Milton's line of 'Fit Audience find tho' few', and
explained that the exhibition could be seen at No. 28 Broad Street in
the corner house. Turner held his one-man shows in Harley Street
and, later, Wilkie would exhibit in Pall Mall, while Haydon was able
to hire the Egyptian Hall in Piccadilly; Blake, however, had no choice
but to use his brother's hosiery shop.

Hardly anyone came. There was a charge of one shilling for entry –
that had been Cromek's fee for those who wished to see Stothard's
painting in Newman Street – and a 'Descriptive Catalogue' was also
available at the price of half-a-crown. James Blake was deputed to
welcome any customers, and one or two contemporaries remember
him in the sober dress of an old-fashioned shopkeeper with knee
breeches and worsted stockings. It must have been a curious
spectacle, as the hosier showed visitors such works of his brother as
'The Spiritual Form of Pitt guiding Behemoth' and 'The Bramins'.
There were nine temperas and seven watercolours on display; for
those who might have had difficulty in interpreting Blake's visionary

scenes, he had written the 'Descriptive Catalogue', which, as it turned out, was his first and last public testament. He sent a copy of it to Ozias Humphry, perhaps because as a miniaturist Humphry was more likely to understand and applaud the 'Minute Discrimination' of Blake's style; he also sent a note with it, in which he declared, 'Till the Venetian & Flemish are destroy'd, the Florentine & Roman cannot Exist; this will be shortly accomplish'd.'[8]

The catalogue was bound in blue-grey wrappers, and it is unlikely that more than a hundred were ever printed: only a handful of copies have survived. It seems not to have been very carefully proof read, and one important detail was omitted; Blake was forced to write in pen on the title page 'At No. 28 Corner of Broad Street – Golden Square'. He also arranged for his neighbourhood printer to make up an advertisement to the catalogue proclaiming 'These Original Conceptions on Art, by an Original Artist'. It is quite clear that these 'conceptions' were properly formulated only after he had experienced the revelation of early art, and the rediscovery of his own 'light', at the Truchsessian Exhibition five years before; that is why he ridicules oil painting and proclaims the supreme merit of 'Fresco' (which occasionally he confused with panel painting). 'Till we get rid of Titian and Correggio, Rubens and Rembrandt, We never shall equal Rafael and Albert Durer, Michael Angelo, and Julio Romano.'[9] He elaborated upon the meaning of each exhibited work in turn, and explains his depiction of the 'spiritual forms' of Pitt and Nelson as a result of 'The Artist having been taken in vision into the ancient republics, monarchies, and patriarchates of Asia'; here he saw works of art 'some of them one hundred feet in height . . . all containing mythological and recondite meaning, where more is meant than meets the eye'.[10] He is still concerned, then, to create a sacred and public art that will be the proper foundation of what he used to call 'Empire'; but his most instinctive concern is with a new form of medievalism or Gothic that he had recreated in the painting he now exhibited as 'Sir Jeffery Chaucer and the nine and twenty Pilgrims on their journey to Canterbury'. One of the striking characteristics of English art, and English writing, has been the creative use of past styles; but for Blake it was also an aspect of the historical vision he had acquired as an apprentice in Westminster Abbey. He consulted Speght's seventeenth-century edition of Chaucer's complete works, and felt able to write in the catalogue that 'The characters of Chaucer's Pilgrims are the characters which compose all ages and nations: as one age falls, another rises, different to mortal sight, but to immortals only the same . . . nothing new occurs in identical existence; Accident ever varies, Substance can never suffer change nor decay.'[11] This was also the context of his growing sense of England's spiritual power, of which his public paintings would be the true ornament; he described one of his exhibited works, 'The Ancient Britons', now lost, as representative of 'all his visionary contemplations, relating to his own country and its ancient glory, when it was as it again shall be, the source of learning and inspiration'.[12] This is what he meant by 'Empire', whose ruler he named as Albion. The adventures of Arthur were, as far as he was concerned, a shadowy allegory of Albion – while the ancient Druid past of England was established by Adam, Noah and Abraham. He went on to mention the poem he had just completed, The Four Zoas, as an account of the 'spiritual agency' he saw working through history – history itself being 'nothing else but improbabilities and impossibilities'.[13]

His was a vision of an eternal reality, open to spiritual sight, glimpsed in the beams of sexual love but only fully revealed in the 'determinate and bounding' line of true art.[14] That is why he felt so aggrieved by the humiliation and neglect to which he was constantly subjected and, in his description of his own painting of the pilgrims, he launched a direct attack upon Stothard's version – 'To be sure Chaucer is a little difficult to him who has only blundered over novels and catchpenny trifles of booksellers.'[15] It is really no wonder that the mild and pacific Stothard was never able to forgive him. Blake also launched into a caustic attack upon Cromek's prospectus, and was at great pains to contradict and disparage everything his former publisher had to say about Chaucer and Stothard's own painting. Blake's work had been completed, moreover, 'in self-defence against the insolent and envious imputation of unfitness for finished and scientific art; and this imputation, most artfully and industriously endeavoured to be propagated among the public by ignorant hirelings', by whom he means men such as Stothard and Schiavonetti. This was Blake's lot, 'to get patronage for others and then to be left and neglected, and his work, which gained that patronage, cried down as eccentricity and madness; as unfinished and neglected by the artist's violent temper'.[16] So these were the 'calumnies' now being spread about him – that he was eccentric, or mad, and that he had a violent temper. It was no doubt why Flaxman and Fuseli never saw him now, and why Cromek and other booksellers refused to deal with him. Yet he was defiant: 'I have been scorned long enough by these fellows, who owe to me all that they have; it shall be so no longer.'[17] In Blake's painting there seems to be an idealised image of himself as the Ploughman, wearing the type of broad hat he preferred, 'thin with excessive labour, and not with old age, as some have supposed'.[18] Looking backwards at him, with a most ferocious expression, is the Miller, who may be intended to be a portrait of Cromek – 'a terrible fellow, such as exists in all times and places, for the trial of men'.[19]

Since this was Blake's testament he did not confine his wrath to those artists and booksellers who now avoided him; he also defends himself against criticism, and especially the assault of Robert Hunt in *The Examiner*, who had described his attempt to delineate souls or spirits in *The Grave* as 'absurd'. It was a standard attack upon the visionary artist; in the same period Turner was being derided for his theatrical use of nebulous forms and was himself accused of madness. Blake lived in a city where the extremes of the human condition met, where mercantile power and financial speculation were the single most important elements, where degradation of every kind was visible; but this was the city where he saw his visions. Why should he not, as he supposed, delineate them as Hogarth had once delineated the citizens of the natural, rather than the spiritual, city? 'A Spirit and a Vision are not, as the modern philosophy supposes, a cloudy vapour or a nothing: they are organized and minutely articulated beyond all that the mortal and perishing nature can produce. He who does not imagine in stronger and better lineaments, and in stronger and better light than his perishing mortal eye can see does not imagine at all.'[20] It is the most powerful defence of his own artistic and visionary practice, which he had rediscovered, as he says, after being diverted and confused by such 'Demons' as Correggio and Titian. He demonstrated the spiritual continuity of his art, also, by exhibiting one of the watercolour drawings he had completed nearly thirty years before – it is that of 'The Penance of Jane Shore', which he had painted while still at the Royal Academy Schools. The exhibition in Broad Street was, therefore, a reaffirmation of his art and of his genius through all the years of neglect. It was a way of establishing or maintaining his identity when it was close to being hidden from all, and he ended the catalogue on a triumphant note: 'If a man is master of his profession, he cannot be ignorant that he is so; and if he is not employed by those who pretend to encourage art, he will employ himself, and laugh in secret at the pretences of the ignorant, while he has every night dropped into his shoe, as soon as he puts it off, and puts out the candle, and gets into bed, a reward for the labours of the day, such as the world cannot give, and patience and time await to give him all that the world can give.'[21]

There would be no other reward, not in his own world; none of the pictures was sold, and there was only one review. It was in *The Examiner* again, that vehicle of *bien-pensant* radical opinion – he was described as an 'unfortunate lunatic, whose personal inoffensiveness secures him from confinement' and whose catalogue exhibited 'the wild ebullitions of a distempered brain'.[22] The few who visited the hosier's shop in Broad Street seem to have agreed. Robert Southey called him a 'painter of great but insane genius' and described 'The Ancient Britons' as 'one of his worst pictures, – which is saying much';[23] the depiction of Nelson, however, might have spurred that author towards his own *Life of Nelson*.[24] A journalist who was to provide valuable information about Blake's later life, Henry Crabb Robinson, considered him to be a prize psychological specimen and made an especial visit to the exhibition: 'I was deeply interested by the Catalogues as well as the pictures. I took four – telling the brother I hoped he would let me come in again – He said "Oh! as often as you please" – I dare say such a thing had never happened before or did afterwards.'[25] George Cumberland's son, also named George, was one of the friends who must have visited Broad Street out of loyalty, and wrote to his father that the Descriptive Catalogue 'is a great curiosity. He has given Stothard a compleat set down . . .'[26] Cumberland asked to see a copy and then reported back to his son, 'Blakes Cat. is truly original – part vanity part madness – part very good sense.'[27]

Of the paintings, there is no other known comment. Some of them have been lost or destroyed, but others are now hanging in the galleries of Britain or the United States at a time when the work of Flaxman or Stothard is quite forgotten. They still possess a kind of strangeness, which his contemporaries called 'wildness', but that is much more accurately to be seen as a deliberate return to primitive forms of art. In the two paintings devoted to Nelson and to Pitt, for example, he reverts to the style of what he called 'Hindoo' or 'Persian' originals. It was his way of affirming the idea of sacred art in a nation that had more conventional notions of reputation and monumentality. Flaxman had designed memorials for both Nelson and Pitt and, in accordance with his usual doctrine of 'contraries', Blake no doubt chose them in direct confrontation with his erstwhile friend's

A draft of certain 'Songs of Experience' in Blake's Notebook: notice 'The Tyger' in the bottom right-hand corner.

No. 17 South Molton Street (below) and No. 3 Fountain Court (right) in the Strand: these were the last two houses in which Blake lived. He died in Fountain Court.

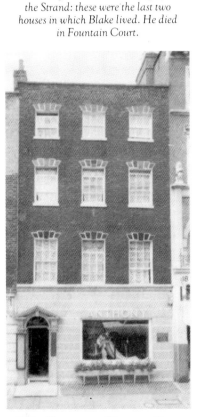

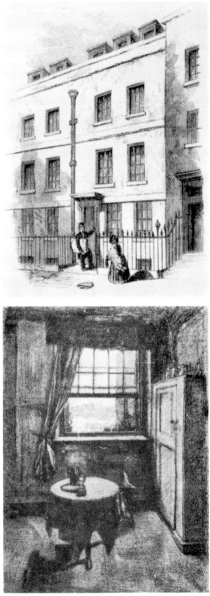

Right: The interior of Fountain Court; from the window he could see the Thames 'like a bar of gold'.

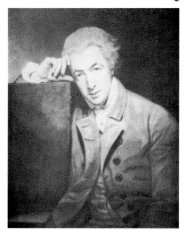

William Hayley, Blake's employer, benefactor and, according to Blake himself, 'spiritual enemy'.

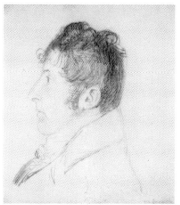

Thomas Hartley Cromek, the patron and publisher whom Blake called privately a 'Sneaking Knave'. He wasn't.

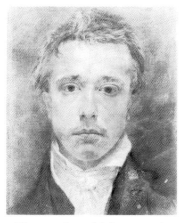

The young Samuel Palmer, one of 'The Ancients' who adored Blake: he used to kiss the bell-handle of the poet's lodgings.

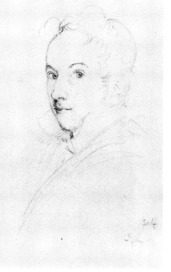

A self-portrait by John Linnell, who protected and assisted Blake in the poet's old age.

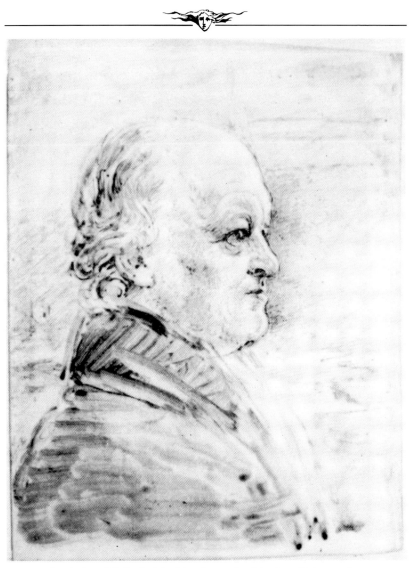

A painting of Blake, by John Linnell, completed in 1821. Blake was then sixty-four years old, but he still possesses that vigorous and pugnacious look he had as a child.

Opposite: The life-mask of Blake made by Deville in 1823. The somewhat grim expression may be the result of having straws stuck up his nostrils.

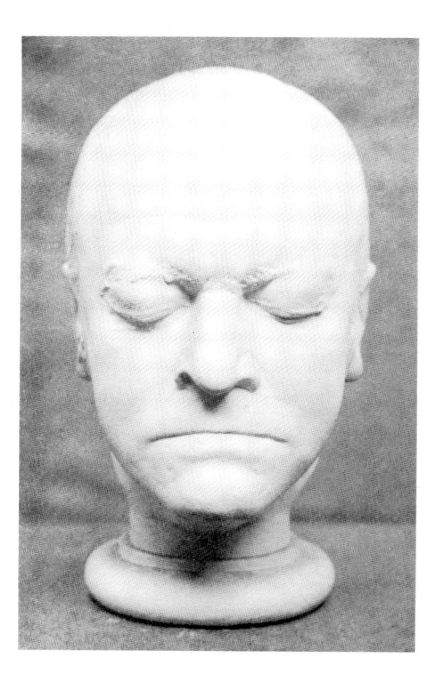

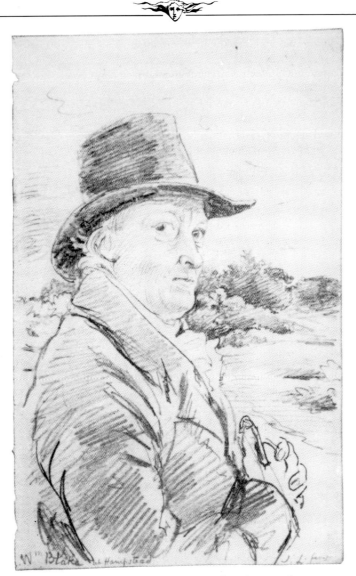

A sketch by John Linnell on the heath at Hampstead:
notice Blake's old-fashioned broad-brimmed hat.

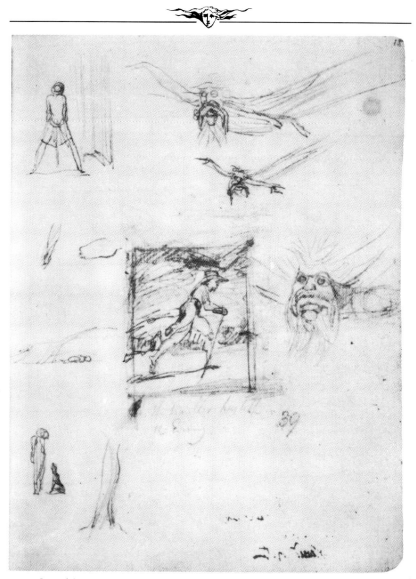

One of the sketches in his Notebook: the 'traveller' was an enduring image with which Blake seems to have identified himself. In the upper left-hand corner a man urinates against a wall.

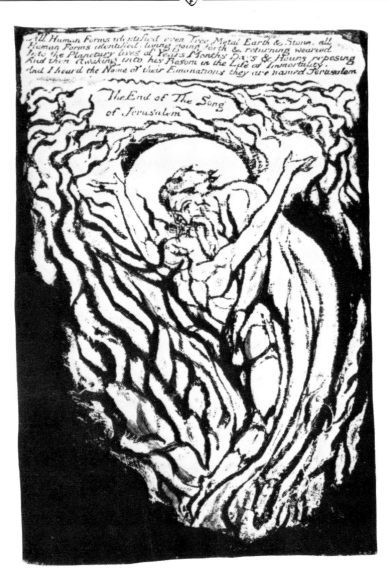

The last page of Jerusalem.

own work. They are remarkable pictures, infused with a kind of barbaric splendour, with the central figure in each case posed like some sacred object of a lost cult while around it are depicted various images of primeval savagery, worship and destruction. They also demonstrate Blake's ability to deploy a shallow space to maximum pictorial effect, since his apprenticeship with the graver meant that he knew precisely how to exploit and amplify the surface of his canvas. Another work on display, 'The Bard, from Gray', has a singular and numinous quality; with the confidence and exuberance of its drawing, with its sweeping contours like long lines of energy emanating from the artist himself, it affords an extraordinary sensation of power, of violence and of exaltation. Blake saw many of his compositions in visions of the past, and this painting could well have adorned the walls of one of those lost cities of Albion that Geoffrey of Monmouth mourned.

The painting of 'The Ancient Britons' has been lost, but it is known to be the largest work he ever finished with a size of some ten feet by fourteen feet. Swinburne recorded the description of one who had seen it with its 'fury and splendour of energy there contrasted with the serene ardour of simply beautiful courage; the violent life of the design, and the fierce distance of fluctuating battle'.[28] It was this painting, or a copy, which he completed for William Owen Pughe two years later – the Welshman was an expert on folklore and bardic literature, and had provided Blake with some ancient 'triadic' verses to describe the painting. Southey confirmed the nature of Pughe's relationship with the artist: 'Poor Owen found everything which he wished to find in the Bardic system, and there he found Blake's notions, and thus Blake and his wife were persuaded that his dreams were old patriarchal truths, long forgotten, and now re-revealed. They told me this . . . I came away from the visit with so sad a feeling that I never repeated it.'[29] Pughe was one of Joanna Southcott's 'Elders' and was open to all forms of millenarian belief; he had once been a political radical, during the revolutionary years of the previous century, but now espoused the complicated mixture of Druidic allegory, Arthurian lore and comparative mythology that made so powerful an appeal to Blake himself. It seemed to Southey, and others like him, to be no more than foolish superstition and tawdry nonsense; but it represented for Blake a refuge from the 'System' that now dominated the early nineteenth century.

Of course the central work of the exhibition in Broad Street was the painting of Chaucer's pilgrims, depicted by Blake leaving the Tabard Inn on their way to Canterbury. The size and dimensions of this tempera on canvas are much larger than those of Stothard's painting, and there is no doubt that Blake completed his in overt competition to the artist he now considered a rival. His composition is in the form of a frieze, with the pilgrims suitably travelling in the opposite direction from those of Stothard, and it has been suggested that Blake was influenced by the first sight of the Elgin Marbles, which were put on public display two years before. The truth is, however, that he did not think very highly of them – Samuel Palmer remembered his saying that they did not 'as ideal form, rank with the very finest relics of antiquity';[30] he is much more likely to have found the source of his inspiration where he always found it, in the art he admired as a youth. The Chaucer painting, in particular, bears a strong resemblance to the kind of historical work which his old master, Basire, had executed in Great Queen Street. Blake's subsequent engraving renders the similarity even closer, and in his advertisement for it he claimed that he was working in the tradition of Dürer, Aldegrave 'and the old original Engravers'.[31] It is clear that he wished to return to the antiquarian hardness and firmness he had once been taught in the workshop in Great Queen Street; this, too, was an element of the 'light' by which he had been refreshed in the Truchsessian Gallery. The picture is indeed like some piece of antiquity restored, and again the nearest analogy must be with Chatterton's creation of a medieval literary style; one contemporary observer actually stated that it 'might in its character and execution have passed for a performance or work of Art, contemporary with the times of Chaucer'.[32] In this context, however, 'English Blake' is doing no more than reflect one of the most significant characteristics of national art and literature. So this large painting took its place among 'Satan, Calling up His Legions' and 'The Goats', both works quite free of that 'blotting and blurring' manner he had espoused before his enlightenment. One of the finest watercolours on exhibition, however, was that of 'The Body of Abel found by Adam and Eve' in which the rich colouring, the striking postures, and the vigour of the dramatic composition possess a vivid intensity. It is as if Gillray had been repainted by Michelangelo.

But there were no purchasers for this, or for any painting other than the 'Ancient Britons', which Owen Pughe had already commissioned – despite the fact that Blake kept the exhibition open for some months after its advertised close. It had been, in the expression of the period, a 'dead failure', and it is significant that in future years his art was largely confined to book illustration. Once more he had fallen at the precise moment when he thought he might rise. Every public project, from his experiments with relief etching to the fiasco over *The Grave*, had gone wrong; he would have been forgiven for thinking that his career in the world was over. But that is to misunderstand the combative instinct he always possessed: he had advertised that he intended to execute an engraving from his Chaucer painting by September of the following year and, unusually for him, he managed to complete it only a fortnight later than promised. There were times when he was very determined.

He was also working on another project at the same period. As he continued with the engraving he wrote out in his notebook, in large letters, 'Chaucers Canterbury Pilgrims Being a Complete Index of Human Characters as they appear Age after Age'.[33] Then he began writing. Sometimes he jotted down independent paragraphs that look as if they had been scribbled in a fit of inspiration, or anger, or both; then he composed consecutive pages of writing, always carefully arranged around pre-existing drawings or verses, and remarkably free of revisions or corrections. This projected prose work was much more than a simple description of his Chaucer engraving, and it turned into a detailed defence of his methods with the same spirited polemic that had marked the defence of his painting in the Descriptive Catalogue. It was ostensibly addressed to the Chalcographic Society, 'respectfully', although there was nothing respectful about it at all – this was a society of engravers of which Blake's enemy Robert Cromek was Secretary. Blake was not a member, but he would have known that at one meeting a toast was given to Stothard's painting of Chaucer; he would also have known that Robert Hunt, the critic who had attacked him in *The Examiner*, was now enthusiastically publicising Cromek's efforts on behalf of the English engravers. It was one such scheme that specifically aroused Blake to fury – Cromek proposed a subscription whereby various connoisseurs or noblemen would buy shares at a hundred guineas each in a venture to subsidise twenty engravings of British paintings. The idea came to nothing, but it was enough to prompt Blake into an elaborate and extensive attack upon current artistic practices. He may have meant it to be published at the same time as his Chaucer print but it remained in his notebook. Nevertheless it is still one of the most important and perceptive accounts of the industrial and commercial systems that were changing the very practice of art in his lifetime.

It is immediately obvious that he feels himself to be isolated and marginalised; he talks about 'Secret Calumny and open Professions of Friendship', and specifically attacks both Stothard and Flaxman. On two occasions he refers to the fact that he has been called a 'Madman' but then issues a challenge to other English engravers: 'for these thirty two Years I am Mad or Else you are so both of us cannot be in our right senses Posterity will judge by our Works'.[34] But his personal frustration and sense of neglect were, in a writer who knew his own genius, symptoms of a much wider disorder – 'Resentment for Personal Injuries has had some share in this Public Address But Love to My Art & Zeal for my Country a much Greater',[35] since he truly believed that 'Engraving . . . as an Art is Lost in England'.[36] The reasons he advances for the decay of true art are various but related, and one of the first objects of his contempt is the state of fashionable opinion in England. He understood well enough how 'taste' was created and in his own oblique manner connected 'Advertizements in Newspapers' with 'Gentlemen Critics' and 'English Connoisseurs' as well as with 'Picture traders' and 'Picture dealers'; here he is attacking what was essentially a middle-class or genteel interest in art, propagated by the newspapers and the art dealers, a fashionable taste known for its liberality and correctness but one quite unable to understand or appreciate the work of a visionary such as Blake. He knew very well that he was being marginalised by an artistic coterie, whose standards were those of a diluted Europeanism, which is why he makes a point of attacking 'the Contemptible Counter Arts . . . set on foot by Venetian Picture traders Music traders & Rhime traders' to the detriment of truly native genius.[37]

But the obeisance to fashions, whether intellectual or cultural, is seen by him to be one aspect of a general movement towards uniformity and standardisation in a commercial economy: 'Commerce Cannot endure Individual Merit its insatiable Maw must be fed by What all can do Equally well'.[38] The villains of this encroaching market are those who manage 'the Arts of Trading Combination', 'the Monopolizing Trader' as well as 'Booksellers & Trading Dealers'. It is in their interests to promote the kind of art that can be easily and mechanically produced, and Blake anticipates the worst aspects of industrialism in his assault on their reliance upon 'Manual Labour' in the production of standard engravings, which is 'a work of no Mind'. That is why he is so intent upon destroying the belief that there is some distinction between conception and execution – 'I have heard many People say Give me the Ideas. It is no matter what Words you put them into & others say Give me the Design it is no matter for the Execution. These People know Enough of Artifice but Nothing Of Art . . . Execution is only the result of Invention.'[39] It is in this context, also, that he makes two separate attacks. The first is upon those engravers, such as Woollett or Strange, who employed journeymen for the more mechanical aspects of any engraving before giving it the 'finishing' touch themselves. But he also condemns the more fashionable and recently developed techniques of stipple or mezzotint, which similarly relied upon mechanical execution to attain their effects. In one of his strokes of genius he relates these techniques to Dryden's rhymes as opposed to Milton's blank verse – 'Monotonous Sing Song Sing Song'.[40] Blake in turn wanted to return to the art of 'Drawing', which was the 'true Style of Art' comprising the invention and energy of the individual artist – 'Painting is Drawing on Canvas & Engraving is Drawing on Copper & Nothing Else'.[41] In an age that was becoming increasingly uniform and standardised, he tried to affirm the originality of artistic genius. He realised that, if the division between invention and execution is made, an 'Idea' or 'Design' can simply be produced on an assembly line. Art then is turned into a 'Good for Nothing Commodity' manufactured by 'Ignorant Journeymen' for a society of equally ignorant consumers. It becomes part of that 'destructive Machine' into which all life is presently being turned – 'A Machine is not a Man nor a Work of Art it is Destructive of Humanity & of Art'.[42]

These ideas are very closely related to his speculations on knowledge and perception – 'To Generalise is to be an Idiot,' he had said in his annotations on Reynolds, whom he also described as a 'Hired Knave . . . His Eye is on the Many. or rather on the Money'.[43] In those same annotations he had asserted that 'Demonstration Similitude & Harmony are Objects of Reasoning'.[44] When 'Spiritual Perception' is denied or downgraded, therefore, society itself becomes the prey to generalising and commercial forces that destroy the knowledge of true art – this is his central theme. A secular society is an industrial society which creates the 'Ratio' of all that exists and calls it knowledge. The uniformity it breeds affects both the nature of art and of human beings themselves, so that in any one remark Blake can be talking about engraving, about machinery and about human society: 'One Species of General Hue over all is the Cursed Thing calld Harmony it is like the Smile of a Fool'.[45] That is why he was opposed to the 'Demonstrative Science' of Newton, which worshipped the outward form of atoms and particles, just as the Greeks worshipped the outward forms of their Gods instead of finding them within the human breast. That is also the reason for his attack upon the epistemology of Locke, which proposed a version of rational and generalised truth that denied intuition and inspiration, whereas Blake believed that 'Invention Identity & Melody are Objects of Intuition'.[46] Original form and true outline are the work of the inspired artist, and of the imagination; they cannot be the work of 'journeymen' like those that Rubens hired. All art is individual and particular, based upon 'Minute Discrimination', because only then can it partake of the divine.

His public address to English engravers was, in essence, not new. John Landseer had attacked the commercialisation of engraving (and in particular Boydell) in a series of public lectures, while artists such as William Sharp and Benjamin West had criticised the beginnings of what we would now term 'mass' production. But none of them had taken their analysis as far, or as deep, as Blake. It is yet another example of his clairvoyant understanding of his age that he is able to draw the connection between art, industrial economics and what would become the 'consumer societies' of modern civilisation in an analysis that was not otherwise formulated until the present century. It is as if his own sense of helplessness and despair had broken him open, and he could speak clearly about the world that had come close to destroying him; it was not madness at all, but a peculiar kind of lucidity which springs from those who have nothing left to lose. But he realised well enough what this encroaching industrial society was about to forfeit – all imitative techniques and mechanical perceptions 'turn that which is Soul & Life into a Mill or Machine'.[47] And what was now all around him? An 'automatical exhibition' in St Martin's Lane that included a female figure playing a harpsichord, cork models in Lower Grosvenor Street, mechanical panoramas in Spring Gardens and Leicester Square, clockwork waterfalls and mechanical pictures at Vauxhall or Ranelagh Gardens, advertisements for a new 'COFFEE MADE IN ONE MINUTE',[48] while 'Mathematical instruments, and every thing curious in that science, appear in abundance';[49] these would include the new chronometers and pedometers and alarm watches, while a steam engine had been demonstrated in the fields by Euston Road during the summer of 1808. All this time Blake continued work on his engraving of Chaucer's pilgrims, redolent of a more spiritual state of England and executed by him in a style that imitated the great 'Gothic' masters of the sixteenth century.

He had also begun work upon two new prophecies, entitled *Milton* and *Jerusalem*, in which Albion will arise from his couch of death. The nature of these poems will be explored in a later chapter, but it is important to note here that the two greatest of his epics were created intermittently over a period of sixteen years; in fact they were not necessarily 'written' at all, unless Blake jotted down first drafts on pieces of paper, but created with quill and graver on the copper plate itself. The title page on both has the date '1804', no doubt quickly inscribed in the period of visionary excitement that followed his visit to the gallery in the New Road; but he seems now to have considered his poetry to be the occasional work of those hours when he was not preparing for the exhibition in his brother's shop. A few months before it opened, he had told George Cumberland that he had neither the time nor the opportunity to print out a set of his illuminated books for an interested customer because he had 'now so long been turned out of the old channel into a new one . . . New profits seem to arise before me so tempting that I have already involved myself in engagements that preclude all possibility of promising anything.' Then he goes on to describe 'my time, which in future must alone be devoted to Designing & Painting'.[50]

He worked occasionally on *Milton* even as he completed *The Four Zoas* – no doubt falling upon the copper in 'the Heat of my Spirits', but he did not begin the actual printing of the poem until he had finished his work on the Chaucer engraving in the autumn of 1810. He adverts to it in his notes on the engraving itself when, in his attack upon those who had 'blasted' his character, he states, 'the manner in which I have routed out the nest of villains will be seen in a Poem concerning my Three years Herculean Labours at Felpham which I will soon Publish'.[51] *Jerusalem* was an even more extensive project – Cumberland had noted in the summer of 1807 that 'Blake has engd. 60 Plates of a new Prophecy!', so he was clearly intent upon it before he began to plan the exhibition of his own paintings.[52] Southey was shown 'a perfectly mad poem called Jerusalem' in 1811, but it was not until 1820 that eighty of the hundred plates had been completed.

The spirits were around him still, through the period of his exhibition and his public addresses. He wrote an entry in his notebook during the summer of 1807 – 'My Wife was told by a Spirit to look for her fortune by opening by chance a book which she had in her hand it was Bysshes Art of Poetry. She opened the following.'[53] He then transcribed a poem by Aphra Behn on the joys of sexual intercourse and 'The immortality of Love'. 'I was so well pleased with her Luck that I thought I would try my Own & opend the following' – he lighted upon some lines from Dryden's translation of Virgil, which depict the sturdiness of a tree that withstands all the fury of the elements because of its 'fixd' foundations. Here Blake saw some analogy with his own state, and in one of his poems on the same page of the notebook he declares that 'I am in Gods presence night & Day'.[54] He knew the reality of spiritual influence, therefore, and he was keen to defend those who might also have some awareness of it, however mistaken; a few months after his divination he wrote a letter to the editor of the *Monthly Magazine* in defence of an astrologer who had been arrested and imprisoned. The man was Robert Powell of Soho Square, who had been taken to the magistrates at Hatton Garden on the charge of being a 'rogue, vagabond and imposter'; the records show that the man pleaded guilty but asked for leniency on the grounds that he had a lunatic wife and three children. Blake knew nothing of this, and in his letter offered another defence: 'The Man who can Read the Stars often is oppressed by their Influence, no less than the Newtonian who reads Not & cannot Read is oppressed by his own Reasonings & Experiments.'[55] It is a perceptive statement, and again demonstrates how far in advance of his age Blake's understanding now was. A young man who met him in this period through Tommy Butts, Seymour Kirkup, has left a description: 'His high qualities I did not prize at that time; besides, I thought him mad. I do not think so now. I never suspected him of imposture. His manner was too honest for that. He was very kind to me, though very positive in his opinion, with which I never agreed.'[56] The opinion was of 'the truth of his visions', and Catherine Blake herself told the young man, 'I have very little of Mr Blake's company; he is always in Paradise.' Kirkup also stated that 'he was very kind & communicative to me', an opinion complemented by another visitor: 'I had the felicity of seeing this happy pair in their one apartment in South molton st; the Bed on one side and picture of Alfred and the Danes on the wall.'[57] The painting he saw was no doubt that of 'The Ancient Britons', but Blake was often so eager to overwork his art that it may well have been almost unrecognisable.

Some others had less happy experiences with him, however, and there were times when his behaviour seemed erratic even to those who knew him best. George Cumberland, for example, was involved in an argument between Blake and a young man, Charles Ker, who suddenly found himself being harassed. In 1808 he had asked Blake that 'at your leisure you shall make me 2 Drawings and when Ive got it I will pay you for them'.[58] Two years later Blake delivered two drawings to him, together with a bill for twenty guineas which he demanded should be paid within two weeks; the young man was still 'the very Picture of Poverty', but offered fifteen guineas. Blake refused. Then he offered to pay the price that any mutual friend should deem proper, but again Blake refused. Then he offered to pay in instalments, but he still refused – 'and then,' as Ker stated, 'he arrested me'. There are no records of any trial, and the matter seems to have been settled out of court. Ker later wrote that 'Blake is more knave than fool and made me pay 30 Guineas for 2 Drawings which on my word were never ordered'.[59] It was odd conduct on Blake's part, if Ker's statements are to be taken at face value, but it suggests the violence of temper and behaviour that sometimes invaded him at times of crisis or anxiety. But then all was calm again. He wrote in his notebook in the year of this dispute – '23 May 1810 found the Word Golden'; five pages later, in the middle of a description of one of his paintings, he wrote, 'the Nature of my Work is Visionary or Imaginative it is an Endeavour to Restore the Golden Age'.[60]

The painting in question was 'A Vision of the Last Judgment', and it was one of a number of commissions in this period. He had expected to attract a public audience, with his submissions to the Royal Academy and his own exhibition in Broad Street, but he was again dependent upon the help and money of friends. He had also hoped to spend his time on original 'Designing & Painting', as he had explained, but his work over the next few years was almost entirely devoted to book illustrations.[61] They were not necessarily un-congenial to him and, even as he worked on *Milton*, he was working on Milton. The first commission came from the Reverend Joseph Thomas of Epsom: he was already a great admirer of Blake, who, according to Nancy Flaxman, 'wishes to collect all B— has done',[62] and in 1807 he asked him to do a series of watercolour illustrations of *Paradise Lost*. It was a familiar subject, of course; the poem had been illustrated by Barry, Romney, Fuseli, Stothard, among others, and was the stock in trade of such mechanical spectacles as De Loutherbourg's 'Eidophusikon' in Leicester Square. One of the most famous painterly illustrations, 'Satan, Sin and Death', was considered to represent the highest point of 'the sublime' in modern art.

Blake completed twelve watercolours for Thomas. Although he remained consistently faithful to Milton's text, his understanding of the poem was immeasurably deepened and strengthened by the work on his own *Milton*. His are highly symmetrical compositions under the influence of characteristically strong vertical lines, and they represent his enthusiasm for the new medievalism or new Gothic that had been divulged to him at the Truchsessian Exhibition: here, too, are revealed moments of vision where gestures and features are strangely stylised. In works such as 'Raphael Warns Adam and Eve' and 'Michael Foretells the Crucifixion', for example, there is little differentiation between facial types; a series of notes for another work provides the explanation that 'the Persons Moses & Abraham are not here meant but the States Signified by those Names the Individuals being representatives or Visions of those States'.[63] That is why the central figure in these watercolours, untypically for the period, is that of Christ; in Blake's vision he is Christ the Redeemer, but he is also 'the True Vine of Eternity The Human Imagination';[64] he is the 'Divine Humanity' from which all eternity derives,[65] and Blake depicts him here as a majestic figure observed in scenes of revelation. He found the subject of *Paradise Lost* of great personal significance, and in the following year he executed a similar set of watercolour and pen illustrations for Thomas Butts; they were almost twice the size of those he completed for Thomas, and there is a marked increase of power both in composition and execution. The depicted scenes are the same, but they are more accomplished and the figures are more elaborately modelled. Beside one sketch of the sleeping Adam and Eve, he wrote a note to himself – 'Remember to make the thigh of Eve join better to the body & to make her a little bigger and Adam less'.[66] He seems to be bringing to Milton the heroic resonance of Michelangelo, while at the same time he is creating a hieratic and symmetrical art reminiscent of medieval religious motifs. It is an extraordinarily powerful combination, and he is here able to create a wholly original religious landscape in which all the constituents of his art are vividly displayed. In terms of sheer draughtsmanship this series must rank as one of his most impressive performances, with very careful and detailed colouring of orange or violet or green to exemplify the aspects of vision. The watercolours need only be compared with those he executed for Milton's *Comus* to reveal how instinctive and how natural his religious sensibility had become.

But he was not always so successful: the year after he completed *Paradise Lost* for Butts, he began a series of watercolours illustrating Milton's 'On the Morning of Christ's Nativity'; there is again an intense religious feeling in his constant drawing of the infant Christ in the manger, representing the presence of the Divine Humanity, but the compositions are not of his finest. He may well have finished the work hastily or inattentively, however, because in the same year he was engaged on an elaborate and ambitious project to which he would return until the end of his life. It was 'A Vision of the Last Judgment', in which his reverence for medieval sacred art and his devotion to Michelangelo were displayed in a painting reputed to be seven feet by five feet and to contain more than one thousand figures. It was not the first such work he had undertaken – four years before he had completed a 'Last Judgment' for Thomas Butts on a much smaller scale and, as a result of some discreet assistance by Ozias Humphry, he had completed another such 'Vision' for the Countess of Egremont in 1808. Each of his paintings of these scenes grows more elaborate, just as his verse prophecies themselves increased in size and in complexity. He wrote a description of the painting to Humphry, in which he gave a relatively simple allegorical interpretation of its contents, moving around the various compartments of the work just as if he were describing a medieval religious object: 'Such is the Design which you, my Dear Sir, have been the cause of my producing & which: but for you might have slept till the Last Judgment.'[67] Humphry was already going blind, after years of work as a miniaturist, but he was so impressed by Blake's prose description that he sent a copy of it to a friend with a strong recommendation. 'The Size of this drawing,' he wrote, 'is but small not exceeding twenty Inches by fifteen or Sixteen (I guess) but . . . It is one of the most interesting performances I ever saw; & is, in many respects superior to the last Judgment of Michael Angelo.'[68] Humphry no doubt expressed such sublime praise to Blake as well, and thus helped to confirm the artist's often threatened belief in himself. Such praise may, in addition, have been enough for him to start work upon a much larger version of the 'Vision of the Last Judgment' in the following year. He also began to write a long defence of this 'Vision' in the notebook, just at the time he was finishing his 'Public Address', and it is possible that he was planning a second exhibition to display his large new work. Once again, in his notes upon the painting, he was concerned to defend the nature of his spiritual insight – 'This world of Imagination is the World of

Eternity . . . tho on Earth things seem Permanent they are less permanent than a Shadow as we all know too well'.[69] It is in this context, too, that he describes the subjects of the painting itself – 'Imagination is Surrounded by the daughters of Inspiration who in the aggregate are calld Jerusalem . . . an Aged patriarch is awakd by his aged wife He is Albion our Ancestor patriarch of the Atlantic Continent whose History Preceded that of the Hebrews'.[70] Blake's religious art, therefore, incorporated conventional Christian eschatology with his own spiritual vision, whether invented or acquired. Now, too, he made an aesthetic analogy that is one of the most explicit statements of his permanent belief – 'as Poetry admits not a Letter that is Insignificant so Painting admits not a Grain of Sand or a Blade of Grass Insignificant much less an Insignificant Blur or Mark'.[71]

Other works of a similar visionary intensity, commissioned principally by Butts, followed the failure of the exhibition in 1809. 'An Allegory of the Spiritual Condition of Man' was completed in 1811 and, although the iconography is somewhat unclear, it represents Blake's constant attempt to return English art to its medieval and sacred origins; the holy figures are laid within various compartments of the painting, and once again he was trying to convey a vision of eternal reality while using a 'tempera' that he believed to be close to the materials of the early masters. Two of the most striking works of this period, however, are the temperas of 'Adam' and 'Eve' that Blake also finished for Butts. 'Adam Naming the Beasts' depicts the face of a sacred figure, wide-eyed, with the look of divinity; he seems to be gazing at the spectator but on further study it becomes clear that he is entranced with some inner vision of the world. There are animals behind him and he holds up the forefinger of his right hand in a gesture both of command and of recognition. Blake once told the spectator of his art that if he 'could Enter into these Images of his Imagination approaching them on the Fiery Chariot of his Contemplative Thought . . . then would he arise from his Grave then would he meet the Lord in the Air'.[72] We can arise and meet the gaze of primordial Adam, then, and see in that blessed moment the very origin and meaning of the Divine Vision by which all things were known and named. Boehme's words are appropriate here, in his description of this luminous primordial man 'who knew the language of God and the angels . . . And Adam knew that he was within every creature, and he gave to each its appropriate name.'[73]

It was one of the last commissions Blake received from Thomas Butts. As one biographer put it, 'The patron had often found it a hard matter *not* to offend the independent, wilful painter, ever the prouder for his poverty and neglect, always impracticable and extreme when ruffled or stroked the wrong way. The patron had himself begun to take offence at Blake's quick resentment of well-meant, if blunt, advice and at the unmeasured violence of his speech, when provoked by opposition. The wealthy merchant employed him but little now, and during the few remaining years of Blake's life they seldom met.'[74] Butts's last payment was recorded at the end of 1810, and they do not seem to have resumed proper relations for something like ten years. This was the shape his life had now taken: his humiliations at the hand of Cromek, his unmerited assaults upon Stothard, his estrangement from Fuseli and Flaxman, the termination of Hayley's patronage, the failure of his public exhibition, the newspaper attacks upon his sanity, now culminated in the alienation of his greatest patron and supporter. Yet never had his spiritual vision been so intense; the more condemned and neglected by the world, the more he shook its dust from his feet. It is sometimes as if he enjoyed his anguish, as if he wanted the crucifixion. He is on the cross, while the world goes by laughing. In his account of the great 'Vision of the Last Judgment' he repeats one of the central tenets of his vision – 'Mental Things are alone Real what is Calld Corporeal Nobody Knows of its Dwelling Place it is in Fallacy & its Existence an Imposture'.[75] Some might consider these the words of a misguided man, railing against a world that refused to notice him; as a result they might find here enough pathos and sorrow to justify calling Blake's life a tragedy. But that was not at all how it seemed to him, and at the close of this unpublished description he breaks out into one of his finest songs of joy: 'What it will be Questiond When the Sun rises do you not see a round Disk of fire somewhat like a Guinea O no no I see an Innumerable company of the Heavenly host crying Holy Holy Holy is the Lord God Almighty'.[76]

TWENTY-THREE

arise with Exultation

'The Last Judgment' is a vision of apocalypse and of revelation, as expounded in the last line of *Milton*: 'To go forth to the Great Harvest & Vintage of the Nations'.[1] He drew or painted this sacred subject at least seven times, and he kept the last one by him until his death. He worked upon the final version for some seventeen years, and at the end it was so blackened with over-painting that little of it remained visible. George Cumberland wrote to his father in 1815 that Blake 'has been labouring at it till it is nearly as black as your Hat – the only lights are those of a *Hellish Purple*',[2] although J. T. Smith remembered a work containing 'upwards of one thousand figures, many of them wonderfully conceived and grandly drawn', with blue wash over gold that gave an extraordinary effect of silvering.[3] Blake had always been haunted by last things, ever since he had engraved the exultant soul parting from the body in memory of his own brother's death. His preoccupation with mortality and resurrection may have its source further back, in the drawings of the royal tombs within Westminster Abbey, and in his own paintings of Judgment he returns to the medieval archetypes which informed that first vision. Within the relatively small scale of these paintings hundreds of finely defined allegorical figures are fashioned in harmonious symmetry and placed within clearly defined 'compart-ments' of the picture; each of these figures is, in Blake's words, 'organised and minutely articulated' with 'minute discriminations', while at the same time every element of the composition flows together to lend a bounding line and contour to what Blake knew to be 'Spiritual Perception'. These are pure circular forms, the image of ideal order, composed, hierarchic, harmonious, unified, eternal.

They might even be said to represent the apotheosis of his own visionary experiences, in which he saw the clear lineaments of the spiritual beings before him. Here in the paintings, then, are Noah and Albion, Abraham and Apollyon, Elijah and Mary, Seth and Jesus, Elohim and the Eternal Female, Araunah and Eliakim, Adam and Cain, clouds of women and children, falling devils and rising angels. It presents what might be called divine theatre, or a revelatory spectacle in which the lineaments of the human form reveal their divine origin. It is an art of gesture and of expression, of scenic light and darkness, of ornamental space and formal intricacy, which act as emblems of the divine pattern.

It has been said that Blake's art is one of process and movement, and in these apocalyptic vistas the main suggestion is one of continual activity and change. The vital motion is of course an intrinsic element of the painterly composition, but it is in turn animated by his profound sense of the energetic interplay between contraries and oppositions. The twin poles of blessing and retribution, of heaven and hell, are placed here in communion within the great body of the painting, which itself represents the Divine Humanity. Will and desire, love and hate, the Resurrection and the Fall, are seen coming from the Saviour and returning to the Saviour. It resembles Blake's recognition of the dialectic between 'the light world' and 'the dark world', which Jacob Boehme established; these in turn move 'the wheel of anguish' and 'the wheel of birth'. 'The wrath and the anger,' Boehme wrote, 'together with the abyss of hell, stand in the centre of the Father'; and out of that 'fierceness' springs 'mobility', which is the turning circle of Blake's Last Judgments.[4] It is an aspect of the greatness of these paintings that they reveal such abstract themes within works of much richness and intricacy; here Blake has managed to combine multiplicity and coherence, variety and harmonious unity, within the perspective of one grand vision.

These spiritual figures, the just and wicked alike, are also close to Swedenborg's vision of life after death when the lineaments of the human form are revived or reawakened in a spiritual sense; they are not necessarily meant to be individual figures, however, but representations of the states through which the human being passes in his journey towards the Redeemer. They are 'Images of Existences', 'States Signified by those Names' such as Og and Abel.[5] There is one other intimation of Swedenborg within the paintings. In *Heaven and Hell* the philosopher had declared, 'an angelic society sometimes appears as one man in the form of an angel' and that Jesus appears as 'one in an angelic form'.[6] It is very close to Blake's depiction of his own Last Judgments in which 'these various States I have seen in my Imagination when distant they appear as One Man but as you approach they appear Multitudes of Nations'.[7] And then, to complete the trinity of spiritual influences vouchsafed to Blake in his youth and fulfilled in the work of his maturity, we might here recall the words of Paracelsus – 'The centre of all things is man, he is the middle point of heaven and earth . . . Heaven is man, and man is heaven. and all men together are the one heaven, and heaven is nothing but one man.'[9] It is perhaps not coincidental, then, that Blake's paintings of the Last Judgment have often been thought to outline the shape of a human figure which is itself the 'Divine Humanity'.[9] All will be restored in Jesus and in the Imagination, which is 'One Man'. Thus from one man, William Blake, springs the vision of eternal life.

TWENTY-FOUR

I [was] am hid

It was as if the brightness of his spiritual vision had blotted out the world, and he was left with his wife alone. '[A]t present I have no intercourse with Mr Blake,' Flaxman wrote in 1808 and when in the following year Joseph Johnson died Blake was not a mourner at the funeral.[1] Fuseli had no 'intercourse' with him either, and now had his own engraver residing with him in his house. Thomas Butts was no longer his patron and Ozias Humphry, his great admirer and supporter, died in 1810. Even James Blake appears to have turned against him and 'looked upon his erratic brother with pity and blame, as a wilful, misguided man, wholly in a wrong track'.[2] It is interesting, then, that he should give up his hosiery business in Broad Street and start work as a clerk in Butts's government office. No doubt they talked of poor 'Will' or 'William' often, and may even have formulated plans to assist him in the event of real poverty.

But Blake knew the world well enough and, as he continued his labours in South Molton Street, the city maintained its external life of identity and change – 'nothing new occurs in identical existence,' he had written, '. . . Names alter, things never alter'.[3] So once again there were riots over the price of bread and demonstrations against the various Ministries. The great comet of 1811, leaving a trail of light across the London sky, might have been in Elizabethan fashion an augury of blood and suffering: the bad winters of 1812 and 1813 (the latter was the worst of the century), disappointing harvests and the effects of the Napoleonic blockade meant that London was once more becoming a city of famine. Over 45,000 inhabitants of Spitalfields alone pleaded to be allowed to enter the workhouse because of their want of bread. It was a time when insurrection, and the fear of insurrection, once again emerged in the capital and in the regions; the violent Luddite protests of 1812 and 1813 were aspects of a general movement among radicals, and what were known as the 'industrious classes', against 'The Thing' or 'Old Corruption'. This was the time of such periodicals as Pig's Meat, Black Dwarf and Axe to the Root; it was once more a period of ale-house meetings and public demonstrations, of government spies and state repression. The victory celebration of 1814 did nothing to alleviate the pressing crisis that threatened to overturn all civil order; in fact the demobilisation of troops only added to the vast number of the unemployed and to the legion of beggars now to be seen in London (so powerfully portrayed by Géricault), while the combination of further bad harvests, the Corn Laws of 1815, and general trade depression led to sporadic revolts such as that led by Watson from Spa Fields to the Tower. The attempted assassination of the Prince Regent in 1817 led in turn to the Seditious Meetings Bill, known as the Gagging Acts, and the suspension of Habeas Corpus. It must have seemed to Blake like a re-enactment of the Jacobin demonstrations of the 1790s, which had themselves led to general social and political repression; in that other time, he claimed to have put on the cap of liberty. Now, when the same pattern of events was restored within the city, we have only one extant remark: 'I am really sorry to see my Countrymen trouble themselves about Politics. If Men were Wise the Most arbitrary Princes could not hurt them If they are not Wise the Freest Government is compelld to be a Tyranny. Princes appear to me to be Fools Houses of Commons & Houses of Lords appear to me to be fools they seem to me to be something Else besides Human Life.'[4] It is a version of political quietism, perhaps, but it is also close to the visionary idealism or anarchism of his youth; he had not retreated from his earlier beliefs, and it was rather that his distaste for 'System' on every level had been intensified and deepened. Certainly he had not, like his near contemporaries Wordsworth and Coleridge, turned into a political reactionary.

Now the events of the world simply passed over his head. His mid-Victorian biographer claims that there was a time when 'for two years together, he never went out at all' except to 'fetch his porter';[5] it is not necessary to believe such an extravagant claim in order to understand the life of a man sometimes lost within his visions and his inspired introspection. There were still visitors, however, and, when a young sculptor from Liverpool came to the door of South Molton Street without a letter of introduction, he was received well enough: Blake 'showed me his cartoons, and complained sadly of the want of feeling in England for high art, and his wife joined in with him and she was very bitter upon the subject'.[6] Indeed he and his wife in this period offer the material for much contemplation – both of them now in late middle age, sharing a life of poverty if not privation, with Catherine attending to the household while at the same time ministering to her husband's nervous anxieties and fears. But she also shared his dreams and his inspiration, implicitly believing in the substance of her husband's visions. Cumberland had said that she was 'maddest of the Two', but that is only because she accepted the existence of Blake's spirits and angels without necessarily understanding the mythology he had single-handedly created.[7] When he explained to visitors the nature of his second sight, she 'would look at her husband with an awe-struck countenance, and then at his listener to confirm the fact. Not only was she wont to echo what he said, to talk as he talked, on religion and other matters – this may be accounted for by the fact that he had educated her; but she, too, learned to have visions.'[8] She was now poorly clad in 'common, dirty dress', but 'vulgarity there was none';[9] she had lost all of her beauty, 'except in so far as love made her otherwise, and spoke through her gleaming black eyes'.[10] She worked with her husband on his art; she sat with him 'motionless and silent' when he needed her presence to comfort him; she fed him and made his clothes.[11] It is a story of the utmost devotion, virtually without parallel in the history of English letters, and it can fairly be said that without Catherine Blake none of the great works of her husband would have appeared. We can salute her now, two hundred years later, as we see her sitting beside her husband in their small room off Oxford Street.

And still he worked on. 'Oh,' he told one young visitor, 'I never stop for anything; I work on, whether ill or not.' And then again he remarked, 'I don't understand what you mean by the want of a holiday.'[12] He had enough with his work, and he laboured through all the years of neglect. 'Poor dear man,' one friend exclaimed after his death, 'to think how ill he was used, and yet he took it all so quietly.'[13] There was greatness in that and greatness, too, in the manner in which he continued with even the humblest of engravers' tasks. Swinburne later wrote that 'he was apparently unconscious how noble a thing was his own life' in this period, but perhaps we may be able to find something of that nobility in the work he completed.[14]

Much of it was the task of the journeyman, largely in commissions from friends or acquaintances who still wished to support him – and who had already been viciously lampooned in his own private epigrams. The publisher Bowyer, for example, who had been secretly attacked by Blake, helped to arrange his work on an engraving from Thomas Phillips's portrait of Earl Spencer. Flaxman, who had been steadily attacked in the notebook, also came to his rescue in three different and important projects; it was not simply the case of a highly successful artist helping an unfortunate contemporary and colleague, however, since Flaxman still had a very high opinion at least of Blake's technical abilities. He described him to one potential client as 'the best engraver of outlines'.[15] That is why he asked him to work upon thirty-seven of his 'Compositions from the Works Days and Theogony of Hesiod', a long and lucrative project that earned Blake almost two hundred pounds over a space of three years; they are very delicate works, closely modelled upon Flaxman's original pencil drawings, but they are executed in an uncharacteristic manner; Blake has used 'stipple', or lines of fine dots, as a way of suggesting the nervous purity of Flaxman's own style. In the same period Flaxman also asked him to illustrate essays on sculpture and armour that he was preparing for The Cyclopaedia; or Universal Dictionary of Arts, Sciences and Literature; Blake engraved images of Jupiter Pausanius and a Chinese figure, but the most familiar and congenial work came in his copying of the statues he had admired as a youth. He visited the Royal Academy in order to make drawings from the plaster casts there of the Hercules Farnese and the Laocoön group. While working on his sketches he was approached by Henry Fuseli, then Keeper of the Academy: 'What! you here, Meesther Blake?' he said. 'We ought to come and learn of you, not you of us!' Nevertheless he took his place with the other students, and drew from the antique: it was the same work he had done thirty years before and yet, according to the same report, he continued now 'with cheerful, simple joy'.[16]

In certain respects he was still very much a child who needed to be comforted and complimented, who could sulk and hide away, but who could also break out in joyous and energetic high spirits. It may in part be related to the defining experience within his own family in Broad Street; but it also throws an intriguing light upon his relationship with Catherine, who remained otherwise childless. So he could draw the Laocoön with that 'cheerful, simple joy'. Flaxman also procured him work of a less cultivated but nevertheless profitable kind; he was commissioned to engrave from Flaxman's drawings almost two hundred pieces of crockery from the factory of Josiah Wedgwood. It was for a 'sample book' used by the salesmen, and the great author of Eternity was obliged to illustrate egg cups, tureens, candlesticks and coffee pots. 'I ought to have mentioned when the Terrine was sent to you,' Wedgwood's son wrote to him, 'that the hole for the ladle in the cover should not be represented & which you will be so good to omit in the engraving.' And Blake replied, in turn, 'I send Two more drawings with the First that I did, altered, having taken out that part which expressed the hole for the ladle.' Then he ended, 'Any Remarks that you may be pleased to make will be thankfully reciev'd by, Sir, Your humble Servant'.[17] This was the poet now writing

> And all this Vegetable World appeard on my left Foot,
> As a bright sandal formd immortal of precious stones & gold:
> I stooped down & bound it on to walk forward thro' Eternity.[18]

These are lines from *Milton* and, as he completed the poem, he was illustrating that poet's works with another series of watercolours which are as accomplished and as beautiful as anything he had previously achieved. It is not clear when or by whom they were commissioned – if they were commissioned at all – and there is some reason for believing that he worked upon them in his moments of liberty as a form of painterly interpretation that complemented the literary interpretation within his own verse. He was largely redeploying old motifs, from poems he had already illustrated, and it may be that he was hoping for a quick sale to his remaining admirers. He designed eight watercolours as an illustration of *Comus*, but these are more elaborately and vividly imagined than the series he had executed for Joseph Thomas at Felpham. They are still not among his best compositions, however, since he was always more intensely affected by Milton's spiritual rather than secular poetry. Another series of watercolours, 'On the Morning of Christ's Nativity', displays a much more passionate and impassioned response to a writer who seemed to Blake to be his forerunner – a prophet and poet who trusted in his divine inspiration and who kept faith with his destiny. But these works are more delicately and finely conceived than the first set of illustrations of that poem; they are freer in execution, with a wonderful range of luminous colouring, and it is clear that Blake has liberated himself from the stern dictates of 'the bounding line' and 'determinate and bounding form' that had been so much an aspect of his exhibition catalogue.[19] He is less inclined to linearity, and is therefore more painterly. The same fluency and fluidity are to be seen in the set of twelve illustrations to *Paradise Regained*, but the freer manner is not achieved at the expense of Blake's spiritual intensity: the figure of Christ here is illuminated with an extraordinary radiance and, with such watercolours as 'Christ in the Wilderness' and 'Christ's Troubled Dream', we explore the art of a man who has removed himself from the world and from all worldly hopes. It is a spiritual art, too, because of the extraordinarily posed and poised figures surrounded by the blue and yellow of vision; the hieratic and numinous qualities of each scene are powerfully evoked, since this is a true nineteenth-century spiritual art that has no counterparts and no proper successors.

The best of Blake's illustrations from Milton were the last, when he painted twelve watercolours of subjects drawn from 'L'Allegro' and 'Il Penseroso', while interpreting those poems in terms of visions and visionary experience. He made his own transcription of the verses from which he was drawing, and appended a commentary as if he were revising Milton in a spiritual sense; his watercolour 'Night Startled by the Lark' is a vigorous but delicately coloured composition in which Milton's description of morning has been turned into an allegorical drama with Night as an ancient man lurking behind a watchtower, the lark as a bright angel, the dawn a young girl with arms outstretched and the earth itself a woman looking up in yearning at the gradually brightening sky. Blake then adds a commentary that begins 'The Lark is an Angel on the Wing . . .', and one might append here some wonderful lines from his own *Milton* about 'the Lark':

> Mounting upon the wings of light into the Great Expanse:
> Reechoing against the lovely blue & shining heavenly Shell:
> His little throat labours with inspiration; every feather
> On throat & breast & wings vibrates with the effluence Divine
> All Nature listens silent to him & the awful Sun
> Stands still upon the Mountain looking on this little Bird.[20]

The painting and the poetry once more come together in a visionary synthesis. That is why he was able to execute these watercolours while working upon *Milton* itself, an epic in which the great poet returns to earth and redeems his Emanation, while also entering William Blake in an effort to redeem the world. The action may be said to take place in that moment of birdsong Blake had heard in his cottage garden. 'Milton was in Earnest,' he had once written, and in this poem he sets out to restore the lost primacy of the poet by reuniting him with his own self in an act of inspired vision.[21] There was much in Milton with which he was closely in sympathy, and Milton's understanding of his sacred vision was directly comparable with that of Blake. Both of them were in the line of inspired poets whose mission was to arouse England from spiritual slumber and fulfil its Covenant; both of them asserted the primal grace of this country when, as Milton put it, 'our ancient Druids' created 'the cathedral of philosophy'. God, he wrote, 'hath yet ever had this island under the special indulgent eye of his providence'.[22] Or, in Blake's words, 'All things begin & end, in Albions Ancient Druid Rocky Shore.'[23] There were other resemblances he may not have noted. Both poets were stubborn and occasionally self-righteous, given to polemical abuse when criticised; both also possessed an element of London hardness in their nature that allowed them to withstand the forces marshalled against them.

'Milton lov'd me in childhood & shew'd me his face,' Blake had once told Flaxman,[24] and, at a later date, he informed another acquaintance, 'I have seen him as a youth. And as an old man with a long flowing beard. He came lately as an old man'[25] – by which he may also have meant that Milton's inspired example first visited him when young. The seventeenth-century poet was in any case 'in the air' of the period; the 'Eidophusikon' included 'Scenes from Milton' among its mechanical effects, while at the Lyceum there was a moving panorama that had as its central attraction 'an Embellished Recitation of Milton's "L'Allegro" '.[26] His works had been painted by the leading artists of the day, including those so much admired by Blake as Barry and Fuseli, while passages from _Paradise Lost_ were always used as token examples of what was then known as 'the sublime'. Yet Blake wished to do something other than imitate or praise Milton: he wanted to rewrite _Paradise Lost_ with the same vigour and visionary intensity with which he had illustrated 'L'Allegro' and 'Il Penseroso'. He wished to change the epic of the Fall into the prophecy of Man's faculties restored, and in so doing allow Milton to re-enter the world, where he might reclaim Satan as part of his own self. Thus the 'solitary flight' of Satan in _Paradise Lost_ becomes the journey of Milton into the vortex of eternity where 'I will go down to self annihilation and eternal death'.[27] The idea for such a journey may have come from Hayley, who in his biography of the poet had written, 'But could he [Milton] revisit earth in his mortal character . . .'[28] In Blake's poem he comes back as a 'Shadow' but then in turn he is united with Blake in a joint celebration of spiritual vision and poetic genius that may redeem the world:

> Then first I saw him in the Zenith as a falling star,
> Descending perpendicular, swift as the swallow or swift;
> And on my left foot falling on the tarsus, entered there.[29]

Such is Blake's understanding of his role that in the course of this long and complex poem he turns his own life into a species of allegory. There is a remarkable engraving of this moment of incarnation, placed between the two books or episodes of the poem, in which 'William' is seen naked with arms outstretched in an attitude of ecstasy as the star of Milton falls towards him: in one copy he is shown with an erect penis, as if to represent Blake's own rejection of Milton's supposedly repressive ethic. But the allegorical significance with which Blake now invests his life has longer and more complex ramifications when, in the course of his narrative, he uses the conflict of Satan and Palambron to deal obliquely with his own struggles against such men as Hayley and Cromek who helped him at the cost of his inspired work. In one letter to Hayley he had put himself in the role of the prophetic outcast, and Milton opens with a polemical address which bears all the marks of being written at the time when he was reflecting upon the failure of his exhibition and the general neglect of his work – 'Painters! on you I call! Sculptors! Architects! Suffer not the fashionable Fools to depress your powers by the prices they pretend to give for contemptible works or the expensive advertizing boasts that they make of such works'.[30] It is the voice of a poet who aspires to Milton's prophetic role and who in his remarks here on 'the Sublime of the Bible' wishes to return to a more ancient faith than that represented by classical literature with its 'Daughters of Memory'.[31] That is why Milton becomes for him a type of ancient epic, and why he prefaces his text with that most famous of his spiritual lyrics, 'And did those feet in ancient time'.[32] To build 'Jerusalem' is to build a city of holy art in which the Divine Humanity creates works of bliss; she is the Emanation of Albion whose foundations lie in 'Lambeths Vale', where the poet began his immortal task and which now are 'laid in ruins'.[33] Scofield appears in the poem, as does South Molton Street and the name of 'Hand' to represent the reviewers who had written against him. The text itself is also in a continual state of movement and revision as if he were in the process of reinventing his own life as he worked upon it. It is not an entirely autobiographical poem, however, and in the course of this long and sometimes difficult work he returns to the main outlines of his myth with its account of the struggle against the fallen world – 'this earth of vegetation on which now I write'.[34] There are passages of great beauty:

> Seest thou the little winged fly, smaller than a grain of sand?
> It has a heart like thee; a brain open to heaven & hell,
> Withinside wondrous & expansive; its gates are not clos'd,
> I hope thine are not: hence it clothes itself in rich array;
> Hence thou art cloth'd with human beauty O thou mortal man.[35]

But in this poem, more than in any other of Blake's works, he is concerned with 'the deceits of Natural Religion',[36] and there are passages of powerful intensity and lucidity where he sees through the entire fabric of his age which harbours 'A Female hidden in a Male, Religion hidden in War / Namd Moral Virtue'.[37] In the course of this he rejects all the scientific technology of his time as a satanic delusion and fraud:

> The Microscope knows not of this nor the Telescope. they alter
> The ratio of the Spectators Organs but leave Objects untouchd
> For every Space larger than a red globule of Mans blood.
> Is visionary: and it is created by the Hammer of Los
> And every Space smaller than a Globule of Mans blood. opens
> Into Eternity of which this vegetable Earth is but a shadow:
> The red Globule is the unwearied Sun by Los created
> To measure Time and Space to mortal Men.[38]

This is an extraordinary passage of visionary perception where the globe of blood is seen also to be an emblem of the cosmos, and where Blake directly addresses the problems of perception in the early nineteenth-century world. Some of his own most striking illustrations, therefore, are also to be found in the poem. In particular there are four white-line etchings – this had been the style he had used for *The Grave*, which Cromek had rejected as too crude, and it is as if Blake was determined to assert his own art in the face of humiliation and disappointment. These etchings are of a wonderful radiance and display naked forms in various acts of worship or exaltation; there is a suggestion of homosexual fellatio in one of them, just as there is in one of the relief etchings, thus adding a quality of strangeness to

Blake's association with Milton. Only four copies of the poem exist but they are richly and intricately coloured in predominant blues, pinks and pale yellows: to look at any one of them is to experience something close to a new form of religious art, drawn from the sacred works of the quattrocento but imbued with a heroic neoclassicism, affected by mannerism, and mediated through Blake's extraordinary and intense imagination. There are times when the delirium of the images – figures swathed in flame, or standing before a great sun – is reminiscent of the illustrations in the alchemical text books of the sixteenth and seventeenth centuries. There is no reason why Blake should not know of such work but, in any case, the hieroglyphic nature of his religious art can bring together spirituality, alchemical knowledge and sexual vitality in quite new ways. He has created his own synthesis out of the millenarianism of the period and his own private impulses – *Milton* is his book of knowledge wherein all is revealed.

'Poor Blake,' George Cumberland reported in 1814, 'still poor still Dirty'.[39] In the following year his son had a similar impression: 'We call upon Blake yesterday evening, found him & his wife drinking Tea durtyer than ever.'[40] If it was dirt, it was the dirt of his work; it is like the story of Turner with a visitor who said that he was a painter. 'Show me your hands,' Turner demanded. They were entirely clean, and Turner whispered to an assistant, 'Turn the fellow out. He's no artist.'[41] And, as Blake had explained to Cumberland's son, 'his time is now intirely taken up with Etching & Engraving'.[42] For, while working on *Milton*, he was also intent upon *Jerusalem*. He had shown an example of it to Southey, who had considered it 'perfectly mad . . . Oxford Street is in Jerusalem',[43] and he exhibited 'Detached Specimens' of his 'original illuminated Poem' at an exhibition of the Associated Painters in Watercolours in 1812 – at least he tried to do so, but the landlord of the premises seized the contents of the gallery when he received no rent. It might be considered another example of Blake's bad luck in the public world.

That world, too, was still changing around him. The sites of his boyhood expeditions were slowly being swallowed by the encroaching city, while there was much noisy building work in his own neighbourhood as Regent Street was constructed and Park Crescent begun.

> What are those golden Builders doing
> Near mournful ever-weeping Paddington.[44]

It is mournful, perhaps, because the bones of Tyburn victims were found there while it was being dug up and developed in 1811. So these two lines became part of *Jerusalem*, which he was writing now in South Molton Street. When he had mentioned that street in *Milton*, he drew three great stone trilithons beneath it – as if these ancient sources of power were still at work in the thoroughfares of the city, and his own bardic strength linked to the visionary wisdom of London. In the same spirit he gives names to the 'daughters of Albion' that he had found in Geoffrey of Monmouth's *Historia Regum Britanniae*. That is why he had begun *Jerusalem* so joyfully:

> Trembling I sit day and night, my friends are astonish'd at me.
> Yet they forgive my wanderings, I rest not from my great task!
> To open the Eternal Worlds, to open the immortal Eyes
> Of Man inwards into the Worlds of Thought: into Eternity.[45]

This was the eternity he saw in the streets of the city, as he described it in this last and greatest of his epic poems: 'I behold London; a Human awful wonder of God!'[46] This is 'the spiritual Four-fold London eternal' where every call and sound are preserved for ever because they lie within us;[47] that is how Blake can invoke 'An aged Woman raving along the Streets',[48] 'the Cry of the Poor Man',[49] and 'the poor indigent' who 'in his hallowd center holds the heavens of bright eternity',[50] the drunken woman 'reeling up the Street of London' who in turn leads Blake towards a vision of material reality as a refuge from 'The Hermaphroditic Satanic World of rocky destiny'.[51] The streets of the city offer sudden vistas and illuminations, scenes and visions against the background of immensity. Here are the furnaces of affliction, the brick fields and the dark courts, 'the pillar of smoke', tumult through 'the unbounded night', the 'clouded banks' of the river, with the great starry night of the heavens revolving above the city: 'I behold them and their rushing fires overwhelm my Soul, / In Londons darkness'.[52] It is a memory of the eternal time when 'London coverd the whole Earth',[53] and where all the scenes of his own life are given human and mortal dimension:

> The Corner of Broad Street weeps; Poland Street languishes
> To Great Queen Street & Lincolns Inn, all is distress & woe.[54]

The frontispiece shows Blake, or Los, striding through a portal into some dark place; he carries the sun as a lamp, because he is beginning a progress through the shadowy city. That journey may be said to have been conceived by South Molton Street and Tyburn's brook, when 'the Divine Vision like a silent Sun' began to set behind 'the Gardens of Kensington'.[55] Los must take up his 'globe of fire', then, and begin his travels from the fields of Highgate and the lead mills of Hackney until he 'came to old Stratford & thence to Stepney' and then on to the unlucky Isle of Dogs where the kennels are only the open streams of filth and sewerage running down towards the Thames.[56] Then he journeys on to where 'the Tower of London frownd dreadful over Jerusalem', and from there north towards the 'Dens of despair', which are Bedlam in Moorfields.[57] Then on to Westminster, to the fields of Marybone which he had known so well as a child, to 'the ruins of the Temple' and thus to London Stone in Cannon Street where finally he sits and listens to 'Jerusalems voice'.[58] He has walked the boundaries of the city, sometimes staying close to its ancient wall, and sees now the vision of it in divine form:

> My Streets are my, Ideas of Imagination.
> Awake Albion, awake! and let us awake up together.
> My Houses are Thoughts: my Inhabitants; Affections,
> The children of my thoughts.[59]

The stones are 'pity' and the bricks are 'well wrought affections', and yet in the fallen vegetative world the city itself is also an emblem of reasoning power, of law and false morality, of war and mechanism:

> . . . of the iron rollers, golden axle-trees & yokes
> Of brass, iron chains & braces & the gold, silver & brass
> Mingled or separate: for swords; arrows; cannons; mortars
> The terrible ball: the wedge: the loud sounding hammer of destruction
> The sounding flail to thresh: the winnow: to winnow kingdoms
> The water wheel & mill of many innumerable wheels resistless.[60]

There is an image in *Jerusalem* taken from 'London', the poem he had written so many years before, which may be said to represent this fallen city of the imagination: 'I see London blind & age-bent begging thro the Streets / Of Babylon, led by a child'.[61]

Yet there is always 'a Moment in each Day that Satan cannot find / Nor can his Watch Fiends find it';[62] it is also the 'Grain of Sand in Lambeth', which is 'translucent & has many Angles'.[63] If we were to drive into it within the chariot of imagination we would arrive at Golgonooza, Blake's great city of art and science. But, before entering, it is as well to turn back to the material world to find images or resemblances of such a place in the streets of London. Models of ancient building, manufactured out of cork or wood, were often displayed at exhibitions: one, representing the Temple of Solomon, was thirteen feet in height. But there were even more elaborate examples at hand: Sir John Soane's Bank of England was being constructed in Threadneedle Street over a period of some thirty-seven years and, in its complexity of arches and panels, has been described as 'the Gothic miracle rediscovered at the heart of the Roman tradition'.[64] In Flaxman's lectures on sculpture at the Royal Academy in 1810 he had described the great palace of Carnac, which contained 'colossal statues' and which was 'approached by four paved roads', bordered on each side by figures of animals fifteen feet high.[65] Similar descriptions were included with Flaxman's essay on sculpture for Rees's *Cyclopaedia*, which Blake was illustrating at the time he was writing *Jerusalem*. There were also great schemes for the building of public galleries, domes, pillars and monuments as part of the city's renovation. All these are reflected in Golgonooza, but there is another more familiar source. The antinomian prophets of the age, such as Richard Brothers, had described in minute detail the rebuilding of the sacred city of Jerusalem as a home for the lost English tribe.

So we can return through the hidden Moment or Grain to the great City of Art which dwells within the bosom of London. It is built upon four sides but, since it does not exist within the material vegetated universe, each of its four gates open into each other; only when the spectator redeems his perception and acquires 'Four-fold Vision', then 'you behold its mighty Spires & Domes of ivory & gold'.[66] But around it lies 'the land of death eternal',[67] bounded by the Mundane Shell, and ruled by the Twenty-Seven Churches, which are the official religions of earth's fallen history, reaching as far as Luther – religious creeds that have excluded the pity and mercy of the 'Divine Vision' and have thus become 'Synagogues of Satan'.[68] Here are to be found 'Pits of bitumen deadly', 'Lakes of Fire', 'Trees of Malice', 'The land of snares & traps & wheels & pit-falls & dire mills'.[69] Yet if you can shake off the dust of the earth, 'whatever is visible to the Generated Man', then you may approach the great City of Art and Manufacture where every lovely form exists in fourfold splendour. Within the courtyard there burns the moat of fire protecting Cathedron, or the home of the golden looms, which weave all created things and in which 'every Human Vegetated Form is in its inward recesses'. Here also is to be found the palace and the forge of Los, the great maker:

> And all that has existed in the space of six thousand years:
> Permanent, & not lost not lost nor vanishd, & every little act,
> Word, work, & wish, that has existed, all remaining still . . .

> For every thing exists & not one sigh nor smile nor tear,
> One hair nor particle of dust, not one can pass away.[70]

It is the vision of immensity seen in terms of a great city; but this place is also the Incarnation. It is the Divine Humanity that exists within each created being. It is the idealised society, also, and the vivid representation of that moment of creation within the lark song. It is unfallen London. It is *Jerusalem*.

It is his last testament, one in which all the resources of his poetry and art find their culmination. He worked on it intermittently over a period of sixteen years, using both sides of the copper plate to save material, and was sometimes forced to employ used plates that had discarded images or marks on them. He completed an early sequence of sixty pages over an initial period of three years, but then worked sporadically on the remaining forty, with a sudden fit of labour towards the end of his task. Some entirely decorated pages seem to have been issued separately while other 'Specimens' were, as we have seen, put on private exhibition. It was not a haphazard work but it grew by accretion, and there are occasions when he copies material from his unpublished *Four Zoas*: it was, in that sense, an informal endeavour but there came a point when he lent definite shape to the poem by consciously increasing its length to one hundred plates so that it became exactly twice the size of *Milton*. There is also evidence of his disaffection and despair during the long years of composition, since at some point he took his engraver's tool and erased certain words that had once been addressed 'To the Public'. He had originally written 'My former Giants & Fairies having reciev'd the highest reward possible: the love and friendship of those with whom to be connected, is to be blessed'. But then he removed 'love', 'friendship' and 'blessed' as if he wanted to impart no compliments to those people such as Flaxman and Stothard who owned copies of his illuminated books. There was also a more general turning away from the 'Dear Reader', once described as 'lover of books! lover of heaven' where in both cases the 'lover' is gouged out; the 'Dear' has also been removed

in an act of rage or defiance. It is as if he were now embracing his
isolation, and addressing himself only to eternity.

Yet the paradox is that, of all Blake's illuminated epics, this is by far
the most public and accessible. It is his own revelation, his own vision
of apocalypse, and those with any interest in the biblical prophets will
understand at once the directness and severity of the poetry; like his
tempera paintings of 1810 and his Descriptive Catalogue, this is an art
of form and outline rather than of softness and shadow. The difficulty
lies only in his attempt to create dramatic characters out of human
faculties and instincts, but he did so because there was no other
language to name or define his understanding of the psyche. Once the
basic principles are grasped, however, there is no need to follow every
complex and sometimes inconclusive or contradictory turn in his
narrative of the human soul. It is possible simply to enjoy the
visionary poetry within such passages as this:

> He who is an Infant, and whose Cradle is a Manger
> Knoweth the Infant sorrow: whence it came, and where it goeth:
> And who weave it a Cradle of the grass that withereth away.
> This World is all a Cradle for the erred wandering Phantom.[71]

Blake's poetry has great natural power when it is read aloud; it
seems to demand the range and breath of the voice – not simply as a
text to be read, but also as a corroboration of his belief in the unity of
all the human faculties. In many respects Jerusalem is an epic drama,
therefore, with a number of voices alternating and competing with
one another. Blake's interest in 'Contraries' and in 'Mental Fight' is
expressed here and, as an aspect of that interest, the poem is carefully
organised into four separate chapters addressed in turn to the Public,
the Jews, the Deists and the Christians. Indirectly it resembles the
'order of the Seales' and the 'Synchronisme' that had been recognised
in the Book of Revelation, a work which nevertheless was considered
by biblical scholars to be filled with 'diverse shews and apparitions', a
'wild and visionary' work made up of 'Circles or Spheres'.[72]

The poem begins with the struggle of Los and his Spectre to protect
Albion; this is followed by visions both of Golgonooza and of the
fallen world while Albion, Jerusalem and Vala lament the 'sleep of
death' in which creation has been cast. There is then a narrative in
which Albion is snared within the net of Moral Law and the
Reasoning Spectre; the fallen world is thus created while the
derangement of the 'four zoas' into four warring material elements is

an emblem of the dissolution of the Divine Human. Albion sickens, despite the efforts of Los to save him, while States and Limits are created in order to fix error and thereby allow it to be one day overthrown. Then there follows Blake's own powerful religious vision in which he relates spiritual myth to chronological history, and translates Judaea and the Holy Land to England. It is the context in which he launches a fine polemic against commercialism and war, industrialism and science, all seen as aspects of the fallen 'Vegetated' universe:

> . . . a wondrous rocky World of cruel destiny
> Rocks piled on rocks reaching the stars: stretching from pole to pole.
> The Building is Natural Religion & its Altars Natural Morality
> A building of eternal death: whose proportions are eternal despair.[73]

In such passages he confronts what he believed to be the full evil of his age; sometimes it seems to be some manifestation of the Female Will, but it is essentially an attack upon the thwarted or concealed sexuality that leads to war, industrialism and perverted science. He laments the occlusion of the Imagination, and of the Divine Vision, which has led to the narrowing of human faculties; he denounces the mills and wheels of industrialism, which are for him intimately related to the cruel religion of Jehovah; he attacks the precepts of rational morality and the moral law that names 'good' and 'evil', just as he attacks phallic sexuality. What is present in work such as this is not some proto-Freudian vision of the world, however, but a general sense of loss and attenuation, of faculties dimmed, of possibilities and energies unrealised. But then in turn the poem is one of apocalypse, which ends in final celebration and triumph. He asserts the true significance of Los, the prophet, who preserves the image of the Divine Vision and labours to keep it from eternal death; he praises contraries and the divine hunt of truth; he celebrates the continual forgiveness of error that is the spirit of faith.

Yet the drama of his narrative is not confined to the polemic of denunciation or celebration, and one of the most intriguing aspects of *Jerusalem* is the variety of its forms. He employs the various powers of lyric, panegyric, epic, dialogue, song and dramatic verse, with these prosodic changes as an important aspect of the 'Contraries' he pursued. Such heterogeneity of forms and procedures seems indeed to be an authentic aspect of the English sensibility, and *Jerusalem* can be placed in the tradition exemplified by Shakespeare or by Dickens. In the same way Blake used by far the most extensive and elaborate number of graphic variations in his illuminations of the text with deliberate ink-wiping, white-line and black-line relief, reverse writing, and a series of full-page relief etchings, which are some of the most remarkable he ever produced. Images of fallen creatures, such as Hand and Vala, are seen in various states of mourning or despair, as if the heroic figures of Michelangelo had grown tired of their life and vitality so that they now remained bowed, weeping, over the ground. The simplicity and intensity of Blake's visions are here strongly in evidence; it can almost be felt in the strokes of the graver, and the fixed emblematic quality of his figures suggests that the whole of religious iconography is somehow being channelled through the artist. Four of the five known contemporary copies of the poem are printed in black ink and remained uncoloured; the last, finished near the time of his death, is very finely painted. The effects in each case are remarkable: the monochrome copies are depicted in the deepest black and the purest white, which, with the use of grey wash, allows the exploration of different kinds of darkness and shadow. Thus he was soon to write:

> Both read the Bible day & night
> But thou readst black where I read white.[74]

The coloured version of the poem is an altogether different production; it is so marvellously ornate and brightly decorated, with such intensity of colour, that it is quite a different experience from that of his other illuminated books. It is as if he had managed to transcend all his previous experiments and difficulties with colour, having gone through the various series of temperas and watercolours, and had emerged with some quite new synthesis. He has even reached beyond the medieval splendours that he had once tried to recapture, into a form of illumination which was quite new and unique to him. In that sense his illustrations complement the text, which is itself a formidably inventive achievement. He had to write it in this manner because he was expressing sentiments and thoughts so original that they could not be contained within the inherited forms of verse; no conventional prosody could have held it, and no cadence could represent it.

Jerusalem is an epic of extraordinary power and beauty, which suggests no less than a sea-change in our understanding of human history and human personality; it is clear that the message is unique because, after two hundred years, it has still to be properly understood. It establishes the truth of all that Blake had written, and painted, before.

And I heard the Name of their Emanations they are named Jerusalem

The End of The Song
of Jerusalem[75]

TWENTY-FIVE

not drawing, but inspiration

Blake was seen at a dinner given by Lady Caroline Lamb at the beginning of 1818 – 'another eccentric little artist,' one of the guests, Lady Charlotte Bury, wrote in her diary;[1] she did not mean to be dismissive, however, since she also described him as being 'full of beautiful imaginations and genius'. She went on to say that 'Mr Blake appears unlearned in all that concerns this world, and from what he said, I should fear that he was one of those whose feelings are far superior to his station in life. He looks care-worn and subdued; but his countenance radiated as he spoke of his favourite pursuit, and he appeared gratified by talking to a person who comprehended his feelings. I can easily imagine that he seldom meets with any one who enters into his views; for they are peculiar, and exalted above the common level of received opinions.' In that, of course, she was more correct than she realised. It is difficult to imagine what Blake was actually doing at Lady Caroline Lamb's party – so unknown as he was and so 'subdued' – except that he told the diarist she had been kind to him. This may well mean that she had purchased work from him but, if so, it has not survived. Perhaps it was bought out of charity, and discarded later. 'Ah!' he said to Lady Charlotte, 'there is a deal of kindness in that lady.' 'Every word he uttered,' she wrote, 'spoke the perfect simplicity of his mind and his total ignorance of all worldly matters.' One may imagine him quiet, but direct and simple when spoken to; one may even imagine him, on such an occasion, distracted by his own visions, which surrounded him night and day. The tenor of his conversation to passing acquaintances can be gauged from a later report: 'I do not believe that the world is round. I believe it is quite flat' was one of his more straightforward remarks. 'I have conversed with the Spiritual Sun,' he explained in the same conversation, 'I saw him on Primrose Hill. He said, "Do you take me for the Greek Apollo?" "No," I said, "that [and Blake pointed towards the sky] that is the Greek Apollo – he is Satan".'[2] It is easy to see why, then, he was shunned by the worldly and the worldly wise.

Yet it had been his only good fortune to find, in various periods of his life, those who would support him through his unworldly ways – in this same year, for example, he met a young artist who for the rest of Blake's life acted as a friend and as a patron. George Cumberland's son had brought John Linnell to see Blake in South Molton Street – 'they like one another much,' he reported to his father, 'and Linnell has promised to get him some work'.[3] Linnell was twenty-six years old at the time of this first and auspicious meeting; he was a Londoner, born in Hart Street, Bloomsbury, in 1792, the son of a carver, gilder and print-seller. He exhibited a talent for drawing and design at an early age, and his father employed him to copy watercolours by the more fashionable artists of the day. He studied for a while with John Varley, who will reappear later in this chapter, but in 1805 he entered the Royal Academy Schools, where Henry Fuseli was still the Keeper. In later life Linnell could imitate Fuseli to perfection, and it may well have been of his impersonations that Fuseli made the remark 'It is very good, it is better than I could have done it myself.'[4] But the most important lessons he learned there were of course artistic ones; he was given an award for his life drawing in 1810 and, in particular, he came to adore Michelangelo and Dürer. He also had a fine collection of engravings by Marcantonio, Bonasone and Dürer himself. Their artistic principles were, then, much in accordance; but there was also more to recommend him to Blake. Linnell had what his biographer called 'great individuality' and was not 'deterred by the opinions of those around him, or by modern art practice'.[5] This was clearly the man for Blake, even though Linnell was something of a puritan in doctrinal matters. He had joined the Baptist church in Keppel Street six years before he met Blake, and throughout his life he remained a severe, practical and professional man who fully earned his title as a 'Puritan democrat'. By the time he met the older artist, he had become so professional that he was able to turn his art to landscapes, portraits, miniatures and engravings with no loss of power. He was also short – at five feet five inches approximately the same height as Blake. And so these two small Londoners, both sons of tradesmen, both artists with a religious sensibility, became close friends.

Linnell kept his promise to 'get him some work' and, after their first meeting, Blake visited him and his wife in Rathbone Place. 'We soon became intimate,' Linnell wrote in his unpublished autobiography, '& I employed him to help me with an engraving of my portrait of Mr Upton a Baptist preacher which he was glad to do having scarcely enough employment to live by at the prices he could obtain.'[6] It is not at all clear how much work Blake did upon the plate itself, and it may be that he confined himself to drawing the outline of the head while Linnell worked upon its texture and finish. Nevertheless he received fifteen guineas for his contribution and, again as Linnell promised, he began to introduce him to various potential patrons such as Lord Suffolk, Lady Ford and the Duke of Argyll; Linnell was a man of business, in every respect, and he had decided to take in hand the unworldly and recalcitrant Blake. But their expeditions were not merely mercenary; they visited many art exhibitions together, including those at the British Gallery and at Somerset House; they also visited the Drury Lane theatre on more than one occasion to see the latest dramas. As Linnell's biographer said of their joint visits, 'They were both equally ardent admirers of a good play or opera, as of a good picture.'[7] Of course the days of the Gothic theatre had been in the 1790s, at the time of revolutionary enthusiasm, and those plays of sublime chaos, heroic irrationalism and sadistic energy, which seem to have affected Blake so much, had been replaced by the vivid representations of Shakespeare engineered by Kean and a steady diet of such dramas as Sheridan's *Pizarro* and Payne's *Thérèse, or the Orphan of Geneva.*

There were difficulties between them, but not necessarily because of the disparity of thirty-five years in their respective ages. 'I soon encountered Blakes peculiarities,' Linnell wrote in his autobiographical sketch, 'and [was] somewhat taken aback by the boldness of some of his assertions. I never saw anything the least like madness . . . I generally met with a sufficiently rational explanation in the most really friendly & conciliatory tone.'[8] This was the familiar experience of those who did not try to patronise or belittle Blake's beliefs and visions; they were for him the most natural thing in the world (at least the world as he saw it) and far removed from the inflictions of paranoia or hallucination. But Linnell was nevertheless not happy with his pronouncements on matters of religion; he said, some years after Blake's death, 'With all the admiration possible it must be confessed that he [Blake] said many things tending to the corruption of Christian morals, even when unprovoked by controversy, and when opposed by the superstitious, the crafty, or the proud, he outraged all common sense and rationality by the opinions he advanced, occasionally indulging in the support of the most lax interpretations of the precepts of the Scripture.'[9] It is clear that Linnell is not referring here to Blake's visions, in which he himself seemed to share some faith, but rather his general views on the subject of good and evil. Although in some of Linnell's descriptions (and in those of his young contemporaries) Blake emerges as some kind of gentle and benign patriarch, it is clear that he had lost none of the antinomianism and vigorous enthusiasm of his youth. Some suggestion of his beliefs is to be found in a series of conversations recorded by the young journalist Crabb Robinson, and it is obvious enough how Blake would have offended a rather puritanical and single-minded Baptist of Linnell's kind. 'Christ he said – he is the only God – But then he added – And so am I and so are you.'[10] Here, clearly stated, is his belief in the Divine Humanity of which the whole of creation partakes; he further added, of Jesus, that 'he was wrong in suffering himself to be crucified'. In a later conversation with Crabb Robinson, he declared, 'What are called vices in the natural world, are the highest sublimities in the spiritual world.' He seems here to be reverting to the subject of sexual religion or sexual magic, because then 'he went off on a rambling state of a Union of Sexes in Man as in God – an androgynous state in which I could not follow him'.[11] Crabb Robinson may not have been able to follow him, but it is the plainest possible indication that Blake had not lost the belief in sexuality as a form of divine energy, which he had promulgated in his first illuminated prophecies. He also reiterated his belief that wives could be held in common, and went on to say, 'he had committed many murders, that reason is the only evil or sin, and that careless gay people are better than those who think &c &c &c'.[12] It is clear then, from the tenor of such remarks, why the young John Linnell was sometimes alarmed by his older friend's utterances.

Yet he remained both companion and patron principally because he had some notion of Blake's true genius. It is not necessarily the case that he learned very much from him, however, and Linnell's biographer has suggested a quite different relationship – 'By his thorough mastery of the art of engraving,' he wrote, 'Linnell was enabled to aid Blake greatly in the improvement of his method, which had become hard and severe, albeit very correct, and left much to be desired in regard to the expression of poetic feeling.'[13] This has generally been dismissed as the bias of a fond biographer, but there are plausible grounds for suggesting that Blake's engraving style did indeed alter after his acquaintance with Linnell; the engraved portrait of Upton, upon which Blake worked, shows that the younger artist was a bold and inventive engraver who used white space and free line to great effect. In the engravings that Blake executed in the last ten years of his life he abandons some of the deliberate formality and 'Gothicism' which had marked his style at the turn of the century, and he develops a freer, more delicate hand. Even in the last commercial works he undertook, such as the portrait of Mrs Harriet Quentin (the mistress of the Prince Regent) and Mr Robert Hawker, he adopted the stipple effect that he had previously condemned in the work of Bartolozzi and Schiavonetti. He also began to rework some of his old engravings, such as the Chaucer plate and 'Mirth' – in each case he has selectively burnished the plate, so lightening it that there are patches of brightness which surround the figures and impart an air of much greater freedom. They seem almost unfinished in comparison with the original engravings, but this is the effect of Blake adopting 'flick-work', a phrase which is perhaps self-explanatory, and leaving areas of white that illuminate the inked lines of the burin. We may also date from this period three wonderful pencil sketches of a baby's face; it was probably the child of Linnell himself, and suggests how in his new sense of liberty and recognition Blake felt free once more to recognise the world.

It may be that he would have moved in the direction of delicacy and variation in any case, since his later paintings had already shown less emphasis upon firm outline; and the effect of Linnell's presence was more pervasive than the simple adoption of a style. There can be nothing more exhilarating for an older artist, who believes himself to be utterly forgotten, than to be taken up and praised by an artist of a much younger generation. It affords a sense of relief and release, and the years of neglect seem to be lifted away; it also inspires a new measure of self-confidence, and a new sense of worth, which may in turn lead to a revival of the youthful energy and ambition that prompted the artist's early work. It must be more than a coincidence, therefore, that in the months following his friendship with Linnell Blake reprinted ten copies of his illuminated prophecies, among them *Songs of Innocence and of Experience, The Marriage of Heaven and Hell,* and *The Book of Urizen;* he used a novel reddish-brown or orange ink that suggests a new sense of decorative purpose, and he deliberately created these late copies as works of art rather than simply illustrated texts. [14]

The original inspiration for this revival of his past achievements may have come from an enquiry by an admirer and collector, Dawson Turner, to which Blake responded with a list of works and prices. 'The few I have Printed & Sold,' Blake wrote, 'are sufficient to have gained me great reputation as an Artist, which was the chief thing Intended. But I have never been able to produce a Sufficient number for a general Sale by means of a regular Publisher.'[15] Certainly he intended to recoup some of his costs now, since most of the items on sale were ten times their original price – *The Book of Thel* had gone up from three shillings to two guineas, while *Songs of Innocence and of Experience* had climbed from five shillings to three guineas. But if Dawson Turner acted as the original prompter for the restoration of Blake's old skills, there were other patrons who retained their interest in him. One of the most important of them, Charles Augustus Tulk, had been introduced to him by Flaxman; he was a Swedenborgian of an unorthodox kind and an agitator for social reform. In this period he was particularly involved in the Bill for the Relief of Children in the Cotton Factories, and he saw in the Blake of 'The Chimney Sweeper' and 'The Divine Image' an artist who shared his concerns. He was also one of those patrons who seems to have weathered Blake's occasional storms of doubt and aggression – Nancy Flaxman had written to her husband about one such disagreement between the two men and reported that 'It is true he [Tulk] did not give him anything for he thought It would be wrong to do so after what pass'd between them, for as I understand B— was very violent Indeed beyond *all credence* only that he served you his *best friend* the *same trick* [some] time back as you must well remember – but he *bought a drawing* of him, I have nothing to say in this affair. It is too ticklish, only I know what has happened both to yourself & me & other people are not oblig'd to put up with B's odd humours.'[16] Here again is testimony to Blake's peculiar and combative behaviour even with those who knew him best – perhaps especially with those who knew him best. How he was 'very violent' is another matter but, given the evidence of his conduct in the past, the supposition must be that he was insistent upon being paid more than the purchaser thought the work was worth; it was the only way of asserting his value in, and to, the world. Crabb Robinson was to remember him speaking 'Of his turning pale when money had been offerd him', and this contradiction is just another aspect of his sometimes hysterical nature.[17] Nevertheless Tulk continued to patronise him in the best sense, and in 1818 he purchased a copy of *Songs of Innocence and of Experience*, which Blake, uncharacteristically, signed for him; it was this volume that Tulk lent to his friend Samuel Taylor Coleridge, who later wrote an interesting if unenlightened commentary upon it in a letter.

It was said by Tulk's daughter that 'William Blake, the Poet & Painter, with his wife, were rescued from destitution by Mr C. A. Tulk'.[18] There is an element of filial exaggeration here, however, since it was John Linnell who effectively protected Blake in the last years of his life. He was instrumental in finding Blake such new patrons as James Vine and Robert Thornton – Thornton being Linnell's doctor, who, within two years of meeting Blake, was to give him one of his most interesting commissions. But Linnell also assisted him in more direct fashion, and by August 1818 began to pay him regular sums of money – it was an arrangement that, with a few gaps, was to last for the rest of Blake's life. It was Linnell's money 'on account' that assisted Blake in the preparation and printing of *Jerusalem*, in which appears the line 'And they conversed together in Visionary forms dramatic . . .'[19] Which is precisely what Blake, sometimes in the company of Linnell, now began to do.

The events surrounding what have become known as the 'Visionary Heads' began when he was introduced by Linnell to John Varley in the autumn of 1818. Varley had been Linnell's first teacher, and was himself a very fine watercolourist of the early nineteenth-century English school; he had been one of the founders of the Society of Painters in Watercolours and, two years before he met Blake, had written a *Treatise on the Principles of Landscape Design*. He specialised in landscapes, rural or classical according to theme, and instilled in Linnell one rule – 'Go to Nature for everything'. Such an attitude was hardly likely to inspire Blake, of course, who regarded Nature as no more than the Mundane Shell or Vegetative Universe that was the vesture of Satan. But there were other reasons why Varley endeared himself to Blake. He was thirty years old when they met, a large man of some seventeen stone who according to one biographer was 'full of life and vitality, generous and unsuspicious to a fault'.[20] He possessed great energy and is supposed to have worked fourteen hours a day for most of his professional life; it could not have been all work, however, since he loved the growing and fashionable sport of boxing. He would don gloves and go a few rounds with his pupils and, when he tired of this pastime, his scholars would divide into two teams and toss him to one another across a wide table. He was imprudent in other respects, also; he was imprisoned many times for debt, and his house was burned down on more than one occasion. He also had an 'idiot son' but, as he told Linnell, 'all these troubles are necessary to me. If it were not for my troubles, I should burst with joy!'[21] He was unmistakable in the streets of London, especially because he wore a large old-fashioned tail coat whose 'sail pockets', as they were known, were stuffed with papers and almanacs. For there was one study he practised above all others, and stood on a level with his love for watercolour painting – he was a professed believer in judicial astrology and zodiacal physiognomy.

It was this aspect of his life, in particular, that came to interest Blake. Whenever Varley met anyone, he would soon be asking for their time and place of birth; with the help of the almanacs stuffed in his pocket he would quickly make out a horoscope. Claims about his astrological skills cannot at this late date be substantiated, but there is a surprising amount of evidence to suggest that he was taken very seriously indeed. He correctly prophesied the time of death of the artist William Collins; and a mid-Victorian biographer recalled how 'Scriven, the engraver, was wont to declare that certain facts of a personal nature, which *could* be only known to himself, were nevertheless confided to his ear by Varley with every particular'.[22] He worked up his own horoscope each morning and, on one particular day, realised that the malign influence of the newly discovered Uranus was to affect his life in a disruptive manner. Its effect was to reach its peak at midday, so Varley took the precaution of remaining in bed. But at the appointed time there was a cry of 'Fire!' outside; he rushed downstairs to find that his own house was in flames. 'He was so delighted,' his son recalled, that he had accurately prophesied his own disaster.[23] He told his nephew to avoid playing sport 'as you are likely to receive a Ball or a blow that might prove *fatal*' and a few months later the boy died after being struck by a cricket ball.[24] He once cast the nativity of an artist, A. W. Calcott, which was then sealed. Many years later it was opened and the prophetic sentence read out – 'Calcott will remain single until he is fifty, and then will marry and go to Italy.'[25] All three events had come to pass. So we may at least be permitted the luxury of suspending disbelief in such matters, even though Blake himself was not particularly interested in astrology alone. 'Your fortunate nativity I count the worst,' he once told Varley. 'You reckon to be born in August, and have the notice and patronage of kings, to be the best of all; whereas the lives of the Apostles and martyrs, of whom it is said the world was not worthy, would be counted by you as the worst, and their nativities those of men born to be hanged.'[26] In fact he is not questioning the accuracy of Varley's prognostications here, only the judgment applied to them; in any case, he did not object to having his own horoscope cast and then printed in an astrological magazine. The first (and, as it turned out, the last) edition of *Urania* commented that 'the extraordinary faculties and eccentricities of ideas which this gentleman possesses, are the effects of the MOON in CANCER in the twelfth house (both sign and house being mystical), in trine to HERSCHELL from the mystical sign PISCES . . . The square of MARS and MERCURY, from fixed signs, also, has a remarkable tendency to sharpen the intellects, and lay the foundation of extraordinary ideas.'[27] Astrology was becoming an unusual interest, in these early years of the nineteenth century, precisely because the influence of scientific enquiry and the effectiveness of mechanical development were eclipsing all previous forms of knowledge. But Blake wished to keep that knowledge alive and, in Varley, he found a charming if somewhat prolix and (if the adjective is permissible in this context) unpredictable companion. Linnell has described them together: 'I have a sketch of the two men as they were seen one night in my parlour near midnight, Blake sitting in the most attentive attitude listening to Varley who is holding forth vehemently with his hand raised. The two attitudes are highly characteristic of the men for Blake by the side of Varley appeared decidedly the most sane of the two.'[28]

And yet the two men embarked upon a series of extraordinary experiments or seances. They began in the autumn of 1819, when Blake walked the short distance from South Molton Street to Varley's studio in Great Titchfield Street, where, between nine in the evening and three or four in the morning, he would sketch his visions of the long dead. They would come before him – Herod, Socrates, the Empress Maud, Mahomet, Edward I, Voltaire, Owen Glendower – and Blake would whisper 'There he is!' Varley would sometimes sleep during these seances but Blake always remained wide awake, watching in the darkness. 'Sometimes,' as one of his biographers wrote, 'Blake had to wait for the Vision's appearance; sometimes it would not come at all. At others, in the midst of his portrait, he would suddenly leave off, and in his ordinary quiet tones and with the same matter-of-fact air . . . would remark "I can't go on, – it is gone! I must wait till it returns" or "It has moved. The mouth is gone" or "he frowns; he is displeased with my portrait of him".'[29] There were occasions when Varley would ask for a certain personage to be drawn, and it seems that the illustrious departed would oblige by appearing to Blake's eye. At a quarter past midnight on 14 October 1819, Richard Coeur de Lion appeared; four nights later, Blake saw 'The Man who built the Pyramids'. Some of them appeared on more than one occasion, and King Saul emerged from death twice so Blake could more easily copy his elaborate armour. The visionary heads were drawn in a small sketchbook that Varley had given to him (and which contained some of Varley's own work), and it seems Blake sometimes literally did 'converse in Visionary forms dramatic' since there are transcriptions of messages beneath some of the drawings. 'The Empress Maud,' he wrote, 'said rose water was in the vessel under the table & said there were closets which contain all the conveniences for the bed chamber . . . Can you think I can endure to be considerd as a vapour arising from your food? I will leave you if you doubt I am of no greater importance than a Butterfly . . . Hotspur Said he was indignant to have been killd by trusting the Stars [words illegible here] by such a Person as Prince Henry who was so much his inferior.'[30] Edward III volunteered the following comment upon his 'butcheries' – 'What you and I call carnage is a trifle unworthy of notice; that destroying five thousand men is doing them no real injury; that, their immortal parts being immortal, it is merely removing them from one state of existence to another; that mortality is a frail tenement, of which the sooner they get quit the better, and that he who helps them out of it is entitled to their gratitude.'[31] It is all very suggestive, and it is quite understandable why Varley should implicitly have believed in the truth of Blake's visions. Many of the heads were then drawn on the pages of a second and larger notebook, in which Varley wrote 'List of Portraits Drawn by Wm Blake from visions which appeard to him & Remaind while he completed them'; these heads are more elaborate than those in the smaller notebook, and Blake sometimes finished them with black chalk. In this second book he seems to have arranged his portraits according to Varley's laws of zodiacal physiognomy, so that he groups together the heads of several female murderers as well as of saints and historical villains such as Jack Shepherd and Colonel Blood. Varley 'counterproved' some of these drawings, thus making copies, while he persuaded John Linnell to work one or two up into paintings.

They are indeed very interesting exercises. They are not at all a joke, or an attempt to satisfy the credulous Varley, as most commentators have suggested; they have the hypnagogic quality of faces hovering or dissolving in a dream, and they seem to emerge from the paper before retreating with expressions strangely distant from ordinary human concerns. One drawing in particular is worthy of attention – 'Joseph and Mary, and the Room they were Seen in' is a remarkable study of the blessed couple. It is so different from the conventional representations that it strikes the observer with the force of revelation and the eyes, as in so many of Blake's visionary heads, have an extraordinary quality of brightness and longing. It is as if they, like Blake himself, were looking into a world that is part memory, part inspiration, part divination and part invention. 'The Room' in which Joseph and Mary were seen is drawn in foreshortened perspective and is strangely reminiscent of one of Blake's more mysterious compositions of the period, which itself had been seen in vision. A friend of Blake has written beneath it: 'I suppose it to be a Vision. Indeed I remember a conversation with Wm Blake about it.' It is thought to represent 'Elisha in the Chamber on the Wall',[32] the holy man of God who worked miracles and who brought back to life a child who 'sneezed seven times' and then 'opened his eyes'.[33] It is not a literal interpretation of any biblical scene, however, but a genuine portrait of some past age, as a tiny candle burns in a bare room. The power of Blake's visionary imagination is such that these images seem to spring unimpeded from him without preliminaries or hesitations.

He was quite candid about the faculty at his disposal. He claimed only to have acquired a gift which all might possess and, as John Linnell put it, 'Blake would occasionally explain unasked how he believed that both Varley & I could see the same visions as he saw making it evident to me that Blake claimed the possession of some powers only in a greater degree that all men possessed and which they undervalued in themselves & lost through love of sordid pursuits – pride, vanity, & the unrighteous mammon.'[34] It is quite likely that Blake was right in this belief and, as we examine the visionary heads more closely, a surprising fact emerges. In many cases the spirits which he drew are very close to the painted or engraved images that he had once seen or drawn. His portrait of Queen Eleanor is remarkably similar to the effigy he had delineated in Westminster Abbey; his picture of Ossian is very much like a sketch he once completed to illustrate Gray's 'The Bard. A Pindaric Ode'; his spiritual portrait of Gray himself seems to be taken from William Mason's frontispiece to the poems; the image of Edward I is highly reminiscent of a portrait in Goldsmith's *History of England*. The list could be extended, but the point is clear: the spirits he observed were real enough, but his visual and imaginative powers were so strong that he literally projected them in front of him. The angels which he saw were, at least in part, the angels of his childhood reading. The prophets and saints sprang from his reminiscence of biblical illustrations, just as Queen Eleanor and Thomas Gray were pictorial recreations of his own visual memory. Perhaps he did not realise the extent of what is a natural human gift; certainly, at times of crisis or despair, he truly believed that he was entering a spiritual world where he would be safe from all possible harm. He wished for eternity, and so he found it.

One of the most memorable, and most grotesque, of his visions is that entitled 'The Ghost of a Flea'. He made two sketches of it in the notebook, and then thought so well of the image that he painted it in tempera upon a panel when he returned to South Molton Street. It is indeed an extraordinary conception of malign presence, with the body of the strange flea-human flecked in green and gold as it puts its tongue towards a bowl in apparent greedy haste. It has been suggested that the vision is in part based upon the 'Flea . . . little busie creature' which Robert Hooke delineated in his *Micrographia*, and there are certain resemblances; but Blake's creation is of another order of intensity. Varley recalled him as he waited for the second visitation of this particular spirit – 'here he is – reach me my things – I shall keep my eye on him. There he comes! his eager tongue whisking out of his mouth, a cup in his hands to hold blood and covered with a scaly skin of gold and green.'[35] So he portrayed the creature, and the anecdote has the ring of authenticity with one of Blake's characteristic phrases – 'Reach me my things'. Varley added to this account in his *Treatise on Zodiacal Physiognomy*, where he disclosed that Blake started to draw the image but 'left off, and began on another part of the paper, to make a separate drawing of the mouth of the Flea, which the spirit having opened, he was prevented from proceeding with the first sketch, till he had closed it. During the time occupied in completing the drawing, the Flea told him that all fleas were inhabited by the souls of such men, as were by nature blood-thirsty to excess, and were therefore providentially confined to the size and form of insects; otherwise, were he himself for instance the size of a horse, he would depopulate a great portion of the country. He added, that if in attempting to leap from one island to another, he should fall into the sea, he could swim, and should not be lost.'[36] It is chilling enough but Blake's tempera also has all the elements of a dramatic creation, complete with a drawn curtain and a backdrop of falling stars. In certain respects, it is also reminiscent of the vision he had once had of Satan. He was climbing the staircase of his lodgings when all at once 'a light came streaming amongst my feet'; when he turned, he saw the thing at the grating. He called for his pen and ink and his wife hurried to him, thinking 'the fit of song was on me', and then at once he began to draw the phantom. It had large eyes like coals, with long teeth and claws, but Blake added, interestingly, 'It is the gothic fiend of our legends – the true devil – all else are apocryphal.'[37] It is indeed a 'gothic fiend' of a flea that he painted, and once again we may see how close Blake remained to the popular imagination. Even when 'the fit of song' was upon him, when he wrote as if in a trance, he stayed close to the theatrical and literary inheritance of his city.

But there were other kinds of vision far removed from those of the late eighteenth-century stage – 'visions,' Samuel Palmer wrote, 'of little dells, and nooks, and corners of paradise; models of the exquisite pitch of intense poetry'.[38] He was referring to another commission for which John Linnell was responsible in this period; it came from Linnell's doctor, Robert Thornton, who was engaged in the publication of Latin texts for schools. One of these was *The Pastorals of Virgil* and, since Thornton did not believe in assisting the schoolboy with direct translations, it was accompanied by Ambrose Philips's 'Imitation of Eclogue 1'. Thornton, with the encouragement of Linnell, commissioned Blake to decorate that somewhat mournful poem with a number of small illustrations.

It could hardly be said that Blake lacked stubbornness and persistence, when required; despite the failure of his relief-etching experiments for *The Grave*, he set out to create a similar effect on a smaller scale for Thornton's publication.[39] The designs were delivered, and met with as firm a refusal as Cromek had given twelve years before – 'the publishers, unused to so daring a style, were taken aback and declared "this man must do no more"; nay were for having all he had done re-cut by one of their regular hands. The very engravers received them with derision, crying out in the words of the critic, "This will never do".[40] Blake's technique, at once strangely antique and curiously 'modern', had again been disparaged by the commercial engravers of his day; his style was too expressive, too individual, for the standardised print productions of the mechanical era. There was one other, more technical, difficulty; the rest of the illustrations were to be fashioned in woodcut, so that they could be more easily placed with the text inside the printing press, and Thornton asked Blake to rework his illustrations in that medium. It was new to Blake – he had not engraved images in wood before, but he went to work in his usual professional fashion. He prepared a piece of box wood by scraping and polishing the surface, and then began to engrave the small images in groups of four; the cuts themselves are done with such finesse that he is likely to have used his ordinary engraving tools, the difference in quality largely due to the manner in which he held the graver. Nevertheless the designs were still too large to fit easily upon the page, so they were pared down to an appropriate size.

It was not the most glorious start to a career as a wood-engraver, but his work upon Philips's 'Eclogue' has generally been considered a model of its kind. In fact the small prints are of considerable beauty. He had once said of Claude Lorrain that 'there were, upon the focal lights of the foliage, small specks of pure white which made them appear to be glittering with dew which the morning sun had not yet dried up'.[41] That same effect of silvery brightness is visible in his woodcuts, where each 'flick' becomes a ray of light spreading a visionary gleam across the surface. Here are images of disconsolate shepherds, of gates and streams and setting suns, where the figures seem to be part of some close dark harmony in which light and shade are aspects of Blake's gentle lines. In some of them the fields and trees seem to be illuminated by the sun, and yet a crescent moon is to be seen through the branches; there must be some other source of brightness here, since Blake well understood the spiritual dimension of light.

In certain respects these woodcuts have the simplicity and concentration generally associated with seventeenth-century emblem books and, like his work in aphoristic poetry, his connection with the popular tradition is clear enough. Certainly he had no interest in the sentimental pastoral mezzotints that were popular with the middle classes. But his is also a much more personal vision. He remains very close to the text of Ambrose Philips's poem but, in his depiction of Colinet's complaints about mockery and neglect, it is hard not to see an element of private involvement; the theme of patronage is also raised in this Virgilian imitation and, apparently instinctively, Blake has used a landscape similar to that of Felpham. These are often bleak vistas, quite unlike Samuel Palmer's description of them, with single or lamenting figures beneath the moon. In one of them a traveller, with staff and broad-brimmed hat, walks away from a distant gleaming city; in his solitary journey there emerges once more an image of Blake himself as he pursues his own lonely course through the world.

It is not clear what Thornton thought of these works. Blake was hardly complimentary to him, when at a later date he annotated his *The Lord's Prayer, Newly Translated* and in the same volume he adverted to the poem itself – 'Caesar Virgils Only God See Eclogue i & for all this we thank Dr Thornton'.[42] But he worked for him again, and there is reason to believe that Thornton himself came to accept, if not to admire, his work. There is the story told of how on his 'meeting one day several artists at Mr Aders's table – Lawrence, James Ward, Linnell, and others, conversation fell on the Virgil. All present expressed warm admiration of Blake's art, and of these designs and woodcuts in particular. By such competent authority reassured, if also puzzled, the good Doctor began to think that there must be more in them than he and his publishers could discern.'[43]

Others were more enthusiastic about Blake's work, however, and Thomas Wainewright gave a 'puff' for *Jerusalem* in the *London Magazine* – 'my learned friend Dr Tobias Ruddicombe, M.D. is, at my earnest entreaty, casting a tremendous piece of ordnance, – *an eighty eight pounder*! which he proposeth to fire off in your next. It is an account of an ancient, newly discovered, illuminated manuscript, which has the name "Jerusalem the Emanation of the Giant Albion!!!" It contains a good deal anent one "*Los*", who, it appears, is now, and hath been from the creation, the *sole* and fourfold dominator of the celebrated city of *Golgonooza*!' It is obvious that Blake talked to Wainewright about his epic, which, according to the antiquarian fashion of the time, he has advertised here as 'ancient, newly discovered'. Wainewright himself was soon exposed as a malignant and subtle poisoner, which perhaps lends added poignancy to a remark Blake is reported to have made in this period – 'that there are probably men shut up as mad in Bedlam, who are not so: that possibly the madmen outside have shut up the sane people'.[44] It is one of those remarks of his that seem almost 'modern' in their emphasis, but it is really only a reminder of his percipience in an age when such perceptions were not common. Another comment of a more humble nature might be added here as evidence of his distance from the ordinary vocabulary of the period, but it has further interest as the only recorded conversation between Blake and John Constable. 'The amiable but eccentric Blake looking through one of Constable's sketch books, said of a beautiful drawing of an avenue of fir trees on Hampstead Heath, "Why, this is not drawing, but *inspiration*;" and Constable replied, "I never knew it before; I meant it for drawing".'[45]

'Inspiration' was, then, the key. George Cumberland records in his diary how he read out extracts from the *Courier* to Blake, concerning the progress of Queen Caroline towards England in order to claim her title. 'Mr Linel came in . . .'[46] But as they come and go, with the news of the day, Blake dreamed and saw his visions. He was painting one of his most elaborate compositions, 'Epitome of James Hervey's "Meditations among the Tombs" ', in which the author of that popular if melancholy work stands before a great and elaborate scene of angels, prophets and resurrected souls. It is a relatively small watercolour, measuring some seventeen inches by twelve, but once again Blake has created such intricate figural arrangements across the surface that it might seem to be some monumental piece of art. Each figure is named, and on the top of the painting he has written 'God out of Christ is a Consuming Fire'. It is a variant on St Paul's words to the Hebrews, 'For our God is a consuming fire',[47] and suggests Blake was once more reaffirming the spiritual vision that had been granted him in the reading of Jacob Boehme so many years before. Charles Tulk seemed to think of Blake as a fellow Swedenborgian, however, and it is clear that he had lost none of his radical spirituality; he did not, like Wordsworth and Coleridge, forswear his beliefs of the past in an attempt to accommodate himself to the present. He began writing quickly, in his old notebook, passages of a poem which he called 'The Everlasting Gospel'. That was the ancient title for the gospel of those millenarians who believed in a 'Third Age' of the Spirit when all men would become part of the divine presence.

> If thou humblest thyself thou humblest me
> Thou also dwellst in Eternity
> Thou art a Man God is no more
> Thy own humanity learn to adore.[48]

The metre is that of iambic tetrameter but the cadence is best seen as that of the popular and radical verse of the period, such as

> The time is come you plainly see
> The government opposed must be.[49]

He wrote out the poem in nine separate sections, composed at different times when no doubt 'the fit of song' came upon him; some of the lines were scribbled on scraps of paper which he then stitched into his notebook with the other verses, and he revised hastily as he carried on writing. So it is that, while working on the elaborate and spacious *Jerusalem*, he felt the need to compose these short, sharp lines of radical dissent. His is still a prophetic, as much as a poetic, voice. In 'The Everlasting Gospel' it has been chastened into restricted shape, just like his woodcuts and his temperas. There is always a fierce and ironical aspect, both to his work and to his temperament – yet it must be kept in check by tight restraining forms:

> The Vision of Christ that thou dost see
> Is my Visions Greatest Enemy
> Thine has a great hook nose like thine
> Mine has a snub nose like to mine
> Thine is the Friend of All Mankind
> Mine speaks in parables to the Blind
> Thine loves the same world that mine hates
> Thy Heaven doors are my Hell Gates.[50]

Soon enough, those gates of heaven and of hell would be opened to him.

TWENTY-SIX

the words fly about the room

In the spring of 1820 the landlord of the Blakes' lodgings in South Molton Street sold his business in order to emigrate to France, and so they were compelled to move on. Londoners rarely move far, however, and they found their new quarters in Fountain Court, a small area on the south side of the Strand; the house was owned by Henry Banes, who was married to Catherine Blake's sister, so the arrangement was easily negotiated. It was here that Blake was to spend the rest of his life.

Fountain Court acquired its name from the Fountain Tavern that had been situated there in the early eighteenth century – it had been the meeting place of a political society known as the 'Fountain Club'. But the court was now entirely residential; No. 3, to which the Blakes moved, was a plain red-brick house of three storeys with a basement area and a set of railings before it. They lived in two rooms on the first floor, overlooking Fountain Court itself with a narrow vista of the Thames between the buildings. One room was used as a 'reception room', where his temperas and watercolours were hung around the walls; the second room was workshop, bedroom, kitchen and study, where they led their ordinary lives. They placed their bed so that, when they lay upon it, they could glimpse the Thames from their window – 'like a bar of gold,' he said. There was a small fireplace in the opposite corner, a table and chairs, and, by the window, his own working table where he engraved. On one side of him, as he laboured, were placed a number of portfolios and drawings while, on the other, there was a pile of books; he had no bookcase. He kept a print of Dürer's 'Melancholia' on the wall beside him. Plain lodgings, like those of the artisan he was, but, as Samuel Palmer described it, 'there was no squalor. Himself, his wife, and his rooms, were clean and orderly; everything was in its place.'[1] Another friend reported, 'there was a strange expansion and sensation of FREEDOM in those two rooms *very* seldom felt elsewhere'.[2] Children often played in the courtyard below, and on one occasion Blake took a visitor over to the window and pointed to them. 'This is heaven,' he said as they listened to their voices.[3]

He was close to his own childhood, too, since the drawing school he had attended fifty years before was just around the corner in the Strand; it was now Ackermann's Repository of Arts, a gas-lit emporium of prints and watercolours. In many respects the Strand had changed since his childhood. The tradesmen still put signs and large advertisements outside their doors but it was rare to find such old-fashioned messages as 'Children Educated Here' or 'Foreign Spirituous Liquors Sold Here'; by the 1820s there were advertising posters for 'Fox's Vegetable Cream for Improving the Growth of Hair' or 'Portable Soups and Gravies' or 'Trotter's Oriental Dentifrice' as well as signs for the perruquier, perfumer and draper. As he walked eastward to his lodgings from Charing Cross, he would have passed Caldwell and Russell the biscuit-makers, a shell-fish warehouse and oyster room, an Irish linen-ware shop, Martin's wine cellars and various other establishments with their glass shop fronts and brightly lettered names. The street was also well known for its newspaper offices. The end of the Strand closest to Fountain Court had been widened nine years before, and a few yards from his lodgings was the Royal Menagerie of Exeter Change; here he might once more have seen a tiger, if he so wished. There is a curious irony, too, in the fact that the young Charles Dickens was at this time working in a blacking factory just off the Strand, by Hungerford Market, and there is some pleasure in the thought of these two London visionaries passing one another along the busy thoroughfare.

His habits were 'very temperate', but when he drank wine he 'liked to drink off good draughts from a tumbler'.[4] His wife was a proficient cook, but they ate simply. One day Fuseli came to visit him and found him eating a piece of cold mutton for his dinner. 'Ah by God!' Fuseli is reported to have said, 'this is the reason you can do as you like. *Now I can't do this.*'[5] Blake was sometimes noticed in the Strand. He went every day to a neighbouring tavern to buy the porter that soothed him, and on one occasion he was snubbed by the artist William Collins, who did not think it proper to greet a man carrying a pot of ale in his hand. A young girl saw him walking there, noticed his 'uncommonly bright eyes', and asked her father who he was. 'He is a strange man,' she was told. 'He thinks he sees spirits.'[6] That is why he could inform a friend that he had struggled with the devil on the stairway in Fountain Court 'to obtain the coals' from the cellar.[7] But sometimes he spoke figuratively about such matters. When a young musician visited him here he told him 'he had a palace of his own of great beauty and magnificence. On Mr Rundall's looking round the room for evidence, Blake remarked, "You don't think I am such a fool as to think this is it".'[8] So he knew very well the true meaning of what he wished to say. And there were now those who wished to hear him.

There was a group of artists who called themselves 'The Ancients', in the belief that ancient man was somehow superior to his modern counterpart. Their catchphrase was 'Poetry and Sentiment'; they wore long cloaks and went for excursions in the woods where they recited Virgil; they sat up on camp-stools to watch the sun rise; they improvised tragedies; they wandered through thunderstorms singing. Once, they entered Bromley churchyard for the purposes of meditation, and were suspected of taking part in the then lucrative practice of grave-robbing. They were all young – Samuel Palmer, Edward Calvert, George Richmond, Francis Finch, Frederick Tatham, John Giles were, at most, in their early twenties; but they discovered William Blake, and almost immediately he became their sage and mentor. It was wonderful for him to be taken up by a group of young English artists who considered his work so highly; at the end of his life, it might almost have made up for the many years of neglect that he had already suffered from his contemporaries. Here, at last, was a generation which adored him. It is not at all clear that they properly understood him, however; they were political quietists touched with religious speculation, reactionary in a rather old-fashioned spirit. John Linnell had been the man who introduced Samuel Palmer and the others to Blake, but he was somewhat dismissive of their conduct. 'I ought to remember,' he once wrote to Palmer, 'that I was not one of the monthly meeting elite when at the platonic feast of reason and flow of soul only real Greeks from Hackney and Lisson Grove were admitted.'[9] It is unlikely that any of them really understood the nature of Blake's social and sexual radicalism. He was of a different generation, an enthusiast who had lived through the period of the French Revolution and endless wars: he was harder and tougher than they were but, most importantly, he was a visionary of genius. They were a religious generation, but their piety was a form of escape; it was not at all what Blake had once envisaged. They were also, with the sole exception of Samuel Palmer, rather minor artists. And yet they possessed qualities that endeared them to him.

Samuel Palmer was a London boy of Houndsditch and Blooms-bury, who had begun to paint and draw as a child. He had never forgotten some lines his nurse once recited to him –

> Fond man! the vision of a moment made!
> Dream of a dream! and shadow of a shade!

From an early age, perhaps as a result, he evinced what he called 'a passionate love – the expression is not too strong – for the traditions and monuments of the church'.[10] He was small, nervous and sensitive. Here, then, was an artist whom Blake could understand. Palmer met him in the autumn of 1824, after the move to Fountain Court, where Blake 'fixed his grey eyes' upon him;[11] he was only nineteen years old but he was himself already something of a mystic, and his acquaintance with Blake strengthened his interest both in medievalism and in sacred art. 'Genius,' he wrote the year after he had met him, 'is the unreserved devotion of the whole soul to the divine.'[12] The other members of 'The Ancients' shared his piety. Edward Calvert, who was at the Royal Academy Schools, had been sitting in his grandmother's garden when he 'presently felt posses- sed of a wonderful sense of blessedness – in his own words – "as of a loving spirit taking up his abode with him, and seating himself beside his own soul" '.[13] This is an experience that Blake would certainly have understood. Another member of the group, the young painter John Giles, used to call him 'divine Blake', who 'had seen God, sir, and had talked with angels'.[14] George Richmond, only fifteen when he met him, used to say that before 'Blake began a picture he used to fall on his knees and pray that it might be successful'.[15] When he walked home with him one night he said that it was 'as if he were walking with the Prophet Isaiah';[16] during that walk, Richmond remembered, Blake spoke of his own youth and of his visions. On another occasion Richmond complained of his distress in not being able properly to work, and Blake turned to his wife: 'It is just so with us, is it not, for weeks together, when the visions forsake us? What do we do then, Kate?' And Catherine replied, 'We kneel down and pray, Mr Blake.'[17] His visions were not necessarily of an exotic kind, however, and he once told Richmond, 'I can look at a knot of wood till I am frightened at it.'[18]

Amongst themselves they called him 'dear old William Blake' or, more reverentially, 'Michael Angelo Blake'; but when they addressed him they called him 'Mr Blake'. It is clear that in the presence of the young he felt unconstrained, at liberty to speak about his life and art in an atmosphere in which he knew he would not be criticised or judged; it was an exhilarating experience, as it had been with Linnell, to feel that the opinions of the young might be a true anticipation of the judgment of posterity. But he was never grand or difficult. The son of one of them said, in a later memoir, that Blake was always 'approachable, kind and natural . . . amenable to all the little interruptions of domestic life'.[19] Edward Calvert, at the end of his life, declared, 'I want to take a little pilgrimage to Fountain Court that I may once more gaze upon that divine window where the blessed man did his work';[20] and Samuel Palmer has left several descriptions of days in what they all called 'The House of the Interpreter' – the bell- handle of which he used to kiss before he pulled it. 'He was fond of the works of St Theresa,' he said in a letter to one of Blake's first biographers, 'and often quoted them with other writers on the interior life. Among his eccentricities will, no doubt, be numbered his preference for ecclesiastical governments . . . In politics a Platonist, he put no trust in demagogues . . . He loved to speak of the years spent by Michael Angelo, without earthly reward, and solely for the love of God, in the building of St Peter's, and of the wondrous architects of our cathedrals . . . He had great powers of argument, and on general subjects was a very patient and good-tempered disputant; but materialism was his abhorrence; and if some unhappy man called in question the world of spirits, he would answer him "according to his folly" by putting forth his own views in their most extravagant and startling aspect.'[21] In Palmer's memories of Blake we can even hear him talking again. On their first meeting Blake asked him, 'Do you work with fear and trembling?' On another's work he would say, 'As fine as possible! It is not permitted to man to do better . . . Blake told me that we were one century behind the civilisation which would enable us to appreciate Fuseli's Oedipus . . . I remember, young as I was, presuming to demur to an assertion of Mr Blake's that our old cathedrals were not built to rule and compass; but now I see that, like many of his art statements, although literally a stretch or violation of the truth it contained or suggested a greater truth.'[22] Blake told 'The Ancients' stories of his past life – stories of Tom Paine, of Basire, of Flaxman and of Fuseli – and sometimes he even drew little sketches of his contemporaries to give the young men a better impression of them. He even gave a copy of his old Exhibition Catalogue to one, as another memorial of his earlier years. One of those who listened to him, Frederick Tatham, wrote down the most accurate description of Blake's childhood and apprenticeship, which, we can be sure, came from Blake and his wife.

His conversation in the last years of his life was also recorded by Crabb Robinson, who seems to have considered him an interesting 'case'. Robinson had a particular affection for German literature, and had become involved with those among the English 'Romantic' poets who, largely through the agency of Coleridge, had become interested in German idealism. Blake, reputedly 'mad' and possessing 'genius', was a tempting study. They had first met at a dinner party given by a German couple, the Aderses, to whom Linnell had introduced him. Charles Aders was a banker and merchant, but his collection of fifteenth-and sixteenth-century Northern art was probably the finest in the country at that time. It was the kind of painting by which Blake always wished to be surrounded and, in the Aderses' residence in Euston Square, in the work of van Eyck, Memling, Schongauer, Dürer and others, covering the entire wall surface of the house, he found the ancestors of his own style. When he brought around a copy of his Chaucer engraving, the Aderses remarked upon its affinity with the works in their collection. 'There is no wonder in the resemblance,' he told them, 'as in my youth I was always studying that class of painting.'[23] But he was not simply known to the Aderses as a painter, and Linnell remembered how 'The Tyger' was recited to the assembled company in Euston Square. It would seem, then, that Blake had at last found that 'Fit Audience . . . tho' few' to which he had always aspired.

It was in this company that Crabb Robinson met him, and he was so intrigued by his conversation that he wrote it down immediately afterwards. 'He is now old,' he wrote, 'pale with a Socratic countenance and an expression of great sweetness but bordering on weakness – except when his features are animated by expression.' The main theme of his description then emerges: 'And when he said my visions it was in the ordinary unemphatic tone in which we speak of trivial matters that every one understands & cares nothing about – In the same tone he said – repeatedly "the Spirit told me".' There ensued a dialogue between them:

CRABB ROBINSON: You used the same word as Socrates used. What resemblance do you suppose is there between your Spirit and the Spirit of Socrates?

BLAKE: The same as between our countenances. I was Socrates . . . a sort of brother. I must have had conversations with him. So I had with Jesus Christ. I have an obscure recollection of having been with both of them.[24]

Then, a little later in the conversation, he considered his own life.

BLAKE: I should be sorry if I had any earthly fame for whatever natural glory a man has is so much detracted from his spiritual glory. I wish to do nothing for profit. I wish to live for art. I want nothing whatever. I am quite happy.[25]

They talked on about art and religion, on the mistakes of Jesus Christ and the follies of Plato, until they were called to dinner. It is easy to understand the fascination he could exert upon those who chose to listen to him, and Crabb Robinson subsequently visited him several times in Fountain Court to make further notes; from the first, however, he believed, 'I fear I shall not make any progress in ascertaining his opinions and feelings – that their being really no system or connection in his mind.'[26] But there was at least one 'connection' that Blake made throughout his life. During a visit he spoke of Milton appearing to him on many occasions, and added, 'Of the faculty of Vision he spoke as One he had had from early infancy – He thinks all men partake of it – but it is lost by not being cultivated.'[27] In a later conversation he informed Robinson that Voltaire had appeared to him and told him, 'I [Voltaire] blasphemed the Son of Man and it shall be forgiven me. But they (the enemies of Voltaire) blasphemed the Holy Ghost in me and it shall not be forgiven them.'[28] It is an arresting perception, and one of many that he made in the company of the journalist. He also said that he wrote only when commanded to do so by his angels, 'and the moment I have written I see the words fly about the room in all directions'.[29] Yet after five or six visits Crabb Robinson began to find him tiresome and repetitive; in a letter to Dorothy Wordsworth he calls him 'poor Blake' yet at the same time recommends his 'genuine dignity & independence' as well as 'native delicacy in words'. What was it, then, that had caused his neglect? Crabb Robinson had no doubt that he suffered an obscurity 'to which the constant hallucinations in which he lives have doomed him'.[30]

They had also doomed him to poverty. John Linnell assisted him in various ways, principally by buying single copies of his old illuminated books and by giving him money 'on account'. He continued to introduce him to patrons such as James Vine, a Russian merchant who lived in Grenville Street and who bought two of his illuminated books. He and Linnell visited exhibitions together; he dined with the Linnells regularly on Sunday nights, and they still visited the theatre. Linnell made a note of one such performance – 'Mr Varley, Mr Blake & myself were much entertained Thursday Evening last by witnessing a representation of Oedipus at the West London Theatre as it much exceeded our expectations as to the effect of the Play & the performance of the Actors. I see it sneered at in one of the public papers but you know what petty motives govern all . . . Public criticism.'[31] The horrors of 'Public criticism' were not, of course, lost upon Blake.

But John Linnell also commissioned new works. He asked Blake to engrave one or two plates after his own design and, soon after the move to Fountain Court, he requested him to complete another version of the Job watercolours that he had finished for Thomas Butts fifteen years before. The idea may have been prompted by Butts himself, since the coolness between him and Blake seems to have been dispelled in these last years. He must have been aware of his poverty, too, and he returned his set of watercolours so that the artist might copy them for the new commission – except that it was John Linnell himself who did the copying. He drew the pencil outlines from the original, and then Blake finished them before working upon the colouring. This new set is more freely modelled, which may be the result of Linnell's own initial intervention, but in addition Blake has used much more ornate and vivid colour than in the originals. The Butts set had been marked by a certain delicacy and almost Georgian restraint but now, employing an entirely different sense of the luminous surface, he deploys bright pastel shades and rich tones.

Linnell's patronage, however, was not yet enough to save him from poverty. Within a short time of their move to Fountain Court, Blake felt compelled to sell his collection of old prints to the firm of Colnaghi's. He had acquired some of them in his childhood – his father had bought them for him – and they had remained with him all his life as a model and inspiration. But they had to be sold so that the

Blakes might live; he retained only the Dürer, which was placed on the wall above his engraving table. Knowledge of the sale came as a shock to Linnell, who had not realised the extent of Blake's poverty, and he approached members of the Royal Academy to solicit a donation. They granted him twenty-five pounds on the grounds that 'Mr William Blake an able Designer & Engraver [is] laboring under great distress'; Linnell himself, out of delicacy for Blake's feelings, collected the money and brought it to him. A month later the two artists visited the fashionable and wealthy portrait painter Thomas Lawrence, and in a memoir William Etty declared, 'Mr Blake, came to a friend's of mine, who lives near Charing Cross, one morning, with tears of joy and gratitude in his eyes – on being asked the cause, he told my friend that Sir Thomas had sent him a 100£ bill which had relieved his distresses, and made him and his wife's heart leap for joy.'[32]

Other assistance was also at hand, and it was soon after this period that Linnell commissioned him to work on a series of engravings of the Job watercolours. It was 'in hopes of obtaining a profit sufficient to supply his future wants,' Linnell wrote, 'that the publication of Job was begun at my suggestion and expense'.[33] A formal agreement was drawn up in the spring of 1823, by which Blake was to receive one hundred pounds in advance for twenty engravings. Five pounds for each engraving was not an extravagant sum but, as Linnell also remembered, his 'means were not adequate to pay Mr Blake according to his merit, or such a work should have placed him in moderate independence'.[34] Blake began by making reduced pencil drawings from the watercolour series in a sketchbook, which he then bound up with two proof sheets of Hayley's Ballads. It is a small book but he numbered its pages in the right-hand corner, as was his methodical habit; there are twenty-seven drawings altogether, but each with different levels of finish. Some have been executed quickly, but others have been worked up with great care and with many corrections -- sometimes Blake pressing down with the graphite so hard that the effects can be seen on the other side of the page. He often starts a sketch gently and tentatively, works it over again hesitantly, and then suddenly finds the composition he wants in a sudden and almost ferocious burst of invention. On other occasions he seems to find the structure of the composition immediately and works it out with the hard pressure of the pencil, finishing off the sketch with more leisurely strokes and jagged lines. It is not at all like the work of a man trained as a reproductive engraver, so free and elastic his late drawing style has become.

He did not lay the drawings directly on the plates for transposition, but instead used them as rough models while he composed his designs upon the copper with chalk or pencil. That is how he had created his illuminated books, after all, with the direct and unmediated invention of the brush. He made no preliminary etching of lines, either, so that the effect is almost like that of drawing or painting rather than simple engraving work. There are borders around each composition, which allow his images to be framed by sacred texts: these notes and phrases were a late addition, drawn straight on to the copper with very few and sketchy preliminary designs, but they represent once again his passion for uniting word and image in all his works of art. It is as if he could not see words without images, and images without words; in that sense he returns to a much earlier sense of language *as* imagery, and can once again partake of the sacredness of representation. That is why he seems so close to medieval illuminated manuscripts, and on the eleventh engraving of the Job series he has added, 'Oh that my words were printed in a Book that were graven with an iron pen and lead in the rock for ever'. Here are globes, and tears, and mandalas, as well as elongated figures that might have come out of a psalter. Of course he has also interpreted the biblical narrative in order to convey his own sense of Job's sufferings; he has, for example, emphasised the visionary revelations vouchsafed to the patriarch in the midst of his trials. The fate of Job has already been seen to be one of the great themes of his life; there can be little doubt that he felt a sense of prophetic identification with him, and it is this private spiritual significance which lends this series of engravings its peculiar and fierce intensity. It can be seen to full effect in one composition entitled 'The Just Upright Man is Laughed to Scorn', where the pressure of self-identification is an intrinsic part of its power. The narrative of Job's sufferings has always been difficult to interpret, open to any number of plausible analyses, but Blake is the first artist to have lent it a fully consistent meaning; he has rejected the legalistic and deterministic attitudes to faith and suffering that were an aspect of the original story, and has instead concentrated upon eliciting its interior or spiritual meaning.

He had sought Linnell's advice on certain technical aspects of the engraving, and there is even evidence to suggest that he would leave half-completed plates at his friend's house for any comment or suggestion. Blake said, at a later date, 'If you should put on your considering Cap, just as you did last time we met, I have no doubt that the Plates would be all the better for it.'[35] But on this occasion he hardly needed an instructor, since the Job series marks the fine, high point of his work as an intaglio engraver. He deployed all the techniques he had learned over the last fifty years, with variable lights and textures playing over the surface of the engraving so that they seem to have a dynamic life of their own. He once said of the work of one historical painter, 'Ah! that is what I have been trying to do all my life – to paint round – and never could', but in fact the modelling within the Job series is at once so firm and so exquisite that there is a definite sense of volumetric space as well as linearity.[36] Neither does he despise the use of stipple, of 'flick' or 'dot', but on each occasion they are used only to emphasise the larger composition of light and hardness, softness and shade. Ruskin said of this work in his handbook *The Elements of Drawing*, '[it] is of the highest rank in certain characters of imagination and expression; in the mode of obtaining certain effects of light it will also be a very useful example to you. In expressing conditions of glaring and flickering light, Blake is greater than Rembrandt.'[37] It is the effect of flame and of twilight, of fire and dawn, in these engravings that adds to the mystery of Job's visionary experiences; it represents what Blake had said in *Jerusalem* of 'darkness immingled with light on my furrowd field'.[38]

His words convey something of the radiant brightness within these engravings, which does not necessarily appear in reproductions, an extraordinary silver light that comes from a very fine distribution of highlights and burnishing as well as the delicacy of the engraved lines. These effects are part of a formal and technical control which derives from a lifetime of practice, using a highly stylised and ritualised series of images that are aspects of a highly stylised and ritualised technique; the starkness and restraint of these powerfully expressive human forms comes from the exigencies of the medium itself. In that sense it is one of the most characteristically Blakean of Blake's major works. The great circular movements within the engravings lend them a feeling of powerful weight and majesty, while the changes of light and texture suggest for a moment that the composition moves and breathes before you. What is most striking, however, is the dramatic intensity conveyed by the pure outlines. These might be the engravings of some lost world commemorated by Bryant or by Stukeley where, within a landscape of stone and distant mountains, ancient humans of heroic stature and fine proportion address each other with hieratic gestures. They might, as Blake always claimed, have been copied from some lost or unknown original. But having described the general vision it is necessary to look at the particulars – to look, for example, at the woman bent over in mourning within 'Let the Day perish wherein I was Born'. The delicate lines of her hair, the texture of her dress, are established upon the absolute certainty of the cross-hatching, the flick of the burin, the burnishing and moulding of form; yet the vigorous certainty of this line was possible only with Blake working directly upon the copper as if he were engaged in a pencil drawing. And, in the penultimate engraving of the series, he celebrates Job the artist showing his daughters the scenes of his life in visionary forms dramatic.

Of course there were immediately those contemporaries who considered the work old-fashioned, too 'hard' or too 'dry', and altogether too close to engravings in the Gothic mode. But that was precisely the effect he wished to create. It is significant that he decorated the covers of the Job sketchbook with his monogram 'WB' arranged in the same shape as Dürer's own 'AD'; it was a means of asserting some kind of identity with the German master, and it is likely that his knowledge of that work had been materially increased by the collection of Northern art which the Aderses had assembled in Euston Square. It was for him a gesture of historical retrieval as well as celebration, a way of reaffirming the spiritual art of the past as well as of the present in that moment of Eternal Imagination where all true art coexists.

The series was printed at Lahees – some one hundred and fifty sets, at a price of three guineas, but little more than thirty copies were sold during his lifetime. They were stored in two great piles in Linnell's house in Cirencester Place, from which they were despatched to country purchasers by coach. Some were returned, however, and there were complaints about the quality of the binding as well as doubts about the work itself. No profits were ever derived from the venture, and the actual sales only just covered the expenses; but Linnell kept the plates and the stock, in hope of better days. In the meantime he could not let Blake starve, and he continued to pay him a weekly allowance of between two and three pounds. 'I do not know how I shall ever repay you,' Linnell recalled his saying. 'I do not want you to repay me,' Linnell replied. 'I am only too glad to be able to serve you. What I would like, however, if you do anything for me, is that you should make some designs for Dante's Inferno, Purgatorio and Paradiso.'[39] So after Job he began another extended project; but he showed his gratitude in a different way by presenting Linnell with the only manuscript copy of the long poem *Vala*, which he had kept by him for so many years without thought of printing or publication.

Blake was not unoccupied on other work during these years at Fountain Court. He had completed three copies of the watercolours from his *Paradise Lost* set for Linnell, no doubt as recompense for money received, and a study of these late watercolours shows how much more fluent his style had now become. He seems to have liberated himself from the formal restraints of his own aesthetic, to which he returned only when he was engaged in the reconstruction or restoration of an ancient style. His late temperas are also much lighter and more lucid than their predecessors at the beginning of the century; he used a much thinner paint laid upon a white ground so that the characteristic brightness and radiance of his late engravings are carried into his art. Many of them are also laid upon wood – there is one entitled 'Winter' painted upon pine – and once more it seems that he was strongly affected by the kind of painting he saw at the house of the Aderses. But the art is all his own. In works such as 'The Body of Abel Found by Adam and Eve', 'Satan Smiting Job with Sore Boils', and the provisionally entitled 'The Sea of Time and Space', there is an extraordinary broadening of his palette into a range of brilliant pastel blues and pinks and yellows. The history of his painting might in some sense be seen as the history of his exploration of colour, until he reaches this point where he creates visionary hues; these are colours which seem to be not of this earth, but of that imaginative landscape he carried with him everywhere.

'The Body of Abel Found by Adam and Eve', in particular, is one of his most powerful late works. The expression of horror and despair upon the face of Cain is illuminated by the smoke and flame that seem to trail from him and pass across the red globe of the sun; his figure takes the form of an inverted triangle in opposition to the figures of Adam and Eve who take up hieratic postures of mourning. The freedom and delicacy of colouring are complemented also by the intensely dramatic nature of the scene. A moment of shame has been given eternal shape in a piece of visionary drama, and once again we may glimpse an aspect of Blake's relationship with the London theatre in the entry on 'astonishment' in a contemporary actors' handbook: '. . . the whole body is actuated: it is thrown back, with one leg set before the other, both hands elevated, the eyes larger than usual, the brows drawn up, and the mouth not quite shut.'[40] This is the stance which Blake's subjects also adopt, and in his static monumental figures we may see a passing resemblance to an actress such as Sarah Siddons, who, as Euphrasia in *The Grecian Daughter*, remained perfectly still in the same attitude for five minutes as the applause mounted around her. Indeed the theatrical emphasis upon statuesque pose, idealised passion, rhythmical speech and elaborate spectacle suggests the connection with Blake's own urban art. It is not the only source, however, and perhaps the best commentary upon his use of hieratic shapes and radiant unearthly colours comes from his own words at this time: 'Nature has no Outline: but Imagination has. Nature has no Tune: But Imagination has! Nature has no Supernatural & dissolves: Imagination is Eternity.'[41]

The story of Cain, and its attendant themes of guilt and forgiveness, was one that much exercised Blake in this period. He produced two pages of illuminated printing, or relief etching, which might almost be a commentary upon the painting itself; it is a short verse drama, entitled 'The Ghost of Abel. A Revelation in the Visions of Jehovah Seen by William Blake', and he produced a very limited number of copies in a brilliant glossy black. The words quoted in the last paragraph are part of its epigraph. He dedicated it to Lord Byron, whose own verse drama *Cain, A Mystery* was under threat of prosecution for immorality and blasphemy; in Byron's drama the outcast Cain becomes a type of the Romantic anti-hero who destroys the limits that God has placed upon him and spurns the conventional inheritance of sin. There is no doubt that Blake sympathised a great deal with Byron's reading of the biblical story, and in his own short piece he repeatedly denies the reality of sin and vengeance while emphasising the necessity for forgiveness. But there was an interior sadness in the adumbration of such a theme, which is revealed in an anecdote by Samuel Palmer -- how, when Blake recited the story of the Prodigal Son, he broke down and wept. He 'began to repeat a part of it; but at the words "When he was yet a great way off, his father saw him", could go no further; his voice faltered, and he was in tears'.[42] It is worth noticing here his fascination for a German fable, *Sintram and His Companions*, which, he told Crabb Robinson, was 'better than my things!'[43] It was a Gothic fable of the early nineteenth century, written by Friedrich de la Motte Fouqué and using Dürer's 'The Knight and Death' as its frontispiece. It concerns the adventures of a fierce and wilful young man who has strange dreams or presentiments, and who is accompanied by visionary companions through a frozen wilderness; he is characterised by 'the fearful wildness of his spirit' and by 'dark melancholy' since he lives in the shadow of his father's evil, but, eventually, son and father are reconciled. Was there now some subdued sense of guilt, in these last years, at the way his life had gone? He had created himself, beyond the bounds of his family, but he had found in recompense nothing but a life of neglect and isolation. Only now, with young men who had become almost surrogate sons, had he found any kind of recognition. Had he, in a sense, become a father at last and thus could perhaps understand his own? But this is speculation. It is clear only that, in Blake's vision, God's forgiveness of Cain could turn the 'Marks of weakness, marks of woe' into the signs of redemption and eternal life.

He made one other exercise in illuminated printing at this time, and there is some reason to believe that he did so almost as an act of territorial possession. At the bottom of 'The Ghost of Abel' he had inscribed '1822 W Blakes Original Stereotype was 1788' – and this in contradiction of an account in the Edinburgh Philosophical Journal of a 'New Style of Engraving on Copper in Alto Relievo, invented by W. Lizars'. George Cumberland had alerted him, through his son, to the presence of this claim to 'Blakes Method';[44] he could not let it pass, he was too stubborn and self-assertive for that. And so he produced another piece of illuminated printing. It was on one sheet only and was clearly designed to be distributed to friends; he entitled it 'On Homer's Poetry', with a second section 'On Virgil', and in the space of a few sentences restated the essentials of his visionary aesthetic. 'Goodness or Badness has nothing to do with Character. an Apple tree a Pear tree a Horse a Lion, are Characters but a Good Apple tree or a Bad, is an Apple tree still: a Horse is not more a Lion for being a Bad Horse. that is its Character; its Goodness or Badness is another consideration. It is the same with the Moral of a whole Poem . . .' Then, at the end of this short document, he restates one of his most essential principles: 'Grecian is Mathematic Form Gothic is Living Form'.[45]

He also mentions the Laocoön, which was one of the works of classical sculpture he had engraved for Rees's Cyclopaedia; now, in illustration of all these theories, he created his own visionary image of the famous group of sculpted figures. It is an extraordinary line engraving, in which he has remodelled the bodies and attitudes to express his own artistic intent, and he seems to have restored the 'original' that the Greek sculptor had once used. As Blake put it at the bottom of the engraving, it had been 'copied from the Cherubim of Solomons Temple by three Rhodians'; now he wished to revive the lost art of remote history and, in the process, infuse the present with the eternal significance of the past. That is why he surrounded the engraved image with phrases and sentences which express the heart of his vision, among them one that states, 'The Eternal Body of Man is The IMAGINATION . . . Jesus & his Apostles & Disciples were all Artists . . . Art degraded Imagination Denied War Governed the Nations'.[46] In particular he denies the importance of money in any great activity, which suggests he had now come to understand the meaning of his own poverty. But there was another, and more curious, note upon the Laocoön engraving: 'Is not every Vice possible to Man described in the Bible openly All is not Sin that Satan calls so . . . Art can never exist without Naked Beauty displayed'.[47] In the same period he did five rough sketches to illustrate the 'Ethiopian Book of Enoch', which had been published in an English translation in 1821. It narrates the history of how the 'Sons of God' became enamoured of the 'Daughters of Men' and begot monsters upon them, and in Blake's sketches he has emphasised the huge phalli of the Sons at the same time as he has lent added significance to the orgiastic potential of the original text. It is clear that he had lost none of his sexual radicalism, and that he remained preoccupied with a kind of mystic sexuality which saw in the penis and the vagina some emblem of eternal life. It had remained one of the major inspirations for much of his work. In this context it is interesting that Linnell is supposed to have admired all of his conversation, except those occasions when he spoke of sexual matters; in many ways Blake remained very much a product of the mid-eighteenth century, and he cannot be said to have adopted any of the moral attitudes of the new century, which would soon be labelled 'Victorian'.

Even in appearance he seemed now of a different era, with his black worsted stockings and his thick shoes which tied, his black knee breeches and buckles, his broad-brimmed hat. He looked, Samuel Palmer wrote, 'something like an old-fashioned tradesman', from which stock he had of course come.[48] There have been suggestions that there were times when he became impatient or bored with the company of The Ancients – Palmer's son wrote that 'The old couple had therefore to listen to the drone of talk, dogmatic assertion and

contradiction and complaints at all times in the midst of their work
. . . [George Richmond] became a severe trial to Blake and his wife
when the old man's course was nearly run. Shrewd and sardonic
Linnell was greatly amused at the great discoveries in art which the
boy poured forth.'[49] But there is no evidence that Blake was ever
really annoyed with them – with these young men he could relive his
own impetuous past, and in their arguments relish the faint echo of
his own. He had generally lost the anger and sporadic violence so
characteristic of his youth and middle age, so truly did he now
understand his destiny, but there were still moments when his old fire
returned. 'It is false!' The Ancients remember him crying out on more
than one occasion, and when he was once shown the first number of
the *Mechanic's Magazine* he replied, 'Ah, sir, these things we artists
HATE!'[50] There was actually no reason for him to be alarmed by the
journal at all, since it contained rather useful information on 'How to
Boil Potatoes Nicely without Waste' as well as 'An Address to a
Blacksmith on His Birthday'.[51] There were also articles that mention
the invention of roller skates, of an alarm clock for workmen which
lights a candle, and a patent for waterproof cloth.

Blake participated in a little experiment of another kind when he
submitted to having a life mask made of his head by the manager of a
lamp shop close by him in the Strand. Mr Deville was an amateur
phrenologist and, knowing Blake's reputation, wished to make a cast
of his head as an emblem of the 'imaginative faculty'. Blake looks
rather grim as a result but, since this was Deville's first attempt, he
may have been understandably alarmed at the process. His head was
covered with wet plaster which then hardened, while two straws were
stuck into his nostrils so he could breathe; since the hardening plaster
became uncomfortably hot, it is really no surprise that Blake's mouth
is turned down in an expression of apparent pain. When the plaster
was removed, it also 'pulled out a quantity of his hair';[52] yet at least
now we have some representation of him as he seemed upon the
earth, with his broad forehead and large eyes, what he called his 'snub'
nose and wide mouth, the small ears slightly low and what George
Richmond termed his 'stubborn English chin',[53] the whole head
seeming somehow as powerful and expressive as the imagination that
once possessed it.

His health now was beginning to weaken, and there were periods in
1823 and 1824 – he was approaching his seventieth year – when his
handwriting seems badly to deteriorate. Some contemporaries were

not even sure that he was still alive, and Charles Lamb wrote to a friend in 1824, 'Blake is a real name, I assure you, and a most extraordinary man, if he be still living.'[54] In fact some of his most important art was yet to come, and when Samuel Palmer called on him in the autumn of that same year he found him hard at work 'lame in bed, of a scalded foot (or leg)'.[55] He could not continue with the Job engravings in such a situation but, propped up with pillows, he was able to work upon pencil sketches and designs for the Dante series that Linnell had just commissioned. Linnell was in one way simply following the taste of the age, which took a decidedly Italianate turn in the second decade of the new century with such works as Leigh Hunt's *Story of Rimini*, Byron's *The Prophecy of Dante* and Keats's *Isabella*. Of course many artists had illustrated Dante before, notably Botticelli and Michelangelo (whose drawings in his edition of Dante were lost at sea), while both Reynolds and Fuseli had chosen for special illustration the plight of Count Ugolino, who was starved to death with his four sons in the 'Torre della Fame'. This was a favourite English theme, indebted to a native taste for the Gothic, and Blake himself illustrated it on more than one occasion. But he seems to have come to Dante rather late in life; he had started learning Italian in 1802, with Hayley, specifically to read the poet in the original, and at one point he even began making small corrections to Boyd's translation of the *Inferno*. He was also studying Cennino Cennini's *Trattato della Pittura*, which Linnell had given to him – he 'soon made it out', according to Linnell himself, thus testifying again to his ready grasp of foreign languages.[56] Now, when the commission from Linnell came, he started reading Dante in earnest with the help of Cary's famous translation. Linnell had given him a folio volume of fine Dutch paper, measuring some twenty-five inches by fourteen, on which he could finish his watercolours. He made some 102 compositions altogether, in various stages of preparation – some are complete watercolours, some are half-finished, some have been prepared only with grey wash, while others remain simple sketches. It was clear that he was also planning some kind of 'Dante Gallery' with a series of engravings, but only seven (in various stages of workmanship) were actually prepared.

The preliminary drawings display once again his extraordinarily fluent and inventive draughtsmanship at the end of his life; many of them are very intricate compositions, combining direct clean strokes of the graphite with more nervous lines and shading. There are times, however, when he is so absolutely sure of his figures that he pencils in the outlines darkly and heavily; the entire shape of the composition often emerges immediately, too, with his characteristically firm, long and curving lines lending it breadth and life. Indeed this combination of long waving strokes with occasional short dark markings resembles the movement of his verse, with its combination of long free lines with epigrammatic brevity. It also resembles the light and shade that he brought to his engravings. Some of the pencil sketches are in the shape of diagrams, which are accompanied by his own pencil comments in the margin; by his drawing of the circles of Hell, for example. he has written, 'In Equivocal Worlds Up and Down are Equivocal'. Identifications are written on the bottom in the plainest style – 'HELL Canto 8' – while he scribbles messages to himself on the back about the order of the works. These are almost incomprehensible, however – 'No 29 next at page 82. This will be 35' – and it is important to realise only that he tended to use the same palette and the same range of mood or theme within any given sequence.

The compositions are recognisably Blakean, with their use of strong vertical symmetries and formal parallels as well as his characteristic concern with the shape of the human figure – it was indeed the 'Human Form Divine' representing all the forces and balances of eternity. But in the Dante watercolours and engravings there is a new ease and fluency; it is as if, while still working with the firm linearity of the Job engravings, he was relieved to take advantage of a looser mode of composition. Although he stays faithful to Dante's text, the possibilities of free association and inventive fantasy were clearly greater than those available in his scriptural model.

Some of the drawings have only been prepared with wash and outline, but this preliminary work creates some wonderful effects. Within 'Dante and Virgil on the Edge of the Stygian Pool', from the seventh canto of the *Inferno*, he has created an expanse of grey wash upon which he has pencilled 'Stygian Lake'; it is worthy of Whistler at his most crepuscular. But the glory of the Dante illustrations lies in the freshness and radiance of their colour. His training as an engraver had taught him how to convey brightness, but in the cold and light tonality of these works he has achieved an extraordinary intensity; they are almost translucent, with the variation of pinks and yellows and blues like colours first seen at dawn. But they can also be very fierce and, in 'The Centaurs and the River of Blood' from the twelfth canto of the *Inferno*, there is an imposing sweep of purple between green to suggest the bloody river running between its banks. It seems likely that he added various layers of watercolour, allowing one to dry before laying on another, and this in turn lends a further element of intensity to the surface of the works. It is often said that he was not a 'pure' artist, but these late watercolours suggest that he was one of the greatest colourists of his age.

His is a visionary landscape in which he has tried to reproduce the effect of Dante's poetry by creating a wonderful stillness conveying majesty. It is a landscape of rocks constructed out of petrified human forms, of vast underground lakes, of burning seas, of large sculpted mountains, of occluded suns, of endless stone terraces and staircases, but all of them touched by the light and colour from some spiritual source of brightness. In his depiction of monumental figures bowed in postures of woe, and in his illustrations of Dante and Virgil wandering among prodigious inhuman forms, we can understand his belief in a great prehistoric art of which the classics were copies. Various sources for these images have been identified in classical sculpture, Hindu compositions, and medieval painting; but this range of effects testifies to the fact that, in his last works, he has assimilated and redefined all the art that moved him during his lifetime. He fails only with his monsters and serpents, which, since they are not touched by any human configuration, are essentially beyond his scope —although perhaps he derived his massive snake from the 'serpent idol' displayed at an exhibition of Mexican art, held in the Egyptian Hail during the spring of 1824.

He made the engravings in 'dry-point' – that is, by drawing immediately upon the plate with an etching needle. They are more impressionistic than most of his original engravings, but this is because they are not so highly finished; nevertheless they have an extraordinary lightness and freedom, as if he were trying to reproduce the freshness of his drawings. He is improvising more, making better use of the surface whiteness of the paper, and these seven works are filled with energy and violence and a kind of impersonal gaiety. They are like the work of a young artist who is discovering the possibilities of his medium for the first time, and they evince all those qualities that he taught to The Ancients: 'UNBROKEN MASSES; UN-BROKEN LINES; UNBROKEN COLOURS'.[57] Here is emotion given shape, and spirituality lent form. It is true that he tends to concentrate upon the more infernal aspects of Dante's vision, and he does not have the artistic means to register the passages of love and yearning tenderness; instead he has created a coherent and enduring landscape of the imagination that is related both to his own vision and to that of the Italian poet. It has a ludic quality which suggests that, at the end of his life, he had found the highest reaches of art.

The same qualities are to be seen in the twenty-nine watercolours illustrating The Pilgrim's Progress that remained uncompleted at the time of his death. A few of these seem to have been retouched and coloured by another hand – most likely that of Catherine Blake – but there are some which are unmistakably from Blake himself. He has used the same technique as that for the Dante watercolours; the pencil sketches are outlined in ink, then given a light wash, then deftly touched by watercolour. Again they are very free compositions, highly coloured or bathed in a mild effulgent light; the violet and purple and orange give indications of a visionary landscape, and it is also significant that at the end of his life he should have turned to the illustration of such religious artists as Bunyan and Dante. His true affiliations lay with them, not with the commercial work he had done for Thornton's Virgil or Flaxman's classical outlines. Yet there is reason enough to remember one last commission –Thornton asked him to make a small engraving of 'Moses Placed in the Ark of the Bullrushes' in order to illustrate an essay in his pocket annual, Remember Me! It is a fine engraving in its own right, with the delicate composition of space that is also evident in his late temperas, but it is worthy of notice as the last truly commercial work of his career. He had begun his life as a journeyman engraver forty-five years before, starting upon a routine of continual labour which left him perilously exposed to the demands of the market place; he completed some 580 commercial plates, and indeed they comprise the bulk of his production. He was never successful enough to keep an apprentice, or to join his guild, but remained a labourer who was forced to work within very strictly defined limits. Perhaps his frustration helped to fuel his extravagant and visionary imagination, but there is no doubt that throughout his life he was impeded and weighed down by the economics of a new age. There is an image of him, given by Palmer, as he worked in Fountain Court – 'his clothes were threadbare, and his grey trousers had worn black and shiny in front, like a mechanic's'.[58] So he remained until his death.

TWENTY-SEVEN

I will arise

The ancient man, bearded and naked, leans out from a bright orb and with his compass divides the material world; his long hair is being blown by some unknown force, and the nature of the fiery sphere or circle behind him is indeterminate. It may be a planet, or a globe of human blood. It may be a sun, since its colours vary from pink and red to ochre and golden. It was one of the last images upon which Blake worked, in the hours before his death. 'Blake finished it to the utmost point,' according to his mid-Victorian biographer, 'making it beautiful in colour as already grand in design; patiently working on it till within a few days of his death.'[1] But it had also been one of his earliest compositions. He had used it as the frontispiece to his Lambeth poem, *Europe*, although it is possible that he originally intended to place it within *The Book of Urizen*, where the 'dark power . . . divided, & measur'd'.[2] Some of its detail may come from *Paradise Lost*, when 'in his hand / He took the golden compasses',[3] or from the seventh chapter of Daniel, where 'I beheld till the thrones were cast down, and the Ancient of days did sit, whose garment was white as snow, and the hair of his head like the pure wool: his throne was like the fiery flame, and his wheels as burning fire.'[4] The form of this giant deity is certainly also related to the figures of Michelangelo and Tibaldi, and the image of the measuring compasses had long been known to him. He had seen them in Dürer's 'Melancholia', which hung in his workroom until his death, and on the frontispiece to Motte's translation of Newton's *Principia* (where indeed you would expect to find them). But perhaps the most obvious source lies in the Freemasonry with which he became acquainted while he was an apprentice engraver in Great Queen Street.

Compasses are to be found in many of his works, from 'Newton' to 'Christ in the Carpenter's Shop', from 'Jacob's Dream' to 'The Spirit of Plato'.

These conjectures can be left aside, however, since all of the past images may have been concentrated in that one moment of vision when Blake saw 'The Ancient of Days' hovering 'at the top of his staircase; and he has frequently been heard to say, that it made a more powerful impression upon his mind than all he had ever been visited by'.[5] But he had seen it once before, on the wooden canopy over the tomb of Richard II in Westminster Abbey, where the old man raises his hand in benediction. In Blake's painting the arm is lowered in a gesture both of power and despair, marking out the limits of the Mundane Shell. If he were to straighten up and turn his face towards us, what would we see? It is the God of the Old Testament. It is the terrible father that haunted Blake all his life. It is Satan. It is Moses. It is the Druid. It is the Great Architect. It is the evil god of this world. It is the Ratio. It is the Moral Law, representing the 'dividing rule' and 'scales' of abstract rationalism.[6] But it is also Urizen in Blake's own mythology, representing the horizon, your reason, whose emblem is the Eye.

Yet why was it that he returned to this same image again and again, redrawing and repainting it as if it were some oblique representation of his own life and genius? Blake himself on occasions used a compass; the mark of its point is clearly to be seen on one proof sheet. But, more importantly, there is in his pride, his ambition, his desire to control the world by creating his own mythological system, some shadowy resemblance to Urizen's own endeavours. Urizen is terrible precisely because Blake realised that those same characteristics had profoundly damaged and impeded him. In that sense 'The Ancient of Days' may be as much an idealised self-portrait as the images of Los or of Orc. Urizen is, after all, a maker of books and is always associated with them -- his 'book of iron on his knees' on which 'he tracd the dreadful letters' might be an image of Blake himself at his copper plates.[7] Urizen writes 'in horrible fear of the future', which must be controlled with 'pen obdurate', again like Blake, and in the depiction of Urizen's painful labour we find an allegorical presentation of Blake's own life in the world.[8] But he is the worst part of Blake -- the earthly part, the unhappy and thwarted aspect of his life, which led him to calculate and to systematise, sometimes losing his inspiration in a mire of obsessive detail and repetition. It is the ambition that sometimes led him to emulate others, and it is the pride that made him rage; it is all the vainglory, and the fear, and compulsiveness which invaded him. That is why 'The Ancient of Days' remains such a powerful and persuasive image, and why he remained half in love with it for all of his life. But even here there is the hope of redemption. Urizen was a being who began in light, even though he ended in restriction, privation and dread. He may be able to cast off these States in which he has resided, and thus reclaim his true self, his true glory. In the last 'Night' of *The Four Zoas* he discards his 'labours void':

> . . . he shook his aged mantles off
> Into the fires Then glorious bright Exulting in his joy
> He sounding rose into the heavens in naked majesty
> In radiant Youth.[9]

It is the image of 'Glad Day' that Blake conceived in his own exultant youth; it is the emblem of glory and of freedom, to which he himself would soon return.

TWENTY-EIGHT

The Imagination which Liveth for Ever

In 1824 Linnell and his family moved to Hampstead, leaving their house in Cirencester Place as the artist's studio; they settled in a small cottage that was part of Collins's Farm, a rambling red-roofed dwelling between North End and a public house called The Spaniards; it looked out upon the gorse hills of the Heath on one side, and upon meadows on the other. The air of Hampstead was supposed to be healthy and refreshing, although Blake insisted that it always gave him 'a cold in my stomach';[1] nevertheless it became his custom to visit the Linnells each Sunday. He walked there from Fountain Court because the Hampstead carriage provoked diarrhoea in him, his constitution already enfeebled by age, and on many occasions he picked up Samuel Palmer in Broad Street along his route. The Linnell children waited for him as he came within sight over the brow of the hill, and would then hurry down to meet him. There is a drawing of Blake at Hampstead, executed by Linnell, which shows him standing alert among the hills, with his broad-brimmed Quaker-like hat and frock coat.

There are descriptions of his visits to a place where even he commented upon 'the beauty of the view' – how he played with the children, how he argued with John Varley on the merits of astrology, how he stood gazing in reverie at the hills, how he liked to sit in the arbour at the end of the garden at dusk 'while the cows, munching their evening meal, were audible from the farmyard on the other side of the hedge'.[2] In the evening, too, he would be moved by the singing of Mary Ann Linnell at the pianoforte, 'tears falling from his eyes, while he listened to the Border Melody'.[3] This is the melody that begins

O Nancy's hair is yellow like gowd
An' her een like the lift are blue
Her face is the image o' heavenly luve
An' her heart is leal and true.

He had always loved popular song, as his own work testifies, although
he was not apparently impressed by 'music of more complicated
structure'.[4] Sometimes he sang himself, in his old voice reciting
ballads or his own songs with their own melodies. It is a reminder of
the young man who had sung his lyrics at the house of the Mathews in
Rathbone Place, more than forty years before. Sometimes he brought
Mrs Linnell gifts, such as his copy of Percy's *Reliques of Ancient English
Poetry*, and on one occasion he showed her 'a Sketch Book, of Copy
from Prints & which he made when about 14 yrs old'.[5] The children
remembered a picture of a grasshopper among its pages.

He always played with the children, and in later life they recalled
him as 'a grave and sedate gentleman, with white hair, a lofty brow,
and large lambent eyes . . . a kind and gentle manner'.[6] He would
take them on his knee and tell them stories, 'readily falling in with,
and taking part in, their amusements'.[7] He explained to them how he
preferred a cat to a dog 'because she was so much more quiet in her
expression of attachment'.[8] Perhaps he told them the true story of the
walnut oil: a connoisseur had sent him a sample for some kind of
artistic experiment but he 'tasted it, and went on tasting, till he had
drunk the whole'.[9] There was to be no artistic experiment at all. And
then there was the story of the lambs. 'The other evening . . . taking
a walk, I came to a meadow and, at the farther corner of it, I saw a fold
of lambs. Coming nearer, the ground blushed with flowers; and the
wattled cote and its woolly tenants were of an exquisite pastoral
beauty. But I looked again, and it proved to be no living flock, but
beautiful sculpture.'[10] It has been said that 'his conversation warmed
the listener, kindled his imagination, and almost created in him a
new sense . . . His description of some clouds I shall never forget. He
warmed with his subject, and it continued through an evening
walk.'[11] It is no wonder that the children loved him.

In the evening Linnell's guests would sit and talk after dinner.
There is a sketch by Linnell of Blake and Varley together at table –
Varley has his arm outstretched in the full sweep of his conversation,
while Blake leans back with an expression somewhere between
interest and amusement. Did he realise at the close of his life, then,
that he could easily have razed that wall which once existed between

him and others? When the party ended, in the cold night air, Mary Ann Linnell would wrap him in an old shawl 'and sent him on his homeward way, with the servant, lantern in hand, lighting him across the heath to the main road'.[12]

Constable had lodgings in Hampstead during this period, and it is likely that he also visited the Linnells: he knew them well enough, and he knew Blake. It was in these last years, too, that Blake became acquainted with Samuel Taylor Coleridge. The unorthodox Swedenborgian Charles Augustus Tulk brought Coleridge to Fountain Court, where, he reported, the younger man examined 'The Last Judgment' – upon which Blake was still working – and 'poured forth concerning it a flood of eloquent commentary and enlargement'.[13] At a later date Tulk observed that 'Blake and Coleridge, when in company, seemed like congenial beings of another sphere, breathing for a while on our earth'.[14] Crabb Robinson also wrote to Dorothy Wordsworth with the news that 'Coleridge has visited B. & I am told talks finely about him'.[15] Blake's opinions of the younger writer are not known, although he has left one or two suggestive remarks about Wordsworth. He thought him a fine poet but remarked to Crabb Robinson that 'Wordsworth loves Nature – and Nature is the work of the Devil'.[16] He also said that Wordsworth's account of passing Jehovah 'unalarmed' in The Excursion had provoked in him a bowel complaint, and later he added this note to his copy of the poem: 'Solomon when he married Pharaohs daughter & became a convert to the Heathen Mythology talked exactly in this way of Jehovah as a very inferior object of man's contemplation, he also passed by him unalarmed & was permitted. Jehovah dropped a tear & followed him by his Spirit into the abstract void. It is called the divine Mercy. Satan dwells in it, but mercy does not dwell in him.'[17]

The difference in language and perception here is enough to mark Blake off for ever from the Romantics with whom he is often associated. He emerges from a much older faith, and when he transcribed passages from The Excursion he characteristically converted them into eighteenth-century capitals and spelling. But this is not to suggest that he was in any way 'out of date'; the remarks in the preface to the Lyrical Ballads about a simple language of feeling, as of 'a man speaking to men', would have seemed otiose to Blake. In poems such as 'The Everlasting Gospel', and in the lyrics from Songs of Innocence and of Experience, he had already proved himself to be closer to a genuinely popular tradition of literature than any of his contemporaries. He was also moving within a deeply rooted literary inheritance in his revision of the emblems he had composed many years before – he had then entitled them 'For Children: The Gates of Paradise', but now he wrote, 'For the Sexes: The Gates of Paradise'. The emblems have been altered but not wholly changed, and Blake has added verses beneath some of them in order to explain the mythic import of the series. Once again he is deploying a popular, and immediately accessible, form for his own purposes; there never was a time when he did not wish to find a public audience and he remained something of a populist, a prophet and a didact until the end.

Now he was coming to the close of his earthly travels. There were months in the autumn of 1823 and the summer of 1824 when his weak and quavering hand suggests illness or general debility. In the spring and summer of 1825 he was attacked by 'shivering fits' that left him prostrate in bed.[18] It may have been gallstones causing an inflamed gall bladder, but there is no authentic medical description of his condition – in the language of the time there was 'mixing of the gall with the blood',[19] and 'bile was mixing with his blood'.[20] Blake simply called it 'this abominable Ague, or whatever it is'.[21] There was some portent of his fate in the death of his old friend Henry Fuseli, in April 1825; the artist's body was laid out in Somerset House with many of his paintings around him, but it is not known if Blake visited him in his final mortal state. Of course there was no finality in death for Blake – commenting upon the demise of another, he told Linnell, 'Every death is an improvement of the State of the Departed',[22] by which he meant, in the words of Swedenborg, that 'every perfection in the heavens increases with increase of numbers'.[23] Yet he was well enough in September to visit The Ancients, who had established a little community in Shoreham, where Samuel Palmer's grandfather had a house. The Blakes travelled down with Edward Calvert and his wife in an old-fashioned covered wagon, and were put up in a neighbour's house. Calvert's son recalls how Blake and the 'old Palmer', once a bookseller and now a minister of the Primitive Baptist church, discussed 'Art and Letters' by the hearth of the cottage.[24] Two small incidents are worth recording. It soon transpired in conversation that 'Blake believed in ghosts', and so an expedition was organised to a half-ruined mansion nearby which was supposed to house one such spiritual occupant.[25] Some time after their arrival they heard 'a curious rattling sound' and in frightened but expectant silence Palmer and Calvert moved towards the source of the unearthly noise. It was a snail crawling up an oriel window. So ended the adventure. Powers of another sort were more in evidence later, however, when Blake sat at a table in the cottage. He put his hand to his forehead.

BLAKE: Palmer is coming. He is walking up the road.

CALVERT: Oh, Mr Blake, he's gone to London; we saw him off in the coach.

BLAKE: He is coming through the wicket.

Then, sure enough, 'Samuel Palmer raised the latch and came in amongst them. It so turned out that the coach had broken down near to the gate of Lullingstone Park.'[26] It was in a period of relative good health, too, that Blake visited the Calverts at their house in Russell Street, Brixton, where, on one occasion, the two artists managed to set fire to the chimney while experimenting with some etching-ground. He had lost none of his youthful enthusiasm for the techniques of his craft. Certainly he was well enough by the September of 1825 to have an animated conversation with Linnell, who was making a journey by coach to Gloucester, and so forgot himself that he started travelling with him and was forced to leave the vehicle after a few miles. In the following month he took his Job engravings to Flaxman, who evidently approved of them, and Blake went off to Hampstead in order to break the good news to Mrs Linnell.

He was ill again by November, however, and in the early months of the following year complained of 'torment of the Stomach', which he blamed again upon the Hampstead air. It was 'Easily removed, but excruciating while it lasts & enfeebling for some time after'.[27] The attack also provoked in him one of his characteristic moments of vision – 'Sr Francis Bacon would say, it is want of discipline in Mountainous Places. Sir Francis Bacon is a Liar. No discipline will turn one Man into another, even in the least particle, & such discipline I call Presumption & Folly. I have tried it too much not to know this, & am very sorry for all such who may be led to such ostentatious Exertion against their Eternal Existence itself, because it is Mental Rebellion against the Holy Spirit, & fit only for a Soldier of Satan to perform.'[28] The sequence of his perceptions here also suggests something of the flavour of his conversation, in its sudden flights and leaps, in its certainty of tone, and in its prophetic or denunciatory quality.

During all of this period he was the prey to attacks of diarrhoea and other stomach ailments for which Dr Thornton, the Linnells' family doctor as well as Blake's erstwhile employer, could prescribe only modest remedies. In January he visited the house of William Upcott, the illegitimate son of Ozias Humphry, and left an entry in the young man's autograph album. 'William Blake one who is very much delighted with being in good Company Born 28 Novr 1757 in London & has died several times since' – by which he meant the sensation that he shared with Swedenborg, of dying to the material world and being transported into the company 'of angels and spirits to the life'. [29] In the album he has also drawn the image of a nude youth holding a scroll that winds around these words; once more he has instinctively placed words and image in the same field. He then questions whether he has written an autograph at all – normally this is 'Writ helter skelter like a hog upon a rope' and is 'very different from that which a Man Does with his Thought & Mind & ought not to be Calld by the Same Name'. [30] He ends by quoting part of Wordsworth's translation of one of Michelangelo's sonnets, 'Heaven born the Soul a Heavenward Course must hold'.

By the end of March he was once more 'very ill' and in a 'tottering state'; 'the Chill of the weather soon drives me back into that shivering fit which must be avoided till the Cold is gone', [31] and two months later he succumbed to 'another desperate Shivering Fit' that 'spread a deathly feel all over the limbs'. [32] He seemed to be getting better in May, when he went to a supper party at the house of Crabb Robinson; the Flaxmans came, too, and Robinson noted, 'I doubt whether Flaxman sufficiently tolerates Blake.' [33] Linnell was so concerned about his health, however, that he arranged for the Blakes to spend some of the summer at Hope Cottage, near his own house in Hampstead, but for the whole of July Blake was plagued by 'paroxysms' and intervals of painful 'delirium'. He could not sit up for more than six hours at a time, was terribly susceptible to cold, and sometimes 'in Pain too much for Thought'. [34] Then, no doubt because of the constant diarrhoea, he developed piles. In August he was well enough to travel at last to Hampstead – 'Our Carriage will be a Cabriolet, for tho' getting better & stronger, I am still incapable of riding in the Stage, & shall be, I fear, for some time, being only bones & sinews, All strings & bobbins like a Weaver's Loom.' [35] He did some drawing here, sitting beneath the trees with his portfolio, but his condition soon deteriorated – perhaps he was right about the deleterious effects of the Hampstead air, after all – and in December was suffering from 'another desperate attack of the Aguish trembling', which, if he ventured out, might prove 'fatal'.[36] He had already heard of the death of his old friend Flaxman, at his house in Buckingham Street only a few days before. Crabb Robinson broke the news to him – 'he had himself been very ill during the Summer and his first observation was with a Smile – "I thought I should have gone first" – He then said "I cannot consider death as any thing but a removing from one room to another" '.[37]

He continued working while there was still day. He had spent some of his last years in completing a number of paintings on commission or at his wife's urging, although he did not find purchasers for all of them. In some cases he seemed to be reinventing or revising old work. He finished a watercolour of 'The Vision of Queen Catherine' based upon a painting he had completed eighteen years earlier, and he began another version of 'The Parable of the Wise and Foolish Virgins', which he had depicted twice before. This latter was commissioned by Sir Thomas Lawrence, who seemed still eager to help him in his penury, and in the stages of the various paintings from 1805 to 1825 it is possible to see the movement of Blake's style. The late work is distinguished by its delicate modelling and freer handling; the colours are at once softer and richer, which heightens the more sensitive and painterly aspects of his genius.

But his preoccupation with sacred art had not in any sense diminished, and in the last few months of his life he began work on an illuminated version of the Bible; he was commissioned by Linnell to illustrate the sacred text with his own designs, but he managed only partially to complete some eleven leaves of the work. He used the King James version of Genesis but added his own textual references with such chapter headings as 'The Creation of the Natural Man' and 'How Generation & Death took Possession of the Natural Man & of the Forgiveness of Sins written upon the Murderers Forehead'. Each page has an illustration, and the pencilled text of the first three has been gone over in green or red watercolour. The title pages have been carefully composed, with a great deal of attention being paid to the religious symbolism of flowers. It is not clear whether this illuminated work is related to the 'Version (for so it may be called) of Genesis "as understood by a Christian Visionary" ', which Crabb Robinson mentioned in his diary,[38] but the important fact is that at the end of his life Blake was reverting to the original source of his inspiration. He had returned to the beginning.

In his last few months he was suffering from a variety of debilitating complaints; he had constant diarrhoea, his ankles were badly swollen and he had a succession of chest infections. Yet he had lost none of the sharpness of his perceptions, and he annotated Thornton's *The Lord's Prayer, Newly Translated* in tones of prophetic denunciation – 'I look upon this,' he wrote, 'as a Most Malignant & Artful attack upon the Kingdom of Jesus By the Classical Learned thro the Instrument-ality of Dr Thornton The Greek & Roman Classics is the Anti-christ'.[39] It was that part of his temperament which The Ancients rarely, if ever, saw; if they had seen it, they would not have understood it. 'Spirits are Lawful but not Ghosts especially Royal Gin is Lawful Spirit . . . I Nature Hermaphroditic Priest & King Live in Real Substantial Natural Born Man & that Spirit is the Ghost of Matter or Nature & God is The Ghost of the Priest & King who Exist whereas God exists not except from their Effluvia'.[40] This parody of Thornton's deistical prayer represents one of his most powerful accounts of human perception, and it is paralleled by a letter he sent to George Cumberland five months before his death. 'I know too well,' he wrote, 'that a great majority of Englishmen are fond of The Indefinite which they Measure by Newton's Doctrine of the Fluxions of an Atom, A Thing that does not Exist. These are Politicians & think that Republican Art is Inimical to their Atom. For a Line or Lineament is not formed by Chance: a Line is a Line in its Minutest Subdivisions: Strait or Crooked It is Itself & Not Intermeasurable with or by any Thing Else. Such is Job, but since the French Revolution Englishmen are all Intermeasurable One by Another. Certainly a happy state of Agreement to which I for One do not Agree . . . God keep me from the Divinity of Yes & No too, the Yea Nay Creeping Jesus, from supposing Up and Down to be the same Thing as all Experimentalists must suppose.'[41] It is an astonishing act of intuition in which the religious, scientific and political perceptions of his period are considered in their full aspect, in which the concept of 'intermeasurability' is seen to be both a scientific and social creed with equally baneful results.

He laboured till the end. He continued work upon his Dante watercolours, and upon his illuminated version of the Bible, although both works were left incomplete. He was still putting the finishing touches to his vast canvas of 'The Last Judgment', now lost; he had darkened it to please the taste of a fellow lodger in Fountain Court, a Frenchwoman, but believed that he had spoiled it as a result. Yet one who saw it described it as 'wonderfully conceived and grandly drawn. The lights of this extraordinary performance have the appearance of silver and gold; but upon Mrs Blake's assuring me that there was no silver used, I found, upon a closer examination, that a blue wash had been passed over those parts of the gilding which receded, and the lights of the forward objects, which were also of gold, were heightened with a warm colour, to give the appearance of the two metals.'[42] The use of gold and of 'warm colour' was now an intrinsic part of Blake's artistic practice, and the last illuminated books he sold were illustrated in an enormously rich and decorative manner so that they no longer resemble texts but works of art; as a result connoisseurs were becoming more interested in him. Even scholars such as William Young Ottley, who had written Inquiry into the Origin and Early History of Engraving, were now buying his works. He used gold, and brilliant colours, as if he were working upon a medieval manuscript for the honour and glory of God; yet he has also gone beyond his medieval examples, and created an art all of his own. He worked until his death upon an exquisitely coloured copy of Jerusalem, and of course upon that last image of 'The Ancient of Days'. But he had not lost his skills as an engraver, and one of the final tasks he performed was upon a visiting card for George Cumberland in which the images of children, and of spirits holding the threads of life, act as an allegory for human existence itself. Yet the late drawings, even though they are as elaborate as any he ever accomplished, show a quavering hand.

In February 1827 he was 'feeble & tottering'. Linnell had suggested that he and Catherine should move to his old house in Cirencester Place, where they might be more easily and properly assisted, but Blake was, in his age and debility, terrified of any change. 'I have Thought & Thought of the Removal,' he told Linnell, '& cannot get my Mind out of a state of terrible fear at such a step; the more I think, the more I feel terror at what I wish'd at first & thought it a thing of benefit & Good hope; you will attribute it to its right Cause – Intellectual Peculiarity, that must be Myself alone shut up in Myself, or Reduced to Nothing. I could tell you of Visions & dreams upon the Subject. I have asked & intreated Divine help, but fear continues upon me . . .'[43] So his visions had not left him, and even at the end he communed with his spirits.

His brother James died in March. In April he believed himself to 'have been very near the Gates of Death'; he was 'very weak . . . but not in Spirit & Life, not in The Real Man The Imagination which

Liveth for Ever'. He spoke of Flaxman's death now, and added, 'we must All soon follow, every one to his Own Eternal House, Leaving the delusive Goddess Nature & her Laws to get into Freedom from all Law of the Members into The Mind, in which every one is King & Priest in his own House'.[44] Already he could not wait to leave his physical body behind, and rise into his true state within eternity. Yet he seemed to have some terror of himself in his extremity, and told Linnell his 'only fear that I may be Unlucky to my friends & especially that I may not be so to you'.[45] So he was still conscious of his misfortune in the world, like some curse or contagion. He visited Hampstead in late June but then suffered a relapse. Linnell visited him in early August and wrote in his diary that he was 'not expected to live'.[46] Underneath he drew a sketch of Blake lying upon his bed, propped upon a pillow, 'great dark eyes dominant'.[47] His only thought now was completing his work on Dante, and 'one of the very last shillings spent was in sending out for a pencil'.[48] On the day of his death he stopped work and turned to Catherine, who was in tears; 'Stay, Kate!' he said, 'keep just as you are – I will draw your portrait – for you have ever been an angel to me.'[49] When he had completed it he put it down, and then began to sing verses and hymns. 'My beloved, they are not mine,' he told his wife as she listened to what she later called 'songs of joy and Triumph', '– no – they are not mine'. He was singing out of gladness, and no doubt he was happy to leave a world which had treated him so ill. Then he told his wife that they would never be parted, that he would be with her always. At six in the evening, he expired 'like the sighing of a gentle breeze'. A female lodger, also present, said, 'I have been at the death, not of a man, but of a blessed angel.'[50] George Richmond wrote to Samuel Palmer, a little later, 'He died on Sunday night at 6 Oclock in a most glorious manner. He said He was going to that Country he had all His life wished to see & expressed Himself Happy, hoping for Salvation through Jesus Christ – Just before he died His Countenance became fair. His eyes Brighten'd and He burst out into Singing of the things he saw in Heaven.'[51]

As soon as he heard news of the death John Linnell came to Catherine and, in his usual efficient way, arranged the details of the funeral and burial. He lent her the money to pay for the ceremony, which was of a relatively modest sort, and five days later – on the day before the Blakes' forty-fifth wedding anniversary – the poet was taken to the Dissenter's burial ground in Bunhill Fields. It had been his wish to lie there, since his parents were both interred in the same place. It was a small elm coffin, some five feet nine inches in length, of the English kind that tapered gradually from the middle like the case of a violin. He lay in a common grave, which cost nineteen shillings, and was buried nine feet under the earth and gravel; already beneath him lay the remains of Margaret Jones, Rees Thomas and Edward Sherwood while, over the next few years, another four bodies would be placed above him. Edward Calvert, George Richmond, Frederick Tatham, John Linnell and Catherine Blake were at the cemetery; but it was, in its way, an anonymous burial. His great friend George Cumberland did not learn of his death for four months.

Catherine moved to Linnell's studio in Cirencester Place as a housekeeper, but in old age she seems to have had a suspicious and difficult temperament. After a few months she moved in as housekeeper to Frederick Tatham but it seems that 'she was opposed to everything he did for her benefit & when she submitted to his views it was always with the words "Had no help for it" '.[52] Eventually they had a fierce argument, but on the following morning she told Tatham that 'William had been with her all night' and desired the breach to be healed. Blake had told her that he would never leave her, and indeed she saw him continually when 'he used to come and sit with her for two or three hours every day. He took his chair and talked to her, just as he would have done had he been alive; he advised her as to the best mode of selling his engravings.'[53] She did in fact keep up the business in her husband's work, selling illuminated books and paintings to erstwhile patrons who wished to assist her, but she always maintained that she could do nothing 'until she had an opportunity of consulting Mr Blake'.[54] Eventually she moved from Tatham's house and took up lodgings at No. 17 Charlton Street. On the day of her death, in October 1831, she was as calm and as cheerful as her husband had been – 'repeating texts of scripture and calling continually to her William, as if he were only in the next room, to say she was coming to him, and would not be long now'.[55] She was also buried in Bunhill Fields, but not in a grave near her husband.

There have been numerous rumours about Blake's 'lost' works; he said himself that he had written 'Six or Seven Epic poems as long as Homer and 20 Tragedies as long as Macbeth'.[56] We may take this to be the pardonable exaggeration of an artist trying always to prove his worth. There are reports, however, that Frederick Tatham destroyed many manuscripts which he had inherited from Catherine. He had become a committed 'Irvingite', one of the many fundamentalist creeds of the mid-nineteenth century, and it is believed he rejected any work that smacked of blasphemy or eroticism. But this is conjecture. What remains is enough, and more than enough, to demonstrate the true genius of William Blake, who lived in a world which distrusted and despised him. After his death George Richmond kissed him, and then closed his eyes 'to keep the vision in'.[57] Yet there was really no need to do so. That vision had not faded in his pilgrimage of seventy years, and it has not faded yet.

SOURCE NOTES

Abbreviations
BR *Blake Records*, edited by G. E. Bentley jnr (Oxford, 1969)
BR(S) *Blake Records Supplement*, edited by G. E. Bentley jnr (Oxford, 1988)
Complete *The Complete Poetry and Prose of William Blake*,
edited by David V. Erdman (New York, 1988)
Gilchrist *The Life of William Blake* by Alexander Gilchrist (London, 1863 and 1880)
Letters *The Letters of William Blake*, edited by Geoffrey Keynes (Oxford, 1980)
Notebook *The Notebook of William Blake*, edited by David V. Erdman (Oxford, 1973)

Chapter 1: O why was I born with a different face?

1 Complete, 479
2 Ibid., 502
3 Symons, *William Blake*, 27
4 Complete, 173
5 BR, 452
6 E. P. Thompson, *Witness Against the Beast*, 121
7 Lecky, *History of England in the Eighteenth Century*, Vol. II, 452
8 Hindmarsh, *Rise and Progress of the New Jerusalem Church*, 83
9 Complete, 479
10 Ibid., 561
11 Ibid., 554
12 Ibid., 191
13 Ibid., 371
14 Gilchrist, 275
15 Complete, 392
16 Gilchrist, 95
17 *Coriolanus*, V.iii.36–7
18 Quoted in Robert Gittings, *John Keats*, 628

19 Gilchrist, 345
20 Complete, 173
21 BR, 508
22 Ibid.
23 Ibid., 509
24 Letters, 20
25 Ibid., 23
26 BR, 508
27 Ibid.
28 Ibid., 481
29 Ibid., 548
30 Ibid., 510
31 Ibid., 540
32 E. P. Thompson, *Witness Against the Beast*, 87
33 Complete, 656
34 Letters, 69
35 Complete, 498
36 Ibid., 660

Chapter 2: The Whole Bible is fill'd with Imagination & Visions

1 Ezekiel 28:14, 16
2 Ibid., 7:5–6

3 Hebrews 12:29
4 Revelation 4:1–2
5 Jeremiah 44:22
6 Complete, 347
7 Job 28:12–13
8 Complete, 325
9 Isaiah 11:6
10 Johannes Albrecht Bengel, *Gnomon of the New Testament,* 1734
11 Ezekiel 7:15
12 Zechariah 8:4–5
13 Jeremiah 1:5–7

Chapter 3: All that we See is Vision

1 Gilchrist, 6
2 Notebook [N 67 transcript]
3 Stanley Gardner, *Blake's Innocence and Experience Retraced,* 5. Mr Gardner also provides some very interesting material on the nursing care provided by St James's Parish which might have played a part in Blake's *Songs of Innocence and of Experience*
4 Ibid., 3
5 Complete, 99
6 *Old England,* 2 July 1748
7 Lecky, *History of England in the Eighteenth Century,* Vol. II, 131
8 Pennant, *Some Account of London,* 170
9 Complete, 243
10 Letters, 158
11 Ibid., 41
12 BR, 529
13 Ibid., 510
14 Complete, 171–2
15 Grosley, *A Tour to London,* Vol. I, 38
16 Smith, *A Book for a Rainy Day,* 23
17 Ibid., 19
18 Thale (ed.), *The Autobiography of Francis Place,* 58
19 John Brown, *An Estimate of the Manners and Principles of the Times,* 95
20 Thomas Babington Macaulay, *The History of England in the Eighteenth Century,* 109
21 Complete, 318
22 Gilchrist, 7
23 BR, 543
24 Ibid., 519
25 Ibid., 318
26 Complete, 35
27 Gilchrist, 7
28 BR, 318
29 Ibid., 510
30 Ibid., 499
31 Quoted in John Livingstone Lowes, *The Road to Xanadu,* 62 and 432
32 Quoted in Read, *Education Through Art,* 43
33 Mentioned in Harrison, *The Second Coming*
34 P. Jaensch, *Eidetic Imagery,* 2
35 Quoted in Read, *Education Through Art*
36 Letters, 65

Chapter 4: I devoted myself to Engraving in my Earliest Youth

1 BR, 456
2 Complete, 412
3 'Memoirs of Thomas Jones', *Walpole Society,* Vol. XXXII, 21
4 Reynolds, *The Literary Works of Sir Joshua Reynolds,* Vol. I, 98
5 BR, 311
6 D. G. C. Allan, *William Shipley: Founder of the Royal Society of Arts,* 76–88. I am indebted for this quotation to David Bindman's excellent *Blake as an Artist*
7 BR, 422
8 Ibid.
9 Complete, 637

10 BR, 422
11 Ibid.
12 Complete, 550
13 Ibid.
14 *The Private Papers of Henry Ryecroft*
15 Complete, 571
16 Ibid., 413
17 BR, 510–11
18 *London Tradesman*, 104
19 Gilchrist, 13
20 Complete, 35
21 BR, 9
22 Ibid., 10
23 Complete, 568
24 Letters, 10
25 Quoted in Robert Hamlyn, 'The Apprentice Years', Tate Gallery catalogue
26 Quoted in Godfrey, *Printmaking in Britain*
27 Complete, 572
28 These instructions have been adapted from *The Art of Graving and Etching* by William Faithorne
29 Complete, 574
30 Ibid.
31 Complete, 575
32 I have here appropriated the words of Amiel, as quoted by Linssen, 35
33 Complete, 572
34 Ibid., 638
35 Gilchrist, 15
36 Berger, *William Blake, Poet and Mystic*, 54
37 2 Chronicles 2:14
38 Complete, 575
39 Job 19:23–4

Chapter 5: Each Identity is Eternal

1 Hebrews 11:37–8
2 Complete, 438

Chapter 6: a Temple built by Albions Children

1 Letter to the Dean of Westminster, quoted in Appendix A of Kerry Downes's *Hawksmoor*.
2 Thale (ed.), *The Autobiography of Francis Place*, 72
3 BR, 422
4 Lister (ed.), *Letters of Samuel Palmer*, 508
5 BR, 283
6 Complete, 241
7 BR, 422
8 Ibid.
9 *The History and Antiquities of Westminster Abbey* (London, 1971), 47
10 Complete, 411
11 Ibid., 532
12 BR, 512
13 Ibid.
14 Ibid., 13
15 *Archaeologia* (1775), III, 376
16 Complete, 278
17 Ibid., 549
18 Ibid., 649
19 From 'Cath-Loda', 'Oithona', 'The Songs of Selma', 'The War of Inisthona', 'Fingal' and 'Dar-thula'
20 Complete, 665–6
21 From *The Story of Wyllyam Canynge* by Thomas Chatterton. Quoted in Ackroyd, *Chatterton*, 79
22 Meyerstein, 465
23 Mallet, xvii
24 Bryant, ii
25 Ibid., xvii
26 Complete, 660–1
27 Ibid., 657
28 Winckelmann, *Reflections*, 62
29 Ibid., 254
30 Quoted in Lowery, *Windows of the Morning*, 134

31 Complete, 417

32 Ibid., 846

33 Ibid., 410

34 Complete, 442 and 447

35 Complete, 550

36 Ibid., 433

37 BR, 423

38 Ibid.

39 Quoted in Erffa and Staley, *The Paintings of Benjamin West*, 68

40 *Literary Works*, Vol. I, 86

41 Ibid., 69

42 Complete, 630

Chapter 7: We do not want either Greek or Roman Models

1 BR, 16

2 *Literary Works*, Vol. I, 54–5

3 Smith, *A Book for a Rainy Day*, 9

4 *Literary Works*, Vol. I, xlvii

5 BR, 17

6 Complete, 81

7 *Literary Works*, Vol. I, 200

8 RA Council Minutes, Vol. I, 4–6

9 BR, 318n

10 Ibid., 423

11 Complete, 454

12 *Literary Works*, Vol. I, 11

13 Ibid., 16–17

14 Ibid., 80

15 Ibid., 164

16 Ibid., 271–2

17 Quoted in Bray, *The Life of Thomas Stothard*, 12

18 *Literary Works*, Vol. II, 3–4

19 Ibid., 7

20 These quotations are taken from Blake's annotations to Reynolds's *Discourses*, Complete, 635 ff

21 Gilchrist, 95

22 Complete, 531

23 Gilchrist, 314

24 Complete, 639

25 Quoted in Ellis Waterhouse, *Painting in Britain, 1530–1790*, 213

26 Complete, 636

27 Smith, *Nollekens and His Times*, Vol. II, 282

28 Essick and Pearce (eds.), *Blake in His Time*, 179

29 Bray, 4

30 Ibid., 79

31 Letters, 50

32 Constable, *John Flaxman*, 1

33 Ibid., 58

34 Smith, *Nollekens*, Vol. II, 353

35 Letters, 45

36 Ibid., 20

37 Smith, *Nollekens*, Vol. I, 152

38 BR, 362

39 George Cumberland, *Thoughts on Outline*, 1

40 E. P. Thompson, *The Making of the English Working Class*, 179

41 Thomas Day, *The Desolation of America*, 6

42 Gilchrist, 93

43 Bray, 21

44 Ibid.

45 *Miscellaneous Works*, Vol. II, 241

46 De Castro, *The Gordon Riots*, 125

47 Complete, 65

48 De Castro, 91

49 Ibid., 92

50 Gilchrist, 36

51 BR, 17

52 George Cumberland, *Some Anecdotes of the Life of Julio Bonasone*

53 Complete, 242

54 Ibid., 325. I am indebted for this reference to Robert Essick, who deals very well with the subject of Blake's engraving in 'Blake and the Tradition of Reproductive Engraving' in *Blake Studies*, Vol. 5, No. 1

55 Complete, 82

Chapter 8: My Eyes are always upon thee

1 Gilchrist, 37
2 Thale (ed.), *The Autobiography of Francis Place*, 51
3 Quoted in Altick, *The Shows of London*, 55
4 Thale (ed.), *The Autobiography of Francis Place*, 14 and 72
5 Ibid., 228
6 BR, 517
7 Ibid., 518
8 Letters, 50
9 BR, 526
10 Ibid., 548
11 Complete, 50
12 Letters, 8
13 Complete, 222
14 Ibid., 223
15 BR, 487
16 BR(S), 74
17 Complete, 596
18 BR, 471
19 Ibid., 276
20 Gilchrist, 59
21 BR, 509
22 Mrs Mathew, in *Notes and Queries*, April 1958, 172
23 Smith, *A Book for a Rainy Day*, 169
24 Complete, 463
25 *Notes and Queries*, April 1958, 172
26 BR, 457
27 Complete, 36
28 Ibid., 189
29 BR, 315
30 Swinburne, *William Blake*, 5
31 *Literary Works*, Vol. I, 191
32 Complete, 460
33 Quoted in Tyson, *Joseph Johnson: A Liberal Publisher*, 92
34 Raine and Harper (eds.), *Thomas Taylor*, 138
35 Ibid., 159

36 BR(S), 94–5
37 Complete, 322
38 BR(S), 95
39 Complete, 42. I am indebted to G. E. Bentley jnr for these references
40 Richard Clarke, *Signs of Times*, 2
41 Raine and Harper (eds.), *Thomas Taylor*, 153
42 Ibid., 159
43 Ibid., 440
44 Ibid., 443
45 Ibid., 131
46 Complete, 462
47 Ibid., 455–8
48 Ibid., 462
49 Smith, *A Book for a Rainy Day*, 45
50 Complete, 500
51 Ibid., 180
52 Ibid., 465
53 *Blake Books*, 482
54 Complete, 446
55 Ibid., 203
56 BR(S), 8
57 Complete, 572
58 Letters, 3
59 BR(S), 1
60 BR, 28

Chapter 9: The Ocean of Business

1 Complete, 463
2 Campbell, *The London Tradesman*, 104
3 Sir John Hawkins, quoted in Nichols, *Illustrations of the Literary History of the Eighteenth Century*, Vol. VIII, 243
4 BR, 459
5 Gilchrist, 59
6 BR(S), xxxiii
7 Letters, 15
8 *Heaven and Hell*, paragraph 440
9 Hindmarsh, *Rise and Progress of the New Jerusalem Church*, 81

10 Quoted in *Blake: An Illustrated Quarterly*, Fall 1992, 43
11 Quoted in Hindmarsh, 81
12 *The Wisdom of Angels Concerning Divine Love and Wisdom*, 10–11
13 Complete, 13
14 Letters, 20
15 Schiff, *Henry Fuseli*, 38
16 Complete, 507
17 Schiff, 45
18 Ibid.
19 Bruce, *William Blake in this World*, 64
20 Quoted in Tomory, *The Life and Art of Henry Fuseli*, 73
21 BR, 53
22 From Cunningham, quoted in BR, 481n
23 Bruce, 66 and 67
24 'Two Biographies of Keats', *Pall Mall Gazette*, 27 September 1887
25 Farington's Diary, 24 June 1796
26 Gilchrist, 2
27 Ibid., 52
28 BR, 39
29 Gilchrist, 66
30 All the annotations for Lavater are to be found in Complete, 583–601
31 Complete, 642
32 Ibid., 636
33 Letters, 101–3
34 Complete, 599
35 Ibid., 285
36 *Life of Caedmon*, IV, 24
37 BR, 460
38 Gilchrist, 69
39 *William Blake's Commercial Book Illustrations*, 42
40 My discussion here is indebted to Joseph Viscomi's *Blake and the Idea of the Book*
41 Complete, 153
42 I am indebted for this insight to Viscomi's *Blake and the Idea of the Book*

43 Complete, 692
44 Ibid., 465
45 Ibid., 39
46 Ibid., 272
47 Ibid., 3
48 Ibid., 1
49 Ibid., 3
50 Ibid., 4
51 Ibid., 7
52 BR, 470
53 Complete, 13
54 Ibid., 9
55 Ibid., 697
56 *Heaven and Hell*, paragraph 110

Chapter 10: And so he was quiet

1 Grosley, *A Tour to London*, Vol. I, 183 (see Vol. VIII, 649 for title)
2 Southey, quoted in Glen, *Vision and Disenchantment*, 97–8
3 Quoted in Glen, 98
4 Quoted in M. Dorothy George, *London Life in the Eighteenth Century*, 42
5 Proposition 79
6 Complete, 23
7 Ibid., 9

Chapter 11: From Lambeth We began our Foundations

1 Letters, 169
2 Complete, 20 and 26
3 Ibid., 45
4 *South London Observer*, 29 June 1912
5 BR, 512 and 521n
6 M. Dorothy George, *London Life in the Eighteenth Century*, 341
7 Complete, 243
8 Ibid., 183
9 Ibid., 122
10 Ibid.
11 Ibid., 26

12 King-Hele, *Erasmus Darwin and the Romantic Poets*, 57
13 Complete, 95

Chapter 12: the crushing Wheels

1 Complete, 97
2 Ibid., 98
3 Ibid., 3
4 Ibid., 406
5 Ibid., 125
6 Ibid., 97
7 Ibid., 210
8 Giorgio de Santillana and Hertha van Deckend, *Hamlet's Hill*, 111
9 Complete, 239
10 Ibid., 42

Chapter 13: Jerusalems Inner Court

1 BR, 522
2 Ibid.
3 Altick, *The Shows of London*, 108
4 Bindman, *Blake as an Artist*, 33
5 Letters, 5
6 Introduction to 'The Economy of Vegetation'
7 Complete, 3
8 BR, 45
9 Ibid.
10 Letters, 4
11 Ibid., 34
12 E. Alison Peers (ed.), *Collected Works*, Vol. I, 188
13 Ibid., 178
14 Ibid., 179
15 Ibid., 177
16 BR, 523–4
17 Zechariah 8: 4–5
18 Complete, 32
19 Ibid., 26
20 Ibid., 25
21 Erza Pound in *Vorticism*, quoted in Ackroyd, *Notes for a New Culture*, 35

22 Lichentritt in *Music and Ideas*, quoted in Bronson, *Some Aspects of Music and Literature in the Eighteenth Century*, 44
23 Complete, 34
24 Quoted in Humphrey Carpenter, *W. H. Auden*, 308

Chapter 14: eyes of fury

1 These, and other revisions, are to be found in Notebook [N 108–N 109]
2 Goldsmith, quoted in Colin Pedley, *Blake's Tiger and the Discourse of Natural History*, in *Blake: An Illustrated Quarterly*, Summer 1990, 242
3 Amos 3:4
4 Job 41:19–21
5 Buffon, quoted in Pedley, 361
6 Stedman, Vol. II, 50–1
7 Complete, 314. I am indebted to J. H. Prynne's lectures, 'Stars, Tigers and the Shape of Words', delivered at Birkbeck College in 1992, for my understanding of this reference in connection with 'The Tyger'
8 Quoted in Asa Briggs, *The Age of Improvement*, 134–5
9 Pedley, 245
10 Ibid.
11 Quoted in Hartmann, *Jacob Boehme: Life and Doctrines*, 117

Chapter 15: walking among the fires

1 Letters, 20
2 Complete, 43
3 Hindmarsh, *Rise and Progress of the New Jerusalem Church*, 142
4 Complete, 609–11
5 Hartmann, *The Life and Doctrines of Paracelsus*, 24
6 Weeks, *Boehme*, 50

7 Complete, 231
8 Quoted in Hartmann, *Paracelsus*, 172
9 *Philosophy Reformed and Improved*, trans. H. Pinnell, 57
10 Hartmann, *Paracelsus*, 67 and 265
11 Complete, 1
12 Letters, 168
13 Rosenblum, *Modern Painting and the Northern Romantic Tradition*, 45
14 BR, 313
15 Ibid.
16 Hartmann, *Boehme*, 20
17 Ibid., 33
18 BR, 41n
19 Hobhouse (ed.), *Selected Mystical Writings of William Law*, 268
20 *Threefold Life*, 6: 71
21 Hobhouse (ed.), *Selected Mystical Writings of William Law*, 369
22 Quoted in Davies, *The Theology of William Blake*, 72
23 Complete, 95–6
24 Ibid., 35–8
25 Ibid., 39
26 Ibid., 44
27 Ibid., 34
28 Ibid., 45
29 Lister (ed.), *Letters of Samuel Palmer*, 663
30 Complete, 44
31 BR, 53–4
32 Gilchrist, 112–13
33 Quoted in Morton, *The Everlasting Gospel*, 52
34 Payne Knight, *A Discourse on the Worship of Priapus*, 173
35 *Heaven and Hell*, paragraph 280
36 BR, 524–5
37 Ibid., 521
38 Ibid.
39 The story is told by Swinburne, quoted in Wilson, *The Life of William Blake*, 215
40 Gilchrist, 93

41 Lecky, *History of England in the Eighteenth Century*, Vol. VII, 460
42 Nichols, *Illustrations of the Literary History of the Eighteenth Century*, Vol. VII, 490
43 St Clair, *The Godwins and the Shelleys*, 46
44 Ibid., 45
45 Complete, 44–5
46 Erdman, *Prophet Against Empire*, 214
47 Lecky, Vol. VI, 51–2
48 Notebook [N 109]
49 *Rights of Man*, Vol. I, 38
50 Ibid., 78
51 *Rights of Man*, Vol. II, 20
52 Quoted in Erdman, *Prophet Against Empire*, 248
53 Ibid., 278
54 Tyson, *Joseph Johnson*, 122
55 Quoted in Erdman, *Prophet Against Empire*, 161
56 Gilchrist, 94
57 BR, 530–1
58 Stephen, *The History of English Thought in the Eighteenth Century*, 463
59 *Vindication*, 270–2
60 Complete, 458
61 Lister (ed.), *Letters of Samuel Palmer*, 663
62 Complete, 580
63 Letters, 20
64 Nichols, Vol. VIII, 325
65 Letters, 20
66 Complete, 285–6
67 Ibid., 292
68 Ibid., 299
69 *Areopagitica*, in *The Selected Prose of John Milton*, ed. C. A. Patrides, 213
70 Complete, 55
71 Ibid., 52
72 Notebook [N 4]
73 *Vindication*, 75

Chapter 16: The Bible of Hell

1 Complete, 692
2 Ibid.
3 Ibid.
4 Ibid.
5 Crabb Robinson, BR, 318
6 Notebook [N 116]
7 Ibid.
8 Complete, 693
9 Ibid., 46
10 BR, 50–5
11 Ibid., 49
12 Ibid.
13 Complete, 51
14 Ibid., 50
15 Ibid., 47
16 Ibid.
17 BR, 33–4
18 Complete, 44
19 Aaron Hill, quoted in Roston, Prophet and Poet, 85
20 Nathaniel Halhed, quoted in Crehan, Blake in Context, 275
21 Complete, 70
22 Ibid., 83
23 Ibid., 70–1
24 Ibid., 78
25 Ibid., 79
26 Ibid., 82
27 Ibid., 72
28 Quoted in Mee, Dangerous Enthusiasm, 182
29 Complete, 70
30 Ibid., 71
31 Ibid., 72
32 Blake Books, 176
33 BR, 452
34 Complete, 84
35 Ibid., 94
36 Quoted in Ranger, Terror and Pity Reign in every Breast, 2
37 Complete, 85
38 Thale (ed.), The Autobiography of Francis Place, 146
39 Complete, 611
40 BR(S), 13
41 BR, 24
42 Thoughts on Outline, 48–9
43 Letters, 6
44 Ibid.
45 Ibid., 11
46 Thoughts on Outline, 2
47 Ibid., 5
48 Some Anecdotes of the Life of Julio Bonasone, 4
49 Quoted in Rosenblum, Transformations in Late Eighteenth Century Art, 167
50 Complete, 370–1
51 Ibid., 63
52 BR, 470–1
53 Gilchrist, 125
54 Ibid., 163
55 Complete, 67
56 Tatham, quoted in Gilchrist, 421
57 W. M. Rossetti (ed.), Rossetti Papers (London, 1903), 16–17
58 BR, 472
59 Complete, 554
60 Ibid., 157–8
61 Letters, 142
62 Complete, 560
63 Gilchrist, 414–15
64 Complete, 581
65 Linguistic Inquiry, Vol. 1, No. 1, January 1970, 8
66 Roger Murray, in Studies in Romanticism, Vol. 13, No. 2, Spring 1974, 103
67 Ronald Clayton Taylor, in Essential Articles for the Study of William Blake, 1970–84
68 Complete, 645

Chapter 17: Newtons sleep

1 Complete, 405–6
2 Ibid., 337
3 Ibid., 96
4 Opticks (London, 1704), 64 and 75

5 Complete, 99
6 Letters, 46
7 Complete, 60
8 Ibid., 712
9 Ibid., 314
10 Ibid., 138
11 Ibid., 77
12 Curry, Prophecy and Power, 131
13 BR, 547
14 Letters, 168

Chapter 18: Go on & on

1 BR, 183
2 Ibid., 50
3 Ibid., 58
4 Ibid., 51–2
5 Ibid., 52
6 Ibid.
7 Night the Fourth, lines 535 and 538
8 Night the Eighth, line 1317
9 Complete, 269
10 Jules Heller, quoted in Viscomi, Blake and the Idea of the Book, 385
11 Complete, 845
12 Ibid.
13 The Four Zoas (facsimile), Magno and Erdman (eds.), 115
14 Night Thoughts (facsimile), Erdman, Grant, Rose and Tolley (eds.), 419
15 Complete, 325
16 Ibid., 627
17 Night Thoughts (facsimile), 4
18 BR(S), 14
19 Complete, 482
20 'Ode for Music', line 56
21 Abraham Raimbach, quoted in Erdman, Prophet Against Empire, 342
22 Mrs Hunt, quoted in Lindsay, William Blake, 130
23 BR, 561
24 Complete, 122
25 Letters, 11

26 Ibid., 93
27 Ibid., 11
28 Lister (ed.), Letters of Samuel Palmer, 179
29 BR, 283
30 Letters, 8
31 Complete, 611
32 Ibid.
33 Boehme, Mysterium Magnum, vii, 5
34 Complete, 619
35 Ibid., 575
36 Quoted in Altick, The Shows of London, 104
37 Letters, 101
38 Quoted in BR, 54
39 All quotations are from Letters, 8–9
40 Ibid., 8
41 Ibid., 26
42 Ibid.
43 BR, 50
44 I am indebted for these remarks to the research of Marsha Keith Schuchard, and in particular to three articles: 'Blake's "Mr Femality": Freemasonry, Espionage and the Double-Sexed' (Studies in Eighteenth Century Culture, Vol. 22, 1992); 'The Secret Masonic History of Blake's Swedenborg Society' (Blake: An Illustrated Quarterly. Fall 1992); and 'Blake's Healing Trio: Magnetism, Medicine and Mania' (Blake: An Illustrated Quarterly, Summer 1989)
45 Complete, 500
46 BR, 180
47 p. 6
48 Reid, The Rise and Dissolution of the Infidel Societies in this Metropolis, 91
49 Quoted in Hartmann, Paracelsus, 165
50 Letters, 6

51 Ibid., 9
52 Ibid., 11
53 Ibid.
54 Complete, 631

Chapter 19: Felphams Vale

1 Quoted in Bishop, *Blake's Hayley*, 93
2 BR, 51
3 Ibid., 51n
4 Ibid., 64
5 Ibid.
6 Letters, 12
7 Ibid., 13–14
8 Ibid., 15–16
9 Complete, 70
10 Letters, 16
11 Swinburne, *William Blake*, 29
12 Quoted in Bruce, *William Blake in this World*, 93
13 Quoted in Bishop, 20
14 *Memoirs of the Life and Writing of William Hayley*, Vol. I, 407
15 Ibid., 305
16 Letters, 17
17 Quoted by G. E. Bentley in *Studies in Bibliography*, Vol. 12, 1959
18 Letters, 19
19 Ibid., 20
20 Ibid.
21 Ibid., 21
22 Ibid.
23 Quoted in Worrall, *Radical Culture*, 44
24 Ibid., 45
25 Letters, 22
26 Ibid.
27 Ibid., 23
28 Ibid., 24
29 Ibid., 22
30 Ibid., 23
31 Ibid.
32 Ibid.
33 Ibid.

34 Ibid., 24
35 Quoted in Owens, *William Blake and Felpham*, 8
36 Complete, 137
37 Letters, 28
38 Ibid., 29
39 Ibid., 55
40 Gilchrist, 158
41 Ibid., 160
42 Introduction to *The Poems of William Blake*, xlix–l
43 Complete, 694
44 Letters, 31
45 Quoted by G. E. Bentley in *Review of English Studies*, 268
46 Complete, 505
47 Quoted in Bindman, *Catalogue of the Collection in the Fitzwilliam Museum*, 60
48 Swinburne, 2
49 Ibid., 18
50 Letters, 32
51 *Review of English Studies*, 268
52 Letters, 32
53 *Review of English Studies*, 269
54 Ibid., 274
55 Ibid., 271 and 270
56 *The Task*, Book III
57 Complete, 663
58 Ibid., 153–4
59 Letters, 45
60 Ibid., 46
61 Ibid., 36
62 Ibid., 37
63 George Richmond, reported by H. H. Gilchrist on a visit in 1887
64 Ibid.
65 *Memoirs*, Vol. II, 126
66 Thomas Wright, *The Life of William Blake*, 105
67 Letters, 80
68 BR(S), 18–19
69 Complete, 95
70 Letters, 46
71 Complete, 95
72 Gilchrist, 162

73 Quoted by Gilchrist, 170
74 Letters, 57
75 Ibid., 30
76 Ibid.
77 *Memoirs*, Vol. II, 155
78 Quoted in Bishop, 291
79 Gilchrist, 174
80 I am indebted for this information to Mr George Lawson of Bertram Rota Books
81 Letters, 53
82 *Memoirs*, Vol. II, 28
83 BR(S), 20
84 Complete, 634
85 Letters, 43
86 Complete, 500
87 Ibid., 501
88 *Confessions of an English Opium Eater*, 64
89 Ibid., 52
90 Letters, 51
91 Complete, 400
92 Letters, 80
93 Ibid.
94 Gilchrist, 160–1
95 Quoted in *Harvard Library Bulletin*, Vol. 20, No. 3, July 1972
96 Ibid., quoting from the *Examiner* of 31 July 1808
97 BR, 93
98 Ibid.
99 Letters, 51
100 *Letters of Dante Gabriel Rossetti to William Allingham, 1854–1870*, ed. G. B. Hill, 158
101 BR, 114
102 Letters, 45
103 Ibid.
104 Ibid., 40
105 *Review of English Studies*, 274
106 BR, 103
107 Ibid., 101
108 Ibid., 105–6
109 Ibid., 106
110 Complete, 506
111 I am indebted for this information

to Viscomi's *Blake and the Idea of the Book*
112 Letters, 47
113 Ibid., 42
114 Ibid.
115 Ibid., 47
116 Ibid., 48
117 Ibid.
118 Ibid.
119 Ibid., 50
120 Ibid., 52
121 Ibid., 58
122 Samuel Warren, quoted in Lindsay, *William Blake*, 102
123 Letters, 61
124 Ibid., 48
125 Ibid., 53
126 Ibid., 55
127 Ibid.
128 Complete, 492
129 Ibid.
130 Letters, 55
131 BR(S), 22–3
132 Letters, 58
133 Ibid., 51
134 Ibid.
135 Ibid., 55
136 Ibid., 42
137 Ibid., 58
138 Ibid., 51
139 Ibid., 55
140 Ibid.
141 Ibid., 57–8
142 Ibid., 57
143 *Vala* (facsimile), 184 [page 70 of text]
144 Complete, 337
145 Ibid, 342
146 Ibid.
147 Ibid., 355
148 Ibid., 354
149 Ibid.
150 Ibid., 333
151 Ibid., 355
152 Ibid., 390
153 Letters, 55

154 Ibid., 34
155 Ibid., 41
156 Ibid.
157 Ibid., 40
158 Ibid., 47
159 Complete, 378
160 Letters, 38

31 Gilchrist, 199
32 Hayley, Memoirs, Vol. II, 47
33 Letters, 106
34 Complete, 120
35 Ibid., 121
36 Ibid., 147 and 162
37 Ibid., 149 and 185

Chapter 20: Scofield the Accuser

1 Letters, 62
2 Ibid.
3 Ibid., 63
4 Complete, 502
5 BR, 236
6 Letters, 170
7 Ibid., 74
8 Ibid., 65
9 Ibid.
10 Ibid.
11 The information has been kindly supplied to me by the antiquarian booksellers Pickering and Chatto Ltd
12 Letters, 23
13 Ibid., 65
14 BR, 135
15 Quoted by G. E. Bentley in 'Blake as a Private Publisher', BNYPL, LXI, 1957, 56
16 Complete, 98
17 Ibid., 181
18 Ibid., 180
19 Letters, 69
20 Ibid., 71
21 Complete, 390
22 Quoted in Gilchrist, 196
23 BR, 145
24 Letters, 75
25 Ibid., 78n
26 Catherine Blake's words, as reported in Gilchrist, 196-7
27 Gilchrist, 196-7
28 Ibid.
29 Letters, 118
30 BR, 145

Chapter 21: Despair

1 Letters, 79
2 Ibid.
3 Ibid.
4 Ibid., 85, 106 and 109
5 Ibid., 85, 98 and 89
6 Ibid., 87
7 Ibid.
8 Ibid.
9 Ibid., 82
10 BR, 150
11 Letters, 80
12 Ibid., 86
13 Ibid., 100
14 Ibid., 93
15 Ibid., 106
16 Ibid., 101
17 Complete, 547
18 Letters, 104
19 Ibid., 101
20 Complete, 547
21 Ibid., 559
22 Ibid., 536
23 Ibid., 562
24 Ibid., 549
25 Ibid., 372
26 Letters, 101
27 Notebook [N 12]
28 Letters, 105
29 I am indebted for these references to 'Blake and Electrical Magic' by John Adlard in Neophilologus, October 1964
30 I am indebted for these and following references to 'Blake's Healing Trio: Magnetism, Medicine and Mania' by Marsha

Keith Schuchard in *Blake: An Illustrated Quarterly*, Summer 1989

31 Complete, 134
32 BR, 159
33 Letters, 110
34 Ibid., 116
35 Complete, 561
36 BR, 167
37 BR(S), 31
38 Ibid.
39 Quoted by G. E. Bentley in 'Blake and Cromek: The Wheat and the Tares' in *Modern Philology*, Vol. 71, No. 4, May 1974, 367–8
40 Ibid., 370
41 Letters, 124–6
42 Quoted by G. E. Bentley in 'Blake's Engravings and Flaxman' in *Studies in Bibliography*, Vol. 12, 1959, 185
43 Letters, 120
44 Gilchrist, 246
45 Thomas Dibdin, BR, 242
46 BR, 208
47 Ibid., 424
48 Ibid.
49 Knowles, *The Life and Writings of Henry Fuseli*, 293
50 'Blake and Cromek' in *Modern Philology*, 344
51 BR, 207
52 Ibid.
53 Letters, 120–1
54 Complete, 585
55 'Blake's Engravings and Flaxman' in *Studies in Bibliography*, 189
56 Wright, *The Life of William Blake*, 8
57 Letters, 120
58 Complete, 506
59 Ibid., 505
60 Ibid., 507
61 Ibid., 508
62 Ibid., 509
63 Letters, 124

64 BR, 464
65 Ibid.
66 Letters, 128
67 Ibid.
68 Ibid.
69 Ibid.
70 Ibid.
71 Ibid., 129
72 Ibid., 130
73 Bray, *The Life of Thomas Stothard*, 140
74 Complete, 180
75 Ibid., 504
76 Letters, 65
77 Complete, 488
78 Ibid., 498
79 Ibid., 496
80 *Heaven and Hell*, paragraph 79
81 *Medieval English Lyrics*, ed. R. T. Davies, 115
82 Complete, 490
83 Ibid.
84 Letters, 120
85 Complete, 361
86 Ibid., 374
87 Ibid., 406
88 Ibid., 390
89 Ibid., 364
90 Letters, 101
91 Complete, 372
92 Ibid., 385
93 Ibid., 388
94 Ibid., 407
95 Ibid., 372 and 388
96 Ibid., 380
97 Ibid., 556
98 Pevsner, 41
99 Complete, 366
100 Ibid., 360
101 Ibid., 407

Chapter 22: organized and minutely articulated

1 Letters, 101
2 BR, 212

3 The volume is now housed at the
British Library, shelf mark
C.45.e.18
4 Complete, 255
5 Ibid., 153
6 All these quotations can be seen
in the original volume
7 Complete, 527–8
8 Letters, 138
9 Complete, 530
10 Ibid., 531
11 Ibid., 532
12 Ibid., 542
13 Ibid., 543
14 Ibid., 550
15 Ibid., 539
16 Ibid., 537
17 Ibid., 540
18 Ibid., 536
19 Ibid.
20 Ibid., 541
21 Ibid., 550
22 BR, 216
23 ibid., 226
24 I am indebted for this suggestion
to Tim Heath of Blake House
25 BR, 225
26 Ibid., 219
27 Ibid.
28 Swinburne, *William Blake*, 81
29 BR, 399
30 Essick and Pearce (eds.), *Blake in
His Time*, 187
31 Complete, 567
32 BR(S), 44
33 Notebook [N 65]
34 Complete, 573
35 Ibid., 574
36 Ibid., 571–2
37 Ibid., 580
38 Ibid., 573
39 Ibid., 576
40 Ibid., 581
41 Ibid., 574
42 Ibid., 575
43 Ibid., 655

44 Ibid., 659
45 Ibid., 662
46 Ibid., 659
47 Ibid., 575
48 Quoted in McKendrick, Brewer
and Plumb (eds.), *The Birth of a
Consumer Society*, 184
49 D'Archenholz, Vol. I, 151
50 Letters, 137
51 Complete, 572
52 BR, 187
53 Notebook [N 88]
54 Ibid., [N 89]
55 Letters, 131
56 BR, 221
57 Ibid., 214
58 Ibid., 227
59 Ibid., 228
60 Notebook [N 67] and [N 72]
61 Letters, 137
62 BR, 166
63 Complete, 556
64 Ibid., 555
65 Ibid., 561
66 Quoted in Short, *Blake*, 56
67 Letters, 133
68 BR, 189
69 Complete, 555
70 Ibid., 554 and 558
71 Ibid., 560
72 Ibid.
73 Hartmann, *Boehme*, 144
74 Gilchrist, 327
75 Complete, 565
76 Ibid., 565–6

Chapter 23: arise with Exultation

1 Complete, 144
2 BR, 235
3 Butlin, *William Blake*, 470–1
4 Boehme, quoted in Hobhouse
(ed.), *Selected Mystical Writings of
William Law*
5 Complete, 555 and 556

6 Bellin and Ruhl (eds.), *Blake and Swedenborg*, 95
7 Complete, 556–7
8 *Selected Writings*, ed. Jolande Jacobi, 87–8
9 Complete, 561

Chapter 24: I [was] am hid

1 BR, 190
2 Gilchrist, 275
3 Complete, 532–3
4 Ibid., 580
5 Gilchrist, 295
6 BR, 245
7 Ibid., 236
8 Gilchrist, 359
9 Ibid., 360
10 Ibid.
11 Ibid., 359
12 BR, 234
13 Gilchrist, 352
14 Swinburne, *William Blake*, 64
15 BR, 233
16 Ibid., 238
17 Letters, 141
18 Complete, 115
19 Ibid., 550
20 Ibid., 130
21 Ibid., 658
22 Christopher Hill, *The English Revolution*, 280
23 Complete, 196
24 Letters, 20
25 BR, 317
26 Altick, *The Shows of London*, 199
27 Complete, 108
28 William Hayley, *The Life of Milton*, 218
29 Complete, 110
30 Ibid., 95
31 Ibid.
32 Ibid.
33 Ibid., 99
34 Ibid., 109
35 Ibid., 114

36 Ibid., 137
37 Ibid., 141–2
38 Ibid., 127
39 BR, 232
40 Ibid., 235
41 Quoted in Lindsay, *Turner*, 263
42 BR, 235–6
43 Ibid., 229
44 Complete, 172
45 Ibid., 147
46 Complete, 180
47 Ibid., 99
48 Ibid., 104
49 Ibid., 144
50 Ibid., 126
51 Ibid., 207–8
52 Ibid., 148
53 Ibid., 234
54 Ibid., 243
55 Ibid., 191
56 Ibid., 194
57 Ibid.
58 Ibid., 195
59 Ibid., 180
60 Ibid., 228
61 Ibid., 243
62 Ibid., 136
63 Ibid., 183
64 Quoted in Summerson, *Georgian London*, 157, and in Rudé, *Hanoverian London*, 235
65 Quoted in Essick and Pearce (eds.), *Blake in His Time*, 183–4
66 Complete, 135
67 Ibid., 157
68 Ibid., 137
69 Ibid., 157
70 Ibid., 157–8
71 Ibid., 206
72 All quotations taken from Wagenknecht, *Visionary Poetics*, 39, 41 and 46
73 Complete, 218
74 Ibid., 524
75 Ibid., 259

Chapter 25: not drawing, but inspiration

1 BR, 249
2 Ibid., 313–14
3 Keynes, *Blake Studies*, 245
4 Story, *The Life of John Linnell*, 39
5 Ibid., 110
6 BR, 257
7 Story, 227
8 BR, 257
9 Story, 247
10 BR, 310
11 Ibid., 316–17
12 Ibid., 332
13 Story, 225
14 I am indebted for the technical summary here to Viscomi's *Blake and the Idea of the Book*, passim
15 Letters, 142
16 BR, 241–2
17 Ibid., 323
18 Ibid., 250
19 Complete, 257
20 Story, 26
21 Ibid., 168
22 Gilchrist, 299
23 Quoted in Gettings, *The Hidden Art*, 119
24 Quoted in Curry, *A Confusion of Prophets*, 43
25 Ibid., 44
26 Quoted in Story, 161–2
27 BR, 297
28 Ibid., 263
29 Gilchrist, 300
30 BR, 624
31 Ibid., 299
32 I am indebted for this identification to Robin Hamlyn of the Tate Gallery
33 2 Kings 4:35
34 BR, 257
35 Quoted in Butlin, *The Paintings and Drawings of William Blake*, Vol. I, 525

36 BR, 373
37 Ibid., 498
38 Palmer, *The Life and Letters of Samuel Palmer*, 15–16
39 I am indebted for new information here to Robert Essick's essay on the Virgil engravings in *Blake: An Illustrated Quarterly*, Winter 1991/2
40 Gilchrist, 318
41 BR, 315
42 Complete, 670
43 Gilchrist, 318
44 BR, 268
45 Ibid., 258
46 Keynes, *Blake Studies*, 246
47 Hebrews 12:29
48 Complete, 520
49 Quoted in E. P. Thompson, *The Making of the English Working Class*, 724
50 Complete, 524

Chapter 26: the words fly about the room

1 Gilchrist, 349
2 Ibid., 350
3 BR, 566
4 Gilchrist, 357
5 Ibid.
6 De Morgan, *Threescore Years and Ten*, 68
7 Wright, *The Life of William Blake*, Vol. 2, 32
8 BR(S), 76
9 Story, *The Life of John Linnell*, 215
10 *The Portfolio*, 163
11 Ibid.
12 Grigson, *Samuel Palmer*, 35
13 Calvert, *A Memoir of Edward Calvert*, 4
14 Ibid., 17
15 Grigson, 44
16 BR, 292
17 Ibid., 294

18 Ibid.
19 Calvert, 21
20 Ibid., 30
21 Lister (ed.), Letters of Samuel Palmer, 508–9
22 Ibid., 968, 593 and 957
23 BR, 539
24 Ibid., 310
25 Ibid., 312
26 Ibid., 315
27 Ibid.
28 Ibid., 322
29 Ibid.
30 Ibid., 324
31 BR(S), 77
32 Ibid., 97
33 BR, 395
34 Ibid.
35 Letters, 157
36 BR, 307
37 The Elements of Drawing, 342
38 Complete, 175
39 Story, The Life of John Linnell, 228
40 Thomas Wilkes, A General View of the Stage, 118
41 Complete, 270
42 Gilchrist, 345
43 BR, 337
44 BR(S), 73
45 Complete, 269–70
46 Ibid., 273–4
47 Ibid., 275
48 BR, 281
49 Quoted in Lister, Samuel Palmer, 54
50 BR, 279
51 Mechanic's Magazine, 30 August 1823
52 BR, 278
53 Quoted in Bindman, Catalogue of the Collection in the Fitzwilliam Museum, 60
54 BR, 284
55 Ibid., 291
56 Blake Books, 684
57 BR, 290n

58 Ibid.

Chapter 27: I will arise

1 Gilchrist, 404
2 Complete, 70
3 Paradise Lost, VII, 224–5
4 Daniel 7:9
5 BR, 470–1
6 Complete, 80
7 Ibid., 353
8 Ibid., 354
9 Ibid., 391

Chapter 28: The Imagination which Liveth for Ever

1 Letters, 158
2 Gilchrist, 339
3 Ibid.
4 Ibid.
5 BR(S), 113
6 Story, The Life of John Linnell, 149
7 Ibid.
8 BR(S), 81
9 BR, 308
10 Gilchrist, 362–3
11 James Heath, quoted in Thomas Wright, The Life of William Blake, Vol. II, 95
12 BR, 292
13 'New Light on C. A. Tulk, Blake's 19th Century Patron' by Raymond H. Deck jnr in Studies in Romanticism, Vol. XVI, No. 2, 223
14 Ibid.
15 BR, 325
16 Ibid., 318
17 Ibid., 321
18 Letters, 156
19 Quoted in Swinburne, William Blake, 82
20 BR, 371
21 Letters, 156
22 Ibid.

23 *Heaven and Hell*, paragraph 418
24 BR, 302
25 Ibid., 303
26 Ibid.
27 Letters, 158
28 Ibid.
29 *Heaven and Hell*, paragraph 440
30 Butlin, *William Blake*, Vol. I, 540
31 Letters, 159
32 Ibid., 159–60
33 BR, 331
34 Letters, 162
35 Ibid., 163
36 Ibid., 165
37 BR, 337
38 Ibid., 322
39 Complete, 667
40 Ibid., 668–9

41 Letters, 168–9
42 Smith, *Nollekens and His Times*, Vol. I, 473
43 Letters, 166
44 Ibid., 169
45 Ibid., 170
46 BR(S), 107
47 Keynes, *Blake Studies*, 220
48 BR, 341
49 Ibid., 502
50 Gilchrist, 405
51 Letters, 171
52 Grigson, *Samuel Palmer*, 38
53 BR, 373–4
54 Ibid., 374
55 Ibid., 410
56 Ibid., 418n
57 BR(S), 87

BIBLIOGRAPHY

The complete writings of William Blake are available in two standard editions:
The Complete Writings of William Blake, edited by Geoffrey Keynes
(Oxford, 1966)
The Complete Poetry and Prose of William Blake, edited by David V. Erdman
(New York, 1988)
I have in all cases consulted the original texts or photographic facsimiles but,
for the convenience of readers who do not have access to these originals, I
have given page references to Erdman's edition. It is by far the most
accurate and intelligible. There is also an interesting edition of Blake's
complete poetry:
The Poems of William Blake, edited by W. H. Stevenson (London, 1971)
Those who wish to acquire some knowledge of the illuminated books must
refer to:
The Illuminated Blake, annotated by David V. Erdman (London, 1975)
The Complete Graphic Works of William Blake, annotated by David Bindman
(London, 1978)
There are editions, in monochrome or colour, of individual illuminated works.
The most important project of this nature is now being undertaken by the
William Blake Trust in association with the Tate Gallery. Editions of
Jerusalem and *Songs of Innocence and of Experience* have already been
published. Other editions of William Blake's prose must also be mentioned
in this place:
The Letters of William Blake, edited by Geoffrey Keynes (Oxford, 1980)
The Notebook of William Blake, edited by David V. Erdman (Oxford, 1973)
An Island in the Moon, introduced and annotated by Michael Phillips
(Cambridge, 1987)
Vala, edited by G. E. Bentley jnr (Oxford, 1963)
The Four Zoas, with commentary by Cettina Tramontano Magno and David
V. Erdman (London, 1987)
The most important work of reference concerning the art of William Blake is:
The Paintings and Drawings of William Blake, edited by Martin Butlin
(London, 1981)
Other volumes should also be consulted:
Drawings of William Blake, with commentary by Geoffrey Keynes
(London, 1970)

William Blake's Commercial Book Illustrations, edited by Robert N. Essick
  (Oxford, 1991)
The Grave, facsimile introduced by Robert N. Essick and Morton D. Paley
  (London, 1982)
William Blake's Designs for Edward Young's Night Thoughts, edited by David V.
  Erdman, John E. Grant, Edward J. Rose and Michael J. Tolley (Oxford, 1980)
Blake's Illustrations to the Poems of Gray, edited by Irene Tayler (London, 1971)
Certain other books are invaluable for the study of Blake's life and work:
Blake Records, edited by G. E. Bentley jnr (Oxford, 1969)
Blake Records Supplement, edited by G. E. Bentley jnr (Oxford, 1988)
Blake Books, revised edition by G. E. Bentley jnr (Oxford, 1977)

There now follows a list of books which I found helpful for the preparation of this
  biography:

Abrams A. H., *Natural Supernaturalism* (London, 1971)
Adams, Hazard, *Blake and Yeats: The Contrary Vision* (Ithaca, 1955)
——, *William Blake: A Reading of the Shorter Poems* (Seattle, 1963)
Adams, M. Ray, *Studies in the Literary Background of English Radicalism*
  (Pennsylvania, 1947)
Adlard, John, *The Sports of Cruelty* (London, 1972)
Altick, Richard D., *The Shows of London* (London, 1978)
Ansari, A. A., *Arrows of Intellect* (Calcutta, 1965)
Antal, Frederick, *Fuseli Studies* (London, 1956)
Aubrey, Bryan, *Watchmen of Eternity* (New York, 1986)
Ault, Donald, *Narrative Unbound* (New York, 1987)
Baine, Rodney, *The Scattered Portions: Blake's Biological Symbolism* (Georgia, 1986)
Bandy, Melanie, *Mind Forg'd Manacles: Evil in the Poetry of Blake and Shelley*
  (Alabama, 1981)
Baker, W. S., *William Sharp, Engraver* (Philadelphia, 1875)
Barrell, John, *The Political Theory of Painting from Reynolds to Hazlitt*
  (London, 1968)
Beer, John, *Blake's Humanism* (Manchester, 1968)
——, *Blake's Visionary Universe* (Manchester, 1969)
Behrendt, Stephen, *The Moment of Explosion: Blake and the Illustration of Milton*
  (London, 1982)
Bellin, H. F. and Ruhl, Darrell (eds.), *Blake and Swedenborg* (New York, 1985)
Bennett, Shelley, *Thomas Stothard* (Columbia, 1988)
Bentley jnr, G. E., *William Blake: The Critical Heritage* (London, 1975)
Berger, Pierre, *William Blake, Poet and Mystic* (London, 1914)
Bertholf, R. J. and Levitt A. S. (eds.), *William Blake and the Moderns*
  (Albany, 1982)
Billigheimer, Rachel, *Wheels of Eternity* (Dublin, 1990)
Bindman, David, *Blake as an Artist* (Oxford, 1977)
——, *William Blake: His Art and Times* (London, 1982)

——(ed.), *William Blake: Catalogue of the Collection in the Fitzwilliam Museum, Cambridge* (Cambridge, 1970)

Binyon, Laurence, *The Engraved Designs of William Blake* (London, 1926)

Bishop, Morchard, *Blake's Hayley* (London, 1951)

Blackstone, Bernard, *English Blake* (Hamden, 1966)

Blake Studies

Blake: An Illustrated Quarterly

Bloom, Harold, *Blake's Apocalypse* (London, 1963)

Bluhm, Heinz (ed.), *Essays in History and Literature* (Chicago, 1965)

Blunt, Anthony, *The Art of William Blake* (New York, 1959)

Bottrall, Margaret (ed.), *William Blake: Songs of Innocence and Experience* (London, 1970)

Bray, Anna Eliza, *The Life of Thomas Stothard R.A.* (London, 1851)

Briggs, Asa, *The Age of Improvement* (London, 1959)

Brock, E. (ed.), *Swedenborg and His Influence* (London, 1988)

Bronowski, J., *William Blake* (London, 1944)

Bronson, B. H., *Some Aspects of Music and Literature in the Eighteenth Century* (Los Angeles, 1953)

Bruce, Harold, *William Blake in this World* (London, 1925)

Burdett, Osbert, *William Blake* (London, 1926)

Burke, Joseph, *English Art, 1714–1800* (Oxford, 1976)

Burton, E., *The Georgians at Home, 1714–1830* (London, 1967)

Butler, Marilyn, *Romantics, Rebels and Reactionaries* (Oxford, 1981)

Butlin, Martin, *William Blake, 1757–1827* (London, 1966)

——(ed.), *The Blake–Varley Sketchbook of 1819* (London, 1961)

Calvert, Samuel, *A Memoir of Edward Calvert* (London, 1893)

Campbell, R., *The London Tradesman* (London, 1757)

Chancellor, E. Beresford, *London's Old Latin Quarter* (London, 1930)

Chesterton, G. K., *William Blake* (London, 1910)

Clark, Kenneth, *Blake and Visionary Art* (London, 1973)

Clifford, James L. (ed.), *Dr Campbell's Diary of a Visit to England in 1775* (Cambridge, 1947)

Clutton-Brook, A., *Blake* (London, 1933)

Constable, W. G., *John Flaxman* (London, 1927)

Crehan, Stewart, *Blake in Context* (Dublin, 1984)

Crouan, Katherine, *John Linnell: A Centenary Exhibition* (Cambridge, 1982)

Cumberland, George, *Some Anecdotes of the Life of Julio Bonasone* (London, 1793)

——, *Thoughts on Outline* (London, 1796)

Curran, Stuart and Wittreich jnr, J. A. (eds.), *Blake's Sublime Allegory* (Wisconsin, 1973)

Curry, Patrick, *Prophecy and Power: Astrology in Early Modern England* (London, 1989)

——, *A Confusion of Prophets* (London, 1992)

Damon, S. Foster, *A Blake Dictionary: Ideas and Symbols of William Blake* (London, 1973)

——, *William Blake: His Philosophy and Symbols* (London, 1974)

Damrosch jnr, L., *Symbol and Truth in Blake's Myth* (Princeton, 1980)

D'Archenholz, M., *A Picture of England* (London, 1789)

Davies, J. G., *The Theology of William Blake* (Oxford, 1948)

Davis, Michael, *William Blake: A New Kind of Man* (London, 1977)

De Castro, J. Paul, *The Gordon Riots* (London, 1926)

De Morgan, Sophie Elizabeth, *Three Score Years and Ten* (London, 1895)

De Selincourt, Basil, *William Blake* (London, 1909)

DiSalvo, Jackie, *War of Titans* (Pittsburgh, 1983)

Dorfman, Deborah, *Blake in the Nineteenth Century* (London, 1969)

Doskow, Minna, *William Blake's Jerusalem* (London, 1982)

Dunbar, Pamela, *William Blake's Illustrations to the Poetry of Milton* (Oxford, 1980)

Eaves, Morris, *William Blake's Theory of Art* (Princeton, 1982)

——, *The Counter-Arts Conspiracy: Art and Industry in the Age of Blake* (Ithaca, 1992)

Ellis, Edwin J., *The Real Blake* (London, 1917)

England, M. W. and Sparrow, John, *Hymns Unbidden* (New York, 1966)

Erdman David, *Blake: Prophet Against Empire* (Princeton, 1954)

——, *A Concordance to the Writings of William Blake* (New York, 1967)

——(ed.), *Blake and His Bibles* (Connecticut, 1990)

Erdman, David and Grant, John E. (eds.), *Blake's Visionary Forms Dramatic* (Princeton, 1970)

Erffa, Helmut von and Staley, Allen, *The Paintings of Benjamin West* (London, 1986)

Essick, Robert N., *William Blake, Printmaker* (Princeton, 1980)

——, *Works of William Blake in the Huntington Collections* (Huntington, 1985)

——, *William Blake and the Language of Adam* (Oxford, 1989)

——(ed.), *The Visionary Hand* (Los Angeles, 1973)

Essick, Robert N. and Pearce, Donald (eds.), *Blake in His Time* (London, 1978)

Fairchild, B. H., *Such Holy Song* (Kent, Ohio, 1980)

Faithorne, William, *The Art of Graving and Etching* (London, 1702)

Falk, Bernard, *Thomas Rowlandson: His Life and Art* (London, 1949)

Ferber, Michael, *The Social Vision of William Blake* (Princeton, 1985)

Figgis, Darrell, *The Paintings of William Blake* (London, 1925)

Fisch, Harold, *Jerusalem and Albion* (London, 1964)

Fisher, P. F., *The Valley of Vision: Blake as Prophet and Revolutionary* (Toronto, 1961)

Fox, Celina (ed.), *London: World City, 1800–1840* (London, 1992)

Fox, Susan, *Poetic Form in Blake's Milton* (Princeton, 1976)

Friedman, Albert B., *The Ballad Revival* (Chicago, 1961)

Frosch, Thomas, *The Awakening of Albion* (London, 1974)

Frye, Northrop, *Fearful Symmetry* (Princeton, 1947)

——(ed.), *Blake: A Collection of Critical Essays* (New Jersey, 1966)

Gage, John, J. M. W. Turner (London, 1987)

Gardner, Charles, *Vision and Vesture* (London, 1916)

——, *William Blake: The Man* (London, 1919)

Gardner, Stanley, *Infinity on the Anvil* (Oxford, 1954)

——, *Blake* (London, 1968)
——, *Blake's Innocence and Experience Retraced* (London, 1986)
Garnett, Richard, *William Blake, Painter and Poet* (London, 1895)
Garrett, Clarke, *Respectable Folly* (London, 1975)
Gaunt, William, *Arrows of Desire* (London, 1956)
——, *The Great Century of British Painting* (London, 1971)
George, D. H., *Blake and Freud* (London, 1980)
George, M. Dorothy, *London Life in the Eighteenth Century* (London, 1925)
Gettings, Fred, *The Hidden Art: A Study of Occult Symbolism in Art* (London, 1978)
Gibberd, Graham, *On Lambeth Marsh* (London, 1992)
Gilchrist, Alexander, *The Life of William Blake* (London, 1863 and 1880)
Gillham, D. G., *Blake's Contrary States* (Cambridge, 1966)
Gleckner, Robert, *The Piper and the Bard* (Detroit, 1959)
——, *Blake's Prelude* (London, 1982)
——, *Blake and Spenser* (London, 1985)
Glen, Heather, *Vision and Disenchantment* (Cambridge, 1983)
Godfrey, Richard T., *Printmaking in Britain* (Oxford, 1978)
Gretton, Thomas, *Murders and Moralities: English Catchpenny Prints, 1800–1860*
    (London, 1980)
Griffiths, Anthony, *Prints and Printmaking* (London, 1980)
Grigson, Geoffrey, *Samuel Palmer: The Visionary Years* (London, 1947)
Grosley, P. J., *A Tour to London* (London, 1772)
Hagstrum, Jean H., *William Blake: Poet and Painter* (London, 1964)
Hall, Carol Louise, *Blake and Fuseli: A Study in the Transmission of Ideas*
    (London, 1985)
Hall, Mary, *Materialism and the Myths of Blake* (London, 1988)
Hamblen, Emily S., *On the Minor Prophecies of William Blake* (London, 1930)
Hardie, Martin, *Samuel Palmer* (London, 1928)
Harper, George Mills, *The Neoplatonism of William Blake* (North Carolina, 1961)
Harrison, J. F. C., *The Second Coming* (London, 1979)
Hartmann, Franz, *The Life and the Doctrines of Paracelsus* (London, 1887)
——, *Jacob Boehme: Life and Doctrines* (London, 1891)
Hayley, William, *The Life of Milton* (London, 1794)
——, *Memoirs of the Life and Writings of William Hayley* (London, 1823)
Hill, Christopher, *The English Revolution* (London, 1949)
——, *The English Bible and the Seventeenth Century Revolution* (London, 1993)
Hill, Draper, *Mr Gillray, the Caricaturist* (London, 1965)
Hilton, Nelson, *Literal Imagination* (London, 1983)
—— (ed.), *Essential Articles for the Study of William Blake, 1970–1984*
    (Connecticut, 1986)
Hind, A. M., *A Short History of Engraving and Etching* (London, 1911)
Hindmarsh, Robert, *Rise and Progress of the New Jerusalem Church* (London, 1861)
Hirsch jnr, E. D., *Innocence and Experience: An Introduction to Blake* (London, 1964)
Hirst, Desirée, *Hidden Riches* (London, 1964)
Hobhouse, Stephen (ed.), *Selected Mystical Writings of William Law,* (London, 1938)
Holloway, John, *William Blake: The Lyric Poetry* (London, 1968)

Howard, John, *Infernal Poetics* (London, 1984)

Hungerford, E. B., *Shores of Darkness* (New York, 1941)

Hutchinson, Sidney C., *The History of the Royal Academy* (London, 1968)

James, D. E., *Written Within and Without: A Study of Blake's Milton* (Frankfurt, 1977)

Jenkins, Herbert, *William Blake* (London, 1925)

Jones, Michael Wynn, *George Cruikshank: His Life and London* (London, 1978)

Jugaku, Bunsho, *A Bibliographical Study of Blake's Notebook* (Tokyo, 1953)

Keynes, Geoffrey, *William Blake: Poet, Painter, Prophet* (London, 1965)

——, *Blake Studies* (Oxford, 1971)

King, James, *William Blake* (London, 1991)

King-Hele, Desmond, *Erasmus Darwin and the Romantic Poets* (London, 1986)

Kliger, Samuel, *The Goths in England* (Cambridge, Mass., 1952)

Klingender, F. D., *Art and the Industrial Revolution* (London, 1947)

Klonsky, Milton, *William Blake: The Seer and His Visions* (London, 1977)

——, *Blake's Dante* (London, 1980)

Knowles, John, *The Life and Writings of Henry Fuseli* (London, 1831)

Langridge, Irene, *William Blake* (London, 1904)

Larrissy, Edward, *William Blake* (London, 1985)

Leader, Zachary, *Reading Blake's Songs* (London, 1981)

Lecky, W. E. H., *History of England in the Eighteenth Century* (London, 1878–92)

Lewis, W. S., *Three Tours Through London* (New Haven, 1941)

Lindbergh, Bo, *William Blake's Illustrations to the Book of Job* (Hbo, 1973)

Lindsay, David W., *Blake's Songs of Innocence and Experience* (London, 1989)

Lindsay, Jack, *William Blake: Creative Will and the Poetic Image* (London, 1929)

——, *Turner* (London, 1973)

——, *William Blake* (London, 1978)

Linnell, David, *Blake, Palmer, Linnell & Co.* (Sussex, 1994)

Linssen, E. F., *The Appreciation of Old Engravings and Etchings* (London, 1951)

Lister, Raymond, *Beulah to Byzantium* (Dublin, 1965)

——, *Samuel Palmer* (London, 1974)

——, *Infernal Methods* (London, 1975)

——, *The Paintings of William Blake* (London, 1986)

——(ed.), *The Letters of Samuel Palmer* (Oxford, 1974)

Lowery, M. R., *Windows of the Morning* (London, 1940)

MacDonald, Michael, *Mystical Bedlam: Madness, Anxiety and Healing in Seventeenth Century England* (London, 1981)

Mantoux, Paul, *The Industrial Revolution in the Eighteenth Century* (London, 1961)

Manuel, F. E., *The Eighteenth Century Confronts the Gods* (Harvard, 1959)

Margoliouth, H. M., *William Blake* (London, 1951)

Marshall, Dorothy, *English People in the Eighteenth Century* (London, 1956)

——, *Dr Johnson's London* (New York, 1968)

Martindale, Andrew, *Gothic Art* (London, 1967)

Mason, E. C., *The Mind of Henry Fuseli* (London, 1951)

Mayor, A. H., *Prints and People* (New York, 1971)

McCalman, Iain, *Radical Underworld: Prophets, Revolutionaries and Pornographers in London, 1795–1840* (Cambridge, 1988)

McKendrick, Neil, Brewer, John and Plumb, J. H. (eds.), *The Birth of a Consumer Society: The Commercialisation of Eighteenth Century England* (London, 1982)

Mee. Jon, *Dangerous Enthusiasm* (Oxford, 1992)

Meyerstein, E. H. W., *A Life of Thomas Chatterton* (London, 1930)

Miles, Josephine, *Eras and Modes in English Poetry* (Los Angeles, 1964)

Mitchell, W. J. T., *Blake's Composite Art* (Princeton, 1978)

Monod, Paul, *Jacobitism and the English People, 1688–1788* (Cambridge, 1989)

Moritz, C. P., *Travels of Carl Philip Moritz in England, in 1782* (London, 1795)

Morton, A. L., *The Everlasting Gospel* (London, 1958)

Murry, Middleton, *William Blake* (London, 1933)

Muses, C. A., *Illumination on Jacob Boehme: The Work of Dionysius Andreas Freher* (New York, 1951)

Nanavutty, Piloo, *Blake and Emblem Literature* (London, 1952)

Natoli, Joseph P., *Twentieth Century Blake Criticism* (London, 1982)

Newton, Eric, *European Painting and Sculpture* (London, 1941)

Nichols, John, *Illustrations of the Literary History of the Eighteenth Century* (London, 1817)

Nicoll, Allardyce, *William Blake and His Poetry* (London, 1922)

Nurmi, Martin K., *Blake's Marriage of Heaven and Hell: A Critical Study* (Ohio, 1957)

——, *William Blake* (London, 1975)

Oistriker, Alicia, *Vision and Verse in William Blake* (Madison, 1965)

O'Neill, Judith (ed.), *Critics on Blake* (London, 1970)

Owen, A. L., *The Famous Druids* (Oxford, 1962)

Owens, Norah, *William Blake and Felpham* (Bognor Regis, 1986)

Pagel, Walter, *Paracelsus* (New York, 1958)

Paley, Morton D., *Energy and the Imagination: A Study of the Development of Blake's Thought* (Oxford, 1970)

——, *William Blake* (London, 1978)

——, *The Continuing City: William Blake's Jerusalem* (Oxford, 1983)

Paley, Morton D. and Phillips, Michael (eds.), *William Blake: Essays in Honour of Sir Geoffrey Keynes* (Oxford, 1973)

Palmer, A. H., *The Life and Letters of Samuel Palmer* (London, 1892)

Pennant, Thomas, *Some Account of London* (London, 1813)

Penny, Nicholas, *Church Monuments in Romantic England* (London, 1977)

Percival, Milton O., *William Blake's Circle of Destiny* (New York, 1938)

Pevsner, Nikolaus, *The Englishness of English Art* (London, 1955)

Philipp, Franz and Stewart, June (eds.), *Essays in Honour of Daryl Lindsay* (London, 1964)

Phillips, Michael (ed.), *Interpreting Blake* (Cambridge, 1978)

Pinto, Vivian De Sola, *The Divine Vision* (London, 1957)

Pollard, A. W., *Early Illustrated Books* (London, 1893)

Pressly, William, *The Life and Art of James Barry* (London, 1981)

Price, Cecil, *Theatre in the Age of Garrick* (Oxford, 1973)

Punter, David, *Blake, Hegel and Dialectic* (Amsterdam, 1982)

Raine, Kathleen, *Blake and England* (London, 1960)

——, *Blake and Tradition* (London, 1969)

——, *Blake and the New Age* (London, 1979)

——, *Blake and Antiquity* (London, 1979)

Raine, Kathleen and Harper, George Mills (eds.), *Thomas Taylor, the Platonist: Selected Writings* (London, 1969)

Ranger, Paul, *Terror and Pity Reign in every Breast: Gothic Drama in the London Patent Theatres, 1750–1820* (London, 1991)

Read, Herbert, *Education Through Art* (London, 1943)

Reid, W. H., *The Rise and Dissolution of the Infidel Societies in this Metropolis* (London, 1800)

Reynolds, Joshua, *The Literary Works of Sir Joshua Reynolds* (London, 1819)

Robson-Scott, W. D., *The Literary Background of the Gothic Revival in Germany* (Oxford, 1965)

Rosenblum, Robert, *Transformations in Late Eighteenth Century Art* (Princeton, 1967)

——, *Modern Painting and the Northern Romantic Tradition* (London, 1975)

Rosenfeld, Alvin H. (ed.), *William Blake: Essays for S. Foster Damon* (Providence, 1969)

Rosten, Murray, *Prophet and Poet: The Bible and the Growth of Modern Romanticism* (London, 1965)

Rudd, Margaret, *Organiz'd Innocence* (London, 1951)

Rudé, George, *Hanoverian London* (London, 1971)

Russell, Archibald, *The Engravings of William Blake* (London, 1912)

Sartain, John, *The Reminiscences of a Very Old Man* (New York, 1899)

Saurat, Denis, *Blake and Modern Thought* (London, 1929)

Schiff, Gert, *Henry Fuseli* (London, 1975)

Schinkel, Karl Friedrich, *The English Journey* (London, 1993)

Schorer, Mark, *William Blake: The Politics of Vision* (New York, 1946)

Schwarz, L. D., *London in the Age of industrialisation* (Cambridge, 1992)

Scott, Harold, *The Early Doors* (London, 1946)

Scull, Andrew, *The Most Solitary of Afflictions* (London, 1993)

Short, Ernest H., *Blake* (London, 1925)

Singer, June K., *The Unholy Bible* (New York, 1970)

Singh, C. S., *The Chariot of Fire* (Salzburg, 1981)

Smith, J. T., *Nollekens and His Times* (London, 1828)

——, *A Book for a Rainy Day* (London, 1845)

St Clair, William, *The Godwins and the Shelleys* (London, 1989)

Stanley, Michael (ed.), *Emmanuel Swedenborg: Essential Readings* (London, 1988)

Stephen, Leslie, *The History of English Thought in the Eighteenth Century* (London, 1902)

Stevenson, Warren, *Divine Analogy: A Study of the Creation Motif in Blake and Coleridge* (Salzburg, 1972)

Story, A. T., *The Life of John Linnell* (London, 1892)

——, *William Blake* (London, 1893)

——, *James Holmes and John Varley* (London, 189.;)

Summerson, John, *Georgian London* (London, 1945)

Swedenberg jnr, H. T., *The Theory of the Epic in England* (Berkeley, 1944)

Symons, Arthur, *William Blake* (London, 1907)

Swinburne, A. C., *William Blake* (London, 1868)

Tannenbaum, Leslie, *Biblical Tradition in Blake's Early Prophecies* (Princeton, 1982)

Thale, Mary (ed.), *The Autobiography of Francis Place* (Cambridge, 1972)

Thomas, Keith, *Religion and the Decline of Magic* (London, 1971)

Thompson, E. P., *The Making of the English Working Class* (London, 1963)

——, *Witness Against the Beast* (Cambridge, 1993)

Thompson, Stanbury (ed.), *The Journal of John Gabriel Stedman* (London, 1962)

Todd, Ruthven, *Tracks in the Snow* (London, 1946)

——, *Blake's Dante Plates* (London, 1968)

——, *William Blake, the Artist* (London, 1971)

Tomalin, Claire, *The Life and Death of Mary Wollstonecraft* (London, 1974)

Tomory, Peter, *The Life and Art of Henry Fuseli* (London, 1972)

Treloar, W. P., *Wilkes and the City* (London, 1917)

Tuer, A. W., *Forgotten Children's Books* (London, 1898)

Tyson, Gerald P., *Joseph Johnson: A Liberal Publisher* (Iowa City, 1979)

Vine Steven, *Blake's Poetry: Spectral Visions* (London, 1993)

Viscomi, Joseph, *The Art of William Blake's Illuminated Prints* (Manchester, 1983)

——, *Blake and the Idea of the Book* (Princeton, 1993)

Wagenknecht, David, *Blake's Night* (Cambridge, Mass., 1973)

Warner, Janet A., *Blake and the Language of Art* (Gloucester, 1984)

Waterhouse, Ellis, *Paintings in Britain, 1530–1790* (London, 1953)

Watson, J. S., *The Reign of George III* (Oxford, 1960)

Webster, Brenda S., *Blake's Prophetic Psychology* (London, 1953)

Weeks, Andrew, *Boehme* (New York, 1991)

Werner, B. C., *Blake's Vision of the Poetry of Milton* (London, 1986)

White, Helen C., *The Mysticism of William Blake* (Madison, 1927)

Wicksteed, Joseph, *Blake's Vision of the Book of Job* (London, 1910)

——, *William Blake's Jerusalem* (London, 1953)

Wilkie, B. and Johnson, M. L., *Blake's Four Zoas* (London, 1975)

Wilkinson, A. M., *William Blake and the Great Sin* (Exeter, 1974)

Wilson, Mona, *The Life of William Blake* (London, 1932)

Wilton, Andrew, *The Wood Engravings of William Blake* (London, 1977)

Witke, Joanne, *William Blake's Epic: Imagination Unbound* (London, 1986)

Wittreich, Joseph A., *Angel of Apocalypse* (London, 1975)

——, *Visionary Poetics* (London, 1979)

Worrall, David, *Radical Culture* (London, 1992)

Wright, Andrew, *Blake's Job: A Commentary* (Oxford, 1972)

Wright, Thomas, *The Life of William Blake* (Olney, 1929)

Wroth, Warwick, *The London Pleasure Gardens* (London, 1896)

INDEX

Works by Blake appear under title; works by others appear under the name of the author or artist

Also available in Vintage

Peter Ackroyd

DICKENS

'I couldn't stop reading it: it's absolutely marvellous
. . . an essential book for anyone who has ever loved
or read Dickens'
P.D. James

'Ackroyd's magnificent biography sets the seal on
Dickens's acknowledged supremacy in the English
novel . . . I can do no more than praise, recommend,
insist that you buy and read this book . . . it supersedes
all other Dickens biographies .'
Anthony Burgess, *Independent*

'As scholarly as it is imaginative . . . fully worthy of its
subject'
John Gross, *Sunday Telegrah*

V

VINTAGE

Peter Ackroyd

MILTON IN
AMERICA

'More concise and sardonic than *Hawksmoor* and *Chatterton*, and even more mysteriously brilliant, *Milton in America* fills the reader's mind with images of extraordinary vividness'
John Bayley, *The Times*

'A strikingly clever premise for a novel . . . Ackroyd's prose fizzes and sparkles as brightly as an electrical misconnection'
Lucy Hughes-Hallett, *Independent*

'Consistently funny, Ackroyd's comic genius . . . is allowed to let rip, with wonderfully enjoyable gusto'
A. N. Wilson, *Literary Review*

V

VINTAGE

Peter Ackroyd

DAN LENO AND THE LIMEHOUSE GOLEM

'Mesmerising, macabre . . . this brilliant novel pervades the midnight movies of the mind and makes the blood run chilly'
Daily Mail

'He has pulled off the greatest coup of all, a four-square crime novel . . . as aesthetically satisfying as it is morally shocking'
Independent on Sunday

'He who is tired of London is tired of life, but he who is tired of Ackroyd requires another planet'
Evening Standard

V
VINTAGE

BY PETER ACKROYD
ALSO AVAILABLE FROM VINTAGE